T0315427

Crossing Great Divides

John D. Fairfield

Crossing Great Divides

City and Country in Environmental
and Political Disorder

TEMPLE UNIVERSITY PRESS
Philadelphia • Rome • Tokyo

TEMPLE UNIVERSITY PRESS
Philadelphia, Pennsylvania 19122
tupress.temple.edu

Title page graphic by Martyn Schmoll

Library of Congress Cataloging-in-Publication Data

Names: Fairfield, John D., 1955– author.
Title: Crossing great divides : city and country in environmental and
  political disorder / John D. Fairfield.
Other titles: Urban life, landscape, and policy.
Description: Philadelphia : Temple University Press, 2024. | Series: Urban
  life, landscape, and policy | Includes bibliographical references and
  index. | Summary: "Argues that the habit of thinking of the city and the
  country as opposites is at the root of our environmental and political
  disorder, and suggests approaches to bridge this social, political, and
  ecological divide"— Provided by publisher.
Identifiers: LCCN 2023044373 (print) | LCCN 2023044374 (ebook) | ISBN
  9781439925713 (cloth) | ISBN 9781439925720 (paperback) | ISBN
  9781439925737 (pdf)
Subjects: LCSH: Rural-urban relations—United States. | Political
  culture—United States. | Social conflict—United States. | United
  States—Social conditions, | United States—Environmental conditions, |
  BISAC: SOCIAL SCIENCE / Sociology / Urban | HISTORY / Social History
Classification: LCC HT384.U5 F545 2024 (print) | LCC HT384.U5 (ebook) |
  DDC 307.2/40973—dc23/eng/20240221
LC record available at https://lccn.loc.gov/2023044373
LC ebook record available at https://lccn.loc.gov/2023044374

Printed in the United States of America

9 8 7 6 5 4 3 2 1

To my children,

Sally, Tom, Fran, and Polly,

and the better world they are making

Contents

Crossing Great Divides

Introduction

Confessions of an Urban Historian

The Dangerous Dualism of
City and Country

Among my earliest memories is a shimmering highway heading straight south into a hot sun, climbing a long hill at the horizon. The memory is of U.S. Highway 41, which runs from the Upper Peninsula of Michigan all the way to Miami, Florida. The highway connects Chicago, where I grew up, to Nashville, Tennessee, thirty miles south of which my father's aunt and uncle owned a farm. The family ties were tight, as a brother and sister (my great-uncle and grandmother) married another brother and sister (my grandfather and great-aunt). My father, born in 1927, spent most of his summers during the Great Depression on this farm. The annual summer trips continued through my boyhood.

Aunt Min loved to tell the story of her husband, Uncle John, bringing her home to the Tennessee farm for the first time after their marriage. My father, six years old and known as Buster, leapt up on the running board of the car as they entered the farmyard and bellowed, "Uncle John, I told you not to do it!" The other marriage involved my grandfather Leslie, partially crippled as a young man in a construction accident. Leslie walked stooped over for the rest of his life, but he won the heart of my grandmother, Frances, a much courted college-educated woman.

Incapacitated for physical work, Leslie took a correspondence course in accounting in the mid-1920s and, just before the Great Depression began, moved to Chicago with his new wife to start a small business. He built the business and kept it alive through the Depression, riding the streetcars all over the city, hoisting himself up onto the cars with his strong upper body. But every summer, my grandmother packed up my father and headed to the Tennessee farm to save money on food. The infusions of urban cash must also have helped John and Min save the farm John inherited just as the Depression began.

Although many Americans must share similar experiences of the close connections between city and country, a deep enmity between urban and rural people is the defining characteristic of our time. This book tells the story of the troubled relationships and false divisions between city and country. The costs have been environmental degradation and political paralysis. Having lived and worked on both sides of the great divide, I hope these pages will encourage other Americans to reach across the barriers that make it so difficult for us to address our many challenges.

I loved the farm. It offered a vastly different world from the Chicago suburb where I grew up. Six-foot-five John and Min, a tall and fit college-educated woman who had excelled at track and field, seemed larger than life to me. Uncle John told hilarious stories often involving the year or two he spent bumming around the country. But with marriage and the new farm, he became a resourceful jack of all trades. John and Min grew tobacco and hay; raised cattle, sheep, pigs, and fowl; tended orchards and gardens; and much else. Long after his neighbors bought tractors, John continued to farm with horses and mules. The farm was full of outbuildings, from a tobacco barn and abandoned tenant house to a creamery and a smokehouse. The farmhouse itself dated from 1805.

My father obviously felt at home in this rural world, as a beloved and respected member of his extended family. But I also knew that my father grew up as a tough city kid on the streets of Chicago. He often took me and my siblings to the city, to the Portage Park neighborhood on the city's northwest side where my grandparents lived, to see baseball games at Wrigley Field and Comiskey Park, and to doctor's offices and busy restaurants in the Loop. He knew this world, too, loved it, understood it, felt in command of it. Much of my love of cities came from him.

I recall those summer trips as a time of connection with my extended family, a time for enjoying people and things. My father marked the journey down U.S. 41 by telling story after story, each attached to its own place. We always arrived at the farm at or near dark, inching along the winding, densely overgrown road to the farmhouse, honking the horn at every turn to alert other drivers. The trip meant adventure, a chance to roam and explore a world entirely different from my suburban home.

It would be many years before I could fully make sense of all these experiences. But they shaped my thinking and my values. In those early days, the farm had no indoor plumbing, just a wooden outhouse that both scared and fascinated me. Later I developed an affection for operating the manure spreader, a strange implement that flung chucks of cow dung across the fields. Although I lacked the intellectual tools to notice, the outhouse and spreader also introduced me to ancient patterns of recycling waste. In contrast, my life back in suburban Chicago reflected a newly affluent society, where I cultivated the habits of a throwaway world.

These memories are tinged with nostalgia for the halcyon days of childhood. As I recall my transition to adulthood, and the competitive process of finding my place in the world, the memories are harsher. After a rocky first year of college, I dropped out and hitchhiked across the country, backpacking in various national parks, forests, and wilderness areas. Two years later, in the summer of 1977, now back in college but still enamored of the farming life, I decided to try to hook up with a grain combining crew. Embarking from the Tennessee farm, I hitchhiked out to Oklahoma City on Interstate 40. Unlike U.S. 41, the many interstates I hitchhiked on in those years do not shimmer in my memory or recall local lore. In my mind it is always night on the interstate, the roadway filled with faceless people rushing to indistinguishable places.

I managed to hook onto a crew and cut wheat, barley, and oats from Oklahoma across the Canadian border, following the harvest north. Joining the crew just as the green revolution kicked into high gear, I encountered a radically different sort of farming from what I had seen in Tennessee. The man I worked for talked as much about bank loans as crops. He owned multiple machines, but no farm. His business always seemed on the verge of failure. As we caravanned across the Great Plains with his family, we harvested grain from vast, mono-cultured fields that stretched out for miles. We ran the combines (so named because they simultaneously reaped, threshed, gathered, and winnowed the grain) well into the night of every working day.

We served an industry as mechanized and energy intensive as any in the city. The Great Plains once stored vast amounts of energy in the roots, stems, and bark of a variety of perennial plants. Perennials promoted soil health by fixing nitrogen (taking up free nitrogen in the atmosphere to produce, through chemical reactions, new compounds essential to plant growth) while retaining water in the soil and shielding one another from wind and erosion. But the seed-heavy annuals of our modern diet leave the soil bare over the winter. Erosion takes a heavy toll on the denuded land. The substitution of machines for manure-producing draft animals demands an incomprehensible amount of imported energy—the equivalent of three or four tons of TNT per acre—in the form of chemical fertilizers and fossil fuels from across the globe. The farms of a single state, Iowa, require the energy equivalent of four thousand Hiroshima bombs every year.[1]

Humans now artificially fix more nitrogen than does the rest of the biosphere. Meanwhile the aggressive mining of phosphorus has, due to runoff, deposited much of it at the bottom of the ocean. Estimates of the remaining, recoverable supplies of phosphorus (along with nitrogen and potassium, an essential element in plant growth) range from sixty to two hundred years. Vast amounts of these nutrients are wasted, running off into waterways where they promote algae blooms whose decay consumes so much oxygen that other forms of life perish. Draining the corn and wheat belts, the Mississippi River pours that oxygen-depleted water into the Gulf of Mexico, which now suffers from a dead zone the size of New Jersey. Excess nitrogen on farm fields also produces nitrous oxide, a potent greenhouse gas. Those same fertilizers powered the bomb that blew up the Alfred Murrah Federal Building in Oklahoma City in the 1995 act of domestic terrorism that announced our growing political divisions.[2]

My memories of the farm in Tennessee and my time with the combine crew fall into a pattern described by the Welsh literary historian Raymond Williams in *The Country and the City* (1973). Williams found in British literature recurrent recollections of a golden rural past forever receding into the past. As he traced those memories from the nineteenth century back to the fourteenth century, he recognized that such recollections had their origins in childhood memories. But he did not dismiss them as mere nostalgia. These memories of "directness, connection, mutuality, sharing," Williams wrote, provided a measure of how "a process of human growth has in itself been deformed." As children matured in a competitive world, Williams argued, they entered a divided world that "teaches, impresses, offers to make normal and even rigid, modes of detached, separated, external perception and action: modes of using and consuming rather than accepting and enjoying people and things."[3]

Williams traced the ritual and repeated contrasts between city and country to capitalism's ratcheting up of the exploitation of nature, including human nature. But as Williams made clear, capitalism began not in the city but in the countryside. Ever since, rural settlements have been mined and exploited for profit as fully as urban settlements. "Country Mice or City Mice—The Cat Doesn't Care," as one reviewer of *The Country and the City* put it. Near the end of his study, Williams revealed that recollections of a golden age could also focus on urban memories of the "delights of corner-shops, gas lamps, horsecabs, trams, piestalls." One cannot blame "the city" for capitalism or look to "the country" for the antidote, Williams concluded, because in both places "the needs of local settlement and community are overridden, often ruthlessly."[4]

Once established, however, the city-country dualism took on a life of its own. We use the habitual contrast of city and country, Williams argued, "to ratify an unresolved division and conflict of impulses, which it might be better to face on its own terms." We try to resolve the dilemma between "human ways" and "natural ways," he continued, "by dividing work and leisure, or society and the individual, or city and country, not only in our minds but in suburbs and garden cities, town houses and country cottages, the week and the weekend." One might add other divisions, such as the arcadian and imperial traditions in ecological thought (preaching, respectively, reverent coexistence and bold mastery) and the contrasting desires for pastoral harmony and technological progress that shaped American culture. The "contrast of country and city," Williams concluded, "is one of the major forms in which we become conscious of a central part of our experience and of the crises of our society."[5]

For me, however, those summer trips to the farm in Tennessee suggested not the divisions between country and city but their interdependence. My experiences imparted something nearly the opposite of what the historian William Cronon took from his family's drives from southern New England past Chicago to his grandparents' cottage on Green Lake in Wisconsin. For Cronon, the drive reinforced his sense of city and country as different worlds. For me, the drive from city and suburb to country, and back again, encouraged me to see myself and my family, and my father especially, as not urban or rural or suburban but all these things at once.[6]

That recognition of the interdependence of all these types of settlements helps to explain the origins of this book. On a warm spring night in 2004, I delivered a multimedia presentation on film images of the city to the Cincinnati Seminar on the City. I highlighted the way film culture in the 1930s and 1940s used "the city" as a dystopian symbol of alienation, exploitation, and menace. With reference to post-1945 urban disinvestment, I argued that "the future of the city was at stake in these images." In the question-and-answer period that followed, a woman asked me, with spite in her voice, "Well, why don't you live in the city?" I knew the woman, often conversed with her at the dinners that preceded meetings of the seminar. She knew that I lived and raised a family in the far reaches of the Cincinnati metropolitan area, near Brookville, Indiana. But her accusatory question left little doubt of her disdain for my choices.

I had long accepted good-natured ribbing from colleagues for being an urban historian who lived in the country. But I understood myself to be a good and loyal citizen of the Cincinnati region. I taught at one of Cincinnati's leading universities, led walking tours of its neighborhoods for a variety of audiences, helped to build a Habitat for Humanity house in one of its low-income neighborhoods, and in myriad other ways contributed to the intellectual and social life of the city. In a more prosaic manner, I contributed to the city's well-being through its payroll tax. I also thought of my activities in rural Indiana as contributing to the life of the region. I served as a lector and catechist in one of metropolitan Cincinnati's many Catholic parishes, coached multiple youth sports teams, gave guest presentations in the public schools, and generally served as an ambassador for Cincinnati's civic and intellectual culture in my rural community.

As I commuted thirty-five miles to the city three or four days a week, I sometimes reflected on the structure of the Cincinnati region. Stopped in traffic as I approached the city, I looked dejectedly at the meridian strip on Interstate 74 and wondered why we did not have a light rail system. Cincinnati's early twentieth-century subway project had included plans for interurban rail connections to Brookville. The city abandoned those plans after World War I as the automobile moved toward the center of American life. Much later, in 2002, a proposal for a regional transit system lost more than two to one at the polls. The lack of a regional transit system fueled my argument, delivered in a variety of settings to diverse audiences, that suburban and rural residents should care about the city. I pointed to the importance of the city's schools, universities, hospitals, sports teams, newspapers, and television stations and its markets and innovative entrepreneurs, as well as its public utilities, in creating an integral and productive region.[7]

It never occurred to me that I also needed to communicate to city residents why they should care about the city's suburban and rural hinterland. But the woman's question that night in 2004 brought me up short. The sense I had of an interdependent region could not be taken for granted even in the city. An antipathy between city and country, as strong on the urban side as on the rural side, made it difficult for us to see our common interests.

Although I called myself an urban historian, I came to believe that much of the trouble lay in the city-country dualism that shaped so much of our thinking. Like other dualisms that oversimplify a complex reality and create false separations (society-nature, mind-body), the dualism of city and country obscures a diversity of interconnected landscapes and settlements, ranging from wilderness, farms, mines, woodlands, and fisheries through exurbia, outer ring suburbs, industrial satellites, edge cities, and inner ring suburbs to suburbanized, peripheral city neighborhoods, dense inner-city neighborhoods, and central business districts. The dualism of city and country too often obscured the relationships between those various places. I thought of them all as parts of an integrated—indeed, an ecological—whole, elements of a region in which each settlement played a complementary role. Evidently, this view of things, the region as a functional whole bound together by mutuality, was not as widely shared as I presumed.[8]

The chapters that follow examine how oversimplified modes of thinking led to destructive modes of acting. The dualism of city and country distorted how we planned cities, our patterns of production and consumption, our ways of dealing with waste, and how we treated one another. Today, too many of the proposed solutions to our mounting challenges, even when well meaning, fail to rethink the erroneous assumptions that led us to this point. This study calls for a rethinking of those assumptions as a means of opening new possibilities.

The current interest in promoting denser, more resource-efficient cities has much to recommend it. The enthusiasm for urban sustainability is only the latest chapter in a long history of urban environmental reform that made cities healthier, safer, and more engaging places where people enjoyed rich and satisfying lives. But urban sustainability also tends to share the weakness of previous urban environmental reforms in failing to reach beyond city limits or even across the whole of the city itself.

Nevertheless, the many successes of urban environmental reform, including recent efforts to forestall displacement and gentrification in greening cities, remind us of what is possible. By including broader regions and more diverse populations, we might reach across great divides and create modes of production and ways of life, less dependent on despoilation and manic consumption, that will be worth sustaining. No one said this more clearly than the polymath urbanist Lewis Mumford. "Regional planning asks not how wide an area can be brought under the aegis of the metropolis," Mumford wrote in 1925, "but how the population and civic facilities can be distributed so as to promote and stimulate a vivid, creative life throughout the region."[9]

Crossing Great Divides is a work of synthesis, ranging across the discipline of history and into many other fields, from sociology and ecological science to philosophy and literature. Building on a body of brilliant, impassioned, and hopeful scholarship, much of it challenging the city-country dualism, I have crafted a larger narrative of what all this scholarship tells us when brought together. As a philosophical pragmatist, I also believe that knowledge comes from experience and is therefore also pluralistic. Hence, the several passages of autobiography in this work ground my arguments in the experiences that gave rise to them and serve as reminders of their partiality. My hope is that the following pages will spur other synthesizers, other narrators, to enrich our understanding of the interdependence of all human settlements and their embeddedness in nature.

The book's organization follows the logic of "Where are we now?" "How did we get here?" and "What should we do next?" In Part I, Chapter 1 explores in more detail the origins and consequences of the great divides, from climate change and soil degradation to political paralysis and intellectual confusion. Chapter 2 addresses the limits of a narrowly conceived urban sustainability through a discussion of the metabolic rift (the pattern of growing food and fiber in one place and consuming and disposing of it in a second place). Written from the perspective of Rust Belt Cincinnati, these chapters interrogate current developments in urban sustainability and explore the consequences, some of them deadly, of ignoring the interconnections between city and country.

In Part II, Chapters 3–8 trace the history of urban environmental reform and ecological thinking from the early nineteenth century to the early twenty-first century. The focus of these chapters is predominantly urban. "The country" figures largely as an object of urban ambitions and as, along with lower-income urban neighborhoods, a neglected, poor relation in terms of environmental reform. But these chapters also suggest that it is impossible to understand the successes and failures of American cities without reference to their exploitation of vast hinterlands and their continuing efforts to manage precarious settlements.

Part III returns to the current damage being done, environmentally and politically, by the city-country dualism. With an eye to the future, these chapters begin the task of imagining a different sort of relationship between city and country. Chapter 9 examines Phoenix, Arizona, as an extreme case of the dysfunctional relationship between city and country and the prospects for what has been called the world's least sustainable city. Chapter 10, with reference to recent proposals for a Green New Deal and the history of populism, argues that a green, democratic populism might best help us bridge the great divides. Finally, the Epilogue considers potential sources of the mutual understanding and resilience we will need as we face the daunting challenges the twenty-first century is already pressing on us.

1
City and Country in Environmental and Political Disorder

A View from the Rust Belt

The next two chapters examine the deteriorating relationship among cities, their regions, and the larger biosphere. This involves two intersecting tasks: interrogating the sources of and current responses to environmental degradation and exploring the relationship between cities and the nonurban ecosystems on which they depend. In linking environmental degradation and social inequality, these chapters emphasize the need to rethink the political, economic, and cultural relationships among settlements across broad regions.

My perspective on these matters has been shaped by thirty-eight years living in the Cincinnati region. Cincinnati's influence on my thinking began, however, even before I had any idea I would live there. Just as I began work on my dissertation in 1980, I read Zane L. Miller's *Boss Cox's Cincinnati* (1968). The book ignited a lifelong fascination with the spatial dimensions of urban life. Examining the boss-reformer dynamic through the lens of a conflict between center and periphery, Miller anticipated something of the argument here. Although I did not notice it then, *Boss Cox's Cincinnati* (and its author, who became a mentor) also provided a model for an ecological approach to the city that combined political, social, and geographical analysis.[1]

Beginning in 1984, while busy teaching at Xavier University and raising a family in rural Indiana, I found time to tramp around Cincinnati. One day, I ventured down to Cincinnati's old public landing, a cobblestone expanse that descended from Front Street right into the Ohio River. I had forgotten about that day, and the old public landing, until twelve years ago, roughly the time I started this project. With a shock of recognition and pleasure, I saw those same cobblestones (most long since buried) in the opening frames of the 1950 film noir *The Asphalt Jungle* (a film that hinges on the trope of evil city and redemptive country). With the spectacular Roebling Bridge in the background, the camera lingers lovingly over the cobblestones, then pans upward and across the city's skyline, with the unmistakable Carew Tower (an innovative multiuse city within a city that anticipated New York City's Rockefeller Center) and Union Trust Building (now PNC Tower) standing out in bold relief.[2]

That opening of *The Asphalt Jungle* impressed on me how much change in Cincinnati I had witnessed over the previous thirty-eight years. "In the city, time becomes visible," Lewis Mumford famously wrote. "Buildings and monuments and public ways . . . leave an imprint upon the minds even of the ignorant or the indifferent." That is how it is with me. I now live in the Cincinnati neighborhood of Oakley and make weekly trips back to rural Indiana. Everywhere I go, I encounter the issues examined here.[3]

If I leave my house today and turn right, for example, after passing a grate of Cincinnati's innovative, if troubled, sewer system, I will come upon Madison Road, along which a streetcar ran until 1951. A stroll east along Madison Road will take me to the pedestrian-friendly business district surrounding Oakley Square, once an adjunct to the factory colony of machine tool firms that made Oakley the center of a global mass-production economy. If I turn left as I leave my house, after passing a fire hydrant of Cincinnati's world-class waterworks, I will quickly run up against the rushing traffic of Interstate 71 and the auto-centric commercial developments the interstate made possible. There dozens of retail outlets in the Rookwood Plaza tap niche markets characteristic of the more fragmented world we live in today. None of the matters that follow feel abstract to me.

1

Great Divides

The Origins and Consequences
of a Way of Thinking

The central argument of this book is that the habit of thinking of city and country as opposites is at the root of our environmental and political disorder. That dualism collapses what is a complex reality into a simple choice, an either/or that obscures our true situation. So, too, with many other related dualisms. The most fundamental of these is between society and nature, dangerously suggesting that somehow human society stands outside of nature, independent of it. From that base, other dualisms proliferate, including production and consumption, business and culture, sustainability and justice, settlement and mobility, masculinity and femininity, and the intrinsic and instrumental value of nature. Burdened with deep and ambivalent feelings, these divides are best addressed directly.

The most obvious physical manifestation of how the dualism of city and country misleads is the dependence of cities on extensive hinterlands often hundreds of times larger than the cities themselves. As I write, I can hear the drone of truck traffic on a nearby interstate, part of a vast, largely unseen, and vulnerable global economy that stretches across the planet. The global economy is environmentally destructive, not least in relying on ten thousand container ships, each essentially a floating coal-fired power plant. Burning cheap but dirty "bunker fuel," container ships transport "ninety-nine percent of everything," dumping one billion tons of carbon into the atmosphere every year, more than all aviation and road transport combined. It would be better if those hinterlands were closer to home, less exploited, and more valued.[1]

Early in this century, urban political ecologists coined the term *socionature* to underscore that the social and the natural are never independent. Nature does not disappear as we enter the city, as everything from baking and brewing to hydraulic cycles and the disposal of waste suggests. Similarly, the social does not end when we leave the city, as everything from dams and electric grids to genetically modified plants and resort towns suggests. Yet even as scholars explore the indivisibility of society and nature, the city-country dualism remains ingrained in our culture. Too often we treat nature as an amenity rather than as the inescapable foundation of our lives. A consequent lack of moral realism about the hard and difficult work essential to our lives results in a callousness toward those who do that work. Even environmentalists too often neglect work as a fundamental part of the human relationship to nature.[2]

The great divides of city-country and society-nature are, of course, imaginary. As ecology and a host of other inquiries tell us, everything is connected. But the great divides are no less influential for being imaginary, not least in obscuring great continuities. Climate change, the declining fertility of soils, and disappearing sources of potable water all stem from a failure to recognize and care for our dependence on nature. Growing income inequality, ethnic and racial hatreds, callousness toward the poor, and the political distrust and paralysis that make it impossible to address these mounting troubles are also products of the failure to see the many ways in which all our fates are intertwined.[3]

Born in 1955, I have lived through some of the most dramatic environmental transformations in the history of a country defined by dramatic environmental transformations. The shift from solar-powered to fossil-fueled agriculture, the bulldozing of urban neighborhoods for highways and urban renewal, suburban sprawl, the explosion of wastes associated with an affluent society, and accelerating climate change all happened or reached a critical stage in my lifetime. To take just two specific examples, 80 percent of the human dumping of carbon dioxide into the atmosphere and virtually all plastic pollution have occurred in my lifetime. I write now amid a dangerous political divisiveness that is, at its core, a reaction to these traumatic transformations.[4]

I have lived and worked on both sides of the great divide between city and country. For twenty-five years, I lived in a rural, southeastern Indiana community, a forty-five-minute commute from Cincinnati. I cleared an acre of land, built a house with my own hands, and raised a family there.

I have engaged in agricultural labor off and on my whole life. I know what hard physical work is and I respect those who do it. One measure of the great divide is that for the longest time, I never imagined these experiences could in any way be linked to my love and study of cities. Even in writing this book, it took years to recognize the implicit case for regionalism I had been building. In bringing my personal experiences on both sides of the great divide into conversation with what I have managed to learn as an urban historian, I attempt to cross the great divides. I have no quick or easy fixes to offer in this study, neither about urban nor even less about rural communities. But a lack of solutions is not the issue.

Experiments and proposals abound, from shifting to renewable energy and making cities more walkable to resolarizing our industrialized agriculture and reducing waste in manufacturing. Most fundamentally, we need to repair our relationships with one another and with the rest of the natural world. We must reinvest in our cities as well as in our rural communities, sharing more equitably our vast inheritance of health, wealth, and opportunity. We must change the way we both produce and consume. We need to stop destroying the environment to enrich a small segment of our society. Our obsession with economic growth must give way to an economy premised on sharing, caring, and production for use.[5]

While many Americans remain outwardly skeptical about the dangers of climate change and environmental degradation, our divisive and venomous politics is the best evidence of mounting fears of scarcity. But we lack the political will, the political courage, and, crucially, the political imagination to act. Thinking differently is the crucial step toward addressing our mounting troubles. Seventy years ago, the naturalist and philosopher Aldo Leopold pointed the way in his call for a land ethic to extend ethical action to the treatment of nature. Deeply held beliefs in human mastery and powerful economic interests stood, and still stand, in the way of this shift in thinking. But the development of such an ethic remains an ecological necessity and a political and evolutionary possibility. The good news is that if we do shift, we simultaneously tackle both our environmental and our political challenges. Without a shift, environmental stresses and divisive politics will continue to feed one another.[6]

While these issues are global, my focus is on the United States. For good or ill, the decisions of the United States in the next ten years will have momentous global implications. In their failure to work together to find common ground, urban and rural people empower an oligarchic elite that skews government to its narrow and destructive interests. The list of governmental failures—from the response to Hurricane Katrina in 2005 and the 2008 mortgage crisis to the Deepwater Horizon oil spill in 2010 and the 2020 COVID-19 pandemic—underscores the enormous cost to the well-being of Americans. These failures also help to explain the dangerous skepticism about the value of public action that distorts our politics. If we are to use our collective powers to address our mounting challenges, urban and rural people will need each other. They can each bring important ideas to the effort to find common ground.[7]

An Honest Accounting

To find our way forward, we need an honest accounting of the costs, as well as the benefits, of our modes of production and our ways of life. To provide for the average middle-class family of four, a careful study concluded, the American economy annually "moves, mines, extracts, shovels, burns, wastes, pumps, and disposes of 4 million pounds of material." Too great a share of the costs of those activities falls on rural areas and too great a share of the benefits accrues to urban areas. We must stop distancing ourselves from the disagreeable consequences of our actions. Dividing city and country, society and nature, spares us the shock of looking at the totality of our social and natural relationships. We need to take responsibility for all activities, all our relationships, good and bad. Taken together, they are who we are.[8]

As a privileged middle-class urbanite, I bear more than average blame for where we are. In my sixty-seven years, by the calculation above, I am responsible for sixty-seven million pounds of waste. Perhaps my well-meaning but fitful efforts to live lightly on the land shaved a million or two pounds off that. The resulting pile—or, rather, mountain—of waste would amount to more than sixty Boeing 747 jumbo jets stacked on top of one another. A full accounting of my debt must include my bodily wastes as well as the human labor, much of it poorly compensated, embedded in all that moving, mining, and shoveling. The material impact of my consumption is experienced hundreds and thousands of miles away in forests, farms, mines, and refineries and by the people who work them. Low wages, toxic wastes, and shortened life spans mark these places of production, while the wastes of urban affluence burden both poor urban neighborhoods and more distant communities.[9]

Cities make earnest if fitful efforts to become more energy-efficient, reduce waste, and conserve and protect water. But there is more than a little justice in the charge that the current drive for urban sustainability is a white, middle-class form of upscale consumption. As hard-pressed municipalities struggle to balance budgets, they find it difficult to invest in such requirements of a sustainable community as affordable housing, adequate education, and accessible health care. Instead, bike trails, farmers' markets, and mixed-use zoning provide a cheaper way for cities to claim the green city status that attracts investors and young professionals. Meanwhile, admirable efforts to clean up industrial wastes, increase green space, and improve stormwater infrastructure price low-income residents out of improving neighborhoods. Some municipalities are making laudable efforts to address such inequalities. But too often, urban sustainability fails to address growing inequality within the city and does little to repair the dysfunctional relationship between city and country.[10]

Oakley, the leafy Cincinnati neighborhood where I live, is an illuminating example of the current state of urban sustainability efforts. A lovely place, the neighborhood is graced by Oakley Square, around which cluster an array of amenities. I can walk to at least five different grocery stores, ranging from big box to organic and mom and pop. There are twenty-five restaurants, a movie theater, and a music venue within easy walking distance. Health-care options are also a short walk away. I can walk to work, as well, two and a half miles to Xavier University.[11]

Oakley once served as the machine tool capital of the world, the center of a mass-production economy. But the machine tool industry is entirely gone, a casualty of globalization. The industrial jobs that raised generations of immigrant and working-class families into the middle class are also gone. Instead, the service industry reigns. Shopping malls, office parks, and condominiums stand in place of busy factories. Today, Oakley's walkable mix of residential and retail streets attracts young (and old) professionals looking for a sustainable urban lifestyle. Nearby farmers' markets offer fresh produce. What promises to become a world-class bike trail, Wasson Way, skirts Oakley's southern border and will eventually link residents to hundreds of miles of trails crisscrossing the city and the state of Ohio.[12]

Oakley's contribution to regional sustainability, however, is limited. A landscape of consumption, the neighborhood teems with bars, coffee shops, yoga and Pilates studios, and boutique vegan and popsicle vendors. For all of Oakley's claim to walkability, more than 80 percent of residents drive to work; the average household owns 1.9 cars. Although it retains its walkable center with independent retailers, that center is flanked by newer, larger, chain-dominated, auto-centric developments. Meanwhile, the neighborhood's stock of low-income housing is disappearing. Real estate prices have been rising for a generation and continue to rise. A laundromat that served the remaining low-income renters in the neighborhood closed in 2019. It is rumored to be reopening as an upscale bar.[13]

Oakley is a world away from Cincinnati's shameful, sprawling second ghetto. Despite being part of a city that is more than 40 percent Black and where half the children live in poverty, Oakley is predominately white (more than 80 percent) and affluent. In Black Cincinnati, the median income is less than half of Oakley's; unemployment is twice as high; and infant mortality rates soar to levels found in the poorest places on the globe. The National Urban League rated Cincinnati seventy-third among seven-seven metropolitan areas for racial inequality in household income. In 2015, the Greater Cincinnati Urban League documented huge racial disparities in unemployment, life expectancy, business ownership, home-ownership, child poverty, educational outcomes, and mass incarceration.[14]

Oakley is also a world away from the small towns and rural communities in the Ohio, Kentucky, and Indiana counties surrounding Cincinnati. The same is true of Cincinnati's aging first-ring suburbs. Those areas share few of the benefits of urban life. They suffer from higher rates of poverty, lower incomes, lower rates of graduation from high school and college, and fewer medical care options. With declining numbers of jobs in farming, mining, and manufacturing, employment levels have been slow to recover since the financial crisis of 2008. Food insecurity is also more prominent due to high prices, low availability, and scarcity of fresh produce. Deteriorating infrastructure, particularly water systems, adds to the burdens.[15]

While far from the most affluent community in the United States, Oakley contributes to an urban way of life that is placing tremendous demands on the biosphere. To satisfy urban demand, a giant pool of investment capital in search of profits leaves no natural resource, no ecosystem, no community untouched or undamaged. The results include resource depletion and climate change, the accumulation and spread of pollution and toxic waste, the loss of agricultural land and the destruction of forests through both clear cutting and, increasingly, fire, and the eradication of habitat and reduction in biodiversity. In cities proper, urban standards of living concentrate pollution and waste heat, disrupt the hydraulic cycle, and contaminate soils.[16]

Great Divides and the History of Capitalism

The habit of dividing city from country has a long history, but it first came into prominence with the rise of industrial capitalism. Indeed, the city-country dualism is one of the major ways we have responded to capitalism. As manufacturing concentrated in urban settings, the city came to be seen as the whole of society, the active force that determined the fate of the nonsocial, natural realm of the countryside. The "unity of living and active human beings with the natural, inorganic conditions of their metabolism with nature," the political economist Karl Marx argued early in the industrial era, "requires no explanation." But what does require explanation, Marx concluded, "is the *separation* of these inorganic conditions of human existence from this active existence."[17]

The separation Marx referred to is the root of the city-country dualism, and it had already begun to take shape with the emergence of capitalism in the countryside, two centuries before the industrial revolution. Amid the enclosure movements in early modern England, the effort to prettify rural dispossession generated habits of thought that shaped the later response to industrial capitalism. In works of sycophancy and misdirection, the neo-pastoral poets praised the natural order of newly enclosed country estates, contrasting it with the artificiality of court life in the cities. The poems lauded the gentry for their generosity to their servants, depicting the servants only as they feasted at table, their pains and labor nowhere acknowledged. These idylls of consumption disguised the brute facts of production, obscuring the origins of estates that had been created by devouring whole villages and evicting tenants.[18]

In the eighteenth century, novelists and poets who tried to make sense of the explosive growth of England's capital city also deployed the city-country dualism. Like the neo-pastoral poets, they looked away from the productive basis of society and its consequences. As London filled up with the dispossessed poor who crowded into hovels and back alleys, poets and novelists described the city as a monstrous growth, ritually contrasting it with the supposedly idyllic conditions of the country. But country and city represented two sides of the same social transformation. The destitute and dispossessed, the hordes tramping in search of work, the overcrowded slums could all be traced back to the dispossession proceeding in the countryside. London's law courts, its capital market, even its marriage market all served the consolidating and expanding fortunes of enclosing landlords.[19]

With the rise of industrialization, the dualism of city and country thus provided a means of explaining away or refusing to take responsibility for the social and environmental costs of capitalist development. By treating the city as the source of "progress, modernization, development" and the country as the repository of "old ways, human ways, natural ways," the cultural critic Raymond Williams explained, we pitted the demands of material well-being against the pull of care and compassion. The city-country dualism thus attached desires for harmony and connection to a disappearing, irrecoverable rural past while "linking our desire for affluence and comfort to an irresistible if not entirely desirable" urban future. "Between the simple backward look and the simple progressive thrust," Williams concluded, "there is room for long argument but none for enlightenment."[20]

For us, too, a belief in the irresistible advance of urbanization, combined with a feckless nostalgia for rural simplicity, shrinks political imagination. Even Williams himself neglected, "for longer than seemed possible," the obvious point that a rural economy "simply had to persist" and did persist in the exploited colonies of the British empire. Our belief that the future belongs to urban life, the knowledge economy, and the digital/virtual world distracts attention from the working poor, both urban and rural, who still do the hard work necessary to civilization. The outsized hopes for an urban-based sustainability, and the relative neglect of needed reforms in agriculture, mining, lumbering, fishing, and other extractive industries, mislead in suggesting that the greening of the city will resolve all our environmental troubles.[21]

Even the most advanced societies still need clean air and water, fertile soil, building materials, and food from the oceans. They also need natural ecosystems that produce oxygen, replenish soils, pollinate crops, decompose wastes, and reduce the accumulation of toxins in air, water, and soil even as they control the spread of weeds, germs, and pests. The steady erosion of soil fertility, the growing scarcity of potable water, and the degradation of ecosystems that provide essential goods and services all signal the dangerous pressures we are placing on the carrying capacity of the planet. So do the filling of the atmosphere with carbon dioxide and the reckless destruction of carbon-sequestering forests.[22]

Whatever its contributions in a relatively empty world, capitalism's treatment of the biosphere as loot and dump on a planet of nearly eight billion people threatens us all. Capitalism elevates economic growth, at best a means to some other end, to an end in itself. In the process, it jeopardizes everything we value. The individual accumulation of wealth is prized above all things, with both the natural world and human society left to absorb the costs. The relentless drive for profit endangers the planetary systems that make human life possible as evidenced by disappearing rain forests, melting glaciers, and acidifying oceans. While the drive for profits disrupts or destroys both individual lives and entire communities, our efforts to dull the pain through manic consumption push immediate gratification above concern for people and places.[23]

Our moral traditions have long held that the incessant drive for power, status, and wealth brings only anxiety, stress, anger, envy, and dissatisfaction. Recent research in neuroscience, psychology, and evolutionary biology confirms that wisdom. We overemphasize the minority of extrinsic values (self-advancement, hierarchy, competition) while neglecting the more powerful intrinsic values (compassion, connectedness, kindness) that make us human. Altruism, even more than language or tools, makes our species unique. We have an unmatched capacity for kindness, sensitivity, and concern and the ability to generalize and encourage these values. We evolved as cooperators, using mutual aid to survive. In ignoring this, we suffer from an epidemic of loneliness, depression, paranoia, anxiety, insomnia, fear, dementia, high blood pressure, heart disease, and lowered immunity. The individual costs are multiplied by the rupturing of social bonds and the erosion of civic and community life.[24]

Environmental Degradation and Political Paralysis

Every day, environmental pressures on our lives and communities increase. Even if we set aside the consequences of climate change (rising sea levels, drowning cities, hurricane-force winds on the Great Lakes, record numbers of tornados, floods that delay or even cancel growing seasons), we face daunting challenges. Scientists estimate global topsoil will be depleted in sixty years, resulting in mass starvation. Millions of tons of topsoil flow into the oceans; underground aquifers—irreplaceable "fossil water"—are drawn down; croplands deteriorate from salinization and desertification; fisheries are depleted; and forests are denuded or burn uncontrollably. For many, declining sources of potable water and accumulating toxic wastes present even more immediate threats.[25]

Unfortunately, we cannot set aside climate change. For years, defense officials—no green radicals—have been planning, and occasionally fighting, climate wars. The rise in temperature is already creating havoc in both rural and urban communities around the world. Significant increases above the current global temperature are now inevitable, perhaps 2 degrees or as high as 6 degrees Celsius. Cities will flood even more; croplands will dry up or flood so badly as to be unusable; and soaring temperatures will continue to spread forest fires while reducing the human capacity for work. We already live on a different planet, where every major feature, from ice caps to rain forests, has been dramatically altered.[26]

A series of feedback loops may be placing control of global warming beyond our reach. A warming world is melting Arctic ice, creating heat-absorbing blue ocean where white ice once reflected heat back into the atmosphere. Vast quantities of methane (a much more potent greenhouse gas than carbon dioxide) have been trapped in frozen tundra and in deep ocean methane hydrates (known as "fire ice"). But global warming is melting both sources. This may create runaway warming effects, even in the event of drastic cuts in the use of fossil fuels. Plans are afoot to burn that methane, too, as it represents a vast new supply of fossil fuel, more than has already been burned in human history.[27]

Anyone can find this information on the web. By the time you read this, it may have been replaced by worse news. We have been hearing, and ignoring, the warnings for many decades. In 1972, in the wake of the first Earth Day and the creation of the federal Environmental Protection Agency, a group of systems analysts from the Massachusetts Institute of Technology predicted the likelihood that humanity would "overshoot" the carrying capacity of the planet. Today, the best estimate is that we are exceeding the Earth's biocapacity by a factor of 1.75. That means we will need 1.75 Earths to sustain current consumption even as we destroy the one Earth we have.[28]

In their 1972 report *The Limits to Growth*, these young analysts ran computer models on the depletion of key resources. The results led them to call for a commitment to economic and ecological sustainability that would provide a secure minimum of material needs and social opportunities for future generations. For a time in the mid-1970s, we appeared ready to heed the advice as speed limits fell, fuel efficiency rose, and a sweater-wearing president turned down the thermostat in the White House. More Americans described themselves as anti-growth than pro-growth (31 percent versus 30 percent), while 39 percent described themselves as "highly uncertain."[29]

The Limits to Growth proved wrong on some matters, underestimating the role of innovation and the profit motive in securing more and new resources. But over the quarter-century that followed, we learned more about the carrying capacity of the planet, including its capacity to absorb waste. In 1997, a group of ecologists and economists calculated the dollar value of the goods and services that nature freely provides. In a conservative estimate, they came up with an astounding number, $33 trillion a year, twice the global product, virtually none of which figured in market prices. To drive home the point, they cited the "exceedingly complex and expensive" preparations for space colonies to underscore that the

Earth "is a very efficient, least-cost provider of human life-support services." In the absence of viable substitutes, the value of natural capital is infinite. After all, what would you pay for the last gasp of oxygen?[30]

Today our divisive politics makes the challenges of dealing with environmental stresses even more daunting. Uneasiness about the future is evident in the venomous debates over immigration and other issues. But many still claim climate change is a hoax, while the oil companies that fund the reports that encourage such doubts knew about the threat decades ago. Self-interest and social antagonisms thus paralyze our political system just when we desperately need to use our collective powers to address our accumulating troubles.[31]

The blue state-red state divide that frustrates cooperation is just the most recent expression of the false and pernicious divide between city and country. Like the other dualisms, the blue state-red state divide misleads and oversimplifies. Many so-called red states contain and depend on blue cities, while so-called blue states contain and depend on red rural areas. The red-blue divide, moreover, runs straight through the suburbs of major metropolises. Denser and more demographically diverse suburbs closer to the metropolitan center remain blue while less dense and more homogeneous suburbs remain red. A preference for light rail and other public investments versus auto-centric development and libertarian values map the division, with ominous implications for the use of our public powers.[32]

Most damagingly, the manipulation of blue-red divisions obscures a profound clash of deeply felt injuries. The legitimate upswing in demands among Black people for equality, including an end to police brutality and mass incarceration, encounters an understandably resentful white population in small towns and rural areas who face declining prospects in areas that range from income to life expectancy. These deeply felt injuries are then exploited by a plutocratic minority to defend its privileges. To end our political paralysis, we need a movement that transcends the urban-rural, liberal-conservative, and Democratic-Republican divisions. The revolt of the Yellow Vests in France, based on similar divisions, is instructive. The "concrete reality" underlying this strange movement, a journalist explained, is "that if you want to deal with climate change globally you need first to topple the regimes of the rich locally."[33]

Yet the great divides continue to frustrate efforts at redress. White urban liberals generally recognize the legitimacy of Black people's aspirations, even if they do too little to address them. But those same liberals generally do not even see rural anger as legitimate. When urban liberals think of "flyover country," they think of it, by turns, as a place of retreat and recreation and as the abode of backward, intolerant, and ignorant people. Even as urban liberals depend on the labor of rural workers, they ridicule—rather than engage and debate—their religious beliefs, their attitudes about marriage and family, their cultural values, and their heroes. No wonder demagogic politicians can rouse rural people to a hatred of urban liberals and everything they stand for.[34]

The Perils and Promise of Environmental Reform and Ecological Thinking

Far from ignorant, many rural people—especially those who work the land—are as aware of environmental degradation as urban liberals, even if they resist policies emanating from the metropolis. They detect a certain unreality in the urban understanding of the natural world. Like the wilderness ideal that it resembles, urban life encourages blindness to our dependence on nature. Many experiences that urbanites take for granted—turning on a tap for water or flushing waste down drains, visiting a park or a forest preserve—depend on an elaborate and invisible urban infrastructure that manages our interaction with nature. Obscuring a recognition of nature as the essential, precarious foundation of every aspect of our lives, these experiences encourage a view of nature focused on health, recreation, and preservation, nature as an amenity.[35]

A similar bias toward thinking of nature in terms of consumption has shaped environmental reform. Much of the history of American cities and regions is bound up in two central tasks—specifically, the building of productive (and often exploitative) ecologies and the management of dense, precarious settlements. Cities, especially in the industrial era, built their economies through the often irresponsible exploitation of extensive hinterlands. They left behind blasted landscapes and impoverished communities. Environmental reform has focused much less on reducing the despoilation that results from such productive activities, too often neglecting the fate of communities and individuals caught in the process.[36]

Environmental reformers have been far more energetic and successful in the second, consumer-oriented task of turning cities into healthier, more beautiful, and more satisfying places to live. Such reforms date back to the early nineteenth century. By the early twentieth century, the effort to sanitize and beautify the city provided urban Americans with the best public services in the world and made modern urban culture possible. But the benefits of those reforms have not always been widely shared, neither within cities nor in the vast hinterlands that cities exploit.[37]

There is, in other words, more than a little justice in the charge that an ecological sensibility appeals to those concerned with consumption, with body and home, more than to those engaged in the hard and dirty tasks of production. The combative bumper sticker, "Are you an environmentalist or do you work for a living?" captures the antipathy. Urban liberals' fascination with ecology strikes many rural people as a badge of moral superiority worn by know-it-alls. Urban liberals look to popular forms of ecology as a guide to repairing our relationship with nature. Many argue that we live in the age of ecology, even identifying ecology as the logical replacement for theology. But rural skepticism about ecology points to the need for a more complete ethic—one that engages production as well as consumption and that can guide us toward more responsible use of the natural world.[38]

Of course, we will need ecological knowledge as we rethink and repair the relationships between city and country. As the scientific study of how living organisms interact with and get what they need from their environment, ecology remains an essential tool. But there are multiple reasons to be wary of ecology—or, rather, the misunderstanding and misuse of the science. Too often nonscientists deploy ecological ideals simplistically, as when people assert that "nature shows" or "nature is" or "nature teaches." Nature is not one thing but multiple things, by turns competitive, destructive, and predatory, as well as cooperative, constructive, and interdependent.[39]

Neither ecology nor nature, moreover, can provide a complete blueprint for the reconstruction of society. Yet those who deploy ecological ideas are often pulled toward the deterministic, reducing human affairs to the blind application of the laws of nature. Like faith in the market's invisible hand, this view minimizes the capacity of humans to identify and pursue collective ends. All those who apply ecological ideas to human societies, scientists and historians as well as citizens and activists, should balance two truths about humans. We are biological creatures that operate within physical limits. But we are also conscious, political, and moral agents who, while saddled with limitations and prejudices, nevertheless have extraordinary manipulative capacities.[40]

The development of the science of ecology has tended to favor the deterministic. Initially having some affinity for natural history, ecology moved toward more technocratic and managerial approaches over the course of the twentieth century. At times offering a subversive but ineffectual challenge to the great god of endless economic growth, ecologists more often either directly served the growth machine or ignored it. Ecology also sometimes flirted with eugenics early in the past century, offering race improvement through environmental reform.[41]

Nonetheless, ecology remains indispensable in teaching us that cities and their regions are part of the natural world. Concrete, asphalt, and plastic are derived from natural sources no less than wood, stone, and brick. Cities and regions depend on natural processes, including hydrologic and nutrient cycles; the reproduction of natural resources, including human labor; and the recycling of waste. Human activities are not imitating natural processes; they are natural processes. No other option exists. Cities seem unnatural only because many of the biophysical systems on which they depend are human-built systems that import materials and energy and export wastes. These systems, what the historian Thomas Hughes called "ecotechnological systems," include the urban water supply and sewage disposal systems, streets, transit systems, and the delivery of electricity and natural gas. All are biophysical systems that are part of the natural world.[42]

We urgently need to consider our cities ecologically. Cities, and the extractive industries that supply them, represent the ecology of the dominant animal on the globe today. As urban populations rise and the aspiration for standards of living common in the cities of the West spread, the future of civilization is at stake in the design and operation of cities and regions. In appropriating natural resources, covering land surfaces and modifying landforms, burning fossil fuels, and building artificial drainage systems, city life changes every natural process on which we depend. Population increase, the release of carbon, the withdrawal of water, and deforestation are the most prominent among a host of other human-induced drivers of environmental change.[43]

The Great Divide in Higher Learning and a Pragmatic Corrective

For all these reasons, urban and regional sustainability must be a high priority. Ecological thinking can help in this effort, making cities and entire regions more healthful, beautiful, and just, as well as more resource-efficient. No single line of inquiry, however, can provide sufficient guidance for a question as complex as the proper organization of human society. Any effort to address our mounting environmental and political challenges will need multiple lines of inquiry, from the ecological and economic to the religious and philosophical. Nor can that effort afford a lack of skepticism about all these lines of inquiry, particularly when we recognize that the great divides have shaped even our most advanced thinking, leaving crucial inquiries partial and incomplete.[44]

As the science of ecology developed over the twentieth century, to take a crucial example, it largely ignored humans. The reluctance of ecologists to bring humanity into their science stemmed from their belief that humans could only disturb an otherwise harmonious balance of nature. The principles and processes of that balance could therefore be studied only in places free from human disturbance. Meanwhile, scholars from a variety of other fields laid claim to the study of human ecology. In the most influential of these efforts, the Chicago school of urban sociologists developed a conception of human ecology that ignored its embeddedness in a larger natural world.[45]

This intellectual division of labor, whereby ecologists studied nature untouched by humans and urban sociologists studied cities that stood outside nature, thus recapitulated the great divides of city and country, society and nature. Philosophical pragmatism offers a useful corrective. Pragmatism first took shape in response to the debate over Charles Darwin's theory of evolution. Like those who have looked to ecology as a master guide to reorganizing human society, social Darwinists sought to turn the insights of Darwinian evolution into a complete plan for social renovation. Pragmatists objected. They argued that ideas, including evolutionary theory, are tools, good for some tasks but not for others, just as a hammer is good for driving nails but useless for turning screws. Darwin's theory had been developed to address the question of the origins of species. It could not be presumed to resolve every other question, least of all how human societies should be organized. For that, we needed multiple ideas, multiple lines of inquiry.[46]

By treating ideas as tools, philosophical pragmatism also underscored the crucial role of consciousness in a distinctively human ecology. The Chicago sociologists, by embracing the deterministic elements of ecology, minimized the role of consciousness. As an early critic wrote, even when these human ecologists "occasionally make references to such volitional factors as purpose," it is only "to tell us how hopelessly the iron laws of nature" overrode human purpose. Pragmatism, especially the evolutionary naturalism of John Dewey, offered an alternative human ecology that placed consciousness at its center. Dewey understood the brain as a product of evolution and thinking as a natural, organic function that mediated between an organism and its environment. Consciousness gave human experience a special quality, the possibility of inquiry, knowledge, and judgment to guide action.[47]

Only in the past three decades have ecologists returned to the matter of human ecology and to consciousness. Building alliances with the policy sciences, ecologists theorize that the accumulation of knowledge provides the means "by which order and behavioral predictability can contain a relatively free-ranging species." Ecologists thus deem it "wise to learn from social scientists" about the social and educational features of human life. But urban ecologists should also keep in mind that the confidence of the social sciences in their ability to treat humans as predictable and manageable entities often outstrips their accomplishments, a development that parallels the natural sciences' troubled quest for a mastery of nature.[48]

Social scientists focus on human *behavior*—that is, on the routine, unconscious, and predictable, that which is measurable by statistics. This approach reinforces and is reinforced by technocratic ambitions. Historians, in contrast, chronicle the idiosyncratic, conscious, and unpredictable *actions* of humans. In doing so, historians have shown how the accumulation of knowledge leads humans to attempt to free themselves from natural limits and, in overreaching, bring destruction to themselves and their environment. As we face a perilous future, history becomes an ever more crucial inquiry. While knowledge can lead to overreaching, it is also the source of our ability to act as moral and responsible agents. Knowledge has too often cut the first way; the task is to ensure it more often cuts the other way.[49]

One thing is for sure. The stakes—and the challenges—have never been greater. Our damage to the environment escalates day by day. For the first time in the history of the world, a species has the capacity to make the planet uninhabitable for itself and, remarkably, is going ahead and doing it. City life has produced great intellectual capacity but also enormous squalor. City people excel in interacting, often in cooperative ways but also in competitive and predatory ways. Most telling, city culture encourages a capacity for understanding abstract things but undercuts a rich understanding of the natural world. Our most daunting challenge is to come to terms with ourselves and our relations with the natural world. Our failures raise the question of whether *sapiens*, wise, is the best name for our species. Clever and smart, for sure, but wise? We shall soon know.[50]

2

Metabolically Adrift

The Limits of Urban Sustainability

"Don't touch that railing." My students and I stood on a raised concrete platform perched thirty feet above Cincinnati's Mill Creek, itself encased in a drab, concrete channel 150 feet wide. The creek flowed lazily by us, green-tinged from algae but otherwise unremarkable. A train crept through the railyard on the opposite side of the creek while, downstream, automobiles crossed the crumbling, concrete Western Hills Viaduct that spans the Mill Creek Valley and provides access to the city's west side. Behind and below us, a small trickle of foul-looking water exited a concrete pipe nearly twenty feet in diameter that protruded from the hillside.

"When it rains hard," our guide continued, "the overflow from this pipe reaches up to that railing. You often see toilet paper hanging from it." From where we stood, thirty feet above the bottom of that pipe, it seemed impossible that water could ever fill the vast space necessary to reach that railing. But if you looked up Cincinnati's hilly west side that stretched to the horizon, you might imagine a rush of stormwater and tens of thousands of flushed toilets overwhelming the capacity of the combined storm and sanitary sewer system and spilling 1.7 billion gallons of untreated wastewater into the creek every year.[1]

We stood at Cincinnati's combined sewer overflow (CSO) #5, the worst in the region but only one of more than two hundred in Cincinnati and Hamilton County, Ohio. It stands where Lick Run once emptied into

Mill Creek. Lick Run, part of the three hundred miles of streams flowing through the Lower Mill Creek Valley, disappeared into a concrete pipe in 1910. Only seventy-five miles of those urban streams now see daylight. The rest flow through the six hundred miles of sewer pipes that crisscross the region.[2]

Like many older cities that have combined sewer systems (handling both stormwater and sewage), Cincinnati has failed to meet the 1972 Clean Water Act's goal of "zero water pollution discharge by 1985." In 2004, the Metropolitan Sewer District (MSD) of Greater Cincinnati entered a consent decree with the federal Environmental Protection Agency (EPA) and Department of Justice and the state of Ohio to reduce its overflow by twelve billion gallons annually. Initial plans included the construction of a massive storage tunnel under Mill Creek, at a cost of at least $250 million, with a $1.7 million annual operating cost.[3]

Combined sewer overflows are part of a pressing environmental challenge hardly anyone even knows about: the metabolic rift, or the practice of growing food and fiber in one place and consuming and disposing of it in another. The rift robs soils of fertility while polluting sources of potable water. Nutrients extracted from agricultural soils are not returned to those soils, and fertility declines. Discarded nutrients (food scraps, human and animal excrement, fibers) instead pollute watercourses in cities and towns and spread disease. The metabolic rift is the most immediate, and deadly, consequence of the failure to treat city and country as parts of a greater whole. The failure to take responsibility for this most basic element of human ecology, the proper treatment of waste, highlights the limits of urban sustainability. Our sustainability efforts must reach beyond the city to the hinterlands and the productive and extractive activities that make city life possible.

The Metabolic Rift and the Limits of Urban Sustainability

The metabolic rift is a prime example of how faulty ways of thinking lead to faulty ways of acting. The dangerous belief that city life frees us from dependence on nature clouds our future because city life multiplies, complicates, and intensifies our reliance on nature. Yet too often we speak of urban sustainability without reference to the hinterlands on which cities depend. In part, this is true because municipal departments charged with environmental and sustainability efforts operate on tight budgets and find it difficult to justify regionally based projects. Rural governments with only a handful of employees, and suspicious of policies emanating from big cities, show even less interest in regional cooperation.[4]

The failure of regional cooperation, however, is not just a matter of logistics. It is also an expression of the great divides between city and country, society and nature. As one of the world's largest multinational corporations (Siemens) puts it, urban sustainability "is the idea that a city can be organized without excessive reliance on the surrounding countryside." The creation of resource-efficient cities is a laudable goal. But too many proponents of urban sustainability take for granted an ever increasing urban population and the depopulation of the countryside. In *If Mayors Ruled the World* (2013), the political theorist Benjamin Barber reviewed the dualism of city versus country and concluded that to "choose sides is a hapless and futile strategy." Yet with reference to rural depopulation, Barber remained complacent, asking, "How could it be otherwise in our era of agribusiness?" He said almost nothing else about agriculture (or mining). Barber's proposal for a global parliament of mayors to take the place of the paralyzed nation-state could serve as a useful step toward regional governance. But rural depopulation means rural de-democratization. Without vigilant rural citizens, ever more damaging forms of agribusiness will counter any positive environmental developments in cities.[5]

A generation ago, the urbanist Joel Garreau's influential study *Edge City* (1991) revealed some of the assumptions that underlay the neglect of rural areas. Garreau treated the edge cities that mushroomed outside major cities as reflections of Americans' desire for a closer "connection with nature, the earth, the ground." But he also knew that urban sprawl damaged the countryside and generated heated debates. Garreau interviewed the cultural historian Leo Marx for perspective. The contemporary debate over sprawl, Marx explained, represented the most recent chapter of Americans' simultaneous and contradictory devotion to technological progress and to unspoiled nature. Edge cities, Marx added, represented yet one more attempt to "escape from the negative aspects of civilization. Too much restraint, oppression, hierarchy—you justify building out there in order to start again and have another Garden."[6]

Yet the pastoral dream of living in harmony with nature, Marx concluded, did nothing to restrain an economic system dedicated to unlimited growth. Instead, in encouraging suburban sprawl the pastoral dream only energized an economic system that "does pitifully little to encourage or reward those constraints necessary for the long-term ecological well-being of society." Yet Garreau pushed the argument back to the same dualism of greedy city and soulful country from which Marx tried to free it. "In the unsettled, unsettling environment of Edge City," Garreau concluded, "great wealth may be acquired, but without a sense that the place has community, or even a center, much less a soul."[7]

The 2021 study *Blue Metros, Red States* again reflects the failure to consider the well-being of rural areas. The political scientists who conducted the study rightly point out that blue metros generate most of the nation's gross domestic product and foreign trade, as well as most patents and new technology. They add that the median income of blue districts in the House of Representatives is $8,000 greater than in red districts, and the trend is toward greater divergence. Despite this evidence of economic inequality, however, the authors neglect to ask whether blue metros have anything to offer rural areas—or, indeed, whether blue metros bear any responsibility for the plight of rural areas. They note that economic growth and high-skill workers are concentrated in million-plus metros. But they seem much less interested in questioning the policy decisions and investments that concentrate opportunity in metropolitan areas or in asking how opportunity might be spread more widely.[8]

Such expressions of the great divides obscure the inextricable links between rural and urban life that stretch back to the Neolithic era. The rise of agriculture turned a negative feedback relationship between food and human reproduction into a positive one. Before the advent of agriculture, food shortages led to lower rates of human reproduction through lack of time and energy, longer periods of lactation, and reduction of the fat content necessary to female fertility. The introduction of agriculture changed this negative feedback into positive feedback. An increase in food increased fat, sped weaning, and provided more time and energy for reproduction. More births also meant more labor and thus more food, intensifying the positive feedback loop. Once literally a burden in hunter-gatherer societies, children became assets in agricultural societies.[9]

Over the subsequent millennia, a steady increase in the food supply expanded the population and made cities possible. As cities grew, they multiplied their demands on their surrounding countryside through agriculture and mining. The most explosive growth began with the intensification of agriculture and the beginnings of industry in early modern Britain. Urban manufacturing supplied tools and technology that intensified exploitation of rural lands, generating another positive feedback loop. Meanwhile, the growth of European empires and the increase in long-distance trade widened the metabolic rift and increased the use of fossil fuels. The subsequent release of the carbon sunk in those fossil fuels and its dispersal into the atmosphere created a biospheric rift (a disruption of the normal carbon cycle due to human economic activity) that slowly began to warm the planet.[10]

The scientific revolution, and the associated belief in human mastery of nature, strengthened the great divides and intensified the metabolic rift. To better understand how to manipulate nature, scientists stripped it of the qualities, often captured in organic and maternal metaphors, that once moderated exploitation. But by the end of the sixteenth century, the English philosopher and architect of the scientific method Francis Bacon argued that "nature takes orders from man and works under his authority." Nature must be "bound to service" and made a "slave," Bacon continued, put "in constraint" and "molded" by mechanical means. As scientists, agricultural reformers, and industrialists more aggressively manipulated nature as a set of objects and relationships, they saw themselves as working *on* nature not *in* it.[11]

By the middle of the nineteenth century, however, the degradation of soils and the pollution of water demanded attention, at least to symptoms if not to basic causes of the metabolic rift. Agricultural reformers devised artificial means of restoring fertility. The subsequent mining, manufacturing, and transportation of fertilizers burned yet more fossil fuels. Meanwhile, urban expansion disrupted the traditional recycling of nutrients in the form of "night soil" (human wastes collected from privies and cesspools in cities and returned to farms). Instead, those wastes fouled urban watercourses and groundwater while sanitary engineers struggled to maintain sources of clean water.[12]

A few prescient critics went beyond symptoms to sound the alarm about the dangers of the metabolic rift. The city of London, the political economist Karl Marx wrote in 1867, can "find no better use for the excretion of four and one-half million human beings than to contaminate the Thames with it at heavy expense." It is a strange animal, Marx and others suggested, that fouls its own nest. After reading the German chemist Justus von Liebig's analysis of intensive British agriculture as a form of robbery, Marx called for a reintegration of agriculture and industry.[13]

Like so much in the city, the trail of waste led back to the countryside. "These heaps of garbage at the corners of the stone blocks, these tumbrils of mire jolting the streets at night, these horrid scavengers' carts, these fetid streams of subterranean slime which the pavement hides, what is all this?" the Boston sanitarian Dr. Henry J. Barnes asked in 1884. "It is the flourishing meadow, the green grass, the thyme and sage," he answered. "It is game, it is cattle, hay, corn, bread upon the table, warm blood in the veins." Instead of being returned to the soil to restore fertility, these wastes fouled the water city people had no choice but to drink.[14]

In the United States as elsewhere, the fertility of rural soils flowed into the city and then to the seas. On the verge of his run for the mayoralty of New York City in 1884, the land reformer Henry George warned: "We are cutting down forests which we do not replant, we are shipping abroad, in wheat and cotton and tobacco and meat, or flushing into the sea through the sewers of our great cities, the elements of fertility that have been embedded in the soil by the slow processes of nature, acting for long ages." Fired by "haunting visions of higher possibilities," George's call for a closer relationship between city and country inspired the British reformer Ebenezer Howard's plans for garden cities. Howard hoped garden cities would, among other things, facilitate the recycling of wastes.[15]

The widespread adoption of sewer systems at the turn of the twentieth century complicated matters, as did the availability of cheap fertilizers. The nutrient load from organic waste now came mixed with huge quantities of water, as well as agricultural runoff and industrial waste, raising the cost of transport and generating health concerns. Some sanitarians, including London's Edwin Chadwick and New York City's George Waring Jr., advocated sewage farming (irrigation with sewage) as a means of paying for sewer systems. But the same public health logic that recommended sewers, particularly the germ theory of disease, also warned that sewage farming spread microbes, parasites, and disease-carrying flies. Only a few American municipalities, mainly in the west, adopted the practice. Most cities dumped raw sewage into local waterways with the idea the "running water purifies itself."[16]

With some easing of the immediate symptoms, that metabolic rift receded from view. Beginning in the 1930s and accelerating in the early 1970s, the construction of sixteen thousand sewage treatment plants across the United States produced huge quantities of biosolids (i.e., the sewage sludge left after treatment; the term is a product of the EPA's Name Change Task Force). The accumulation of biosolids added another troubling element to the urban waste stream. No wonder that in 1961, even after the widespread adoption of treatment plants, the urbanist Lewis Mumford described the sewer system as "a backward step ecologically, and so far a somewhat superficial technical advance." To be sure, sewers reduced disease. But they still turned a valuable resource into a problematic source of potentially toxic waste.[17]

In the second half of the century, the accumulation of biosolids and the constant threat of sewer overflows perplexed eight hundred municipalities in the United States. In 1965, reflecting on decades of struggling to supply clean water to Baltimore, the sanitary engineer Abel Wolman brought the challenges of "urban metabolism" to public attention. Defining urban metabolism as all the materials needed to build and maintain the city and sustain its inhabitants, Wolman emphasized that "the earth is a closed ecological system." Yet even he treated metabolism as a one-sided, urban issue. Urban metabolism is "not completed," Wolman wrote, "until the wastes and residues of daily life have been removed and disposed of with a minimum of nuisance and hazard." But removed and disposed of where? For all his insight, Wolman did not challenge the artificial boundary between the city and the larger biosphere or turn a linear process back into a circular one.[18]

In the 1970s, a few environmentalists argued that biosolids should be returned to agricultural fields. In 1971, the biologist Barry Commoner wrote: "Clearly the ecologically appropriate technological means of removing sewage from the city is to return it to the soil." Four years later, the environmental historian Joel Tarr hoped that we had come to recognize that "city and country are one rather than separate." But as more and more toxic materials entered the economy, human bodies, and consequently the sewers, experts debated the safety of returning biosolids to the soil. Meanwhile, rural districts understandably balked at having metropolitan wastes dumped within their jurisdictions.[19]

With support from the EPA, the National Biosolids Partnership today promotes safe practices among wastewater agencies across the country. But public health advocates still warn of human pathogens and worry about the pharmaceuticals, heavy metals, toxic chemicals, and carcinogens found in biosolids. The presence of waste from hospitals and funeral homes, as well as the 100,000 chemicals American industries use, does not inspire confidence. Nor does the well-known role of organized crime in the waste management industry and its illegal dumping of toxic wastes.[20]

But there are few attractive alternatives. Landfills, incineration, and gasification are expensive and merely shift the pollution around, and ocean dumping is illegal (since 1989). Consequently, the EPA both promotes and regulates the use of biosolids. Class A Exceptional Quality biosolids, which a few firms produce by heating the biosolids to 70 degrees Celsius, can be applied in parks, fields, and even schoolyards without notification. But the much more common Class B biosolids contain pathogens and can be used only at a distance from human habitation and on certain crops. Compared with those in many European countries, EPA regulations are lax, and compliance is not well monitored by the minuscule available staff. The most authoritative study, by the National Academy of Sciences, found no documented evidence of a threat to public health. But the study also concluded that uncertainty demanded additional investigation.[21]

Estimates vary, but in the United States today perhaps, at best, 50 percent of biosolids are returned to the soil. The level of recycling may have already peaked as citizen-activists accumulate a mountain of anecdotal evidence on health issues and the courts hear more suits. Most biosolids are incinerated. In 2015, Cincinnati's incinerator went down. The MSD issued a request for proposals to haul to landfills the one million pounds of biosolids produced daily. One of the outlying metropolitan counties, for a time, returned 25 percent of its biosolids to agricultural fields, but development gobbled up much of the farmland while rising transportation and energy costs ended the experiment in favor of incineration.[22]

Due to stringent state and federal regulations, only a portion of waste can even be classified as biosolids. Moreover, deteriorating sewer systems routinely send untreated waste into local waterways before they even reach a treatment plant. And, of course, industrialized agriculture still depends heavily on chemical fertilizers that flow into our rivers and streams. Untreated waste from unregulated concentrated animal-feeding operations add to the toxic load in our water sources.[23]

Environmental Degradation as a Crisis of Culture and Character

In the three decades after 1945, the green revolution intensified the metabolic and biospheric rifts. Artificial fertilizers and pesticides, coming out of military innovations in munitions and nerve gas during World War II, made American farms more dependent on fossil fuels than ever. The green revolution, which also included the development of genetically modified, high-yield crop varieties, increased crop production and, in time and in places, eased global hunger as food became a tool of American foreign policy. But the green revolution also set in motion changes in farming that transformed all of American society.[24]

As the green revolution gained momentum in the 1970s, a few dissident voices linked environmental degradation to a crisis of culture and character. The poet, farmer, and environmentalist Wendell Berry did so with direct reference to the metabolic rift. The modern household, with its "machines and gadgets," Berry wrote, had become "a veritable factory of waste and destruction." The household took in industrial artifacts, whose production already damaged the biosphere, and converted them "into garbage, sewage, and noxious fumes—for none of which we have found a use." Americans, Berry continued, thought little of the "tons of organic matter (highly valuable—and certainly, in the long run, necessary—as fertilizer) that they flush down their drains or throw out as garbage."[25]

Berry recognized the household as our first and essential connection to the Earth. But the idea of the household as a haven from places of production and its consequent "remoteness from work" obscured that connection. The divorce of consumption from production bred irresponsibility and, behind the irresponsibility, anxiety. Multiple commentators noted that Americans consulted an escalating variety of experts to address a host of anxieties, but Berry added that Americans "*ought* to be anxious." The average American, a narrow specialist who could not provide anything for himself but money, lacked the competence to respond to even the most minor disruptions in his routine. His "air, water, and food are all known to contain poisons," Berry observed, and he "feels bad, he looks bad, he is overweight, his health is poor."[26]

Berry traced this disruption of the household upward toward the arrangement of cities and farms. No longer rising "from the earth like a pyramid," Berry explained, American life "scatters itself out in a reckless horizontal sprawl, like a disorderly city whose suburbs and pavements destroy the fields." Farm households suffered the same corruption as metropolitan households. As the administration of President Richard Nixon instructed farmers to "get big or get out," the diversified farm gave way to industrialized monocultures dependent on fossil fuels. By removing animals to feedlots, industrialized agriculture deprived farms of needed nutrients while generating vast concentrations of manure that fouled air, water, and land. Such arrangements, Berry concluded, managed to "take a solution and divide it neatly into two problems."[27]

The "get big or get out" mentality branded skilled, frugal farmers, who produced more per acre than industrialized farms, as too ignorant and too inefficient to survive. Berry found a glaring example of the contempt for small farmers in *National Geographic*'s 1970 celebratory account of "the revolution in American agriculture." Dislocated farmers "drift into cities," the article explained, "where they join past migrants in the ghettos—to become added tinder for the riots that can be labeled one of the social consequences of the agricultural revolution." Yet *National Geographic* remained undaunted by the "hapless millions of rural refugees," black and white, and the rural communities that just "wither away." Not "all small towns are dying," the journal reassured its readers, as harried urbanites repopulated the countryside, attracted by the prospect of "watching kids and crops grow in a handful of acres a man can call his own."[28]

Berry could barely believe what he read. "Here surely is cause for mourning," Berry began, "a forced migration of people greater than any in history, the foretelling of riots in the cities and the failure of human community in the country." How "can one hold the small farm in contempt as the living of a farm family," he continued, "and then sentimentalize over it as the 'country place' or hobby of an executive?" He found the answer in the shallowness of our understanding of what we called "the environment." As soon as we defined the environment as that which is "*surrounding us,*" Berry lamented, "we have already made a profound division between it and ourselves." Rejecting the great divides, Berry beseeched his readers to recognize that "we and our country create one another, depend upon one another, are literally part of one another; that our land passes in and out of our bodies just as our bodies pass in and out of our land."[29]

Berry's study contributed to the cultural history of the metabolic rift, a genre that included Raymond Williams's study *The Country and the City,* discussed earlier. Also writing in 1970s, the American cultural historian Leo Marx made a criticism of culture and character that echoed Berry and Williams. Our industrial, technological society, Marx wrote, "rewards the habit of mind which analyzes, separates, categorizes, and makes distinctions." That society made little room for "the connection-making, analogizing, poetic imagination—one that aspires to a unified conception of reality." At best, such habits of thought gave rise to a conservationism that focused on "the environment beyond the city limits," treating nature as a "world that exists apart from, and for the benefit of, mankind." Our "overall capacity for survival," Marx concluded, depended on embracing the ecological, connection-making perspective that saw humanity as "wholly and ineluctably embedded in the tissue of natural process."[30]

High Water and Low Water, Spigot and Drain

Challenges to the great divides continued into the new century. In *The Cincinnati Arch: Learning from Nature in the City* (2004), John Tallmadge imagined how swimming up from the Gulf of Mexico would give one a pungent sense of how cities are of the earth, taking on specific qualities of the surrounding countryside. On the lower stretches, as you passed New Orleans on toward Memphis, you would smell the clay, feldspar, and mica of the southern reaches of the continent. Later, entering the Ohio River, you would smell the hardwoods, coal, and metamorphic rock of the lower Midwest and upper South as you passed Louisville and reached Cincinnati. But the swim would hardly be pleasant. You would also gag on manure and urine, fertilizer and detergents, solvents and metal filings.[31]

Tallmadge only dreamed of making this suicidal tour of the metabolic rift. Growing up as a conventional environmentalist, he preferred the high, clean water of the mountains to the low, contaminated water of the city. For him, nature meant clear streams, not piped city water, which he associated with a culture of greed. The idea of drinking water from the Ohio River horrified Tallmadge. He shuddered at the thought of the upstream refineries and chemical works, coal mines and steel mills; the raw and treated sewage dumped by small towns and large cities; the household wastes; and the immense load of fertilizers and pesticides dumped into the river with every rain.[32]

Yet like most urbanites, Tallmadge gave little thought to how clean water for drinking, cooking, and cleaning came into his household. While attending to the pressing matter of keeping water out of his household, he gave little thought to where his wastewater went. As he painted, caulked, and puttied, he also drank, cooked, cleaned, and flushed, unthinkingly relying on those fundamental facilities, spigot and drain. None of these activities struck him as related to nature until one day he saw a duck skimming along the filthy Mill Creek. The mindless flushing of wastes, he now saw, was the underside of his flight to the wilderness in search for purity.[33]

Tallmadge resolved to follow city water, upstream and downstream, toward responsibility. First, he visited Cincinnati's world-class waterworks to learn how it provided clean water. Water in Cincinnati is plentiful and cheap, as clean as any in the industrialized world, and as safe as advanced technology can make it. Every day, municipal engineers pump 120 million gallons of water out of the Ohio River from an upstream intake valve. We expect it to come out of the spigot not only clean but tasty (or, at least, not foul). We then not only drink it but wash our cars and clothes and water our lawns with it, thinking little about what in most of the world is a scarce and precious resource.[34]

Tallmadge knew that the water taken from the river is filled with contaminants. He now learned that engineers put it into holding tanks where they aerate it, add coagulants, and allow gravity to help settle and clump the impurities. They then force the water through a filter of sand and gravel to remove remaining particles and then through activated charcoal to absorb organic compounds (some of which are known carcinogens) that form from the chlorine used to disinfect drinking water. In 2013, the waterworks added a third treatment, ultraviolet light, provided by two hundred solar panels, which kills microorganisms resistant to chlorine.[35]

Still, the engineers must be vigilant. Three hundred times a day the water is tested for 148 contaminants, twenty-one of which are found in small quantities. The task is complicated by the 85,000 synthetic chemicals in regular circulation, the use of only six of them restricted. Given sufficient evolutionary time, every waste can become food for some other organism. But for all the new, artificial chemicals we dump into urban watercourses and that find their way into our bodies and those of other creatures, the time frames are much shorter, and more deadly.[36]

Determined also to follow his wastes downstream, Tallmadge enlisted the aid of Stanley Hedeen and Robin Corathers of the Mill Creek Restoration Project (now the Mill Creek Alliance). They started their tour at the highest point in Hamilton County, near Mt. Rumpke, a huge landfill north of Cincinnati, up the ancient Licking River Valley through which the tiny Mill Creek now trickles southward. (The Mill Creek Valley is larger upstream because thousands of years ago the much larger Licking River flowed northward.) Early in the nineteenth century, industry began polluting the creek with a multicolor stream of effluent from slaughterhouses, breweries, distilleries, paper mills, laundries, and a host of other enterprises. Today it is agricultural runoff, household wastes, and leachate from old industrial and municipal landfills that do the most damage.[37]

Where the tour began, some twenty-five miles north of downtown Cincinnati, the creek looked surprisingly clean and full of life. Hedeen pointed out caddisfly larvae and water-penny beetles, creatures sensitive to pollution, as a sign of the creek cleaning itself. The tour continued south toward the city, stopping at Winton Lake, a product of an Army Corps of Engineers flood-protection dam completed in 1952. Here impervious surfaces (as much as 35 percent on the lower reaches of the creek) and the consequent runoff of pollution began to increase. Signs of life remained, however, in saplings, shrubs, even evidence of a coyote (an invasive species from the southwest). Farther downstream, at Reading, the tour examined the Army Corps' channelization project. The project confined the creek to a concrete bed, again designed for flood control.

Upstream lay the last wild stretches of the Mill Creek (at least until it approaches the Ohio River). The corps ran out of money in the 1980s and never finished the channelization, judging levees and zoning regulations more cost-effective.[38]

The next stop came at the General Electric Aviation plant, where rocket parts were made during the Cold War and that now produces aircraft engines. The plant includes a superfund site that still leaks polychlorinated biphenyls (PCBs) and other toxins into the creek, one of more than ninety thousand hazardous waste sites across the nation. Rusty barrels and sprawling factories fill the wide valley here, punctuated by an overflow port of Greater Cincinnati's combined sewer system. The port spouts raw sewage when it rains. But even here there is wildlife, and volunteers plant trees that absorb heavy metal through phytoremediation. Here and elsewhere in the Mill Creek Valley, industrial sites occupy once prime agricultural bottom land. But do not try to grow anything here now—or, at least, do not eat what grows.[39]

Down Interstate 75 lay the next stop, the Elda Landfill, Cincinnati's main dump between 1973 and the late 1990s. Elda finally closed after neighbors complained about health issues from gas emissions. The landfill will continue to leach toxins into the creek for decades at least, probably centuries. Here Hedeen pointed out the physical pollution from channelization, the easy entry of sunlight and heat that eliminated many species that require shade and cool water. But he also pointed out the creek's effort to restore its bed, to create gravel bars and meanders where willows and cottonwoods took root. Bass darted in the pools. Tallmadge looked up and saw industry, but looking down he could imagine a clean river, the same image that kept Hedeen, Corathers, and thousands of others working to protect the creek.[40]

The tour continued downstream to the Procter & Gamble plant, where the creek flows through its concrete channel, past factory piping, tanks, and buildings. Even here, however, the creek deposited silt on the sloping concrete walls, trying to rebuild its bed. But the company regularly bulldozed the recovering bed, protecting its investment from flooding. Farther downstream, the tour visited aging industrial neighborhoods and stopped at Salway Park, where volunteers planted hundreds of trees and constructed two butterfly parks. Corathers pointed out that the creek still served as a migration corridor for ducks, herons, and other birds, undeterred by railway yards and ugly oil slicks on the water.[41]

Finally, the tour arrived at the sewage treatment plant, just downstream from CSO #5. Here the channelization ends, and trees and shrubs again line the banks of the creek. The creek drops its sediment load into a depression called the Ohio River pool. A moist, rank odor filled the air. Nearby, a huge, open concrete tank stood ready to collect raw sewage when the combined sewer filled to capacity. When the raw sewage reaches the top of the tank, heavy steel doors open to allow the sewage to flow into the creek. But just when things looked worst, the tour group saw a black-crowned night heron, a wild and secretive bird, perched on a rock on this wild stretch of the creek. Only one other colony of the species has been identified in Ohio, on an island in Lake Erie; the fenced property of the sewage treatment plant provided this second haven.[42]

Tallmadge found hope in the heron and all the other signs of life along the creek. The wildness of the birds—so unlike the creatures that have closely co-evolved with us and with which we share diseases—gave them immunity from the bacteria and viruses so dangerous to us in the polluted creek. Given time, evolution might even find ways to use the waste for other forms of life. But in the shorter run, it remains pollution, moral corruption as much as physical thing. "Wendell Berry was right to observe," Tallmadge commented, "that our environmental crisis stems from defects in character as well as in culture." It feels overwhelming, but if we see the life that keeps pushing back, we might believe in the possibility of repair that drove Corathers, Hedeen, and Tallmadge to take responsibility.[43]

Two decades after Tallmadge's Dantesque descent, Cincinnati still struggles with its combined sewer system. In the nineteenth century, diluting household waste with stormwater made some sense. But the increase in population, wastes, and impervious surfaces overtaxed the system. Now, to fix it properly appears too expensive and disruptive. Some partial solutions have emerged. Small, intermittently run treatment plants will be installed at overflow points. Elsewhere, storage caverns under the creek will receive overflow and pump it to treatment plants after the stormwaters recede. But it is hard not to see such solutions as more of the out-of-sight, out-of-mind solutions that Tallmadge decried. It is our intelligence, imagination, and sense of responsibility that are being tested.[44]

In responding to the 2004 consent decree, the MSD embraced some more imaginative strategies. The sewer district's $3.2 billion plan includes man-made wetlands, swales, rain gardens, and green roofs to keep as much storm water out of the system as possible. It also includes the daylighting of Lick Run, taking it out of the sewer pipes and making it the centerpiece of a revitalized neighborhood. Begun in 2013, the Lick Run project will cost less than half the cost of building and maintaining the storage caverns and keep eight hundred million gallons of wastewater out of the Mill Creek. Attracting the attention of federal officials when launched, the Lick Run project is justly lauded as a model for Rust Belt cities in the eastern half of the United States.[45]

Another part of the plan, the Twin Creek Preserve, suggests the potential for rethinking not just urban sanitation but the relationship of the city to its region. Funded by the Ohio EPA and coordinated by the regional Mill Creek Watershed Council of Communities, the Twin Creek Preserve is combatting flooding with five acres of wetlands and the aggressive planting of trees. The design includes a tree canopy to cool the water, as well as oxbows, pools, and riffles (man-made rapids) to slow and aerate the water, providing habitat for native species. Opting for less colossal technology and more respect for natural processes, the Cincinnati region might build what one environmental designer calls a civic ecology that brings into popular consciousness the "unfathomable and unseen labyrinth" of biophysical systems that underpin our lives.[46]

Addressing the metabolic rift will require us to take responsibility for the material basis of our lives. The proper care of waste, a basic aspect of human ecology, is crucial to restoring the fertility of our soils and preserving our dwindling sources of potable water. Failure will only further darken our prospects. Of course, the metabolic rift is just one, however fundamental, aspect of the interdependence of all human settlements and their embeddedness in the natural world. But easing the metabolic rift will help us develop an alternative vision and a new set of tools with which to cross the great divides and address our mounting troubles.

Productive Ecologies, Precarious Settlements

Cincinnati's innovative approach to sewer overflows is the most recent chapter in its creative, if sometimes irresponsible, manipulation of the natural environment. From the beginning, the physical site of Cincinnati offered both advantages and disadvantages on which its future depended. Two early efforts to build settlements in the area, Columbia and North Bend, suffered from frequent flooding. The eventual site of downtown Cincinnati, an elevated plateau of glacial outwash deposits, provided some protection from flooding. But hemmed in by hills (the remnants of an eroded plain), the city had limited options for expansion. Until steam-powered streetcars ascended the hills in the 1870s, only the Mill Creek Valley, gently rising from the Ohio River, provided room for expansion. Early settlers established a few water-powered mills along the sluggish Mill Creek, while the rich soils of its valley supported abundant agriculture.[47]

Cincinnati boosters nevertheless aspired to build the greatest city in the Midwest, if not the nation. But how "could Cincinnati," one booster wrote, "situated nearly a thousand miles from the sea, almost in the center of the continent, rival our great seaports?" The answer came in connecting the Ohio River as closely as possible to the seaboard economy. The invention and adoption of the steamboat, a crucial part of the early city's success, made the Ohio River a two-way avenue of commerce. In 1838, when the United States boasted only two thousand steam engines, four hundred of them powered steamboats operating out of Cincinnati. The city soon became a center of steamboat construction, combining craft work and manufacturing. A host of iron foundries, machine shops, and cabinet- and chair-makers produced goods directly for steamboat construction and for the markets the steamboats opened.[48]

Another crucial innovation turned Cincinnati into the Queen City of the West. Begun in 1825, the Miami and Erie Canal connected the city with Dayton in 1830. By 1845, the canal reached Toledo, linking the Ohio River to the Great Lakes. By establishing a commercial artery through densely forested lands, the canal enabled Cincinnati to tap the rich soils and the coalfields of the lower Midwest, just as the Ohio River allowed it to tap soils, resources, and markets to the east and south. By 1831, a recent arrival in the city had already found its commerce "beyond comprehension." "Boats arrive from the interior daily," he observed, "loaded down with thousands of barrels of flour, pork, whiskey, hams, lard, corn, and every kind of produce." As it rose to become one of the busiest inland ports in the world, the city indeed began to resemble a seaport. By 1850, Cincinnati stood as the nation's fastest-growing city and second-largest manufacturing center.[49]

Less happily, Cincinnati's growing population and industrial production, combined with its constrained site, produced dangerous crowding and pollution. The accumulation of filth and decaying refuse on streets and in standing water created conditions conducive to infectious disease. As cholera swept through the city in 1849, the poor state of sanitation raised alarms. The *Daily Cincinnati Commercial* observed that the water from the "hydrants lately had an odorous and dull yellow color." Yet even as deaths mounted, the *Daily Cincinnati Gazette* editorialized that the threat "is mainly confined to the poorer classes," as "the working man is habitually careless and incautious." More than four thousand Cincinnatians died in the outbreak, while the city's Board of Health did little.[50]

Slowly but surely, however, the municipal government shifted its attention from responding to specific emergencies that threatened prosperity to taking on the day-to-day tasks of insuring the health, safety, and well-being of residents. Although the sources of disease were not well understood, the cholera epidemic focused attention on the five thousand hydrants in the city. While the municipality had purchased a steam-powered waterworks and twenty-five miles of pipes from a private firm in 1839 for $400,000, ten years later most residents still depended on contaminated groundwater from these hydrants. In the decades to come, the waterworks would become central to the city's health and well-being. In 1876, a professionalized municipal department replaced the Board of Trustees that had previously overseen the waterworks.[51]

Meanwhile, the growth of meatpacking, distilling, brewing, and other industries turned Mill Creek into an open sewer. By 1913, more than fourteen million gallons of industrial waste and a nearly equal amount of household sewage entered the creek, fully one-quarter of its flow as it emptied into the Ohio River. The stench and the health concerns led municipal officials to begin construction of an interceptor sewer to bypass the creek and send the waste directly to the Ohio River. This eased the local damage, particularly for the squatters along Mill Creek, who "huddled together in their miserable shacks and eked out a . . . barbarous existence." But it was hardly an ideal solution, especially for those urban and rural communities downstream on the Ohio River. Consistent sewage treatment would not come until after World War II.[52]

Environmental reformers had even less success in regulating the coal smoke that arose with the shift to fossil fuels. Nationwide, twenty million tons of unburned coal fouled the air and spread tuberculosis and other respiratory diseases. Yet when municipal officials tried to regulate smoke, they encountered opposition and apathy. Both industries and households resisted regulation, in part because of the association of factory smoke with economic prosperity. Only more technologically efficient means of burning coal and the shift to natural gas eased the burden in the years after World War II.[53]

All cities, in one way or the other, succeed by manipulating their natural environment. They build harbors, dig canals, drain swamps, create new acreage with landfill, import fresh water, and export waste, to cite just a few of the obvious examples. The greatest challenges, especially for industrial cities such as Cincinnati, are to build productive ecologies and manage dense, precarious settlements, tasks that often require tapping vast hinterlands. In doing so, cities have often acted in irresponsible ways, exporting the costs while failing to share fully the advantages of modern urban culture. To anchor just and sustainable regions, cities must act in more responsible ways.[54]

Cincinnati's story has parallels from coast to coast. In 1839, to take a famous example, Henry David Thoreau and his brother witnessed the creative and exploitative manipulation of the natural environment on their trip up the Merrimack River. Expecting to find a peaceful wilderness, the brothers paddled their flat-bottomed boat past masonry and wood dams set below bustling cities and towns in northeastern Massachusetts and southern New Hampshire. The dams channeled Merrimack River water into a network of canals that helped to produce eighty thousand horsepower to turn nine hundred mills. The canals directed the water into the basements of brick mill buildings constructed astride the canals. In those basements, flowing water set in motion belts, shafts, and pulleys and powered the machinery that spun cotton yarn and wove it into cloth.[55]

The Thoreau brothers witnessed the work of the Boston Associates, founders of New England's textile industry. The reach of these Boston investors and others who followed extended far beyond city limits. Appropriating for private ends what had once been understood legally as a common resource, the Boston Associates extended their control of water from nearby Lowell, Massachusetts, to the New Hampshire lakes that fed rivers in Massachusetts. As industrialization extended beyond textiles to lumber, paper, leather, and dozens of other products, new dams, canals, and locks changed the ecology of the region's rivers, harnessing their flow to an industrial ecology while destroying local fisheries.[56]

Industrialization made enormous demands on the rivers of New England. As industrialists appropriated water for energy to power mills, farmers found their fields flooded, the forests they relied on destroyed, and the navigable rivers that linked them to markets obstructed. The rivers also served as a convenient sink for human and factory waste even as they remained the source of water for domestic needs. Urban workers thus felt the impact of industrialization as well, not just in terms of low wages, but also from polluted waters that subjected them to disease.[57]

Creative manipulation of the Columbia River, to take another example, is at the center of the story of the Pacific Northwest. Over the course of the twentieth century, a series of dams on the Columbia River created an "organic machine," a combination of human-made and natural systems that is impossible to disentangle. "Snow melting, dams storing and releasing water, turbines turning, generators producing electricity, lights going on, motors humming all blended together," the environmental historian Richard White explains. Centuries before, the Native American techniques for fishing—creating places for gill nets or dipnets or spear fishing above pale flat stones that made the fish easier to see—represented no less a combination of nature and culture. By the end of the century, Columbia River water cooled the nuclear reactors at Hanford that produced plutonium for Cold War weaponry. The subsequent damages to the health of both salmon and humans remind us that these manipulations often produce unintended effects.[58]

A focus on the creative, if often irresponsible, transformation of nature highlights the connections between cities and their regions and the inseparability of society and nature. For too long, however, our histories obscured these matters. In the famous essay "The Significance of the Frontier in American History" (1893) that helped launch the historical profession, Frederick Jackson Turner told the story of midwestern development in terms of hunters and trappers who made way for farmers who clustered in villages. Cities, in Turner's view, came much later. In 1959, the urban historian Richard Wade turned this on its head. He argued that cities served as "the spearheads of the frontier," the staging areas and guiding force of frontier settlement. "Agriculture is nearly as invisible in *The Urban Frontier*," the environmental historian David Stradling observes, "as cities were in Frederick Jackson Turner's *The Significance of the Frontier in American History*." We need to tell the story of cities and their regions in a different way.[59]

Over the past thirty years, urban scholars have been telling a different story, emphasizing the interrelationship of city and country. Much of this scholarship has shown how city builders, in their reckless manipulation of both nature and human nature, often undercut the foundations of the city's vitality. As important as such stories are, we must also avoid the trap of what the environmental historian Martin Melosi calls "declensionist" narratives. In treating humans as invariably agents of harm, standing outside nature as disrupters, such narratives replicate the great divides. They also discount the possibility of imagining and implementing environmental transformations that preserve and enrich life in all its forms. If we are respectful of the often admirable aspirations of city builders, noting their successes along with their failures, it is possible to extract from our history the beginnings of an environmental ethic that can guide our interactions with the natural world and with one another. We can also find in that history possibilities that point us toward a more fulfilling, more just, and more admirable way of life.[60]

II

An Ecological Narrative for the City and Region

Environmental Imperatives
and Ecological Thinking

The chapters that follow develop an environmental and ecological narrative for cities and regions. One thread examines how cities created far-reaching productive ecologies while also managing dense, precarious settlements to make them prosperous, healthy, and satisfying places to live. The other thread follows the role of ecological thinking, for better or worse, in the development of American urbanism. The arc of the narrative traces an increasing understanding of cities as a part of nature that culminated in a regional moment during the Great Depression and the subsequent dissipation of that understanding in the postwar policies that promoted mass suburbanization and urban renewal. The revival of ecological thinking in response to those policies brings us to the beginnings of our own time.

As with Part I, these stories intersect with my lived experience. My life began in a brick two-flat bordering Portage Park on Chicago's Northwest Side. Portage Park got its name from the Native American use of the area as a portage between the Chicago and Des Plaines rivers. During wet weather, the area provided a navigable path from the Great Lakes to the Mississippi River system. A similar path later served as a key element in the productive ecology Chicagoans built in the nineteenth century. Portage Park, begun in 1913, also contributed to a decades-long effort to make cities more healthful and engaging places to live. The largest public park on the Northwest Side, the thirty-six-acre park features playgrounds, tennis courts, baseball fields, a cultural arts building, and an Olympic-size swimming pool, among other amenities. I recall being raised up, as a small child, to get a drink from the park's magnificent stone water fountain constructed by the federal Works Progress Administration in the 1930s.[1]

At the time of my birth in 1955, my family moved to the Chicago suburb of Arlington Heights. We settled in a subdivision called Virginia Terrace, part of the postwar wave of suburbanization. The subdivision, subsidized by federal mortgages and protected from "inharmonious racial groups" by the practice of redlining, made me part of a privileged, white suburban middle class. The options I have had in life owe much to this privilege. I also vividly recall the day the bulldozers came to clear the prairie behind the subdivision where we neighborhood kids played. The removal of a giant boulder, left there by some long-ago glacier, saddened us, part of the disappearance of open space that did so much to promote a new environmental movement.

Many years later, in the late 1980s, influenced by the counterculture green movement, I built an energy-efficient house in rural Indiana. I thus unwittingly contributed to the deflection of the sustainability movement from public matters of social and racial justice into private matters of home and garden. As part of the project, I used a chain saw to clear an acre of land. I recall taking down a huge pine tree and finding two small trees behind it. Just as I was about to heedlessly take down those trees too, something stopped me. As it turned out, I saved a beautiful redbud and a river birch that I would enjoy for years to come. Not everything about the counterculture was misguided.

In between those experiences, I spent a tumultuous year traveling around the country as a college dropout. As a result of six formative weeks in Phoenix, Arizona, I returned to college eager to learn more about cities. My favorite course was urban sociology, taught by a third-generation University of Chicago sociologist. Initially, I found the Chicago sociologists' interest in human ecology intriguing. I dimly expected something that would combine my interest in environmentalism and cities. But I never could see what all the excitement was about. I found their work boring, even deeply boring, something that seemed to preclude more promising approaches.[2]

I never stopped thinking and writing about the Chicago sociologists. I grew to appreciate and admire their deep investigations into Chicago's many social worlds. But I did not fully understand their significance, or my negative reaction to them, until I read Jennifer Light's astounding *The*

Nature of Cities: Ecological Visions and the American Urban Professions, 1920–1960 (2014). I am indebted to Light's uncovering of the profound influence of the Chicago sociologists on urban policy in the middle decades of the twentieth century. I now believe that the Chicago sociologists did indeed deflect a more promising line of ecological analysis stretching back to the nineteenth century.[3]

In the mid-1990s, when I first began teaching an Ecology of the City course, I encountered the Los Angeles School of urban studies. In launching a challenge to the Chicago School, the Los Angeles urbanists took what seemed to me a more promising approach to human ecology. Sharing the Chicago School's interest in spatial arrangements, they added an emphasis on the city's often disastrous relationship to the rest of nature. Deriding the "little pastel pods of chardonnay lifestyle" that spread into the desert surrounding Los Angeles, the historian Mike Davis saw the city "spilling wreckage and desire in ever-widening circles over a denuded countryside." But I found something dispiriting here, too. The Los Angeles urbanists seemed to take for granted an irresistible trajectory toward a dystopian future of increasing social conflict and environmental collapse.[4]

The Chicago School, ignoring the city's dependence on the natural world and setting out to manage its social conflicts, exuded overconfidence. The Los Angeles School, depicting cities as at the mercy of global forces that lay outside the cities themselves, risked despair. We must reject the Chicago School's complacency about natural limits and social inequality without succumbing to the Los Angeles School's skepticism about alternatives. While we detail the costs of our quest to master nature, we should also highlight our capacity for innovation and creativity.

3

Exploiting Productive Ecologies

Shock Cities and the Transformation of Nature

In 1835, the French aristocrat Alexis de Tocqueville visited the textile city of Manchester, England. Tocqueville found Manchester lacking in all the usual elements of civilization. A "thousand noises disturb this damp, dark labyrinth," he wrote, "but they are not at all the ordinary sounds one hears in great cities." No "clatter of hoofs as the rich man drives back home. . . . Never the gay shouts of people amusing themselves, or music heralding a holiday." Only "the footsteps of a busy crowd, the crunching wheels of machinery, the shriek of steam from boilers, the regular beat of the looms, the heavy rumble of carts." No one had ever seen anything like quite like Manchester, a city given over entirely to industrial production.[1]

One of the early sites of the industrial revolution, Manchester grew explosively at the turn of the nineteenth century. Its population increased nearly sixfold in the sixty years after 1770. By 1850, the population topped 300,000, making it the second largest city in Britain. Yet the city would not be incorporated or inaugurate a system of local government until three years after Tocqueville's visit. An "evident lack of government," Tocqueville observed, explained the "noisome labyrinth" of social extremes, of newly rich and abject poor. "Everything in the exterior appearance of the city attests to the individual powers of man," he concluded, "nothing the directing power of society."[2]

Tremendous efficiencies of scale and the division of labor gave rise to giant textile mills, ruled by rich men but worked by poor women and children. A single mill employed fifteen hundred people, twelve hours a day, six days a week. There "is no town in the world where the distance between the rich and poor is so great," a reformer wrote. "There is far less personal communication between the master cotton-spinner and his workmen . . . than there is between the Duke of Wellington and the humblest laborer on this estate." Yet "from this foul drain," Tocqueville marveled, "the greatest stream of human industry flows out to fertilize the whole world. From this filthy sewer, pure gold flows."[3]

Writing in 1963, the eminent British historian Asa Briggs described Manchester as the "shock city" of the early nineteenth century. By *shock city*, Briggs meant a city that people believed anticipated the shape of the future. In the late nineteenth century, Briggs noted, Chicago emerged as the new shock city. Just as Tocqueville felt he must visit Manchester, so the German sociologist Max Weber visited Chicago in 1904. Weber compared the city to a "man whose skin is drawn back and whose insides you may see working. For you can see everything." The turbulent growth of Manchester and, later, Chicago seemed to announce the future.[4]

Beneath the turbulence lay extraordinary efforts to appropriate nature and organize labor. By transforming natural resources and processes from far-flung hinterlands, Manchester and Chicago built productive ecologies. Place-based investments in cities, the nineteenth-century economist Henry George argued, brought out "a superior power in labor, which is localized in land." The principle applied no less to regions than to cities. The creative incorporation of nature, including human labor, into market economies produced great wealth and rising standards of living.[5]

But the great market transformations of the industrial revolution also threatened the natural and human sources of vitality. The laissez-faire regimes that arose with industry multiplied the danger, proscribing any sort of regulation in favor of a faith in the self-regulating market. The resulting pollution, poverty, and degradation generated the companion notion that the "country," often in the ersatz form of suburban retreat, provided the antidote to a harsh urban society. The separation of the material benefits of industrial ecologies from their social and environmental costs added another dimension to the great divides.[6]

Shock City Narratives

Stories about the shock cities of Manchester and Chicago spread far and wide. They did so, Briggs explained, through the "imaginative power with which people arranged the facts in a pattern," forcing "to the sur-

face what seemed to be intractable problems of society and government."
But each generation has told new stories about what made these cities
shocking. Amid the industrial revolution and its political discontents, the
socialist agitators Frederick Engels and Karl Marx focused on class conflict. The urbanists Lewis Mumford and Briggs, writing in the mid-twen-
tieth century as the regulatory/welfare state expanded, emphasized the
lack of public powers. At the beginning of the twenty-first century, amid
growing anxiety about the state of the biosphere, the historian Harold
Platt emphasized the environmental dimensions of the shock cities of
Manchester and Chicago.[7]

Examining Manchester, Engels and Marx predicted a coming con-
frontation between a suburbanized bourgeoisie enjoying almost total
freedom from the disagreeable aspects of industrial production and a
degraded proletariat subjected to dirt, disease, and poverty. "These plutocrats," Engels wrote of Manchester's lords of the loom, "can travel
from their houses to their places of business in the center of town by the
shortest routes, without even realizing how close they are to the misery
and filth which lie on both sides of the road." Innovators in redesigning
production, Manchester's industrialists thought little of the city as a viable settlement.[8]

Two generations later, Mumford and Briggs emphasized what had
been obvious to Tocqueville: the complete absence of government in
Manchester. "There was no local government," Briggs wrote, "to either
encourage or restrain. All depended on individual enterprise." Manchester's entrepreneurs, Mumford added, "knew no law but their own sweet
will." Dispensing with even the most rudimentary traditions of municipal
service, Manchester lacked every amenity of modern urban culture. The
"essential human achievement of the new urban culture," Mumford
jeered, was that "it worked out a minimum of life. . . . A minimum of
schooling: a minimum of rest: a minimum of cleanliness: a minimum of
shelter." Anticipating Mumford, a nineteenth-century medical examiner
concluded that a lack of regulatory codes or planning principles meant
that Manchester's jerry-built slum housing furnished only "the minimum
amount of shelter and comfort necessary for existence."[9]

In Platt's environmental story, Manchester appeared to have severed
all connection between the human and natural worlds. The very "soil has
been taken away," Platt quoted Tocqueville, "scratched and torn up in a
thousand places." The rivers became sewers "stained with a thousand colors by the factories." A "black smoke" covered the skies, Tocqueville concluded, leaving the sun "a disk without rays." In Manchester, another

observer recalled, one encountered "strange and to a certain extent un-natural conditions of life, not paralleled in any former state of history." Others had recognized the environmental degradation of Manchester, but Platt raised it to a central position, capturing the sense visitors had of "plunging headlong from the natural world into a monstrous inferno."[10]

Finding (and Fleeing) Nature in Manchester

Visitors and residents alike found it difficult to see nature in Manchester. But as Platt shows, nature remained present and played a crucial role in Manchester's rapid growth and its explosive conflicts. With a combina-tion of creativity and callousness, Manchester's industrialists turned a broad region into a productive ecology centered on the city. They did nothing, however, to address the natural hazards that burdened Man-chester with foul and festering slums. Fleeing to the green suburbs they built for themselves, industrialists left their workers to "regret the disap-pearance of the clear stream, the green lanes, the merry songbirds, the smokeless sky" of the preindustrial city.[11]

Humidity, abundant rainfall, and flowing water made the highlands surrounding Manchester a center of textile production as early as the thirteenth century. Humidity kept brittle cotton fibers supple, while abundant, fast-moving water powered mills and facilitated the washing, bleaching, dyeing, and printing of textiles. In the industrial era, human ingenuity put to more intensive use the 650 billion gallons of water that annually flowed through the valleys of the region. In 1761, the Duke of Bridgewater directed the digging of a tunnel deep into the coal-laden hills, exposing submerged veins of coal while releasing a vast supply of water that carried the coal across an aqueduct to the city. By slashing the price of fuel, the duke set in motion a far-reaching transformation of the local economy. Other entrepreneurs followed by building a series of ca-nals, applying steam technology to the mechanization of spinning, and reorganizing the labor process in centralized workplaces.[12]

From damp air and flowing water to coal and steam, nature played a fundamental role in the productivity of greater Manchester. Nature also set limits that the city transgressed at its peril. Flash floods destroyed mills, and perpetual damp created unhealthy conditions, especially in basement dwellings. More ominously, human, animal, and industrial wastes contaminated local water sources with deadly bacteria and toxins. Manchester experienced the first great urban epidemic of the nineteenth century, as cholera ravaged the city in 1832. Cholera returned nearly every decade for the rest of the century. Lung-damaging coal smoke from factories and residences might seem the epitome of the unnatural, but its contribution to sickness and death demonstrated that humans remained subject to the same natural constraints as any other organism.[13]

The unhealthy conditions in Manchester gave rise to the suburb in its classic form. In the decade and a half after the cholera epidemic of 1832, Manchester underwent a higher degree of suburbanization than London did in the century after 1770. Manchester's cotton lords still valued the city center for the face-to-face transactions crucial to their volatile business. But for their residences, the blight of pollution and the dangers of disease recommended suburban retreat. So, too, did class tensions. A parvenu elite, all too obviously securing its wealth by the immiseration of its workers beside whom they once worked, the cotton lords feared a recalcitrant working class given to strikes and riots.[14]

Transforming the entire city according to its logic, suburbanization created the industrial pattern of an urban core devoted to business; affluent residential districts on the periphery; and a zone of factories and workers' housing crowded in-between. Trading their city residences for cheaper land on the periphery, Manchester's cotton lords extracted an unearned increment from the city's growth, then doubled their gains in helping to finance speculative building in the suburbs. A prospectus for suburban Victoria Park, two miles south of central Manchester, promised easy access to the business district but "total freedom from manufacturers and from their disagreeable effects."[15]

Manchester's town council, established in an 1838 referendum that tallied property values rather than votes, catered to public health only where it could be made to pay. Thus, even as exclusive Manchester suburbs such as Victoria Park enjoyed clean air and water, Manchester slums such as Little Ireland suffered from what a local health officer called "every possible abomination." Pollution spread, he added, "until every natural watercourse may be termed a lengthened and gigantic cesspool." Yet early sanitarians blamed the victims. One decried the "contagious example which the Irish have exhibited of barbarous habits and savage want of economy." Such attitudes limited investments in municipal sanitation in favor of lectures on morality.[16]

Suburbanization intensified inequality as escape from the dangerous conditions in the industrial city defined class privilege. Networks of waterlines, drains, and sewers, championed by the sanitarian Edwin Chadwick and others, represented one of the greatest technical and social accomplishments of the age. But they served Manchester's suburbs, not the slums, where life expectancies barely topped twenty-five years. Slum watercourses, a health officer reported in 1848, could be seen "not merely bubbling with the escape of gases, but literally boiling, foaming, throwing up a thick and foul scum like an immense cauldron." Nevertheless, municipal officials set water and sewage rates at levels working families could not afford, even as they collected taxes from those who did not receive the services.[17]

Suburbanization left workers hemmed in between a central district given over to business and suburbs enclosing the rural areas to which workers once enjoyed access. Walls and gates prevented even vicarious enjoyment of the green grounds of Manchester's suburbs. The "general object," a suburban publicist affirmed, is "to shut out everything belonging to the neighborhood" in favor of "exclusive enjoyment." Meanwhile, the hovels of working people competed for space with pigsties as they clung to the filthy canals and riversides in the central city.[18]

Distancing themselves from the horrors of the city, Manchester's uneasy industrialists wrapped themselves in the aristocratic style of rural England's country estates. Like the country houses of those enclosing landlords, Manchester's suburbs were "land organized for consumption," as the historian Robert Fishman argues, "pleasing prospects" meant to disguise the exploitation that made them possible. Everything about their suburban residences intentionally recalled the country estates, from the surrounding wall and gatehouse, curving drives, and ornamental plantings to the towers, battlements, and buttresses and the telltale designation "park."[19]

For all their rural trappings, however, Manchester's suburbs sheltered a decidedly urban elite. The suburbs enabled the industrial elite to enjoy all the power, all the education and culture, and all the material comforts and amenities that the urban-industrial economy made possible, while avoiding its costs. Suburbs have since taken a bewildering array of forms, from elite to working class, residential to industrial. But these classic suburbs represented a refusal to take responsibility for a mode of production. They helped to build what Fishman calls "a divided environment that continues to deform our cities."[20]

Nature's Metropolis: Rethinking the Great Divides

Chicago, the shock city of the late nineteenth century, also built a productive ecology, one that stretched across a continent. New York and European capitalists, in concert with local entrepreneurs, made Chicago the gateway city to the Great West. By investing in multiple railroads, trunk lines heading to New York City and branch lines fanning across the Great Plains, those capitalists linked the Great West to the global economy. Chicago firms then directed the cutting of the great pine forests of Michigan, Wisconsin, and Minnesota and the transport of the lumber to the treeless plains to the city's west, where the lumber turned into railroads and towns, farms and feedlots.[21]

As with Manchester, the rise of Chicago illuminates the intimate connections between city and country and the ways in which cities are embedded in larger natural systems. As in Manchester, however, people speculated about Chicago's relationship to nature in ways that obscured that reality. Some saw nature as a nonhuman force that irresistibly powered Chicago's rise. Others saw nature as a precious nonhuman creation damaged by the city's rise. In his groundbreaking study *Nature's Metropolis* (1992), the historian William Cronon finds in these views anguished responses to capitalism's transformation of nature and human nature. Spun out in such dualisms as country and city, rural beauty and urban ugliness, pastoral simplicity and cosmopolitan sophistication, rural bondage and urban freedom, purity and corruption, childhood and adulthood, past and future, each offered "a compelling token of the divided world we inhabit."[22]

Nineteenth-century boosters proclaimed Chicago the destined site of a great city, as if nature itself called the city and the extraordinary feats of its heroic inhabitants into being. Undoubtedly, Chicago enjoyed some natural advantages, especially good lake transportation that linked two different and economically complementary ecosystems: the north woods, with its vast stores of timber, and the Great Plains, with their fertile soils and need for lumber. The presence of a mid-continental divide, a mere twelve miles to Chicago's west, meant that if that distance could be spanned, Chicago could link the Great Lakes to the Mississippi River Valley and the north woods to the Great Plains.[23]

But Chicago's site also possessed significant disadvantages, beginning with swampy ground and a slow-moving, foul-smelling river. Even at its highest points, Chicago's marshy site lay just a few feet above Lake Michigan. Native Americans visited the area to fish and collect the wild leeks and onions that gave the city its name. But they never settled permanently in the area. The sluggish river and sodden blue clay soils made for poor drainage, a pestilential climate, and, in the rainy seasons, a vast expanse of mud as the lake rose and returned to its ancient outlet toward the Mississippi River. Although Chicago had become the busiest port in the United States by 1870, the site provided for only a cramped harbor, continually filled in with silt from the lazy river. Dry seasons stranded ships while ice and storms made lake travel impossible from November to May.[24]

A city arose on the southern end of Lake Michigan because of the innovative—indeed, manic—artifice of humans. Only massive investments of capital, labor, and ingenuity made Chicago's future greatness possible. The innovations included dredged harbors and breakwaters, raised sidewalks and buried sewers, brick tunnels under the lake and water-pumping stations in the lake, grain elevators, and skyscrapers built on floating rafts suspended in marshy soils. Above all, canals and railroads secured Chicago's future. These innovations created a second nature, nature manipulated for human purposes. "Man must make all" in Chicago, the novelist Robert Herrick put it, "must prepare special foundations for his great buildings; must superimpose good streets of asphalt and brick upon the treacherous bottom . . . for left to herself nature merely hides the plain with a kind of brown scab."[25]

The title of Cronon's landmark study, *Nature's Metropolis*, thus has an ironic meaning. Chicago did not arise spontaneously from the natural world. Its growth depended on the construction of productive ecologies, human-shaped ecologies, a second nature. But Cronon's title has an unironic meaning, as well. Chicago's spectacular rise cannot be separated from its transformation of the far-flung ecosystems on which it depended and from which it grew rich. Embedded in the natural world, Chicago became "urban" just as much of its hinterland became "rural." The farms and resort towns of Wisconsin, no less than cutover forests of Michigan and the feed lots of Iowa, were part of Chicago's growth.[26]

As investments in canals and railroads integrated Chicago into an already established international market system, few alternative traditions and practices stood in the way of complete market transformation. Chicago's population soared from fewer than five thousand people in 1840 to more than one million by 1890. Served by a single railroad in 1850, the city ranked as the greatest railroad center in the world six years later. By 1890, Chicago led the nation in slaughtering and meatpacking, the production of lumber and furniture making, as well as foundry and machine-shop products. A leading producer of iron and steel, Chicago combined metal fabrication and agroindustrial production to command one of the most heavily industrialized regions in the world, as well as a vast hinterland of farms, timber lands, and mines.[27]

Transforming Nature

The transformation of nature in Chicago began with the process of lifting a marketplace out of the mud. Glaciers left Chicago's immediate hinterland a poorly drained mosaic of wetlands, forests, prairies, and savannahs that made it difficult to move agricultural produce into the city. Within the city proper, mud sometimes swallowed wagons and pedestrians whole. Into the 1850s, a weak and impoverished public sector allowed flooding and disease to bedevil the settlement. But where private interests could be served, or government could be induced to pay, Chicago made itself into a marketplace.[28]

Dredging the lake and the river, building docks and piers, lifting the streets out of the muck, and, above all, constructing canals and railroads, Chicagoans created a marketplace. Construction of the Illinois and Michigan Canal, begun in 1836, then slowed by economic depression, reached completion in 1848. The state-financed construction project cut through the mid-continental divide, linking the Great Lakes to the Mississippi River Valley. The construction of Chicago's first railroad, the Galena and Chicago Union Railroad, largely financed by rural communities along the line, also began in 1848. By the same year, a quarter-million dollars in federal funds finally dredged enough sand to provide Chicago with a decent harbor.[29]

Together these improvements, and the many railroads to follow, set in motion market processes that turned forests into lumber, prairies into farms, and Chicago itself into a grid of parcels for sale. The railroads changed everything. Rising above the mud, sheltering goods and passengers from the weather, and accelerating the movement of goods and information, the railroads overcame significant obstacles of geography and climate. The railroads also changed perceptions of time and its value and shattered biological limits by adding fossil fuels to animal and human energy.[30]

The railroads also changed business practices. Mobilizing capital from multiple sources, railroad corporations operated complex enterprises over far-flung territories and in diverse environmental conditions. Railroads pioneered new corporate forms of recordkeeping and statistical analysis. They also employed new types of engineers, accountants, and managers and established new hierarchical forms of organization. But even as they imposed their own logic on Chicago and its hinterland, railroad corporations experienced great vulnerability. With enormous fixed costs in track and rolling stock, railroad corporations tried to minimize risk by setting shipping rates to maximize traffic.[31]

One cannot help but admire the dogged determination and inventiveness of those who built Chicago. But each of the "commodity flows" that Cronon examined involved a transformation of an ecosystem according to market logic, with uncertain consequences. To see a forest in Michigan as "timber" was to imagine its entry into the market. Ingenious methods of transport, all dependent on facts of nature (the freezing point of water, the density of pine logs—i.e., they float), brought logs down iced skidways to frozen rivers and, with the spring thaws, to Lake Michigan and on to Chicago. The arduous labor provided cash for strapped farm families, while the lumber turned the western prairies into farming communities. But there were costs. Stupendous logjams wreaked havoc upstream, while the longer-term consequences included vanished forests; a bare, poorly drained land inhospitable to agriculture; and a depopulated, economically defunct landscape that became a burden on state tax ledgers.[32]

The extraction of resources from one ecosystem fueled the transformation of another ecosystem. On the Great Plains, the arrival of the railroad and the removal of buffalo in favor of cattle meant a change in the ecology of both the shortgrass and tallgrass prairies. In the shortgrass prairies of Colorado, Wyoming, and Montana, fencing cattle near sources of water led to the disappearance of the grasses and other plants that once flourished along watercourses. Instead, native and invasive species (ironweed, goldenrod, thistle) that were less palatable to cattle spread. Market logic also dictated that valuable tallgrass prairie closer to Chicago could no longer be given over the grazing. Instead, the tallgrass prairies of Illinois and eastern Iowa became fenced-in feedlots where biological space intersected with market time.[33]

The market in beef, transformed by Chicago's vast packinghouses, rearranged the natural cycles of reproduction and growth for cattle. Born in one place, cattle were fattened in a second place, killed in a third, and consumed in a fourth. The short period of rapid weight gain for young steers meant that feedlot owners cut their lives short, even as they fed them grain to speed their time to market. The unanticipated results of a grain diet for cattle included vast quantities of untreated wastes and, eventually, the overuse of antibiotics in perpetually sick cattle (genetically unprepared for a grain diet) and the spread of E. coli. But the success of dressed beef (butchered beef eaten a week or more after its death) also represented an extraordinary triumph of market construction. Even after the successful invention of the refrigerated railroad car, consumers found the idea of

week-old beef a "nasty-nice horror." Only cheaper prices and new strategies of cosmetic butchering and display pried opened resistant markets.[34]

The story of dressed beef illustrates how market logic and market
power shaped the flow of commodities extracted from nature. The railroads, eager for large, regular shipments that helped cover their fixed
costs, favored the shipment of bulky live animals over lighter, condensed
shipments of dressed beef. The triumph of dressed beef over live cattle also
threatened the railroads' investment in an immense, nationwide system of
stockyards. In the 1870s and 1880s, the railroads therefore resisted the
technological innovations necessary to dressed beef, forcing the packers
to build their own refrigerated cars. The railroads also offered rebates to
shippers of live cattle in exchange for a guarantee of large, regular shipments. But the creation of the Interstate Commerce Commission in 1887,
and the packers' growing share of the railroads' total shipments, ended
the railroad's manipulation of rates in favor of live shippers. The packers
quickly swept away the resistance of wholesale and retail butchers, centralizing butchering in Chicago and transforming the eating habits of a
nation in the process.[35]

Selling Futures, Naturalizing the Market

As the story of dressed beef illustrates, railroad corporations kept a flood
of commodities flowing through Chicago as quickly as possible. Primary
among the inventions designed to speed the flow of commodities, the
steam-powered grain elevator took the market in unanticipated directions. Getting grain out of the traditional sacks and onto conveyor belts
and into tall elevators produced huge economies of speed and scale. But
the steam-powered grain elevators also represented a new set of fixed
costs. Operators saddled with half-filled bins wanted to mix grain from
different owners. In the momentous year of 1848, the Chicago Board of
Trade began operation as a private organization. By 1856, the Board of
Trade had established categories of grain and uniform standards that
enabled grain elevators to mix grains grown in different places by different people.[36]

Both shippers and farmers deposited grain in the elevators and received a receipt for an equal quantity of equally graded grain. A lively
trade in these elevator receipts soon replaced the purchase of specific
grains from specific producers. But this arrangement increased the potential for adulteration, misrepresentation, and fraud, prompting further
efforts to regulate the grain market. Over the next few years, the Board

of Trade established more and more classifications, including "rejected," as well as an inspection system. In 1859, the Illinois legislature decided to regularize these spontaneous regulations of the market. The legislature granted the private Board of Trade quasi-judicial and legal powers, establishing it as "a body politic and corporate" charged with ensuring the integrity of the grain market.[37]

The elevators and their receipts created a national market for grain. Standardized grades enabled buyers anywhere in the country to purchase Chicago grain, sight unseen, for delivery at some future date at a fixed price. Combined with the telegraph, which provided nearly instantaneous information about grain prices across the country, this new market process erased much of the importance of geography, making grain from one place indistinguishable from grain from another place. This shift from an actual marketplace to the abstract concept of "the market" meant that transactions in Chicago shaped the fortunes of growers and consumers, buyers and sellers across vast distances. It also lessened some risks, saving farmers and small dealers the costs of storing and transporting grain in the face of uncertain prices.[38]

But even as this shift from the market as an actual place to a placeless process limited risks for some, it opened speculative opportunities for others. Nothing illustrated this better than the "to arrive" contract. Betting on the future price of grain, speculators contracted to ship grain at one price in the hopes that when the contract came due, they could buy the grain at a lower price and pocket the difference. As a market in the future price of grain developed, speculators did not even have to deliver the actual grain, so long as the buyer would settle for a cash payment representing the difference between the contract price and the current price. The futures market, a historian explains, became a place where "men who don't own something are selling that something to men who don't really want it."[39]

By 1875, the speculative market in the future price of grain dwarfed the size of the market in actual grain ($200 million against $2 million). Bulls, who bought futures contracts, bet against bears, who sold futures contracts. But when the futures contracts came due, usually on the last day of the month, the market in abstract grain intersected with the market in actual grain. This created yet another speculative opportunity, the corner. Buyers of futures contracts (bulls) could attempt to monopolize actual supplies of grain, forcing sellers of futures contracts (bears) to purchase grain (often from the architects of the corner) at ruinous prices when the contracts fell due.[40]

Successful corners destroyed less well-informed speculators, as well as many small operators. A corner also disrupted and distorted the actual trade in grain, especially in its "skeery" aftermath. An 1868 corner, the *Chicago Tribune* reported, proved as disastrous as "a long continued strike." It had "kept cereal from the city, driven operators away, and forced millers to buy elsewhere." Although the Board of Trade declared corners "essentially improper and fraudulent," it failed to end or even restrain them. A grudging admiration for those who orchestrated a corner played a role. But a growing respect for the market as a principle, something that should not be violated, played an even greater role. After all, the corner exploited the same classification system and the same futures contracts that made Chicago the center of the legitimate grain trade.[41]

Grain traders treated corners as natural and inevitable features of the market. Elevator operators claimed the same for other manipulations of the market. If an elevator operator mixed grains of different grades in such a way as to profit from selling a larger quantity of the higher grade, the operator saw it as intrinsic to the whole grading system. This peculiarity of the market could not be eradicated without destroying the market itself. But farmers, rural merchants, and many members of the Board of Trade found it difficult to see such manipulations as natural and inevitable. Much less did they accept the elevators' fraudulent weighing, the withholding of information on the supply of grain, the issuing of false receipts, and monopolistic arrangements made with the railroads.[42]

Agrarian protest escalated over the course of the 1860s, abetted by the formation of the Grange, an insurgent movement of farmers founded in 1867. As farmers began to organize and educate themselves, they protested what they saw as the unearned profit extracted from honest producers. Downstate agitation eventually produced Article 13 in the new Illinois State Constitution of 1870 and the state's Warehouse Act of 1871. Both asserted the state's power to regulate the elevators and the railroads. In *Munn v. Illinois* (1877), the U.S. Supreme Court agreed that railroads and elevators were "clothed in a public interest" and subject to state regulation.[43]

But the Board of Trade, not agrarian protesters, drafted the actual legislation. The law thus reflected the board's view of the market, attacking fraud but accepting corners and other peculiarities of the market whose rules it defined. Advancing from place to process to principle, the market finally became a power, reshaping everything in its image. Living within a world created by the many benefits provided by Chicago's market, both urban and rural people came to accept as normal the market's rules and consequences. Over the next century, futures trading spread to a wide variety of commodities (even climate change now has its futures market).[44]

Through these years, Chicagoans—and Americans generally—naturalized the market, accepting it as a force of nature. Boosters took for granted, as one proclaimed in 1876, that "a city is an organism, springing from natural laws as inevitably as any other organism, and governed, invariably, in its origin and growth, by these laws." Even the anarchist opponents of Chicago's merchants and industrialists shared this faith in the market as a natural force, even if they envisioned a different result. A "free system, with science for its guide and necessity for its impelling force," the anarchists held, would allow "the laws of nature to have full sway." The self-regulating market beguiled even its fiercest opponents.[45]

The Great Transformation

What the Austrian economist Karl Polanyi called the great transformation from a market *economy* to a market *society* captures much of what people saw in the shock cities of Manchester and Chicago. Markets had existed for millennia, embedded in larger social arrangements to which they remained subservient. Respect for the power of the market, as a source of both mutuality and antagonism, demanded that it be isolated in time and space, a visible and circumscribed place. Even as commerce quickened in early modern Europe, the marketplace remained hedged in by religious, municipal, and guild rituals and regulations.[46]

The emerging potential of machine industry in eighteenth-century Britain, however, raised a demand that society become subservient to the market. For industrialists, the indefatigable machine offered the prospect of twenty-four-hours-a-day productivity, but only if land (i.e., natural resources) and labor could be made available for purchase on the market in limitless quantities. Vast investments in machinery, the prospect of gain, and the danger of ruin if those investments did not pay demanded that land and labor be turned into commodities.[47]

No longer embedded in larger social arrangements, the market instead dictated those social arrangements. However much industrialists professed a faith in the self-regulating market, the task of releasing land and labor from traditional constraints that limited their exploitation depended on public policy. In Great Britain, repeal of the corn laws (creating a world market for grain) and revision of the poor laws (leaving the workhouse or starvation as the only alternatives to wage labor) turned nature and labor into commodities, their price and treatment subject only to the laws of supply and demand. The great transformation brought astounding, if unequally distributed, affluence, as well as dispossession and destitution.[48]

Land and labor are not, of course, commodities. They are not produced to be sold on the market but given by nature and nurtured by families. Their transformation into commodities threatened both nature and society. Nature became a vast storehouse, available for unlimited exploitation. As for labor, the self-regulating market enshrined hunger and gain as the sole motivations for work. Past societies had markets, even fear of hunger and love of gain, but only in a market society did these motivations appear timeless, universal, and exclusive. Polanyi marshaled anthropological and historical evidence of economies organized around religious, aesthetic, customary, honorific, and political motivations. Even in modern market society, he noted, people still worked for a variety of motives, including duty to others and the sheer joy of using one's talents. But market logic, Polanyi concluded, encouraged a great divide between "'real' man, bent on material values, and his 'ideal' better self."[49]

Polanyi knew that no society ever held strictly to the logic of the self-regulating market. The "idea of a self-regulating market implied a stark utopia," Polanyi wrote. If held to strictly, it "would have physically destroyed man and transformed his surroundings into wilderness." Consequently, spontaneous efforts to protect land, labor, and society from market logic never ceased. From the highest financial circles down to the poorest neighborhood, people acted to limit the damage produced by the logic of the self-regulating market. Not only the regulations established by Chicago's Board of Trade, but also the city's labor movement and its struggle for justice, testified to the truth of Polanyi's assertion. So, too, did the efforts of social reformers to protect Chicago's most vulnerable citizens.[50]

Separation versus Connection

In a pattern that would persist, however, the damage done in the creation of productive ecologies would receive less attention than the management of precarious settlements. Even that latter effort would be selectively applied. The widening distance between the place of consumption and the place of production, and between rich and poor, encouraged the pattern. While the links between city and country, and between rich and poor, could be seen easily enough if one wanted to see them, they could also be disguised or ignored.

Montgomery Ward's mail order business, founded in Chicago in 1872, mapped the web of relationships that linked urban and rural places. Cutting costs by eliminating retail stores, Ward's business operated out of a single building ("the busy beehive") on Michigan Avenue. By 1900, Ward's catalog included 1,200 pages, 17,000 illustrations, and 70,000 items gathered from every direction of the compass. As rural people rose to protest the exactions of "middlemen" from the big city, Ward promised—and delivered—wholesale prices to retail customers. Tens of thousands of farm families across the Great Plains gathered at kitchen tables to peruse the vast array of products available from the metropolitan center. Ward's two million customers kept two thousand clerks busy year-round, many of them doing nothing but opening letters, fifteen thousand to thirty thousand a day.[51]

But the most remarkable thing about the building and the catalog is how effectively they obscured the economic relationships they orchestrated. Each product in the catalog stood alone, divorced from the place of production and the people who produced it. Few customers wasted any time wondering where the products came from, who produced them, or under what conditions and with what consequences. The separation of production and consumption also made it easy to ignore the vast debt the city owed to the exploitation—at times, the theft—of natural wealth from the ecosystems it transformed. The city's spectacular growth brushed aside the question of how much the city's wealth and power owed to the continent's abundant natural resources that Chicagoans had no hand in creating, even if they very much had a hand in bringing them to market.[52]

The separation of production and consumption also disguised the damage done to those left behind in the frenzy of market expansion. The casualties included those left with few opportunities in the cutover districts of north woods as well as the victims of financial speculation in the towns and farms of the Great Plains. They also included those urbanites struggling in the crowded, disease-ridden river wards that had never been raised above the muck with the rest of the city. Chicago's affluent classes quickly abandoned those wards for lakefront mansions and distant suburbs. No longer working side by side with their employees, Chicago's manufacturers, like Manchester's, enjoyed a host of urban amenities in well-drained, park-like, "country" settings.[53]

The farther one lived from the sites of production, the more easily one could ignore the costs and consequences of market transformation. As in Manchester, suburban retreat established the domestic realm as a refuge from the market. Suburban women ruled over "the place of Peace," the English social critic John Ruskin wrote following his visit to Manchester in 1864. They made the domestic realm a "shelter, not only from all injury, but from all terror, doubt, and division." Ruskin beseeched such women to extend their healing hands to the "furnace ground" of industrial Britain. But Manchester's affluent women remained sheltered in, or confined to, the domestic realm. The notion of male and female spheres thus joined the separation of production and consumption as two more dimensions of the great divides.[54]

As if answering Ruskin's challenge to the women of Manchester's suburbs, however, the settlement house leader Jane Addams moved into one of Chicago's low-lying, riverfront neighborhoods in 1889. The well-educated daughter of an affluent family, Addams found the conditions in these neighborhoods shocking. "The streets are inexpressibly dirty," she wrote soon after settling, "sanitary legislation unenforced, the street lighting bad, the paving miserable and altogether lacking in the alleys and smaller streets, and the stables foul beyond description." Addams's Hull-House settlement, dedicated by its initial charter "to investigate and improve the conditions in the industrial districts of Chicago," became a meeting ground for those concerned with environmental degradation and social inequality.[55]

As Addams listened to her neighbors, she learned that dangerous and unhealthy conditions and inadequate public services topped their list of concerns. Chicago's practice of keeping property taxes low and paying for infrastructural improvements through special assessments of abutting property left landlords in the river wards free to ignore dangerous conditions. But the adoption of a ward system of politics in 1863 theoretically gave such neighborhoods a local champion. Determined to clean up their neighborhood, the women of Hull-House ran stand-in candidates against the corrupt local alderman and ward boss Johnny Powers in the 1890s.[56]

Powers ruled the ward by providing some measure of protection and assistance to his constituents. His generosity, fueled by graft, and his control of 2,600 payroll jobs, equal to one-third of the ward's electorate, enabled him easily to defeat the Hull-House candidates at the polls. But the women of Hull-House pursued politics by other means. Determined to secure for their neighbors a better quality of life than Powers delivered, Addams and her colleagues unsuccessfully submitted a bid to take over garbage collection. They then convinced the mayor to appoint Addams as garbage inspector for the ward in 1898. Once Powers recognized that improved sanitary conditions exposed his neglect, he had the position cut from the city budget.[57]

Meanwhile, Addams and her colleagues began to produce reports on slum conditions. They included *Hull-House Maps and Papers* (1895) and *Tenement Conditions in Chicago* (1901). Selecting a few representative neighborhoods, the tenement report examined everything from the quality of light and air to sanitary and drainage facilities. Innovative use of maps and photographs illustrated the miserable human costs of squalid slum conditions. The report estimated that 700,000 Chicagoans, 40 percent of the population, lived in substandard conditions. It also documented the links between rising urban death rates and filthy streets, wet cellars, and overflowing sewers and privies.[58]

Addams and her allies then drafted a model tenement reform bill based on the report. The bill expanded municipal powers over the built environment, setting minimum standards of construction governing access to light, ventilation, and sanitation, while requiring indoor toilets and strict adherence to fire safety rules. But given public indifference and the combined opposition of ward bosses, property owners, and building contractors, the City Council buried the bill in committee.[59]

Addams understood why Chicago's elite failed to make the City Council act. It was too "easy for even the most conscientious citizen of Chicago to forget the foul smells of the stockyards and the garbage dumps," Addams later wrote, when she is "living so far from them." But a citywide outbreak of typhoid fever in 1902 provided an opportunity to awaken public concern. A Hull-House survey revealed that its neighborhood, with one-thirty-sixth of the city's population, suffered one-sixth of the deaths from typhoid. The miasma theory of disease blamed decaying organic material in slum neighborhoods, presumably making infection a localized threat.[60]

The miasma theory, however, could not explain why affluent neighborhoods also suffered from the epidemic, even if at lower rates. The emerging germ theory of disease suggested that spring rains might have swept waste into the water supply, contaminating it with microorganisms. But since everyone drank the same water, no one could explain the lower rate of infection in affluent neighborhoods. The microbiologist Dr. Alice Hamilton, a Hull-House resident, provided an answer that connected the fate of the affluent districts to that of the tenement districts. Finding the typhoid bacillus on houseflies, Hamilton used the germ theory to explain why typhoid struck everywhere but at lower rates in the affluent districts. As the city's central produce distribution hub, the river wards sent home delivery vehicles and peddlers' carts into every ward, rich and poor, in the city. With those vehicles and carts came disease-carrying flies. Only the well-screened and drained houses of the affluent limited the severity of the epidemic.[61]

The disease might be more virulent in the poorer wards, Hamilton showed, but it could not be confined there. With an eye to reviving the tenement reform bill, Hull-House issued a pamphlet demonstrating that "the river wards cannot be isolated from the other residence portions of the town." With every home delivery "go the houseflies," the pamphlet ominously concluded, "bearing, as we may believe, the typhoid germ." The subsequent passage and enforcement of the tenement house law enhanced land use regulations, imposed new obligations on landlords, and tightened building and housing codes. Although corruption and neglect continued, Hull-House won at least a partial victory in its effort to improve environmental conditions in the poorer wards.[62]

While Chicago's rapid growth produced an unthinking naturalization of market processes, the efforts of Hull-House represented the spontaneous response to address market ills that Polanyi described. Challenging the reign of laissez-faire, Hull-House residents held public policy and municipal governance responsible for environmental injustice. As political reformers, Addams and the women of Hull-House, and women across the city and the nation, secured an expansion of municipal responsibilities and raised expectations about the quality of public services.[63]

Addams and other advocates of environmental justice tried to awaken the public to the importance of a clean and safe environment for all. They hoped to extend to all classes the benefits arising from the efforts of physicians, sanitarians, engineers, landscape architects, and others who, over the course of the nineteenth century, had made cities healthier and more satisfying places to live. The new attention given to improving the urban environment, a municipal engineer explained early in the new century, "does not lie in the newness of the problem, but rather in the intellectual awakening of the people." The need for environmental reform and justice, however, had long outstripped the successes. It remained to be seen how far reform could be made to reach.[64]

4

Managing Precarious Settlements and Inspiring Civic Loyalty

*Positive Environmentalism and
the City Beautiful Movement*

ities have always been precarious settlements. Population density
and accumulating wastes create immediate issues of sanitation.
Living in close quarters with domesticated and scavenging animals
and other humans, city dwellers encounter all manner of bacteria, viruses,
and other germs. Parasites coevolve and pass between species. As density
rises, humans confront expanding pools of infectious agents and increasing contact with those agents. For thousands of years, humans poorly
understood the dangers of these new urban environments. As recently as
the late nineteenth century, experts ascribed infectious disease to unspec-
ified substances in "bad air" or "miasmas."[1]

In one of the great success stories of American urbanism, however,
nineteenth-century cities gained water and sewage systems, paved and
lighted streets, trash collection, zoning laws, public health regulations,
and green spaces. Their efforts made modern urban culture possible and
inspired visions of even greater possibilities. Tax revenues, the land reformer Henry George argued, should be "applied to the improvement and
beautifying of the city, to the promotion of the health, comfort, education, and recreation of its people." Such improvements could extend to
gratifications of a "social and intellectual nature," including "the realms
of the imagination," and make possible a "wider and fuller, and more
varied life" for all.[2]

Vanquishing laissez-faire assumptions, environmental reform also gave rise to modern urban governance. The "sanitary arrangements of the city," a New York City sanitarian argued in 1845, would secure "the increased health of the population, a much better state of public morals, and, by consequence, a more easily governed and respectable community." By the new century, the standard textbook on municipal sanitation rejoiced that "even the need for sewers has scarcely to be urged by health officers. The public so well appreciates their advantages that they are usually demanded when needed, even if they must be entirely paid for by the abutters."[3]

At the turn of the twentieth century, the City Beautiful movement built on these successes to promote a far-reaching program of positive environmentalism. City Beautiful activists believed that ugly cities, filled with polluting factories and tacky billboards, made for a passive and bewildered citizenry. But tree-lined boulevards, public spaces and parks, and civic monuments would promote civility and civic loyalty. What "are we doing to make our cities a worthy influence?" City Beautiful leaders asked, arguing that a beautiful city would both enrich the life of the individual and nurture a "civic conscience." People are "in large measure what the city makes them," City Beautiful proponents argued, as they campaigned for a beautiful city that would "awaken love, affection, interest" and serve as a "socializing agency" for the creation of good citizens.[4]

Urban environmental reform provided an essential complement to the creation of productive ecologies, securing the city's viability. It also encouraged a deeper ecological understanding of cities and regions. But in its transformation of municipal governance, urban environmental reform also produced a gender divide and a democratic deficit. As male experts and professionals asserted their authority and their priorities, activist women and the engaged public saw their roles diminished and their priorities neglected. Consequently, environmental reform benefited some groups and classes within the city more than others.

The benefits of urban environmental reform, moreover, generally stopped at the city's limits. Rural America grappled alone, and less successfully, with its own issues of sanitation, exacerbated by the disposal of waste from ever escalating urban standards of living. Urban environmental reform also failed to address blasted landscapes associated with lumbering, mining, drilling, and farming.[5]

Meanwhile, the search for water, energy, and the other resources that enriched urban life reached deep into rural hinterlands, demonstrating the falsity of the city-country divide. When cities came looking for water, battles raged between urban and agricultural interests for limited sources. The struggle over the waters of the Owens River, north of Los Angeles, and the tragic failure of the St. Francis dam in 1928 is only the most famous of many such conflicts. New York City, for example, depends on nineteen artificial lakes to supply its population with more than one billion gallons of water every day. (Profligate New Yorkers use four times the per capita rate of Londoners.) The creation of those lakes (off-limits to locals for both swimming and boating) required the expropriation and submersion of some twenty-six villages, along with countless farms, orchards, and quarries, deepening enmity between the empire city and rural upstate New York.[6]

From Moral to Positive Environmentalism: Sanitizing and Greening the City

The challenges of sanitation grew over the course of the nineteenth century. Between 1830 and 1860, early industrialization and a laissez-faire disdain for municipal governance opened everything for exploitation, including land, air, and water. Uncollected garbage, human and animal excrement, and industrial wastes filled the streets, fouled the air, and compromised water supplies. Consequently, cholera, typhoid, diphtheria, and other diseases ravaged urban populations. Coal smoke and sundry pollutants spread respiratory ailments. Solid wastes, buried underground or dumped in huge slag heaps, further compromised both health and quality of life.[7]

The municipal effort to sanitize the city began in the 1830s as the deterioration of urban environments coincided with a scientific receptivity to environmentally based explanations of disease. Edwin Chadwick, secretary of England's Poor Law Commission, pointed the way in documenting the links between rising urban death rates and environmental conditions. As disease undermined economic prosperity, the demand for reform sometimes came from businessmen and boosters. But worried for their cities' reputations, business leaders too often preferred public-relations efforts over health-planning procedures.[8]

What historians call moral environmentalism proved more influential. The upper classes tended to blame the poor for urban conditions and privileged moral reformation over physical improvements. But as the religious concept of the innate depravity of human nature waned, moral environmentalists began to ask how citizens, and particularly recent immigrants unfamiliar with urban life, could possibly lead upright lives amid garbage, human and animal wastes, fetid standing water, and polluted air. An improved environment, they argued, would produce an improved morality.[9]

In the face of rising death rates, concerns about health reinforced those about morality. The anti-contagion theory, advanced by the emerging profession of sanitarian, traced the source of disease to foul odors (or "miasmas") arising from waste-filled water and rotting organic matter in the streets. Despite the resistance of timid or corrupt political officials and vested economic interests, sanitarians secured new public health boards and other public agencies that assumed responsibility for providing clean water, removing wastes, and, less aggressively, protecting air quality and improving conditions in the slums.[10]

The structure of modern municipal government and its expanded responsibilities came out of the effort to sanitize the cities. In the middle decades of the nineteenth century, the courts enabled municipalities to take property for a public purpose under eminent domain; to regulate private and public nuisances; and to wield the police power to protect the safety, health, and convenience of citizens. Municipal governments also regulated building practices and noxious trades, demolished buildings, and removed obstructions. Such legal innovations also made possible the construction of waterworks and sewer systems and the paving of streets.[11]

As existing occupations professionalized and new professions emerged, lawyers, engineers, doctors, sanitarians, architects, and landscape architects filled the ranks of the reformers. Such professionals saw a need for applying their expertise to the dangers they observed every day. As cities made major investments in public works that required long-range planning and broad vision, reformers demanded a nonpartisan, professional administration of municipal affairs that would give their expertise free rein. While reform-minded professionals made mistakes and inevitably had only a limited and biased perspective, they addressed essential and neglected needs in cities.[12]

Water represented the most pressing need for cities and demanded the most urgent action. Most cities relied on private and local sources of water into the 1830s. But as population and congestion increased, disease from contaminated water and the need to flush the streets and fight fires sent cities in search of water far outside their municipal boundaries. New York City's Croton Aqueduct, tapping sources forty miles away, opened in 1842. Other large cities soon followed suit. Urban voters eagerly supported public ownership of waterworks, as private firms failed to provide adequate service or plan for future needs. By 1860, the nation's sixteen largest cities all enjoyed waterworks, a dozen of them municipally owned, often tapping distant, upland sources in rural areas. By 1910, more than 70 percent of cities with more than thirty thousand residents operated municipal waterworks.[13]

Abundant water, however, flooded cities with wastewater. The case of Chicago well illustrates the city's embeddedness in the larger biosphere and the interconnections of city and country. Chicagoans voted for a public waterworks in 1851, and ten years later virtually the entire city enjoyed running water. Chicago drew its water from Lake Michigan, however, which eventually had consequences for urban and rural communities across the Great Lakes region. More immediately, Chicago dumped its waste into the Chicago River. As in cities across the nation, this included human waste due to the widespread adoption of the "water closet" (flush toilet) in affluent households. Household waste now joined wastes from distilleries, slaughterhouses, and other industries to spread infectious disease.[14]

Beset by the highest death rate in the nation, Chicago pioneered the comprehensive sanitary sewer system in the 1855. In the wake of a mass meeting in December 1854, the Illinois state legislature created a three-member Board of Sewerage Commissioners, which then hired the engineer Ellis S. Chesbrough to design the system. Rejecting as too costly Chesbrough's most sophisticated proposal for collecting waste in a reservoir to be pumped out periodically and used to restore fertility to nearby farms, municipal officials chose the cheapest option. Relying on gravity, the city laid sewer pipes at ground level and raised the streets five to fourteen feet above the pipes. Dredging the river and collecting fill from excavated basements provided the means to raise the streets. The plan left it to property owners to lift their structures at their own expense.[15]

Chesbrough also improved the city's waterworks. He praised Lake Michigan as "a fountain inexhaustible, lying at our very feet, requiring us only to provide a means of drawing from its boundless resources." He thus directed the construction of an underground, brick-lined tunnel two miles out into the lake, where a pump station would deliver water of "ever-lasting purity" to the city. The "two-mile crib" opened in 1867. But relying on the lake as both source of pure water and sink for voluminous wastes still proved disastrous. To protect Chicago's harbor from silting, the Army Corps of Engineers had constructed a pier at the mouth of the river, extending into the lake. Local officials soon learned that during heavy spring rains, the pier efficiently directed the river's flow toward the two-mile crib, compromising the city's water supply. The press dubbed the Chicago River "a river of death," with infectious disease rampant along its shores and, due to the contamination of the crib, far beyond.[16]

In the last decades of the nineteenth century, Chicago experimented with various means of addressing the threat. These efforts included periodic flushing of the river and moving the most noxious industries farther out onto the prairie to the city's west. After officials noticed that the pumps that filled the Illinois and Michigan Canal tended to reverse the river's flow, they made intermittent efforts to reverse the river's flow permanently by deepening the channel of the Chicago River and pumping water out of Lake Michigan. These efforts culminated in the opening of the Sanitary and Ship Canal in 1900. Sending Chicago's wastes downstream to St. Louis and other communities required an astoundingly large diversion of lake water, as much as 4.5 million gallons per minute, 6.5 billion gallons a day. Downstream communities looked askance at the stench, the dead fish, and their compromised water supplies. In denouncing the practice, they allied with Great Lakes cities alarmed by the drop in the level of the lakes. Federal and international lawsuits in the early twentieth century, and federal funds in the 1930s for the construction of sewage treatment plants, eventually limited the damage.[17]

As Chicago's example illustrates, misguided public policies could prove as damaging to the environment as heedless economic activity. But in the short run, Chicago's declining death rate led cities large and small to construct combined (storm- and wastewater) sewer systems in the last three decades of the century. Beginning in the 1880s, widespread acceptance of the germ theory of disease (isolating waterborne bacteria as the danger) accelerated the trend. By 1910, virtually every city operated a sewer system, with a nonpartisan expert board overseeing it.[18]

The construction of sewage systems required street improvements. Durable and smooth, easy to patch and clean, asphalt paving supplanted cobblestones and wooden blocks. Paving improved drainage and eased the removal of vast quantities of ashes and animal manure, household and industrial wastes, and scrap metal and rubbish that obstructed maintenance of the sewer system (and compromised health). Beginning in 1895, George Waring's transformation of New York City's ragtag assembly of street cleaners into the famous "White Wings" brought professional standards and military discipline to street cleaning. While directing the removal of two-foot-deep accumulations of wastes in side streets and alleys, Waring also addressed the metabolic rift. By requiring the stabling of horses at night, he facilitated the collection and sale of manure as fertilizer.[19]

Improved paving turned streets from multiuse, if filthy, extensions of domestic, social, and political space into conduits for traffic, commerce, and public utilities. The loss of the street as a public space intensified the demand for neighborhood parks and playgrounds at the turn of the twentieth century. By 1917, more than five hundred cities provided playgrounds, and thousands of reformers attended the conventions of the Playground Association of America. These Progressive-era reformers embraced "positive environmentalism," a strategy that added wholesome recreation, improved housing, and city planning to sanitation as the means of reshaping individual character and improving civic life.[20]

Positive environmentalism emerged first and foremost in park planning. Many cities had included civic greens and public squares from their inception. But population and economic growth overwhelmed these spaces. Beginning with Boston's Mount Auburn Cemetery in 1831, dozens of garden cemeteries opened within city limits, providing relief from urban grids and becoming places of relaxation for harried urbanites. Garden cemeteries pioneered new romantic design concepts, replacing formal, classical designs with informal, curvilinear layouts and picturesque landscapes. The garden cemetery idea expanded in two directions: toward the romantic suburb and the urban park. Even as they designed the first romantic suburbs for the affluent, Andrew Jackson Downing and Frederick Law Olmsted campaigned for public parks for all classes.[21]

Olmsted, who, along with his partner, Calvert Vaux, designed New York City's Central Park (1857), emerged as a leader of the new profession of landscape architecture. In the decades after the Civil War, Olmsted developed plans for dozens of cities to maximize drainage, minimize infrastructural costs, preserve landscape amenities, and protect local waterways from residential development and industrial pollution. In Boston's "Emerald Necklace," Olmsted designed a system of parks, parkways, and waterways to manage stormwater, improve sanitation, and provide beauty and recreation.[22]

The effort to sanitize and green the city engaged the efforts of a host of professionals, artisans, and laborers in an explosion of environmental experimentation and reform. Managing the manifold threats in precarious settlements lowered death rates and improved the quality of life. But technological fixes for pollution, such as sewers and, later, landfills and tall stacks for power plants, just moved waste from one place to another. Such remedies extended the habits of industrialists in treating water, land, and air as free goods where waste could be dumped.[23]

Dystopian and Utopian Visions Conjure Dreams of a City Beautiful

American cities continued to grow rapidly in the second half of the nineteenth century as the extent and scale of industrial production soared. Only sixteen cities exceeded fifty thousand in population in 1860; by 1910, more than eighty did. Despite the reforms in the first half of the century, poverty and social unrest, crime and overcrowding, and increasing pollution burdened these cities. The clang and grind of machinery, snarls of traffic, networks of overhead wires, construction sites, vacant lots, and dilapidated buildings further blighted the cityscape. In the last decade of the century, an avalanche of commercial billboards added to the clutter and chaos of city streets.[24]

As a series of terrifying epidemics in the 1870s spread anxiety up and down the social scale, the potential for explosive social conflicts added to the precariousness of city life and conjured darker fears of urban destruction. Poverty and economic inequality made crime a feature of everyday life and occasionally escalated into large-scale violence. Uneasy members of the upper classes proved less than sympathetic. "If the club of the policeman, knocking out the brains of the rioter will answer," a religious weekly editorialized in 1877, "then all well and good; but if it does not . . . , then bullets and bayonets, canister and grape . . . constitute the one remedy." Such visions depicted the volatile city as a threat to civilization.[25]

Labor unrest lent a hard edge to urban disorder, exploding in massive waves of strikes and armed encounters. Living close to their work in polluting factories and crowded into substandard housing, industrial workers harbored grievances related to both workplace and neighborhood. In *How the Other Half Lives* (1890), the photographer and reformer Jacob Riis described the city's poor as "shiftless, destructive and stupid," just "what the tenements have made them." In what Riis called "the foul core of New York's slums," positive environmentalism had accomplished little. The "sea of a mighty population, held in galling fetters, heaves uneasily in the tenements," Riis continued. The city had already "felt the swell of its resistless flood," he warned in reference to the terrible Draft Riots of 1863. "If it rises once more, no human power may avail to check it."[26]

Sensational newspapers, crime magazines, and dime novels added to the aura of urban menace. With advances in flash photography, exposés such as Riis's provided the affluent with glimpses of places into which they rarely ventured. A suburbanizing middle class, increasingly unfamiliar with actual slums, devoured dystopian novels of urban destruction. Ignatius Donnelly's fictional destruction of New York City, *Caesar's Columns* (1890), dramatized a nightmare of violence between greedy capitalists and the debased poor. It had sold half a million copies by 1906.[27]

Nightmare images of urban life even appeared within the competing utopian literature of the period. Julian West, the fictional hero of Edward Bellamy's *Looking Backward, 2000–1887* (1888), awoke in 2000 to find that Boston had become a city of "large open squares filled with trees, along which statues glistened and fountains flashed in the late-afternoon sun." But horrid visions of a previous Boston reeking "with the effluvia of a slave ship's between decks" disturbed West's sleep, as did chilling images of "half-clad brutalized children" and "starving bands of mongrel curs" fighting over garbage. Bellamy knew that such nightmares too closely resembled the actual conditions for many urbanites.[28]

Political corruption, especially at the municipal level, hampered public efforts to address urban ills. Public service corporations, the agencies on which improved environments often depended, freely distributed bribes among city officials in exchange for municipal franchises to supply transit, electricity, and other utilities. While reformers wished for a spirit of civic loyalty to redeem the city from such corruption, they also feared that American cities lacked the landmarks, symbols, and traditions that might kindle such loyalty. Little in these cities engaged the emotions, the senses, or the imagination—no magic to stir men's blood.[29]

At the same time, the successes of sanitarians and engineers in constructing urban systems raised expectations about technological solutions to urban problems that found their way into the literary utopias. Perfect sewage and water distribution, cooling and heating, rapid transit, and instantaneous communication turned these imagined cities into what one novelist called "immense palaces nicely intermingled with fragrant gardens and luxuriant parks—there being no dirty streets or unsightly habitations of any description." The utopians' civic centers, parks, parkways, and boulevards would soon reappear in City Beautiful plans.[30]

By the end of the century, public opinion, the aspirations of environmental reformers, and literary utopias coalesced around the ideal of a technologically sophisticated city set within and attuned to the rhythms of nature. The literary historian Leo Marx later called this urge a wishful melding of the machine and the garden, a fervent hope that the city might be redeemed through an injection of rural beauty. Utopian novelists argued that the city should be "treated as the canvas of a painter or the marble of a sculptor." Everything should be done "to enhance the beauty of any part of the growing city, or to increase its convenience or the comfort or welfare of its inhabitants." A city of convenience and beauty would reconcile the conflicting desires for technological sophistication and pastoral ease.[31]

From Public Parks to the White City

Public parks brought a middle landscape—neither urban grid nor untamed wilderness but nature ordered and improved by human effort—into the heart of the city. Parks appealed to real estate speculators, who recognized their impact on surrounding land values, as well as citizens, who simply enjoyed them. But Olmsted articulated a more complex philosophy of parks that offered rural beauty as the antidote to urban harshness. Alarmed by the degradation of the physical environment and the coarsening of social relations, Olmsted worried that city life promoted "a peculiarly hard sort of selfishness." The "further progress of civilization," he explained, "is to depend mainly upon the influences by which men's minds and characters will be affected while living in large towns." Parks would bring people together so that each contributed to "the pleasure of the others, all helping to the greater happiness of each." Exerting a "harmonizing and refining influence" on the urban masses, Olmsted concluded, parks were "favorable to courtesy, self-control, and temperance."[32]

Olmsted left a multifaceted legacy. Aside from his championing of positive environmentalism, he designed massive public works that required heavy municipal expense, encouraged the collaboration of artists and professionals, and experimented with strategies for the control of crowds and traffic. Extending his vision to include systems of parks, parkways, and boulevards designed to guide and direct urban development, Olmsted articulated an understanding of the city as a living, complex organism with interdependent parts that informed the City Beautiful movement. He also trained and mentored a fair share of the architects and planners who joined the movement.[33]

Olmsted's landscape design for the 1893 World's Columbian Exposition in Chicago galvanized a movement for urban beautification that had already begun to take shape in municipal improvement associations across the nation. Under the leadership of the prominent Chicago architect Daniel H. Burnham, exposition planners oversaw the transformation of nearly seven hundred acres of swampy land on the city's South Side lakeshore. Managing scores of architects and other professionals, Burnham directed the dredging and filling according to Olmsted's plan. Featuring ponds, lagoons, and green space, the site accommodated four hundred buildings in a melding of the natural and technological.[34]

At the center of the exposition stood the Court of Honor, a collection of neoclassical buildings fronting Olmsted's reflecting pool and dubbed "the White City." The Court of Honor reflected the principles of the Parisian École des Beaux-Arts and its emphasis on proportion, scale, and the balanced arrangement of forms. The White City also represented a culmination of advances in urban engineering, sanitation, transportation, illumination, and public safety. Filtered drinking water, sewage treatment, convenient toilets, and nightly sweeping and cleaning of streets and sidewalks made the White City a wonder. The landscaping and design of buildings, arising from the collaboration of architects, landscape architects, sculptors, and mural painters, built on the experiments of the previous twenty years. Although composed of temporary structures faced with white plaster, the White City left a lasting impression.[35]

In demonstrating that cities could be beautiful, the White City made its greatest contribution. Designed for visual pleasure, the White City invoked an emotional response, akin to religious awe, that American cities so conspicuously lacked. Like many future proponents of the City Beautiful movement, Burnham retained a Protestant religiosity, even a mystical strain, driving his effort to inculcate higher ideals of civic spirit in both elites and, especially, the masses. Commentators marveled at the good behavior of the "obscure and anonymous myriads of unknown laborers" who attended the fair. "It seemed as though the beauty of the place," a Protestant minister wrote, "brought gentleness, happiness, and self-respect to its visitors." The White City heartened those who would redeem cities.[36]

The planning of the exposition, however, anticipated the democratic deficit that would bedevil the City Beautiful movement. Olmsted long struggled to keep park design and park management in the hands of experts and professionals. Chafing under his association with venal politicians, Olmsted saw the profession of landscape architecture as a means for men of intellect and vision to exert an influence usually denied them in municipal affairs. The exposition provided that influence. Authorized by an act of Congress in celebration of the four-hundredth anniversary of Christopher Columbus's voyage to America, and ostensibly overseen by a public commission, the World's Columbian Exposition answered only to a private corporation directed by Chicago capitalists. Winning the trust of the corporate directors, Burnham became the exposition's undisputed manager. His benevolent autocracy ensured the elimination of billboards, the strict control of signage and other communication, and the discrete isolation of deliveries. The exposition's Columbian Guard kept the peace without interference from corrupt politicians.[37]

For some urban elites, the World's Columbian Exposition thus provided a model not only of what a city should look like but also of how it should be governed. But no blueprint existed for replicating the exposition's successes in actual cities, with their messy democratic processes. The White City demonstrated the potential for combining reforms focused on sanitation and parks with those related to civic art and urban design. It also energized new and existing efforts to clean up and beautify cities. But the precise connection between an improved environment and an improved citizenry, and the role of that citizenry, had yet to be clarified.[38]

The City Beautiful and Imperial

The City Beautiful movement coalesced in the decade that followed the Chicago exposition. Improved economic conditions and a lessening of social conflicts in the final years of the 1890s gave the movement an optimistic tenor. More than managing precarious settlements, the City Beautiful movement aspired to make cities more satisfying and stimulating places and, especially, to make them more worthy of civic loyalty. Building on the fame of the White City, the movement united park planning with civic art. Under the motto "To make us love our city, we must make our city lovely," City Beautiful activists joined civic art advocates in making war on crass commercialism and urban disorder.[39]

City Beautiful projects ranged from grand railroad stations and monumental civic centers to processional boulevards and parkways. The huge expense of civic centers and their potential disruption of downtown real estate markets left more centers envisioned than constructed. Processional boulevards and belt parkways proved more achievable. Boulevards punctured the gridiron of streets and improved urban circulation. They also lent grace and beauty to many cities. Paseo Boulevard in Kansas City, Missouri, for example, followed the contours of the landscape, afforded views from atop the bluffs above the Missouri River, and passed through more than two hundred acres of parkland dotted with cultural institutions and Beaux-Arts structures. Such boulevards attracted grand residences, discouraged suburban escape, and promoted urban investment.[40]

Belt parkways linked scattered parks and increased access to open spaces while serving as spines to direct new development and ease congestion. Parkways, the movement's publicist Charles Mulford Robinson argued, also extended the benefits of natural beauty into "busy, workaday sections of the town." Like boulevards, the parkways followed the natural contours of land and provided access to forest preserves. Both parkways and boulevards combined utility and beauty, the watchwords of the movement. As Robinson explained, they provided "shortcuts to traffic" but also contributed "variety in street intersection, revealing pleasant vistas, and making easy the provision of little open spaces."[41]

The boldest City Beautiful plans broke free of the aesthetic framework to offer comprehensive and expansive visions of the urban future. The movement's emphasis on civic life, education, and culture reflected a view of the city as more than an economic machine. Burnham's ambitious plan for San Francisco included an inner ring of streets lined with cultural institutions, parks on every hilltop, and an outer belt parkway featuring spectacular views of the region. While much of Burnham's San Francisco plan remained unbuilt, he had more success with his *Plan of Chicago* (1909), the best-known and arguably the most successful of City Beautiful plans. Devised by Burnham and his young École des Beaux-Arts–trained assistant Edward H. Bennett, *Plan of Chicago* offered an inspiring vision of a gracious and civically adorned city.[42]

City Beautiful visions did not, however, limit the imperial ambitions of the urban economic machine, and in some ways they abetted them. The San Francisco that Burnham proposed to beautify set hydraulic cannons to work blasting apart the Sierra Nevada Mountains and burying rural settlements under silt. When federal courts ended hydraulic mining in the United States, San Francisco's entrepreneurs exported the practice across the globe. Meanwhile, the technology of mining remade the city. The iron ropes and flywheels central to mining pulled cable cars up San Francisco's Nob Hill, tapping bonanza fields of speculative real estate. The electric lighting, ventilators, high-speed elevators, and telephones developed in the mines made skyscrapers feasible. A pioneer in skyscraper design, Burnham visited the Nevada mines in 1868, where the Deidesheimer square set, a heavy timber cube used to hold open mine shafts, offered an architectural model for the steel-frame skyscraper. Skyscrapers, essentially inverted mines that rose above instead of descending below ground, expanded mining fortunes by garnering huge rents. They also served as command centers for the further exploitation of far-flung hinterlands.[43]

In 1904, Burnham produced City Beautiful plans for two cities in the Philippines, one of those far-flung hinterlands of imperial San Francisco. Closer to home, Burnham's *Plan of Chicago* offered a strategy for solidifying and enhancing Chicago's imperial dominance of its region. Sharing the ambitions of the commercial and financial elite who commissioned it, *Plan of Chicago* treated the windy city as "without bounds or limits" and its hinterlands as an "illimitable space now occupied by a population capable of illimitable expansion." In the preceding thirty years, Chicago's growth had increased the value of downtown real estate many times over, but congestion threatened those values. With congestion now bound to "increase in geometrical ratio" to the city's reach, Burnham's plan focused on facilitating movement into and around the urban core.[44]

Burnham's *Plan of Chicago* envisioned regional highways, both radial and concentric, reaching sixty miles into the hinterland. To ease the anticipated congestion, Burnham designed a new freight handling center on the city's far southwestern side that would work as a "perfect machine," serving more than a score of railroad lines entering the city. In the central core, complementary freight distribution and passenger routing systems used existing underground tunnels and linked the railroad terminals to the city's transit system. Such improvements would enable Chicago to accommodate "many times" its current traffic.[45]

For all his allegiance to business interests, however, Burnham embedded his blueprint for commercial dominance in a more expansive vision of city life. "Make no little plans," Burnham is supposed to have said, "they have no magic to stir men's blood." There is nothing little about his *Plan of Chicago*. It promised to turn the city into "an efficient instrument for providing all its people with the best possible conditions of living." Believing that "good citizenship is the prime object of good city planning," Burnham embraced the positive environmentalism and the faith in the harmonizing influence of civic art that the City Beautiful movement did so much to spread.[46]

Burnham saw Lake Michigan as a civic and recreational asset, capable of promoting social unity and contentment. He opposed plans to make it a working harbor. With the Chicago River's pollution of Lake Michigan reduced, if not eliminated, the lakefront also provided a key resource for beautifying the city. Burnham often ended his speeches by invoking the lake to capture the City Beautiful movement's animating vision of a technologically sophisticated city attuned to the rhythms of nature. It seemed "as if the lake has been singing to us all those years," Burnham declaimed, beckoning Chicago to be "merged into nature and become part of her."[47]

Plan of Chicago gave stirring expression to the City Beautiful movement's hopefulness about the city. It expressed Burnham's faith that challenges could be overcome and "a unified city, wherein each portion will have organic relations to all other portions," could be created. The volume itself, with its midnight green cover and title and cipher of the Commercial Club impressed in gold, and weighing more than five pounds, appealed first and foremost to the senses. The publication offered the reader/viewer a vision of a future Chicago, invoking wonder at the cultivated beauty of a serenely civilized place. In arguing that the "cities that truly exercise dominion rule by reason of their appeal to the highest emotions of the human mind," *Plan of Chicago* announced its own ambitions.[48]

The City Beautiful Movement and the Democratic Process

A plan for a well-ordered and convenient city, Burnham and his associates believed, would win over public sentiment and improve life for all. But dystopian scenarios for the future of the city could not be dismissed. Substandard housing, unpaved streets, noise, and pollution taxed the health and well-being of Chicagoans and exacerbated labor and social conflicts. Such fears shaped the City Beautiful movement's approach to the democratic process. The failures of democratic governance, *Plan of Chicago* warned, made slum neighborhoods "a menace to the moral and physical health of the community." The "public authorities," Burnham told his patrons in the Commercial Club, "do not do their duty," but one way or the other "they must be made to."[49]

The elite sponsors of *Plan of Chicago* doubted whether the municipal government could ever address the city's needs. State-imposed limitations on the borrowing capacity of the city, overlapping local governments and boards, and a corrupt political culture made municipal governance hopeless. The Commercial Club favored a semiofficial planning commission with public legitimacy but composed entirely of its own members and insulated from both the voters and elected officials. The Board of Alderman ultimately approved a broadly representative Chicago Plan Commission with 328 members, but the aldermen placed authority in an executive committee of fifteen members, twelve of whom belonged to the Commercial Club. The executive committee's chairman, Charles H. Wacker, a Commercial Club member and veteran of the 1893 exposition, became the effective leader of the effort.[50]

To secure acceptance of a plan that still had no official standing, Wacker made sure every significant public official received a copy of *Plan of Chicago*. The $25 price, however, put it out of reach of most Chicagoans. To secure public support for the plan, Wacker hired the master publicist Walter D. Moody. Cultivating newspaper editors and reporters, Moody blanketed the city with five hundred lantern-slide lectures, reaching 150,000 people, and commissioned a film, *A Tale of Our City*, shown in sixty theaters to 175,000 viewers. Moody also produced several short publications, including *Chicago's Greatest Issue: An Official Plan* (1911), that he provided free to property owners and those who paid more than $25 in rent a month. He also negotiated an agreement to make another of his publications, *Wacker's Manual of the Plan of Chicago* (1911), the required civics textbook for eighth-graders in Chicago's public schools.[51]

The top-down effort to lobby key decision makers while overawing the public with a media blitz betrayed the most promising methods and the most democratic vision of the movement. At its best, the City Beautiful movement relied on a civic-spirited citizenry energized by a vision of a beautiful and generous city. The logical product of that vision would be ample civic and public spaces serving as barriers against the encroachments of crass commercialism. Philadelphia's Benjamin Franklin Parkway, connecting City Hall with the Philadelphia Museum of Art, demonstrated the potential of linking the center of democratic power with the institutions of public culture. The project made a start in asserting the claims of a shared public realm and setting limits to the dominance of private interests. The Boston Public Library off Copley Square, the Detroit Public Library and Institute of Arts, the Denver Public Library and Art Museum, and Cleveland's six-building Group Plan anchored similar public spaces.[52]

The full realization of the City Beautiful movement's democratic vision, however, required more than public spaces. It demanded an engaged and active citizenry using those public spaces for discussion, debate, and deliberation. The City Beautiful movement's encounter with the explosion of commercial billboards, however, underscored the limits of its democratic vision. City Beautiful advocates complained that commercial billboards obtruded into public space with "all sorts of sordid ideas." But they linked the billboard menace to their suspicions of mass democracy, equating the "din" and "shriek" of visual salesmanship with the "riot" of "the mob." Industry spokesmen countered that their billboards offered color, amusement, and companionship to harried urbanites, providing relief from a dreary and monotonous cityscape and a more genuinely public art than elitist civic monuments.[53]

Neither side in the debate over billboards, however, championed an active, deliberating public. Both sides treated the citizenry as spectators.

Industry spokesmen charged that monumental architecture spoke in an authoritarian idiom that demanded obedience, while the billboards spoke in favor of freedom over self-denial. But the advertisers' own efforts to mold mass markets paralleled and ultimately supplanted the effort to use civic monuments to produce a unified and contented citizenry. The *Architectural Record* glimpsed the future when it complained in 1915 that billboards, neon signs, and other commercial images defiled the "permanent, unimpeachable" architectural forms on which civic identity depended. Moody's promotional efforts acknowledged this shift of cultural authority from monumental architecture to advertising.[54]

Even as the City Beautiful movement found itself squeezed by expansive commercialism, it failed to satisfy advocates for participatory democracy. Some in the City Beautiful movement championed civic art to "soothe . . . popular discontent" or advertise the benevolence of a philanthropic elite. As its leading spokesman, Robinson praised imposing civic centers that would "visibly dominate" the city. "To them," he wrote, "the community would look up, seeing them lording over it at every turn, as, in fact, the government ought to do." But others thought civic spaces should promote a "spirit of liberalism and equality" and promote interaction among diverse peoples and "arouse in the individual a keen sense of proprietary pride."[55]

Some City Beautiful activists, disillusioned with the limits of the movement's democratic vision, pursued other strategies. Charles Zueblin, an academic sociologist who rose to a leadership position in the City Beautiful movement, initially believed its program of public improvements could reinvigorate citizenship. Inspired by "the idea of striving for a purification of politics," Zueblin stood with those who wanted public spaces that served as "open-air clubs at which political affairs and questions of art and literature were discussed from varied, individual points of view." But he soon left a movement he found deficient in democratic credentials to promote civic forums as vehicles for popular debate and deliberation.[56]

Without an engaged citizenry, the City Beautiful movement found it impossible to tackle housing reform, land use regulations, and other contentious issues that required greater public control over private interests. Speaking for moderates within the movement, Robinson conceded that "sunless bedrooms, dark halls and stairs, foul cellars, dangerous employments, and an absence of bathrooms" are "sociologically pressing" issues. But regarding such matters, he insisted, "civic art has no responsibility, however earnestly it deplores them." The movement might sometimes warn, as *Plan of Chicago* did, of the eventual necessity of public housing for tenement dwellers "so degraded by long life in the slums that they have lost all power of caring for themselves." But affordable housing and the other social issues surrounding poverty remained off the City Beautiful agenda.[57]

The Gender Divide: From the City Livable to the City Profitable

A gender divide, between the city livable and the city profitable, exacerbated the democratic deficit in the City Beautiful movement. Male reformers relied on the profit motive and private enterprise to address social ills, while female reformers demanded an expansion of municipal responsibilities to secure a richer life for all. The struggle over Chicago's lakefront illustrates the point. Whether focused on the lakefront for industrial and harbor development or recreational and commercial uses, men tended to think in terms of profit. Faced with the male City Club's lakefront plan for a commercial development with restaurant, boardwalk, and plenty of parking, the Women's City Club advocated for a public lakefront, accessible by streetcar extensions and open to all in "a broad and democratic spirit."[58]

Women played a central role in trying to make the City Beautiful and other environmental reform movements more democratic and inclusive. The settlement house leader Jane Addams initially shared some of the attitudes of cultural uplift that shaped the City Beautiful movement. But as she lived among and listened to her neighbors in one of Chicago's worst slums, she came to see that "unless all men and all classes contribute to a good, we cannot even be sure that it is worth having." Addams and other women struggled to broaden the agenda of the City Beautiful movement to include pure water, smoke abatement, careful disposal of wastes, inspection of public markets and supplies of milk and meat, and building regulations to insure adequate light and ventilation. But the effort to clean up public markets revealed the divisions within the movement. An inveterate foe of clutter, Robinson treated public markets as antithetical to clean and efficient cities. Urging their complete removal, he charged them with generating litter, congestion, and odor. Female reformers defended the importance of universal access to public markets and healthful food, recommending regulation and upgrading of public markets rather than their removal.[59]

Women also agitated to broaden the agenda of the City Beautiful movement from physical to social planning. In 1908, women played key roles in designing and launching the public exhibition on poverty and housing presented by the Committee on Congestion of Population in New York (CCP). The women of the CCP also laid the groundwork for the first national conference on city planning, held in 1909. The settlement house leader Mary Kingsbury Simkhovitch chaired the CCP, and Addams's settlement colleague Florence Kelley organized the poverty and housing exhibition. As Simkhovitch explained, the exhibition "pictured graphically what overcrowding meant in New York's tenements." Well acquainted with the challenges of immigrant and working-class neighborhoods, settlement leaders pushed for a bottom-up form of city planning—partially realized in the movement for municipal housekeeping discussed in the next chapter—that addressed issues such as childcare, education, recreation, and health care.[60]

At the first National Conference on City Planning in Washington, DC, in May 1909, the city livable vied for attention with the city profitable. The impassioned arguments of social reformers for "sunlight and pure air against greed" captured the imagination of some City Beautiful veterans in attendance. Simkhovitch, the only woman to address the conference, pushed for neighborhood self-determination and community organization. Although she found proposals for building garden cities on the urban periphery intriguing, she knew her neighbors did not want to lose "the social advantages which a city affords." Rather than give up on distressed neighborhoods, Simkhovitch called for a comprehensive approach to city planning that would preserve and improve them by addressing both social and physical needs.[61]

A battle to shape the emerging profession ensued at future national conferences. A few attendees stood with the insurgents in seeking to make city planning what the architect Frederick Ackerman called "a social and democratic movement." The city must be "the physical expression of social and democratic ideals," Ackerman told the Fifth National Conference in 1913. "Why not arouse interest in the processes of government," he asked, "by relating them to the things of physical nature which [the citizen] can see and feel?" The city, from its squares and monuments down to its sewers, "constitutes the real, vital art of a people," Ackerman concluded, urging that city planning be made a central part of the curriculum of the public schools.[62]

Most conference attendees, however, found the insurgents too radical and feared their proposals would alienate powerful interests. George Ford's address at the Fifth National Conference, "The City Scientific," better captured the future direction of the profession. Fearing that "our

best laid plans may be interfered with by some political or local prejudice," Ford insisted that in "almost every case there is one and only one,
logical and convincing solution of the problem involved." Fortunately,
Ford concluded, "City planning is becoming as definite a science as pure
engineering." A decade later, Ford told the conference that city planning
was "merely doing for the city what every good businessman or manu-
facturer does for his own plant."[63]

Future conferences and the emerging profession narrowed the scope
of city planning. Downplaying the democratic and popular dimensions
of their work, city planners pursued professional status and alliances
with powerful patrons. Their work focused increasingly on economic
efficiency and the protection of residential property values. Where once
the City Beautiful movement depended on women's contributions and
leadership, the emerging city planning profession found the emphasis on
beauty to be effeminate. As male professionals embraced what they called
"the city practical," they closed the doors to women. "There is nothing
effeminate and sentimental about" city planning, insisted a male professional, "like tying tidies on telephone poles and putting doilies on cross-
walks, . . . it is vigorous, virile, sane."[64]

As the purview of planning narrowed, supposedly feminine concerns
such as beauty, sociability, and justice faded. The great divides, now including gender, threatened to stunt the aspirations of environmental reform and city planning. But the struggle for environmental reform had
brought new forms of ecological thinking into prominence and given rise
to various speculations about a specifically human ecology. Some sort of
partnership between human ecology and city planning still seemed possible. Much depended on what shape a distinctively human ecology
would take.

5

In Search of Ourselves

Human Ecology from Urban Reform
to Science of Society

At the turn of the twentieth century, the formal science of ecology took shape against a backdrop of successful urban environmental reforms. Even as the new science matured, sanitarians and other reformers began to think about the city in ecological terms. Treating the city as either a complex organism or what would later be called an ecosystem, environmental reformers described its various processes as forms of metabolism. As a Chicago sanitarian put it in 1880, "A great city is a vast laboratory, in which the energies imported in the food supplies and stored in the atmosphere are transmitted into human life, or rather into thousands of human lives, but which are momentarily and perpetually exposed to that further transmutation which crumbles organized being back to its chemical elements." As other urban experts pushed for public health measures, housing regulations, civic centers and civic art, and parks and playgrounds, they, too, began to think of the city in ecological terms.[1]

In its early years, the emerging profession of city planning shared this ecological approach to the city. As Frederick Law Olmsted Jr. argued in the introduction to an influential manual for the profession published in 1916, city planning arose from "a growing appreciation of a city's organic unity, of the interdependence of its diverse elements, and of the profound and inexorable manner in which the future of this great organic unit is controlled by the actions and omissions of to-day." The planning profession, he concluded, must be guided by "conception of the city as one great social organism." In urging his fellow planners to recognize urban development as "a complex evolutionary process," Olmsted spoke for a profession with roots in environmental reform.[2]

Across a range of fields and endeavors in the early twentieth century, scholars and activists focused new attention on the interactions between organisms and their environments. The prospect of applying ecological knowledge to the reformation of human society seemed to hold especially great promise. Utopians seized on ecology as the foundation for a new social order. Social scientists and planners found in ecology a model for reshaping their own disciplines. Ecologists themselves pointed to a wide range of practical applications in agriculture, fisheries, forestry, and conservation.[3]

A few early leaders of the emerging science of ecology even took the next step of proposing the application of ecological knowledge to the planning and management of cities. "In the field of sanitation men are endeavoring to change a dirty environment into a clean and therefore healthy one," the first president of the Ecological Society of America, Barrington Moore, observed in 1920. He then asked, "What is this but ecology?" Two years later, the society's new president, Stephen Forbes, called for a "humanizing" of ecological science. Forbes urged his colleagues to take "the actions and relations of civilized man as fully into account . . . as those of any other kind of organism." The "relationship of man himself to his environment," he continued, "is an inseparable part of ecology; for he also is an organism and other organisms are a part of *his* environment." To deny this is "setting man outside the general order of living nature in a class by himself."[4]

In the first two decades of the twentieth century, the growing interest in ecological science appeared destined to shape the emerging practice of city planning. Over the rest of the century, however, the science of ecology and the profession of city planning went their separate ways. Recapitulating the great divide, ecologists excluded human actions from their study of nature while city planners redesigned the city without reference to the larger biosphere in which it was embedded. It is not that human concerns played no role in the fledgling science of ecology. Progressive business leaders subsidized the earliest ecological investigations as basic research that would inform the applied science of conservation. In clarifying how plants and animals adapted to their environment, the new science promised to improve human adaptation to new lands and the management of already cultivated lands. However, the underlying assumption that humans inevitably disrupted nature's balance meant that ecologists believed they could study and understand that balance only in areas free of human interference.[5]

For their part, city planners gave little thought to the city's place in nature, even as they moved toward a professional ideal of the "city scientific." In excluding women and their concerns from the profession, they forfeited a promising model of what a union of human ecology and city planning might look like. Early in the century, as noted in the previous chapter, women launched a movement for municipal housekeeping that addressed a host of environmental issues, including cleaner streets and improved sanitation, pure water and smoke abatement, careful disposal of wastes, inspection of public markets and supplies of milk and meat, and regulation of buildings to insure adequate light and ventilation. Dedicated to urban reform, municipal housekeepers tried to infuse city planning with an understanding of human ecology.[6]

Rejecting that model, city planners eventually developed a partnership with the Chicago School of urban sociologists. The most influential of the many scholars and activists who took up the topic of human ecology, the Chicago sociologists showed little interest in the city's relationship to the rest of nature. They said nothing about the topics we now associate with an ecological approach, such as weather and climate, topography and hydrology, flora and fauna, and the extraction of resources and disposal of wastes. In his influential essay "Urbanism as a Way of Life" (1938), the Chicago sociologist Louis Wirth articulated the underlying assumption of the Chicago School. "Nowhere," Wirth wrote, "has mankind been farther removed from organic nature than under the conditions of life characteristic of great cities."[7]

In ignoring the city's embeddedness in the biosphere, the Chicago sociologists took their cue from an expanding, urban-based mode of production at its most energetic as it proclaimed its independence from natural limits. Focused on the social dimensions of the chaotic, explosive industrial city, the Chicago sociologists tried to make sense of its labor, ethnic, and racial conflicts and to manage what their leader, Robert E. Park, called its "chronic condition of crisis." The rapid growth of Chicago, the vast migration of people into the city, and the breakdown of old cultural forms and the emergence of new ones appeared to the Chicago sociologists as natural, irresistible forces that recommended an ecological approach. The Chicago sociologists thus offered city planners exactly what they sought: a dispassionate analysis of social order and disorder in terms of space and position.[8]

The Chicago sociologists' vision of human ecology, however, closed off more promising approaches that were more attuned to the city's place in nature. Not only did they minimize the connection between city planning and urban environmental reform. They also obscured what made human ecology distinct from that of other species. Park might have learned from his one-time teacher, the philosopher John Dewey, that consciousness represented the distinctively human dimension of the universal struggle of organisms to adapt to and alter their environments, to "change the changes going on around" them. Neglecting that lesson, the Chicago sociologists minimized the role of consciousness in human ecology and treated the given distribution and exercise of political and economic power as unalterable. They thus minimized the human capacity for political and moral choice, even as they exaggerated our freedom from natural limits. Their science of society thus constrained us where we might have been more experimental while distracting attention from the environmental constraints that would loom ever larger in the future.[9]

Municipal Housekeeping as Human Ecology

The early twentieth-century movement for municipal housekeeping contributed to a burst of urban environmental reforms that underscored the central role of conscious deliberation and experimentation in human ecology. Engaging in both direct action and political agitation, municipal housekeepers joined the much larger benevolent empire of volunteering women who struggled to make the city more livable and just. Cleaning up nuisances, educating the public, and demanding higher standards of civil service, municipal housekeepers grounded the lofty ideas of the City Beautiful in mundane matters such as garbage cans. "Out of interest in the lamppost," a municipal housekeeper put it, "comes an interest in the causes of crime; proper housing, wholesome amusement, and employment may thus be intimately connected with the artistic lamppost."[10]

Municipal housekeepers challenged the gendered dimension of the great divides by bringing the values of the domestic realm to bear on the larger city. Rather than domesticating politics, their demand for an expansion of municipal responsibilities politicized the environment. They also pointed to the unjust treatment of women as a key source of environmental degradation. "Most of the departments in a modern city," Jane Addams asserted, "can be traced to woman's traditional activity." Yet these duties had "slipped from woman's hands" because of her exclusion from public affairs. Women were "missing the education which the natural participation in civic life would bring to them," Addams concluded, and the city suffered as a result.[11]

Municipal housekeepers did much of the grassroots work that first established widespread support for city planning. They popularized ecological knowledge and worked to engage the entire citizenry in the effort to improve the urban environment. Ellen Swallow Richards, a leader in the movement, introduced American audiences to the term *ecology* in 1892. The first female graduate of the Massachusetts Institute of Technology and a pioneer of the new discipline of sanitary chemistry, Richards brought her technical expertise to the public in a series of popular books, articles, and pamphlets. "The sanitary engineer has a treble duty for the next few years of civic awakening," she wrote in 1911: the duty not only to design and manage sanitary systems but to educate the public about ecological principles.[12]

Worried about the growing specialization of scientific and technical knowledge, Richards conceived of ecology as an integrative science aimed at the transformation of daily life. To preserve and improve our physical environment, she wrote, "there must be inculcated habits of using the material things in daily life in such a way as to promote and not to diminish health." It was of the "greatest importance that everyone should acquire such habits of belief," she concluded, and that ecological knowledge be directed toward "inculcating right and safe ways in daily life."[13]

Richards spoke for a movement that believed that the future well-being of society depended on the education and the participation of all. In Boston, the Women's Municipal League organized neighborhood groups to engage in "study, education, inspection, and cooperation" regarding the enforcement of city ordinances. New York City's Woman's Municipal League produced a pamphlet on ways to keep streets clean aimed at "Young Citizens in City Schools." After women in Kalamazoo, Michigan, secured trash cans for the city, the Junior Civic Improvement League distributed handbills to encourage citizens to use "the wastepaper can at the corner."[14]

To encourage democratic participation and raise awareness of environmental issues, municipal housekeepers held public meetings, staged weeklong civic revivals, conducted surveys and published their findings, held protests and ran political candidates, and served in official positions. They also challenged the pervasive metaphor of municipal government as a business. Elevating the quality of life and social justice above profits, Chicago's Women's City Club pledged allegiance to the principle that "the welfare of human beings is the chief business of a city government."

Environmental reform, one of its members added, addressed "a common dependency from which there is no escape."[15]

Even before women won the vote, municipal housekeepers tried to democratize local politics. Distributing its findings in a "Notice to House-holders," Boston's Women's Municipal League sponsored public meetings that led to new legislation against littering. The league also educated citizens about what they had "a right to expect in the way of sanitary care and cleanliness in the distribution of food." Caroline Crane, another leader in the movement, visited more than sixty cities in every region of the country, insisting on "a thoroughly advertised campaign participated in from start to finish by deeply interested citizens." She always rented large halls, believing that "the people will come . . . when they learn what it is about, and when the selection of a large and popular auditorium makes it plain that they are really *expected* to come."[16]

Beginning in the second decade of the twentieth century, however, the professionalization of sanitary engineering, city planning, and related fields marginalized municipal housekeepers. Meanwhile, the same recognition of the interconnections between environmental and human well-being that drove the effort to sanitize the city also generated an anxiety to police the borders of the home and purify the racial and ethnic composition of the population. Squeezed out of the professions, women still found themselves called on to secure the borders of the home and nation, protecting the purity of both.[17]

Human Ecology and the Eugenic/Euthenic Urge

The confinement of women's activities to the domestic realm—and the exclusion of women from political life—opened the way for a darker vision of human ecology. Minimizing the distinctive role of consciousness in favor of biological determinism led powerful men, and some women, to embrace both immigration restriction and forced sterilization. In less extreme forms, this deterministic view of human ecology gave rise to home economics and a focus on the domestic environment as the source of personal, family, and national health. The same germ theory of disease that undergirded the drive for municipal housekeeping also recommended the scientific, sanitary kitchen and home. Richards, for example, pointed to defective plumbing, poor ventilation, and inadequate housekeeping as sources of disease. Linking exterior to interior, she understood home economics as providing protection from dangers both inside and outside the household.[18]

The economist Charlotte Perkins Gilman shared Richards's concerns and imagined a more complete ecological renovation of society. Gilman's utopian novel *Herland* (which appeared serially in 1915) centered on an all-female nation, isolated from the rest of the world. A maternal utopia, Herland promoted community, education, sanitation, and conservation to create a pollution-free zone of "no dirt," "no smoke," and "no noise." In its parklike, aesthetically pleasing setting and with its carefully managed natural resources, Herland provided a model of the technologically sophisticated city set within and attuned to the rhythms of nature. "Everything was beauty, order, perfect cleanness," Gilman wrote, "and the pleasantest sense of home over it all."[19]

A model of ecological purity, Herland practiced sustainable agriculture and strict population control. Ridding themselves of cattle that took up too many resources, the Herlanders husbanded nutrients. "These careful culturists," Gilman wrote, "had worked out a perfect scheme of refeeding the soil with all that came out of it. All the scraps and leavings of their food, plant waste from lumber work or textile industry, all the solid matter from the sewage, properly treated and combined—everything which came from the earth went back into it." Herlanders also tamped down "child-longing" by sharing child-rearing responsibilities. Where necessary, the Herlanders took control of the choices of those with undesirable qualities, subjecting them to the will of the community that they refrain from procreation.[20]

In several respects, Gilman's vision resembled the suburban communities being planned and settled by the new professional-managerial middle class at the turn of the century. Tired of the pollution, noise, and disease that coarsened city life, prospective suburbanites sought fresh air and cleanliness, cultured company, and a family orientation. But they also demanded all the amenities of modern urban culture. Architects and developers set to work building exclusive suburbs that would satisfy these desires. Using advanced architectural designs and efficient construction techniques, they provided paved roadways and drainage systems, piped water and water closets, electric-generating facilities, and hot water heaters. Housing reformers and domestic advertisers added an emphasis on professional home management. The proper housewife presided over a scientifically designed and mechanized domain, insuring proper hygiene and minimal waste.[21]

The early suburb of Short Hills, New Jersey, graced with wooded areas and vistas of coastal New Jersey and Manhattan, reflected the venerable belief that natural surroundings provided moral uplift and spiritual regeneration. "The social salvation of America," one proponent put it, "rests with the country." But the union of technology and nature required careful planning. Short Hills had its own waterworks; commuter rail; and landscaped, paved roads, and it eventually provided gas lighting, sewers, electricity, telephones, and fire protection. Short Hills even made fertilizer derived from sewage available for greenhouses and nurseries.[22]

Advocates of this suburban ideal offered it, however unrealistically, as a model for those of more modest means. But Gilman's Herland reflected an exclusive commitment to race purity, and a concern about degenerating racial stock, that was all too common in industrial cities with expanding immigrant populations. In Gilman's allegory, Herland originated in an environmental catastrophe that brought down a slave society. When the slaves revolted, women put down the revolt. Later, when three white men stumbled upon Herland, the women's victory over the slaves and their utopian community convinced the men that "these people were of Aryan stock, and were once in contact with the best civilization of the world." In Gilman's vision, racial purity reinforced environmental purity, each overseen by her female heroes.[23]

Richards offered a parallel path to purification. "Eugenics," Richards wrote, "deals with race improvement through heredity. Euthenics deals with race improvement through environment." She thought eugenics awaited "careful investigation" but recommended euthenics as the "preliminary science" on which a more thoroughgoing program of race improvement might be based. While intent on improving the living conditions of urbanites of all backgrounds, Richards also shared the xenophobia common in the era. "Conditions of motion, of rapid intermingling of distant populations," she warned, "make national control a necessity." Like Gilman, Richards saw women in the forefront of such control, maintaining a vigilance against environmental threats, seen and unseen. "Our enemies are no longer Indians, and wild animals," she wrote. "To see our cruelest enemies, we must use the microscope."[24]

The control of borders supported vigilance in domestic settings. In Herland, geographic isolation did the work of border control. One of the men who stumbled into Herland takes a wife and resolves to return to the United States. The Herlanders, "unwilling to expose our country to free communication with the rest of the world," ask that the couple not reveal the location of the utopian community. The task of border control is more daunting in Richards's vision. "Eternal vigilance is the price of safety in sanitary as well as in military affairs," she warned. For both Gilman and

Richards, the stakes were so high that the needs of the collective community overrode those of the individual, whether by calling women to their civic and religious duties (Richards) or subjecting the womb to the needs of the community (Gilman).[25]

The case of the geographer Ellsworth Huntington provides another example of how an interest in human ecology could invite biological determinism and an enthusiasm for eugenics/euthenics. Huntington argued in *Civilization and Climate* (1915) that a temperature range of 38–60 degrees Fahrenheit provided the ideal conditions for civilization. Fascinated by the relationship of race, environment, and social development, Huntington believed that the environmental peculiarities of North America produced a superior civilization. Calling for a union of geography and human ecology, Huntington crafted racial explanations of history and eugenic/euthenic visions of the future. Environmental reforms related to public health, medicine, industrial efficiency, city planning, and, ultimately, eugenics would maintain Anglo-Saxon superiority. His determinism hardened after World War I, as he came to believe that racial differences, which he saw as embedded in genetic endowment, could not be erased. Promoting eugenics, Huntington supported his theories with dubious research that ratified his racial biases.[26]

The eugenic/euthenic urge marred both the movement for municipal housekeeping and, later, the city planning profession. Municipal housekeepers often targeted immigrant entrepreneurs whose activities obstructed or sullied commercial streets and sidewalks while neglecting residential conditions in immigrant and black neighborhoods. City ordinances often singled out "undesirable persons," usually foreign-born, as targets of exclusion, reflecting the belief that downtown should be made safe for middle-class retailers and customers. City planners, deploying racial science that asserted biological inequality, associated urban congestion, disorder, and disease with African Americans and immigrants. Although the U.S. Supreme Court struck down racial zoning in 1917, city planners still encouraged segregation through zoning restrictions on "inharmonious" land uses and restrictive covenants. Real estate professionals and the U.S. Department of Commerce added support for residential segregation for decades to come.[27]

The fascination with eugenics/euthenics illustrates the danger of treating ecology as the master key to human affairs. Validating prejudices, a deterministic human ecology also minimizes our ability to address challenges and secure opportunities through politics. Like economics, ecology can tell us about the means at our disposal, and especially the limits of those means. But neither economics nor ecology can or should determine our ends. Human ecology must stretch in two directions: toward an understanding of the limits of our means and toward the conscious and democratic discussion of ends.[28]

John Dewey as Human Ecologist

The evolutionary naturalism of the pragmatic philosopher John Dewey provided a foundation for a more promising human ecology rooted in consciousness. Moving to Chicago during the convulsive Pullman strike in July 1894, Dewey found the city enormously stimulating. He marveled at and joined in the city's explosion of practical and utopian experimentation, including the "White City" at the center of the 1893 Chicago World's Fair; the industrialist George Pullman's model town; an organized labor movement demanding full participation in the life of the city; and Dewey's own laboratory school at the University of Chicago. Under the influence of Charles Darwin's work, Dewey came to recognize the brain as a product of evolution and thinking as an evolutionary adaptation that helped humans "react upon the environment to bring about modifications to their own future." This conviction could hardly have found greater confirmation than in Chicago's manic artifice and manifold experimentation.[29]

Consciousness gave human experience a special quality, Dewey argued: the possibility of inquiry, of knowledge, of judgments to guide action, especially when confronted with some obstacle, some difficult, challenging, or unprecedented situation. He saw the Pullman strike as just such a situation, one that he hoped would "get the social organism thinking." Supporters of Pullman treated the strike in terms of individualism and a laissez-faire approach to the market. As sole proprietor of his business, Pullman could do whatever he wanted, including fire his workers and close his shop. His workers, also individual proprietors, could sell as much of their labor as they liked for whatever price they could get. But no one else had any business interfering. Acting in combination for ends that transcended one's individual interests, such as the sympathy strike of non-Pullman workers in the American Railway Union, was illegitimate. Moreover, labor's opponents asserted, the Sherman Antitrust Act of 1890 made it illegal.[30]

Yet the magnitude of the struggle transcended the individualistic calculus and underscored the dysfunctionality of laissez-faire policies. The strike brought the economy to a halt and threatened "the starvation of a nation," as a federal judge warned in sending strike leaders to jail. Part of the violent and chaotic nationwide struggles that accompanied the consolidation of corporate capitalism in the late nineteenth century, the strike forced a rethinking of the relationships among industrial workers, corporations, the public, and the state. As Dewey anticipated, the Pullman strike put laissez-faire policy on the defensive. Federal courts and federal troops intervened, in the name of the public interest, to crush the strike. Initially directed against labor, the new concern with the public interest soon placed some limits on corporate power, as well. [31]

Dewey had already joined a group of academics who challenged laissez-faire thinking. Rejecting the social Darwinist credo of the survival of the fittest, reform Darwinists such as Dewey argued that human evolution proceeded through consciousness and the application of intelligence rather than blind submission to natural selection. The botanist and sociologist Lester Ward argued that the brain "has been developed in the same manner as the other anatomical characters," like sharp claws or the opposable thumb, making mind "a natural product of evolution." Ward's credo of "mind as a social factor" became the rallying cry of those who found it perfectly natural for humans to intervene in social development to secure the good. But even more than Dewey's academic colleagues, Jane Addams shaped his thinking about the Pullman strike. Like Dewey, Addams hoped to get the "social organism" thinking as a means of overcoming the "lack of democracy in social affairs." [32]

Favoring cooperation over conflict, Addams opposed the strike. But like Dewey, she also recognized the strike as a rupture in established ways of thinking. Her distinctive contribution was to see that both sides wanted—needed—the same outcome but misunderstood each other, making the strike a tragedy. Pullman wanted to be a great man who did great things, Addams argued, but he left "those ideals unconnected with the consent of [his] fellow men." The strikers also failed to understand how the "new claim on the part of the toiling multitude [and] the new sense of responsibility on the part of the well-to-do, arise in reality from the same source" and must "logically converge into the same movement." Addams encouraged Dewey to see that the resistance the world, including other people, puts up to our actions is not a genuine opposition of interests but a stimulus to creative imagination and experimentation. [33]

Two years after the Pullman strike, Dewey wrote a short, technical, and critical piece on the "reflex arc" experiments in psychology that reflected Addams's influence. In measuring response times to a stimulus (a light going on), the reflex arc experiments broke experience into three distinct parts: stimulus, thought, and response. Dewey objected to this division, as it turned experience into a "herky-jerky series of discrete acts which began with sensational stimuli existing outside" of experience. It thus turned thinking into a passive reaction to random stimuli. Stimulus and response, he countered, are merely "divisions of labor, functioning factors within the single concrete whole." The whole is experience, the conscious effort to cope with and transform the environment, to "fight for ends," as his fellow pragmatist William James put it. In Addams's terms, stimulus is simply the resistance the world puts up to our conscious, purposeful efforts.[34]

As part of experience, thinking mediated between stimulus and response, enabling us—as Addams had it—to cooperate and resolve disputes. Dewey agreed. Thinking mediated between old habits and the tensions created by new situations, he argued, turning "unconscious adaptation and survival" into "conscious deliberation and experimentation." It also enabled people to redirect their impulses, such as turning anger into conviction for social justice. By placing consciousness at the center of human interaction with the environment, Dewey thus provided a place for both human ingenuity and natural limits. Well-conceived and well-considered human action in transforming the natural world gave rise to new knowledge and new values, revealing persistent limits and new possibilities. The knowledge and values gained then enriched future experience by deepening our understanding and appreciation of both human potential and natural limits.[35]

Finding Democracy at the Indiana Sand Dunes

The University of Chicago ecologists Henry Chandler Cowles and Warder Clyde Allee conducted research that complemented Dewey's work. They, too, advanced an evolutionary and experimental paradigm that found the potential for cooperation and democracy embedded in both nature and human experience. But whereas Dewey grounded his democratic faith in the emergence of consciousness, his colleagues grounded their faith in ecological relationships that preceded consciousness, what they called proto-cooperation.[36]

Cowles came to the University of Chicago as a graduate student in 1895. He gravitated to the emerging field of ecology and embraced the Danish scientist Eugenius Warming's concept of commensalism. A thoroughgoing Darwinian, Warming saw aggregations of plants in competition for individual survival. But if one species did not undermine the viability of nearby species, sticking to its own niche, then that species contributed positively to the survival of other species—hence, "commensalism." Along with his colleagues, Cowles extended this insight to "proto-cooperation," the idea that some species might produce conditions conducive to the thriving of other species. This "vague, unconscious, mutual co-operation," Cowles's colleague, the animal ecologist Allee, argued, "should rank as one of the major principles comparable with the better recognized Darwinian principle of the struggle for existence."[37]

Cowles's interest in proto-cooperation came out of his extension of Warming's work on ecological succession. A key concept in the young science, succession referred to the transition, interdependence, and mutual adaptation of various species in associations of plants. Warming's own work on Danish dunes and the suggestion of the landscape architect Jens Jensen directed Cowles toward the Indiana Sand Dunes. At the dunes, Cowles found succession, a process usually worked out over time, laid out in space. Dunes vegetation changed as it moved inland from the water-saturated shores and pounding waves of Lake Michigan. In his dissertation, Cowles described the dunes as an example of succession as well as proto-cooperation. Pioneering associations of organisms provided conditions for other species to thrive. Perennial grasses and shrubs served as "dune-builders," Cowles explained, in a process that "makes all things new," producing "a world for conquest" for other plant species.[38]

Allee, who joined Cowles at the University of Chicago in 1908, found a similar sort of preconscious proto-cooperation in his study of freshwater crustaceans in the ponds of the dunes. In ways analogous to the grouping of immigrants in cities, Allee wrote, "a group of similar animals tend to minimize for each other the disturbing effects of unusual surroundings." World War I intensified Allee's interest in proto-cooperation. Exploring "the problems of group behavior and other mass reactions, not only of isopods, but of all kinds of animals, man included," Allee argued that toleration and cooperation had survival value. Cooperation, he wrote, was a "fundamental trait of living matter," seen in the "beneficial effects of relatively unorganized aggregations of animals."[39]

Cowles went further in his subsequent work, treating the dunes ecology as a model for the future of American democracy. When Chicago's industrial expansion threatened the dunes, Cowles joined a diverse group of scientists, settlement house leaders, landscape architects, poets, and politicians to preserve them as a national park. Steeped in an atmosphere of social reform since his undergraduate days at Oberlin College, Cowles described succession at the dunes using metaphors that invoked a vision of a cooperative commonwealth. In his testimony before a public hearing conducted by the National Park Service, Cowles described the dunes as a "common meeting ground of trees and wildflowers from all directions . . . a marvelous cosmopolitan preserve, a veritable floral melting pot." At the same hearing, the settlement house leader Graham Taylor added that a great park, held in common, would provide "a center for the getting together and unifying of the cosmopolitan people of the world."[40]

It took imagination to see a model of democracy in the stark, wind-blown landscapes of the dunes. But the dunes did their part in suggesting the analogy. Ranging from lake, storm beach, and moving dunes to stable, forested sand hills; shallow lakes; and a marshland of sloughs, rivers, and bogs, the dunes landscape supported an unusually diverse collection of species. Tamarack, jack pine, and Arctic bearberry, left over from the period of glaciation, joined species moving up from the south, including tulip, black gum, and sassafras trees. The western prairies, deserts, and meadows contributed grasses, cacti, and wildflowers. Eastern woodland species—sugar maple, beech, and trillium—took root in the wetter, more protected areas. Wolves and bald eagles, great flocks of waterfowl, deer and smaller mammals, and all sorts of migrating birds populated the landscape.[41]

In combination, the elements at the dunes produced a whole greater than its parts that suggested an ecological model of American democracy. The dunes lay at "the center . . . of the North American continent," the president of the National Dunes Park Association argued. "Here, the north, south, east and west meet geologically, botanically, zoologically, historically, socially, industrially, commercially." The dunes, Jensen added, are "the common meeting ground of friends from all parts of the land." A park, the preservationists believed, would protect this special place and provide inspiration for the moral ideals of democracy and the cooperative commonwealth. The preservationists' efforts resulted in the Indiana Dunes State Park in 1923, the Indiana Dunes National Seashore in 1966, and the Indiana Dunes National Park in 2019.[42]

The seminal work of Cowles and Allee earned the Indiana Sand Dunes the mantle of "birthplace of ecology." The dunes, however, are better seen as one site in a struggle over the future character of the science. In the early twentieth century, a variety of reform-minded inquiries, from the social gospel to the settlement house movement, provided a model for an ecological science that combined objective, theoretical inquiry with moral purpose. Such a fusion could produce insights to inform an ethical and democratic response to the environmental and human costs of industrialization. But at the same time, a contrasting model arose from the rapid accumulation of scientific knowledge, the spread of professionalization, and the expansion of the American university system on the model of Germany's preeminent research centers. This model recommended rigorous research oriented toward immediate, practical results and alliances with policy-making elites.[43]

Frederic Clements and the Chicago School of Urban Sociology

Cowles and Allee worked at an institution, the University of Chicago, known for its dedication to pure research, as distinct from immediate problem solving. More interested in preserving than in controlling nature, Cowles and Allee found moral lessons for human society in the proto-cooperation they found at the dunes. In contrast, the ecologist Frederic Clements, working at the land-grant University of Nebraska, pursued a more utilitarian course, dedicated to immediate problem solving. Rather than sand dunes, Clements studied the grasslands so central to the economy of the Great Plains. He took his cues from state surveys and experimental stations and worked closely with practitioners of agronomy and other applied sciences. A pioneer in the application of quantitative methods to botany, Clements became the nation's most influential ecologist in the first half of the twentieth century.[44]

Clements offered a competing paradigm for ecological succession that ultimately triumphed over Cowles's. A mechanist, Cowles argued that succession could be understood only at the level of the individual habitat of each plant. He also believed that succession had no goal, no direction, and might take different forms or even be reversed. An organicist, much influenced by Herbert Spencer, Clements saw plant communities as functioning organisms. Clements argued that plant communities, under the impact of climatic conditions (rather than individual habitat), went through a developmental process with a definite, progressive direction. Rather than proto-cooperation, however, Clements saw competition as "the controlling function in successional development." Through the invasion of species, competition for scarce resources, and the succession of new species to positions of dominance, the developmental process led irresistibly to a destined formation for each broad climatic region. In the climax stage, competition decreased and gave way not so much to cooperation as to relations of domination and subordination among species and a stable, resilient, and self-regulating natural balance that could last millions of years.[45]

The grasslands of the Great Plains, Clements argued, enjoyed such a climax formation for several million years until disturbed by sod-busting farmers. As a graduate student in the late 1890s, Clements witnessed firsthand the destruction of the grasslands, their biodiversity giving way to a few favored species of commercial agriculture. He saw the human costs, as well, as the land's reduced carrying capacity and drought devastated farmers. But like other ecologists, Clements believed that only once we understood how nature's balance worked could we repair and more effectively manage it. He therefore studied succession in places relatively free of human interference. Abandoned wagon roads and fenced railroad rights-of-way provided those rare places where human intervention did not fully dictate which species lived and died.[46]

Cowles and Clements shared a faith that ecological knowledge could benefit human society, whether through moral speculation or practical application. But whereas Cowles proved willing to move back and forth between ecological theory and human society, Clements placed humans outside of his science and outside of nature, as disturbers of nature's balance. On occasion, Clements acknowledged that the frontier pattern of settlement on the Great Plains, as articulated by the historian Frederick Jackson Turner, shaped his thinking about succession. But he never fully grappled with the consequences of leaving humans out of his understanding of succession.[47]

A full understanding of the fate of the grasslands climax required consideration of human activities. Clements had witnessed the early stages of a clash of two processes of development—the grasslands climax and the maturation of an urban-industrial society—a clash that culminated in the Dust Bowl in the 1930s. The clash of these two processes of development—grasslands and urban-industrial—might easily have been studied in concert. For just as Clements emerged as the leading figure in ecological science, the fledgling Chicago School of urban sociologists cast about for tools with which to explain the explosive growth of the industrial city. Park and his closest collaborator, Ernest Burgess, filled their influential textbook, *Introduction to the Science of Sociology* (1921), with descriptions of the ecological processes that shaped plant and animal communities, especially invasion, succession, and climax, treating them as models of what was happening in the city.[48]

As migrants and immigrants flowed into Chicago and its neighborhoods underwent transformation, Clements's theory of invasion, succession, and climax appeared to make sense of the growth of the city. Burgess's famous concentric zone theory of urban growth built directly on

Clements's theory of succession. The evolution of the plant community, Clements argued in his most influential publication, resulted from "a series of invasions, a sequence of plant communities marked by the change from lower to higher life-forms." Similarly, Burgess described the growth of the city as proceeding through "the tendency of each inner zone to extend its area by the invasion of the next outer zone," resulting in the production of natural areas. Park then described the racial, ethnic, and class segregation in Chicago's neighborhoods as just such natural areas. There are "forces at work within the limits of the human community," Park wrote, "which tend to bring about an orderly and typical grouping of its population and institutions." To "isolate these factors," he concluded, is the essential task of "what we call human, as distinguished from plant and animal, ecology."[49]

Park left unclear what "forces" and "factors" distinguished human from plant and animal ecology. The Park and Burgess text mentioned a process of "competitive cooperation," but Burgess elsewhere cautioned that this cooperation was "without a shred of what the 'spirit of co-operation' is commonly thought to signify." Their younger colleague Roderick McKenzie, who did much to encourage the ecological approach, questioned whether anything at all distinguished human from plant and animal ecology. The "plant ecologist is aware of the effect of the struggle for space, food, and light upon the nature of plant formation," McKenzie argued, "but the sociologist has failed to recognize that the same processes of competition and accommodation are at work determining the size and ecological organization of the human community." McKenzie admitted that the human "ability to contrive and adapt the environment to his needs" represented the "essential difference" between human and plant or animal communities. But he quickly cautioned that "human communities are not so much the products of artifact or design as many hero-worshipers suppose."[50]

Using Clements's theory, the Chicago sociologists thus naturalized Chicago's racial, ethnic, and class segregation, obscuring the role of economic and political power. They used the term *natural areas*, Park explained, because such areas were not products of conscious design but of "the inevitable processes of human nature." But as their early critic Milla Aissa Alihan recognized, what the Chicago sociologists called "natural areas" resulted more often from "conscious planning and communication" than their theory allowed. Their "lack of regard for volitional factors," Alihan continued, left impersonal forces, rather than humans, to do all "the selecting, the sifting, the sorting, the allocating." Even when these human ecologists did address consciousness, Alihan concluded in reference to Mc-Kenzie's comment about hero worshipers, it was only to emphasize how much "the iron laws of nature" overrode human purpose.[51]

The Chicago sociologists neglected much about their own city that might have helped them shape a human ecology that put consciousness—its aspirations, as well as its overreaching—at the forefront. Park did include selections from his former teacher John Dewey in the textbook he produced with Burgess. But Dewey's placing of consciousness at the central part of human ecology made no impact on Chicago sociology. Chicago itself might also have provided evidence of the role of conscious purpose in the city's development, as well as its embeddedness in nature. The sociologists might have considered Chicago's astounding transformation of distant places, including the grasslands that Clements studied, or the city's strenuous, half-century campaign against filth and disease and its implications for communities downstream and across the Great Lakes.[52]

Neglecting all this, the Chicago sociologists used ecology only in analogy. They did not think about cities as actual living systems. Their metaphors remained metaphors, and those metaphors contained troubling ambiguities. Finding urban "organization and disorganization analogous to the anabolic and katabolic processes of metabolism in the body," as Burgess put it, they treated the city as a single organism. But their use of the theory of succession suggested the city should be understood as a community of organisms, or what ecologists would later define as an ecosystem, a collection of organisms along with their abiotic environment. Whether organism or ecosystem, moreover, the sociologists' city grew and yet remained a self-contained, bounded system, unconnected to the external world. It would be hard to be more wrong about Chicago's growth, which depended on the transformation and exploitation of a far-flung hinterland.[53]

The failure to explore the connections between the Chicago sociologists' human ecology and Clements's grasslands ecology recapitulated the great divides between city and country, society and nature. Clements at times glimpsed the connections. "Grazing, irrigation, agriculture, and urban communities," Clements wrote, "are all bound together in such an intricate and vital bond that the interests of any one must be harmonized with the interests of all." But determined to study pristine nature, untouched by human actions, Clements showed little interest in the role of cities in the fate of the grasslands. He thus limited his ability to consider different ways of integrating the cultural and the biological. In contrast,

Cowles's willingness to include humans in his thinking about ecology, and his belief in the multiple forms succession might take, left room for imagining less disruptive and more just ways of fitting human activities into the rest of nature. Cowles's interest in proto-cooperation, moreover, suggested the possibility of something other than blind competition at work in human society, as well as in nature.[54]

The Chicago sociologists did not aspire to be environmentalists, of course, and must be understood on their own terms. It is "not man's relations to the earth he inhabits," Park explained, "but his relations to other men, that concerns us most." Yet even on their chosen terrain, the Chicago sociologists preached the limits of human choice. "The conditions of social change became to them the *facts* of social change," Alihan argued, leaving them the "expounders of the socially 'given,' the realists of the established order." Naturalizing the workings of political and economic power, they thought only of social adjustment. "The city," Park wrote, is "full of junk, much of it human, . . . men and women who, for some reason or other, have fallen out of line in the march of industrial progress and have been scrapped by the industrial organization of which they were once a part." The Chicago sociologists' preferred methods of adjustment to irresistible natural forces left existing injustices in place and perpetuated others.[55]

The neglected issues of environmental and social injustice, however, still animated alternative visions of the intersection of human ecology and city planning. A handful of activists—most notably, the regionalist Lewis Mumford—believed that a reuniting of city and country provided the key to building sustainable communities. Recognizing the embeddedness of humans in "the general web of life" from "bacteria upward," Mumford and his associates looked for benign or even beneficial forms of development. Coming "to terms with the earth," they would work "in partnership with the forces that promote life and the traditions which enhance it." Inspired by Dewey's pragmatism, Mumford also envisioned a democratic form of regional planning that would encourage political participation and environmental consciousness. The Great Depression created a brief opportunity to explore these possibilities.[56]

6

The Regional Moment

Ecological Visions in the Great Depression

"From as far west as Idaho, down from the glacier peaks of the Rockies, from as far east as Pennsylvania, down from the turkey ridges of the Alleghenies," rhapsodizes the narrator of Pare Lorenz's 1938 documentary, *The River.* "Down the Yellowstone, the Milk, the White, and Cheyenne; the Cannonball, the Musselshell, the James, and the Sioux; down the Judith, the Grand, the Osage, and the Platte," the narrator continues. The narration, nominated for a Pulitzer Prize in poetry, lovingly names thirty-eight rivers that flow into the Mississippi River on its way to the Gulf of Mexico. Sponsored by the federal government, the film celebrates the role of the Mississippi River in American life. But it also underscores the repeated disasters from its flooding and ends with praise for the regional planning undertaken by the recently created Tennessee Valley Authority (TVA).[1]

Lorenz's film captured the spirit of the regional moment in American life. His film dramatized an ambitious vision for the reconstruction of American civilization based on ecologically and culturally defined regions. An insurgent group of activists, seeing overgrown cities as dinosaurs, too big and too costly to support a decent culture and quality of life, hoped to deconcentrate population and spread opportunity through broader regions. By addressing the dysfunctional relationship between city and country, the insurgents argued, regional planning might become part of a more conscious and conscientious evolutionary process that promoted the health of both humans and the rest of nature.[2]

The American Institute of Planners' 1939 documentary *The City* considered the regionalist argument from an urban perspective. Filmed and directed by Lorenz's colleagues Ralph Steiner and Willard Van Dyke, it dramatized the vision of the Regional Planning Association of America (RPAA). Founded in the 1920s by the architect Clarence Stein, the RPAA explored alternatives to industrial squalor and metropolitan congestion, including garden cities surrounded by greenbelts. Aaron Copeland's musical score and the RPAA member Lewis Mumford's commentary accompanied an image-based argument.[3]

The City's opening scenes of the public squares and grist mills of an iconic New England town depicted a successful union of city and country. The images that followed of grimy industrial city and frenetic, impersonal metropolis (reinforced by dissonant music and a darker film texture) illustrated the current dysfunction. The final third of the film celebrated the garden cities then being constructed by the federal greenbelt program, presented as an updated version of the New England village. "You take your choice," Mumford's commentary explains. "Each one is real. Each one is possible. Shall we sink deeper, deeper into old grooves . . . or have we vision and courage?"[4]

For a brief time in the 1930s, the interest in regional reconstruction reached the highest levels of American government. Created in 1933, the TVA combined environmental planning and civic renewal to win praise as "democracy on the march." In 1937, with disastrous flooding in the Midwest and devastating drought on the Great Plains recommending an expansion of regional planning, Democratic President Franklin Roosevelt and Republican Senator George Norris of Nebraska announced an ambitious vision of "enough TVAs to cover the entire country." Environmental degradation and economic recession created an opportunity for radical change, especially as Roosevelt stepped up his indictment of "economic royalists."[5]

But Roosevelt never made regional planning a centerpiece of the New Deal. He never showed as much interest in urban revitalization as in the other, "back to the land," half of the regional vision. Moreover, the messy business of holding together a political coalition took precedence over any grand ideological vision. The short-lived Resettlement Administration (1935–1937) reflected Roosevelt's limited ambitions. Offering nothing for urban revitalization, the program also tried to juggle concern for—and constituencies associated with—farm poverty, the collapse of the construction industry, and the application of the most advanced town planning principles to suburban migration. The agency built three green-belt towns that generated impressive citizen participation and cooperative enterprise in their early years. But in the end, the greenbelt towns became little more than well-designed bedroom suburbs. The result satisfied no one, except, perhaps, their fortunate residents.[6]

Mumford's quixotic attempt to distill his lifelong devotion to region-al planning into a short film did not help matters. The film betrayed a lack of sympathy for city life that a fuller engagement with Mumford's written work dispels. Steiner and Van Dyke complained that the greenbelt section produced an "impossible dullness." Even Mumford admitted that "every attempt to show better alternatives in planning and living was commonplace, insipid, conventionally conceived, and entirely unconvinc-ing." Reviews suggested that audiences may have embraced the energy, vitality, and diversity of the city that the film failed to celebrate. The *Architectural Review*, for example, judged the greenbelt section "surpris-ingly flat and lifeless in comparison with the teeming energy of the city." Meanwhile, other reviewers praised the images of steel town and con-gested metropolis as "great movie art," noting that they "pack a wallop." Audiences got "the point because it is put over in terms of traffic jams and hurried meals instead of statistics."[7]

Toward the end of the 1930s, as the regional moment faded, another set of ecological ideas gained intellectual momentum and institutional power beneath public notice. Adapting the ecological concepts of inva-sion, succession, and climax to the study of the life cycles of cities, a group of urban professionals clothed themselves in the prestige of the natural sciences. By comparing cities to farms, forests, and ranges as natural resources, they linked their policies to the conservation strategy embraced by President Roosevelt and his administration. Claiming to have identified natural, predictable laws, these self-styled urban conser-vationists promised to manage urban growth and decay. But their top-down technocratic vision left little room for democratic revitalization.[8]

These two ecological visions—regionalism and urban conservation—offered contrasting roads forward. The one banked on grassroots democ-racy and popular energies; the other, on professional expertise and man-agerial acumen. Neither vision survived the 1930s intact. Despite their interest in democratic revitalization, the insurgent regionalists placed too much faith in technological innovation and failed to win durable popular support for their vision. Urban population would be decentralized but in a more chaotic fashion than the regionalists proposed. By the end of the decade, however, the controversies surrounding federal efforts to manage forests, farms, and parks also undercut the prestige of conservation strategies. The strategy of urban conservation continued to shape urban policy in the late New Deal and postwar periods. But the ecological dimensions of the strategy remained little more than empty justifications for policy makers' prejudices and assumptions.[9]

The Regional Moment

The River joined Lorenz's earlier documentary film on the Dust Bowl, *The Plow That Broke the Plains* (1936), in exposing destructive environmental practices. Celebrating federal responses to environmental degradation, the man known as "FDR's filmmaker" popularized regionalist strategies emanating from the highest levels of government. As social and environmental disorder increased, the regional moment also gave rise to various experiments in communal living and vernacular arts. The New Deal's federal arts, writers, and theater projects funded many of these experiments.[10]

Searching for something to replace the collapsing corporate culture of consumerism, artists from William Faulkner and Willa Cather to Robert Frost and Georgia O'Keefe found it in a regional attachment to place and folk culture. John Steinbeck's *The Grapes of Wrath* (1939) is only the most famous of literary works that bemoaned environmental decay and called for a new respect for the land. The photographic work of Dorothea Lange and Arthur Rothstein, the music of Woody Guthrie, the regionalist paintings of Thomas Hart Benton and Grant Wood, and regionalist investigations such as Walter Prescott Webb's history *The Great Plains* (1931) and Howard Odum's sociology of the South all added to the ferment.[11]

At the same time, President Roosevelt embraced his cousin Theodore Roosevelt's interest in conservation and extended it to human settlements. Within a welter of programs driven by political expediency, President Roosevelt's commitment to prevention, recovery, and restoration at the intersection of natural and social systems gave rise to three innovative New Deal experiments. In its first hundred days, Roosevelt's administration won congressional support for the Civilian Conservation Corps (CCC), the Soil Conservation Service (SCS), and, most ambitious, the TVA. "Could the valley be so transformed by regional planning," Roosevelt asked in promoting the TVA, "as to support not only those living in it, and at a decent standard of living, but also others who moved in, myriads of others who now, jobless and hopeless, walked the city streets?"[12]

Rural in outlook, enjoying an empathy for the natural world, and having some knowledge of ecology, Roosevelt understood land as an evolving set of relationships. As a public official, stretching back to his time in the New York Senate, Roosevelt pushed conservation measures and articulated an ethical obligation to one's neighbors and to future generations. Connecting the health of land to the health of people, Roosevelt described the "opponents of conservation" as the "opponents of the liberty of the people." As governor of New York, he worked to expand state forests, defying energy corporations that wanted to lease existing preserves as reservoirs for hydropower. His Temporary Emergency Relief Program of 1931 created twenty-five thousand conservation-related jobs. Roosevelt also supported an amendment to the state constitution that led to the nation's largest program dedicated to the purchase and reforestation of land no longer fit for agriculture.[13]

As president, Roosevelt saw sustainable land management as a foundation for democracy. His Brains Trust, especially the economist Rexford Tugwell, helped him see land management as also the key to economic recovery. "Our economic life today is a seamless web," Roosevelt explained in 1933. "If we get back to the root of the difficulty, we will find that it is the present lack of equality in agriculture." The CCC, SCS, and TVA all championed careful land management and scientific planning. Roosevelt supported renewed and managed landscapes to repair the relationship between urban industry and rural agriculture that had gone horribly wrong.[14]

In the CCC, Roosevelt brought together two wasted resources—damaged rural land and unemployed urban youth—to preserve both. Employing three million young men (Eleanor Roosevelt and Labor Secretary Frances Perkins campaigned unsuccessfully for what the press coined a "she, she, she" corps), the CCC linked city and country by infusing rural communities with financial and technical aid while providing income assistance to urban families. Four federal departments (War, Labor, Agriculture, and Interior) orchestrated the effort, connecting the federal government with ordinary citizens in new ways. Hiring unemployed woodsmen as supervisors, the CCC provided recruits with employment, training, formal education, and improved health. Recruits gained height, weight, and muscle.[15]

Critics objected to the program as disguised militarism or preparedness training. But the "civilian" corps required military assistance only for logistics. Other critics branded the program "make work," useful only for short-term relief. Such objections prevented its transformation into a permanent program. Before its demise in 1942, however, the CCC had planted three billion trees. This included, at Roosevelt's insistence, a one hundred-mile-long shelterbelt on the Great Plains, anchoring soil, tempering wind, and retaining water. The CCC replanted much of the western grasslands, repaired fences and bridges, and eradicated tree-killing insects. It also constructed eight hundred new parks, plus trails, cabins, and shelters.[16]

The SCS complemented these efforts with five thousand local projects in forty-four states. The agency paid farmers to help save their farms while employing sixty thousand young Americans. A grassroots effort that outlasted the New Deal, the SCS preached conservation efforts in rural districts with an idealistic fervor. In the 1950s, it extended its efforts to reduce erosion in suburban subdivisions.[17]

The TVA, the New Deal's most ambitious domestic project, combined flood control with soil conservation and hydropower. The project covered territory in all or part of the seven states drained by the Tennessee River. The product of political compromise between progressive Republicans and conservative Southern Democrats, the TVA became a unified program of regional development due to Roosevelt's vision. It embraced an integrated approach, hyperaware of interrelationships of all sorts. Its dams and lakes, generating plants, and fertilizer factories not only controlled flooding. The project also improved river navigation, produced hydroelectricity, and contributed to soil revitalization and conservation. Reforestation, eradication of disease, provision of recreation, and encouragement of tourism rounded out the TVA's contributions.[18]

Far from perfect, the TVA provoked controversy as it built forty-nine dams across six states. Critics lambasted the project's expense, intrusiveness, and unconstitutional reach. The TVA also earned the enmity of utility companies for providing electricity through public means more cheaply than private sources. Some questioned both its democratic and environmental credentials. Dams built by the TVA displaced people, usually Black and poor people, disrupting local communities and burying rich soils and traditions. The motto atop every TVA dam, "Built *for* the People of the United States" (italics added), suggested the top-down nature of the project. Top-down management overrode local knowledge and practice such as timing planting from the appearance of leaves on specific types of trees or measuring land by the number of workers needed to tend it (instead of by standardized acre). A sensitive human ecology should have preserved and built on just such detailed, on-the-ground knowledge.[19]

Notwithstanding these criticisms, the TVA showed what planning and cooperation could do, especially when linked to a regional approach. Roosevelt praised the avowedly utopian project as an opportunity "where the people can produce what they use, and where they can use what they produce." The TVA provided the cheapest energy in the country, brought electricity to tens of thousands of farm families, and employed tens of thousands of workers. The project also saved billions in property damage from flooding, pioneered new techniques to improve water quality, produced fertilizers (free to landowners) to renew exhausted soils, and eradicated malaria without chemicals (using water fluctuation to frustrate mosquito reproduction).[20]

The success of the TVA inspired visions of a more complete regional reorganization of American life. Introducing the TVA legislation in 1933, President Roosevelt suggested that if "we are successful here we can march on, step by step, in a like development of other great natural territorial units within our borders." In 1937, however, Roosevelt and Senator Norris's proposal for a nationwide system of TVAs met with stiff opposition from utility companies that doomed the "seven TVAs" legislation. A similar fate befell the Resettlement Administration. Under Tugwell, the member of Roosevelt's Brain Trust most dedicated to regional planning, the Resettlement Administration sought to resettle 500,000 families while moving the Great Plains from factory farming, absentee ownership, and tenant farms to cooperative settlements, diversified agriculture, and participatory politics. Starved for funds by its many opponents, the Resettlement Administration resettled only 4,400 families before its demise in 1937.[21]

Reuniting the City and Country

In the Roosevelt administration's vision of regionalism, the city figured largely as something to escape. While Mumford and his associates in the RPAA also detested the overgrown megalopolis, they nevertheless recognized the crucial role of cities in successful regionalism. The region cannot even be defined, Mumford insisted, "as a geographic, economic, and cultural complex without respect to the essential relationships between city and country." In healthy regions, he added, cities served as "spheres of attraction," focusing "the flow of energies, men, and goods that passes through a region, concentrating them, dispersing them, diverting them, re-routing them, in short, exerting a close and controlling influence over the development of region as a dynamic reality." Even the forester Benton MacKaye, who did so much to bring a rural perspective to the RPAA, emphasized the importance of the regional city in promoting a "giant orchestration of varied life (urban, communal, and even primeval) as against the dull cacophony of standardized existence presented by the metropolis."[22]

Eager to reunite city and country, Mumford and his associates believed neither could thrive independently of the health of the whole. They first worked out their thinking in helping to design and publicize New York State's experiments in regional planning in the 1920s. "To the few the great city gives all," Stein wrote in publicizing the experiments, "to the millions annually it gives less and less." But regionalism, Mumford added, would make economic and cultural opportunities available to all while protecting "human values hand in hand with natural resources."[23]

Over the next decade, Mumford distilled half a lifetime's learning into a grand vision for the regional reconstruction of American civilization. His magisterial *The Culture of Cities* (1938) grounded this vision in a sweeping survey of Western urbanism since the medieval period. Mumford praised the medieval city for its close connections to nature. Enjoying easy access to the countryside and using local resources, medieval citizens grew food within the city walls and in nearby fields. Only later did the rise of the capital cities of the absolutist monarchies disrupt the medieval citizen's "close vegetative relationship to his native soil." In the age of exploration and colonization that followed, imperial cities drained the countryside of its wealth as well as its cultural and political vitality, first at home and then overseas.[24]

The disorder only deepened with the rise of the industrial city. Mumford lambasted the industrial regime of coal and iron, mines and blast furnaces, steamships and railroads that treated the countryside as a mine from which materials could be extracted. "The region considered as a theater for human activity," Mumford charged, "occupied no place in this scheme." Typified by Coketown and the Country House, factory town and rural retreat, industrialization widened the gap between city and country. The subsequent rise of megalopolis offered no relief. Failing "to distribute the benefits that it potentially commands" across an impoverished countryside, megalopolis also further alienated its citizenry from nature. The modern urbanite, Mumford wrote, lived "in a shadow world projected around him every moment by means of paper and celluloid: a world in which he is insulated by glass, rubber, cellophane, from the mortifications of living."[25]

Mumford took heart, however, in the slow development of a conservation ethic of husbanding resources, recycling wastes, and preserving wilderness. Embracing and building on the environmental reforms and ecological thinking of previous decades, Mumford envisioned a future "biotechnic" order based on the application of the biological sciences to technology. The environmental reforms that had made cities healthier, safer, and more satisfying places to live would now be extended across the region. With the melding of the cultural and the biological, city and country would be reunited in a new regional synthesis, restoring vitality and variety and balancing self-sufficiency with specialization.[26]

Following his mentor, the Scottish regionalist Patrick Geddes, Mumford defined the region in terms of intersecting biological and cultural processes. Regional reconstruction therefore required not only a thorough understanding and appreciation of the geographic character of a place— its soil, climate, and vegetation—but also the agricultural and industrial practices built on that foundation. We can "no longer leave soils and landscapes and agricultural possibilities" out of urban plans, Mumford argued; such plans must start with "the barest terms of 'air, water, and places.'" Ecology also underscored "the importance of the environment as a co-operative factor" in the development of all life-forms. Therefore, Mumford concluded, regionalists must also address the question of whether there might be "favorable habitats and favorable forms of association" for humans, as well.[27]

An ever changing product of cultural adaptation, the region combined what Mumford called "primordial" geographic features with "emergent" social differentiations. As humans transformed floodplains into agricultural fields, they magnified the natural features of the region, increasing the number and range of human interactions with them. Technology did not lessen the importance of the natural environment; it multiplied it. A forest became a source not just of game, but of lumber, recreation, soil retention, and scientific observation. Originally the haunt of fishermen alone, Cape Cod attracted artists and scientists, glass makers and cranberry pickers, each new group magnifying a distinctive characteristic of the place.[28]

Understanding regions as cultural adaptations as much as geological facts guarded against environmental determinism. Like the pragmatist John Dewey, Mumford believed that consciousness changed everything, opening the possibility that evolution might become more deliberate and intentional. Neither "finished product in nature" nor "solely the creation of human will," the region represented nothing less than the fundamental relationship of humans to their environment. "In conceiving a region," Mumford explained, we must remember that "our task is to replace the primeval balance that exists in a region" with "a more subtle and many-weighted balance, of human groups and communities in a state of high culture." Imports from other regions, cultures, and historical experiences added complexity to regions. Countering the "metropolitan effort to wipe out every other mode of life except that which reflects its own image," regionalists would cherish and protect the innovations that arose organically out of geography, history, and culture.[29]

MacKaye complemented Mumford's urban rethinking of the region by starting at the other end. Urging city planners to remember the city's "roots in its vast hinterland," MacKaye worked to restore rural communities even before the RPAA existed. His 1919 plan for the restoration of the "stump country" (the cutover forests of the north woods) blossomed into a larger project of turning *forest mining* into a more sustainable *forest culture.* MacKaye's proposal in 1921 for the Appalachian Trail, out of which the RPAA sprang, offered an antidote to the "invasion of an over-wrought mechanized civilization" into rural communities. He hoped the Appalachian Trail would repopulate rural areas with cooperative farms and sustainable forestry.[30]

MacKaye believed that a healthier relationship to the countryside could redirect the energies of urban-industrial society toward human happiness and the public good. For urbanites to get "to the roots of industrial questions," MacKaye believed, they needed interaction with both rural communities and wilderness. An "experience of nature," he wrote, prevented "superficial thinking and rash action" and encouraged a "questioning and rejection of overly materialistic and consumptive" values. Fellow forester and conservationist Aldo Leopold, with whom MacKaye helped to create the Wilderness Society in 1937, shared the belief that an experience of nature could encourage moderation and restraint.[31]

Regionalists sought a balance of urban and rural communities rooted in an understanding and love of distinctive places. MacKaye believed a people with "some vital, common geographic interest" would counteract metropolitan standardization and rootlessness. The philosopher Josiah Royce agreed. A community rooted in place would develop a "consciousness of its own unity," he argued, and a "pride in its own ideas and customs." What Royce called "wise provincialism" could be cultivated to avoid insularity or sectionalism and generate respect for the loyalty others felt to other places. In working for a "common sympathy between the different sections of our country," Royce complemented the rural sociologist Howard W. Odum's vision of "regionalism as a cultural-historical approach" to national integration. An advocate of equal opportunity for all races and ethnicities, Odum envisioned regions as integrated wholes interacting harmoniously with other regions.[32]

A Transformed and Transformative Politics

In his defense of the central role of cities in regionalism, Mumford added the crucial point that cities preserved and facilitated access to a rich social heritage of accumulated knowledge, practices, and institutions. Cities thus served as key agencies of both socialization and individuation. Cities promoted socialization in providing democratic access to the social heritage and its many benefits. By facilitating interaction with one another and the social heritage, cities also encouraged individuation by maximizing opportunities for individuals to find their own distinctive and creative ways to use and contribute to the social heritage.[33]

Exposing another dimension of the great divide, Mumford lamented that we treated socialization and individuation as competing, exclusive alternatives rather than different dimensions of the same thing. Individualistic ideologies monopolized opportunities and appropriated the benefits of social development for the fortunate few (everything from rising land values to the fruits of scientific and technological advances). Socialistic ideologies, in contrast, imposed uniformity on things such as culture, politics, and higher education that should be vehicles for diverse individuation. Mumford believed that the regional city should provide a "generic, equalized, standardized, communal" base (public schools, sewers, parks, civic spaces, and all the things that made cities richer and less precarious settlements) from which "specific, unstandardized, individual, aristocratic" emergents could grow (inventions, innovations, the arts).[34]

Falling far short of this ideal, the megalopolis limited access to the social heritage to its most fortunate citizens. But the question remained as to how the regional vision might be realized. The usual, and potent, criticism of Mumford's regional vision is that it depended too heavily on technological change. Mumford and the RPAA banked too much on the decentralizing effects of electricity, the internal combustion engine, and other elements of the second industrial revolution. They believed such technologies would result in a fourth migration, redistributing population, as well as civic life and cultural resources, into more manageable cities of 200,000. Millions of Americans did indeed depart dinosaur cities in the coming decades. But postwar suburbanization promoted neither the attachment and loyalty to place nor the civic and cultural renewal the RPAA had in mind.[35]

For all Mumford's misplaced (and later regretted) faith in technological change, however, he did not shrink from the task of suggesting
how regional reconstruction might proceed. He understood that in the
face of a standardized metropolitan culture indifferent to place, regionalism needed some means of promoting attachment and loyalty. He believed this might be cultivated by a political culture of collective inquiry
and collaboration focused on regional resources, practices, and opportunities. The construction of regions as "deliberate works of collective art,"
Mumford argued, must become the "grand task of politics."[36]

Skeptical of the nation-state, Mumford placed his faith in a transfor-
mative, grassroots political culture that would produce a transformed
politics. From Geddes and his own experience, he took the idea of a regional survey as the foundation for communal education and civic regeneration. The regional survey engaged both experts and citizens in a sys-
tematic investigation of the region and an imaginative discussion of its
potential. From schoolchildren to specialists, every citizen would be
touched by the "moralizing forces" of the scientific method and cooperative inquiry. The mutual education of citizen and specialist, moreover,
made the regional survey the "central core in a functional education for
political life." Subjecting expert knowledge to democratic scrutiny, the
regional survey transformed both experts and citizens. Experts learned
how to communicate with nonspecialists and how to listen to popular
concerns and aspirations. Nonspecialists, in seeking to understand and
guide the methods and findings of specialists, became well-informed,
public-minded citizens.[37]

The regional survey ultimately provided the foundation for the coordinated planning of agriculture, industry, and community life, infusing
all with larger social purposes. But much of the value lay in the democratic process itself. By conducting the survey themselves, the people demonstrated that "the opportunities for the fullest manifestation of life be-
long, not to an exclusive minority, but to every citizen, up to the limits of
his capacities." The participation of schoolchildren in the survey would,
over time, transform politics from the bottom up. By supplementing textbook learning with activities such as sailing, fishing, hunting, quarrying,
and gardening, primary education gave students a role in regional surveys
of soil, climate, and geology. Exploration of "the immediate region, small
enough to be grasped from a tower, a hilltop, an airplane" also prepared
students for civic life. As citizens who "know in detail where they live
and how they live," Mumford concluded, they would be less susceptible
to sloganeering and demagoguery.[38]

Mumford believed the regional survey could reverse the trend of American politics toward expert administration and passive citizenry. But by the end of the 1930s, a political economy of citizenship (the pursuit of economic and political arrangements that cultivated good citizens) gave way to a political economy of growth (satisfying the expanding desires of consumers). "There was an old dream: the independent man in his own little shop or business," the New Dealer and former head of the TVA David Lilienthal wrote in 1953. "It *was* a good dream," he admitted, but now "a new dream" had come, "a world of great machines" run by experts for the benefit of consumers. With his survey, Mumford attempted to forestall that trend, to restore "human scale in government," to widen "the cooperative processes of government," and to place front and center "the processes of persuasion and rational agreement."[39]

The regional survey provided a concrete example of what Dewey meant by "cooperative inquiry." In *Logic: A Theory of Inquiry*, published in the same year as *The Culture of Cities*, Dewey summed up and refined forty years of work in a way that illuminated Mumford's debt to pragmatism. Dewey's four stages of inquiry paralleled Mumford's four stages of the regional survey. A collective inquiry like the regional survey proceeded from (1) recognition of a problematic situation to (2) the creative generation of theoretical solutions. An imaginative appraisal of the probable consequences of each proposal (3) followed, leading to a judicious choice and implementation of a course of action (4). The knowledge gained from the process and from the assessment of results then guided and enriched future inquiry and experience.[40]

Rejecting the idea of a *planned* society dominated by an elite, Dewey called for a *planning* society that promoted the mutual and continuing education of expert and democratic public. Science became knowledge, he argued, only through "that common understanding and thorough communication which is the precondition of the existence of a genuine and effective public." Without the public, experts became "a specialized class . . . shut off from knowledge of the needs which they are supposed to serve." Experts could take the lead in conducting inquiries, Dewey concluded, but only the public could "judge the bearing of the knowledge supplied by others upon common concerns." Mumford took the same approach. If regional planning were left to experts, he put it, the result would be "old dominants, not fresh emergents."[41]

In responding to the journalist Walter Lippmann's indictment of an uninterested and ill-informed "phantom" public, Dewey admitted that most people lacked access to the accumulated knowledge of modern society. We lived in a vast web of interdependencies reaching around the globe, he explained, but we lacked a democratic public that understood and took responsibility for those interdependencies. Dewey saw this as an indictment of social arrangements, however, not of individual endowments. If individuals engaged in a process of cooperative inquiry in local settings where global developments inevitably impinged, they could gain the knowledge they needed. As MacKaye put it, local communities were "part of an endless chain reaching to the four corners of the earth" that could help citizens makes sense of "a sort of barb-wire entanglement reaching around the world."[42]

A closing of the great divide between city and country could be glimpsed in several New Deal experiments, in Mumford's regionalism, and in his collaboration with MacKaye and the RPAA. It could also be seen in the partnership between MacKaye and Leopold that linked preservation with the remaking of urban-industrial society. But the tiny band of regionalists would prove no match for the social scientists and urban professionals who had been crafting their own strategies in these years. Mumford worried that urban experts thought only of economic efficiency, while "most contemporary treatises on 'urban sociology' in America throw no important light" on the place of the city in a healthy region. By the end of the 1930s, those treatises in urban sociology had begun to shape the actions of urban experts and buried Mumford's regional vision.[43]

Urban Conservation and the Chicago Sociologists

Beginning in the building boom of the 1920s, a series of federal studies on the future of the city tightened the connections among social scientists, planners, and real estate professionals. The Chicago sociologists' use of ecological concepts brought prestige to the partnerships, providing urban experts with scientific principles to guide their work. The onset of the Great Depression added urgency to the partnerships, as urban experts applied ecological concepts to explain and manage the collapse of realty values, neighborhood disintegration, and the migration of industries.[44]

The frequent exchange of concepts and metaphors with multiple meanings between ecology and other inquires facilitated these partnerships. Ecologists borrowed a key concept—community—from sociology. Straddling the line between the natural and social sciences, ecologists described associations of plants and animals as communities in the sense of being a product of interaction among individuals. Now the Chicago sociologists borrowed back, combining the ecological concepts of invasion, succession, and climax to craft a new strategy of urban conservation to manage what they thought of as the urban life cycle. Just as plant and animal ecologists crafted policies to preserve forests, farms, and ranges, so, too, might human ecologists shape policies to save cities.[45]

The Great Depression appeared to confirm the life cycle theory, as well as the ideas of invasion and succession. The Chicago sociologists had long held that the life cycle of inner cities pointed toward decay. The "ambitious and energetic keep moving out," Ernest Burgess wrote in 1925, while "the unadjusted, the dregs and the outlaws accumulate." Citing ecological research, one of his students explained that the "city grows like a tree, taking on new growth at the periphery but dying at the heart." "Residential property is always invaded more or less rapidly by industry and business," another Chicago-trained sociologist explained, "and the old houses of the well-to-do are being turned over, in progressive stages of disrepair," to the poor.[46]

Burgess's famous concentric circle model of urban growth, developed in the 1920s, reinforced the idea that cities went through predictable life cycles. Burgess expressed the conviction of many in asserting that "prediction is the aim of the social sciences as it is of the physical sciences." When sociologists made predictions about the directions of urban growth and decay, they increasingly pointed to ecological research for support. A few scientists and social scientists challenged the applicability of ecological concepts to cities. But generally, ecologists applauded the analogies and invited sociologists to their conferences, while sociologists filled their publications with ecological evidence.[47]

Blight, initially referring to plant disease but finding its way into urban discourse via the Chicago sociologists, illustrates how these ecological analogies often just ratified existing prejudices. Deployed to explain the threat to central cities posed by the building boom and suburban expansion of the 1920s, the term *blight* offered a seemingly objective and scientific way to describe what many saw as a spreading plague of ethnic and racial minorities. In the years to come, planners recommended physical rehabilitation, zoning restrictions, and code enforcement to stop the spread of blight. In such ecological concepts, urban experts, especially planners and real estate professionals, found new explanations for slum creation and new rationales for the racial and economic segregation many already favored.[48]

Staffing federal bureaucracies such as the Home Owners Loan Corporation and the Federal Housing Administration, urban experts brought ecological thinking to key decision-making agencies. In concert with other agencies addressing rural disorder, urban experts might have exerted considerable leverage in healing the great divide of city and country. The economist Richard Ely recognized that possibility when he warned that the "mistakes of the past" resulted from the failure to understand that "the utilization of agricultural, forest, mineral, and urban land is characterized by a network of interrelationships." The New Deal provided an opportunity to address those interrelationships. So, too, did the Chicago school's embrace of Frederic Clements's work on grasslands.[49]

Applying Clements's theories to urban development, an economic historian captured something of the dysfunctional relationship between city and country. "The efficient builder establishes first his radial lines running out in all directions from the center," he wrote in a description that called to mind how Chicago's railroads remade the Great Plains. "Then the concentric fasteners are put in. At last the spider, poised at the center, is ready to do business." Here was a starting point for exploring the linked fates of grasslands and metropolis.[50]

The linkages between grasslands and metropolis included everything from markets and credit to tools and machinery—most notably, the chilled plow that broke the sod (manufactured in South Bend, Indiana), the "farmall" tractor (produced by the Chicago-based International Harvester), and the combined harvester-thresher. Even the introduction of soybeans during the 1930s came at the initiative of a city-based corporation, the Ford Motor Company. Henry Ford hoped to increase the purchasing power of farmers while also turning soybeans into car parts. "There is a bushel of soya beans in every Ford car," *Fortune* revealed in 1933.[51]

Urban-fueled mechanization sped the industrialization and consolidation of farming operations on the Great Plains. Industrialized agriculture and a capitalist culture determined to wring profits out of the land led to dispossession on the scale of the great English enclosures. Even before the Dust Bowl, mechanization forced tenants off the land in the corn-growing, eastern sections of the Great Plains, sending droves of despised "Okies" on the road in search of employment. Meanwhile, the boom in soybean production sped the rise of giant urban-based agricultural processing corporations such as Archer Daniels Midland and Cargill that accelerated the industrialization of agriculture.[52]

The Crisis of Conservation

By the middle of the 1930s, the Roosevelt administration's conservation strategy had begun to come under attack precisely for ignoring such interrelationships. Leopold and others went from ardent supporters of the CCC to harsh critics, complaining specifically about a lack of coordination among projects. As the CCC drained swamps, eradicated insects, cleared forest floors, and built roads into wilderness areas, Leopold charged, no one considered the unintended effects of such changes. As befit a future founder of the Wilderness Society, much of Leopold's criticism hinged on habitat destruction. But he also criticized conservation efforts for ignoring ecological relationships and for failing to develop a "harmonious balanced system of land use." The harshest test for conservation strategy, however, would come in the Dust Bowl.[53]

The winds always howled along the Great Plains, but something new and troubling began in the spring of 1934. As the weather turned hot and dry, dust storms filled the air ten thousand feet high, displacing 350 million tons of dirt. A single storm in 1934 dropped twelve million tons of dirt on Chicago and darkened cities as far away as the East Coast. The Dust Bowl revealed that those neglected connections between city and country could kill. Lakes and other bodies of water shrank; animals died; temperatures soared; and nothing grew. Dust pneumonia and other diseases spread. A plague of grasshoppers blocked out the sun, and one-sixth of the nation's topsoil disappeared. Two-and-a-half-million people migrated west toward California.[54]

By the end of the decade, the National Resources Planning Board estimated that thirty-five million acres of farmland had been destroyed, with many more acres in danger of losing all their topsoil. Drought provided the first scapegoat, but something more than drought troubled the grasslands. The intersection of social and ecological processes proved disastrous on the Great Plains. As early as the 1870s, poor farmers had begun to settle the grasslands. Many of them fled the impoverished South and brought with them a desperate habit of exploiting the land without restraint. Despite warnings from the federal Geological Survey that the land could support only grazing, a series of federal homestead acts doled out the land in small acreages that could only be made to pay by planting row crops. Designed in part to relieve pressure in cities already overcrowded by rural dispossession, the homestead acts set farmers to work, using city-made tools, to bust up the sod.[55]

Urban and rural boosters, from railroad and bank presidents to newspaper editors and land speculators, promised that "rain follows the plow." The theory that human habitation and cultivation turned arid lands humid is now discredited. "Misery follows the migrant" might be more accurate. The legacy of slavery and sharecropping, which burdened white farmers as well as Black, brought to the region a callousness toward both the land and the people who farmed it. That legacy also brought a tradition of specialized monocultures geared to far-flung markets. The spread of monocultures undermined soil fertility, destroyed biodiversity, and buried the knowledge essential to survival. Poor diets left most farmers susceptible to disease. Meanwhile, back east, extractive industries also devastated much of the Appalachian region.[56]

Unusually abundant rain and market demand brought a brief boom during World War I, but the war's end led to a collapse of markets. The all-purpose, affordable tractor now promised relief through economies of scale. On the flat prairies, the tractors invited more sod-busting, more land in production, at larger scale. With each downturn, however, the expense of mechanization brought more dispossession and consolidation. As urban speculators raised the price of land, even the farmers who remained fell deeper into poverty and debt during the 1920s. In the Mississippi River watershed, deforestation intensified flooding, inundating twenty-seven thousand square miles in the flood of 1927, and elsewhere gullied the land. A neglect of education and public health and substandard public utilities added to the burdens of farm families.[57]

By the early 1930s, sodbusters had destroyed much of the grass that held the plains together. Evolved over tens of thousands of years, the deep root systems of the native sod preserved biomass and moisture below ground and provided a buffer against wind. But now the commitment to a single cash crop and harvested fields left bare of vegetation put the Great Plains at the mercy of drought and wind. So, too, did straight furrows, parallel to the wind. The federal Department of Agriculture tried to stabilize the worst areas, purchasing acreage and later leasing it back to local farmers for forage. The department also established soil conservation districts. Contoured planting of native grasses supplemented the planting of billions of trees to stabilize the soil.[58]

Still the misery and foreclosures spread. Three-quarters of a million farm families left the land during the Great Depression. As declining prices left the remaining farmers angry and desperate, they plowed under or destroyed crops even as urbanites faced malnutrition or starvation. At the end of 1936, the federal Great Plains Committee sent President Roosevelt a report titled, "The Future of the Great Plains." It declared the Dust Bowl a man-made disaster, a product of efforts to "impose upon the region a system of agriculture to which the Plains are not adapted." We could no longer assume that "nature is something of which to take advantage and exploit," the report concluded, but must adjust our economy to nature's.[59]

In the wheat-growing regions of the Dust Bowl proper, however, farmers organized to resist federal resettlement programs, pledging never to leave. With the aid and assistance of the SCS, they set out to wring profits once again from the land. The experience of the SCS revealed the limitation of both conservation and New Deal reform. Ecologists and land-use planners called for vast acreages to be returned to grassland and for farmers to grow less soil-depleting wheat and more soil-conserving grasses and legumes. But to profit-hungry and debt-ridden farmers, ecology sounded like surrender. For their part, ecologists never thought much about how a new land ethic might emerge out of a capitalist culture. More attuned to immediate political realities, the agronomists and soil engineers (including former students of Clements) who staffed the SCS assisted farmers bent on increasing production. Advocating contour planting and terracing, built with CCC labor, the SCS endeavored to make two stalks of wheat grow where one, or none, had grown before.[60]

By the early 1940s, with the easing of the drought and the expansion of international demand in World War II, even the mildest of SCS reforms appeared burdensome. Farmers, especially the bigger operators, now found terraces too costly and difficult to plow and shelterbelts a waste of valuable land. Meanwhile, even where the SCS had managed to take some land out of production, it proved difficult to coax the grasslands back into bloom. Farmers plowed even more marginal land, while no one in the SCS wanted to admit that their own advice had distracted attention from the need for more fundamental reform.[61]

Between 1954 and 1957, an even worse drought and dust storms pummeled the plains and shook confidence in the conservation movement's technocratic ability to manage nature. Salvation by technique had proved ineffectual. Meanwhile, Clements's theory of the climax community of grasses had also come under attack. As early as 1937, even Clements had recommended adaptation to cycles of drought rather than a wholesale return to the climax community, admitting that "the climax dominants are not necessarily the most valuable to man." Writing amid the dust storms of the 1950s, the historian James Malin speculated that nature needed plowing, and perhaps even dust storms, to remain vigorous and fertile. Finding records of dust storms as far back as 1830, Malin argued that storms took deep topsoil and deposited it more uniformly. The grasslands had always been in flux; only agriculture brought any measure of order, peace, and harmony.[62]

Clements's theory had also been under attack from within ecological science. In 1935, the British ecologist A. G. Tansley questioned Clements's assertion of the single true climax. He argued that a variety of factors, from grazing animals and fire to human disruptions, led to a variety of climaxes. Tansley also criticized Clements's theory for leaving no room for humanity. "Is man part of 'nature' or not?" Tansley asked. He answered that humanity must be seen as "an exceptionally powerful biotic factor which increasingly upsets the equilibrium of preexisting ecosystems and eventually destroys them." But then humans formed a climax of a "very different nature." Once we rejected Clements's rigid model, Tansley concluded, we might build an anthropogenic climax, human-created but stable and balanced.[63]

Tansley also introduced the idea of an ecosystem as a substitute for Clements's community. Following the American ecologist Henry Gleason, who had questioned whether associations of plants should be understood as organisms, Tansley included the abiotic elements of the environment (such nonliving elements as climate, soil, hydrology, geology) in his concept of the ecosystem. Tansley sought to make the "whole system (in the sense of physics)" the fundamental unit of ecology. Many ecologists came to believe that an understanding of ecosystems would facilitate the rational management of nature. Tansley shared something of that faith, but he also believed that the ecosystem concept would finally facilitate the incorporation of human activities into ecological science.[64]

Ecosystem ecology supplanted the community paradigm over the next decades. But Clements's theory could not be so easily dismissed. Juxtaposed to the disaster of the Dust Bowl, the idea of a stable climax put human disruptions into bold relief and offered a model against which human actions might be judged. Even Malin admitted that the wisdom of human culture in each region must be measured against its "conformity with the requirements of maintaining rather than disrupting environmental equilibrium." On the Great Plains, conservation strategies and technocratic processes struggled to find the most appropriate balance between human culture and the rest of nature. Over this same period, a version of the conservation strategy began to remake the nation's cities.[65]

7

Decentralization and Recentralization

The Environmental Costs of Mass
Suburbanization and Urban Renewal

In the three decades after the end of World War II, the United States underwent one of the most dramatic environmental transformations in its history. A popular desire for decentralization, aided by federal policies aimed at economic recovery, buried visions of regional planning. By facilitating an unplanned, chaotic restructuring of cities and regions, federal mortgage insurance, freeway construction, and fiscal policies encouraged urban sprawl in the countryside while undercutting the vitality and viability of central cities. Strategies of urban renewal and neighborhood conservation, aimed at recentralization, fared no better. Urban renewal failed to revitalize cities, while declining population undercut efforts at neighborhood conservation.[1]

The ecological thinking that informed urban renewal and conservation failed to halt or even acknowledge environmental degradation and, in some forms, accelerated it. Although we tend to assume suburbs thrived at the expense of cities, both cities and the suburban countryside suffered environmental degradation. The organic metaphors that might have encouraged an understanding of the linked fates of cities, suburbs, and the countryside became formulaic. Instead, a new fascination with mechanistic systems encouraged architects, planners, and traffic engineers to believe they could use machine technology to craft a new synthesis between society and nature, between the machine and the garden.[2]

The sprawling metropolis resembled more machine than garden, however, with a complex steel and concrete infrastructure at its center. Knocked down and rebuilt as a rational layout of freeways and feeder roads, high-rise office and residential towers, shopping centers, office parks, cultural centers, and sports stadia, the metropolis came to resemble an immense inhuman system of conduits and energy flows. Planners and engineers treated the metropolis in terms of feedback loops and homeostatic systems but failed to appreciate the complex needs of cities and regions. Even as bulldozers punched new traffic arteries across the city and razed entire neighborhoods, they also drove highways deep into the countryside and turned cornfields into subdivisions. Conflicting responses to urban decline and suburban sprawl among urban, suburban, and rural communities frustrated any effort to reintegrate city and country.[3]

The Totalitarian Threat and the Eclipse of Regional Planning

For a brief, heady time during the New Deal and in the early years of World War II, it seemed as if planners and policy makers might gain broad powers to direct postwar regional reconstruction. "As it was with the land itself, so it was with our cities," the public works administrator Harold Ickes argued in 1935. "Expanding in a time of swift growth, they spread—altogether aimlessly at first, then with only a modicum of direction," Ickes continued, until an urban "fungus took root and its inevitable economic and moral drain began." But Ickes and others believed the situation might be reversed with bold regional planning. Small-scale, piecemeal planning, a modernist architect argued, is obsolete. It must be replaced with "urban biology, or the study of the life of cities and of the living conditions within them." Lewis Mumford even found himself briefly in vogue, consulting with members of the National Resources Planning Board (NRPB), the New Deal agency charged with coordinating planning efforts at the federal level.[4]

Meanwhile, organic ecology enlisted in the popular front against fascism. In September 1941, just months before the attack on Pearl Harbor, Warder Allee's "Ecology Group" at the University of Chicago organized the symposium "Levels of Integration in Biological and Social Systems." The symposium found evolution toward greater integration everywhere, from the simplest multicellular organisms to the world economy. The conferees' emphasis on cooperation as an evolutionary force counteracted the fascist view of war as an extension of "survival of the fittest."

With an eye to the European war, one participant argued that "isolationism is a biological anachronism."[5]

Even at the height of enthusiasm for regional planning, however, some derided it as totalitarianism. In 1936, a member of the NRPB warned that "national planning in America can neither go to the extremes nor employ the methods used in Russia, Germany, Italy or other countries under dictatorship." Once the war came, organic ecology's opponents within the sciences denounced it as "totalitarian biology," whose "aggregation ethics" undermined individualism. The totalitarian threat made the cooperative ant colony seem less attractive than a competitive ethic that left room for individuality, diversity, and dissent. By war's end, conservatives conflated communism and fascism in the specter of "red fascism" and warned that regional planners' dream of "an inexhaustible public purse" paved "the road to serfdom." As Congress dismantled the NRPB in 1943, an angry senator denounced the "dictatorial tactics of the federal bureaucracy" as a "grave menace to society."[6]

The discrediting of regional planning accompanied a larger shift in political culture. That shift doomed Mumford's dream of creating an ecologically responsible citizenry through the regional survey. Abandoning earlier efforts to democratize the economy, New Deal liberals seized on fiscal policy as a less controversial means of promoting economic recovery. "National intervention to stimulate production is the method of the totalitarian state," the New Dealer Leon Henderson put it in 1941. "National intervention to stimulate consumption is the democratic method." Recognizing growth-at-any-costs, consumer-oriented liberalism as a "deflation of American ideals," the political commentator Edgar Kemler lamented: "We withdrew human character from the range of our reforms."[7]

Mumford's hopes for a biotechnic future also faded. Just as oil had begun to outcompete coal, Mumford believed that solar energy would soon outcompete oil. In the meantime, oil powered the cars, trucks, and buses that replaced the centralizing railroad *line* with the decentralizing highway *network*. Combined with electric power, the highway network promised to make possible a balanced regional economy of manufacturing and agriculture. With soil regeneration and conservation, regions could supply themselves with fresh vegetables and fruit in all seasons. With the "effective inter-relation of agriculture with the city," Mumford concluded, even to speak of city versus country would be "to refer to an increasingly moribund division of labor."[8]

Instead, the war catapulted oil to the center of geopolitics as it powered the mechanized slaughter that engulfed the world between 1939 and

1945. After the war, the victorious United States intended to control as much of the world's oil as possible. Massive increases in American foreign investment and military might between 1947 and 1972 secured it. Noting that the United States controlled half the world's wealth but contained just 6 percent of the world's population, the diplomat George Kennan warned his colleagues in the U.S. State Department, "We will have to dispense with all sentimentality and day-dreaming." Only "straight power concepts," he concluded, could help us maintain the status quo. This left little room for utopian experimentation.[9]

Dreaming of a new synthesis between society and nature, Mumford had written enthusiastically about machine technology. The motorcar and the airplane, electric power and modern communications "vastly increased" the potential for regional reconstruction. "Giant power strides over the hills," he enthused, while "the airplane, even more liberated, flies over swamps and mountains, and terminates its journey, not on an avenue, but in a field." But, as Mumford later lamented, the proliferation of oil-powered machines gave rise to a fossil-fueled, drive-in civilization of highways, subdivisions, and shopping centers. With both military and consumer uses generating soaring demand for oil, everything got bigger: the national security state, cars, houses, the plastics industry, and, above all, the amount of oil pumped out of the ground. As postwar suburbanization rose on the ocean of cheap oil, the carefully planned "fourth migration" that Mumford and his colleagues envisioned gave way to rapid, haphazard metropolitan expansion.[10]

Mistaken Analogies: Urban Renewal and Neighborhood Conservation

With the eclipse of regional planning, federal policies favoring suburban development—buttressed by lingering ecological analogies—became the default plan. Postwar suburbanization had its roots in New Deal efforts to end the Great Depression. With half of all mortgages in technical default and the construction industry at a standstill in 1933, Congress created the Home Owners Loan Corporation (HOLC). The HOLC spent $3 billion to refinance defaulted mortgages, shore up the banking system, and put the construction industry back to work. To minimize risk, the HOLC enlisted the aid of real estate professionals and lenders to compile Residential Security Maps and Surveys that ranked neighborhoods according to the risk of default. The HOLC maps put a federal imprimatur on existing practice and the ecological theories that justified it. After its creation in 1934, the Federal Housing Authority (FHA) used the same logic—in some cases, the same maps—for its mortgage insurance program.[11]

The HOLC maps and the FHA program of mortgage insurance received considerable support from the Chicago School of urban sociologists' use of the ecological ideas of invasion and succession. What the FHA called the "infiltration of inharmonious racial or nationality groups" stood as a primary consideration for the rankings. The presence of African Americans immediately marked an area as especially risky, earning it the lowest rating (colored red on the HOLC maps—hence, the term *redlining*). The ecological concept of invasion reinforced such thinking, holding that when a neighborhood began to go Black, the trend would continue, accompanied by an irreversible physical and social decline.[12]

Neither the HOLC nor the Chicago sociologists invented racial and ethnic prejudice or the discriminatory lending practices it encouraged. Indeed, the HOLC provided mortgage assistance impartially and, ironically, saw a better record of repayment in redlined areas. But the FHA, in concert with private lenders, shunned redlined districts. Applying the idea of the urban life cycle, the FHA cited several factors, aside from race and ethnicity, that signaled danger. These included the age and condition of housing, population density, and presence of mixed uses, all factors that favored new suburban subdivisions over urban neighborhoods. Mortgages insured by the FHA thus went overwhelmingly (well over 90 percent) to new, single-family, whites-only suburban developments.[13]

In concert with federal and local agencies responsible for public housing and urban renewal, the FHA thus embedded racial prejudice in the housing market and the built environment. It also encouraged the emergence of a new racialized rhetoric of property rights. Even as public policy favored white homeowners, those same homeowners thought of themselves as upright, property-owning citizens in no need of government handouts. Ecological metaphors helped disguise the role of racial prejudice in those policies as natural workings of the market. Guided by federal policies and the theories that supported them, white homeowners disguised racial discrimination as a defense of property rights and safe neighborhoods. "We have all seen what can happen to a good, well-kept neighborhood when taken over by Negroes," a white suburban woman charged. "Their treatment of property and their behavior is like a slow disease killing off a once healthy neighborhood." As white neighborhoods mobilized to counter the threat of "black invasion," the supposedly inevitable decline of neighborhoods invaded by racial minorities justified every means, violent or otherwise, to resist.[14]

Even as they benefited from vast, new state-subsidized credit markets, white homeowners and their elected officials translated the results of discriminatory public policies into new forms of cultural racism to justify those very public policies. Declining Black neighborhoods provided the fuel for cultural racism. But predictions of the inevitable decline of Black neighborhoods served as self-fulfilling prophecies when lenders denied loans and hard-pressed cities reduced public services. A segregated housing market left African Americans vulnerable to predatory lenders and slumlords who skimped on basic maintenance. With new construction in city neighborhoods virtually halted, African Americans squeezed into already overcrowded structures. Slumlords subdivided their properties into ever smaller units and rented out basements and attics following shoddy conversion efforts.[15]

Polluted air, filthy sidewalks, aging and abandoned buildings, and vacant lots produced additional environmental dangers. The concentration of poverty and poor housing led to fear, resentment, and crime. Lead-based paint in the plaster of crumbling housing produced illness and developmental disorders in children. Researchers later established a correlation between high levels of lead and increases in violent crime. The location of heavy industry, toxic wastes, highways, and the detritus of automobile use and maintenance further burdened low-income and minority neighborhoods. Segregation also made everything else more expensive, from food to services.[16]

The promising African American neighborhoods that emerged in the first half of the twentieth century as launching pads for civic and social equality struggled on. But by the 1960s, environmental deterioration stood at the center of a deepening urban crisis. Public infrastructure decayed and, in cases such as Cleveland's city-owned and -operated Municipal Light Plant, spewed pollution into poor neighborhoods. Deteriorating plumbing and porous basements made rats a constant menace. Uncollected garbage and collapsing outbuildings worsened the trouble. Delinquency, truancy, homicide, and drug abuse reflected what national commentators called a "mood of suspended rage" behind "the invisible wall" of forced segregation.[17]

As policy makers prepared for postwar urban renewal projects, they explained the deterioration of city neighborhoods as a product of blight. "Like a cancer," Homer Hoyt, the real estate economist and associate of the Chicago sociologists, wrote in 1943, "blight spread through all the tissues of the urban body and the urban organism was unable to cure itself except by major surgical operation." But few policy makers troubled to think through these ecological metaphors. The Chicago sociologists' use of *blight* suggested that all the factors that gave rise to slums arose from within the neighborhoods themselves. So, too, did their assumption that cities operated as closed systems. Such concepts made it too easy to ignore disinvestment, deindustrialization, declining tax bases, and systemic segregation and discrimination, none of which originated in distressed neighborhoods.[18]

The jobs programs that poor urban residents clamored for might have reversed decay, especially if coupled with funds for the physical rehabilitation of housing and infrastructure. Instead, bulldozers went to work clearing slums. The postwar strategies of slum clearance and slum prevention (which amounted to slum clearance around more stable neighborhoods) came to be known collectively as urban *renewal*, another term taken from ecological discourse. The logic held that the city, as a climax community, would prove resilient if its diseased portions were cut out. Urban renewal, a legal expert explained in 1953, "represents a complete change from the concept that a city must, of necessity, decay, wear out, and then be abandoned to blight. It asserts the belief that cities can be brought and kept up-to-date—made and kept livable."[19]

The Chicago School's view of the city as a closed system buttressed the policy of urban renewal by implying that investment and population had nowhere else to go. But the city was not closed. With the mechanization of southern agriculture and mining, millions of Black and white southerners migrated to the cities of the North and West in the postwar decades. Even as migrants moved in, however, white middle-class residents, retail, and industry steadily moved out. Nationally, for every two nonwhites who settled in the city, three whites left. With a massive redistribution of population, resources, and opportunity, improved housing had only a limited capacity to improve people's lives and revitalize the city. The narrow focus on physical clearance ignored a host of other environmental, economic, and social factors. Worse, urban renewal exacerbated shortages of affordable housing and disrupted informal economies and social networks, and so tended to produce new slums.[20]

The related policy of neighborhood conservation also relied on the view of the city as a closed system. Unlike urban renewal, which bulldozed declining areas, neighborhood conservation sought to stabilize areas threatened by surrounding slums. The strategy held that strict enforcement of housing and sanitation codes; improvements in public services, schools, and parks; and spot demolition of troubled properties would stabilize conditions and attract new investment. The policy also relied on homeowners' associations, encouraging them to continue their use of restrictive covenants. Local experiments in neighborhood conservation in Baltimore and Chicago initially received positive reviews.[21]

Neighborhood conservation, however, floundered as population and investment flowed out of the city toward the suburbs. At least part of this resulted from white flight. Despite the importance of "invasion" in the Chicago sociologists' theories, neighborhood conservation never effectively dealt with racial conflict. Racial tensions could not be addressed at the neighborhood level—not while redlining threatened property values in transitioning neighborhoods. By bulldozing Black neighborhoods in favor of the expansion of universities and hospitals and upper-income housing, moreover, urban renewal intensified those racial tensions and earned the name "negro removal."[22]

The spread of slums and racial tensions added push factors to the subsidized mortgages, tax advantages, and better public services that pulled whites toward the suburbs. The neighborhood conservation strategy subsequently came to depend on the efforts of Black homeowners, many of whom embraced neighborhood conservation as a means of holding off the bulldozers. But they also left neighborhoods marked for conservation to take up better housing left behind by suburbanizing whites. In turn, lower-income Black people moved into the neighborhoods targeted for conservation. Usually renters, these lower-income residents lacked the resources to implement the conservation strategy. Instead, slumlords continued to subdivide properties.[23]

Automobility and the Environment

Meanwhile, suburbia's low population density and its zoning regulations, separating places for work, residence, and retail, catapulted the automobile to the center of postwar life. As public transit deteriorated, traffic engineers became more consequential public officials than city planners, prioritizing the convenience of motorists and what the cultural critic Marshall Berman called "the flow." The federal gasoline tax provided enormous funds for the elaboration and improvement of the road network, including the interstate highway system, the largest public works project in history. The automobile would eventually be held responsible for urban sprawl and a host of environment troubles, from the loss of open space and ugly strip malls to air pollution and climate change.[24]

Ironically, however, automobility initially promised the new synthesis of society and nature about which Mumford wrote. The Bronx River

Parkway, the nation's first limited-access parkway, completed in 1925, restored a polluted industrial landscape and created what one of its architects called "an environment of unsurpassed beauty." Flanked by thirty thousand newly planted trees and graced with garden strips separating the opposing lanes of traffic, the fifteen-mile parkway ran through a linear park that reclaimed the polluted Bronx River. The parkway's northern end, designed to "inspire civic pride in the citizens of New York," provided a "magnificent approach" to the Kensico Dam, which stored water for the city that had been brought from the Catskill Mountains. Less commuter artery than civic ecology, the parkway encouraged popular awareness and appreciation of biophysical systems.[25]

New York's master builder Robert Moses soon became the preeminent champion of parkways. Three of Moses's earliest parkways provided access to his greatest triumph at Jones Beach State Park on Long Island, opened in 1929. The deft combination of earth, water, and sky at Jones Beach, and the beautifully landscaped parkways, represented a creative synthesis of nature and culture. Moses's parks and parkways provided working-class New Yorkers access to wholesome recreation, at least for the few who owned an automobile. As affluent New Yorkers led the nationwide expansion of automobile ownership from eight thousand vehicles in 1900 to twenty-three million in 1929, however, commuting to work became more popular, choking Moses's parkways with traffic. Each new parkway generated more traffic and created a demand for new roads. Moses subsequently designed the West Side Improvement, opened in 1937, with urban commuters very much in mind.[26]

The West Side Improvement demonstrated Moses's broad vision and feel for a landscape. Carved out of the mudflats, shanty towns, and railroad tracks that lined the Manhattan shore of the lower Hudson River, the West Side Improvement provided a grand entrance to the city. As the motorist drove south toward the city, Moses's biographer Robert Caro explains, the Saw Mill and Henry Hudson parkways offered "mere hints in the midst of a natural setting of the shaping hand of man, mere hints of what the parkway was carrying them toward." A series of bridges, each individually designed and built with stone chosen to blend with local rock formations, carried intersecting roads above the limited-access highway.[27]

Soon after crossing the Harlem River on the Henry Hudson Bridge, the motorist rounded a curve and, suddenly, the George Washington Bridge, with its immense steel towers and thick cables, came into view, announcing the presence of a great city. Now flanked by the terraced lawns of Riverside Park that climbed up toward the stone and brick monuments, mansions, and apartment buildings of the city proper, the motorist could see the spires of the Empire State and Chrysler buildings shimmering in the distance. Looking west, the motorist could enjoy yet another spectacular view, across the Hudson River, of the forest-topped cliffs of New Jersey's Palisades. Ahead, giant ships hugged the city's docks and piers, while others dotted the vast harbor. The spectacular combination of city and nature moved reporters to call the new road "the most beautiful drive in the world."[28]

Anticipating an accelerating postwar flow of population outward, Moses remade New York City for the automobile. "Unfortunately most of the new parkways," Moses told the New York State legislature the year after the West Side Improvement opened, "do not penetrate the city much beyond its borders. *It is now proposed to extend them into the heart of the city.*" Working within a framework established by New York's business elite and fueled by New Deal and postwar funding of public works, Moses laced and punctured New York City with traffic-moving arteries, most without the amenities of the early parkways. Few decisions would have more momentous consequences.[29]

Moses's highways and, later, his contributions to urban renewal accelerated a strategy that had wide support. Although stripped of much of its early twentieth-century insurgency, urban modernism looked to large-scale, technologically rational, and functionally efficient developments to remake the city and improve people's lives. By tearing down tenements, bringing sunlight and air into the city, and easing congestion, postwar urban modernism promised to update the decaying, industrial metropolis. A combination of New Deal idealism and Cold War pressures to address the international embarrassment of urban poverty also encouraged the construction of public housing, especially as the numbers displaced by urban renewal rose. Urban modernism enjoyed considerable success in upgrading housing and transportation, while its open spaces brought sunlight, air, and what one commentator called "the balm of distance" to overcrowded cities.[30]

Business leaders, real estate promoters, construction unions, and civic organizations pursued a strategy that, at its best, sought to preserve central cities as a civic and public space holding the metropolis together. But real estate, retail, and insurance interests focused first and foremost on protecting land values. This put a premium on attracting the middle classes back to the city and led to the fateful strategy of trying to compete with suburbs by making cities more suburban. Public officials argued that improved traffic circulation, combined with more open space and "lessening the nuisance of smoke, dirt and noise," would "capture some of the attractions which pull people in the suburbs."[31]

Urban renewal spread across the country with the passage of the Housing Act of 1949, creating private-public partnerships that provided federal funds to subsidize private development while limiting funds for public housing. Fighting the image of the city as an obsolete locale of poverty, crime, and pollution, urban renewal's tall residential towers set in green spaces beckoned the middle classes, while its spacious expansion of hospitals and universities provided high-paying jobs. Even if middle-class residents did not return to the city, modern freeways and subsidized parking enticed them back as commuters and shoppers.[32]

Punching freeways into the heart of the city thus stood at the center of redevelopment efforts. Even as Moses spread the gospel, a 1944 congressional report sought to allay potential opposition by linking freeways with the earlier parkways. These "new arterial highways may be made," the report explained, "not the unsightly and obstructive gashes feared by some[,] but rather elongated parks bringing to the inner city a welcome addition of beauty, grace and green open space." A more misleading prediction would be hard to imagine, especially after the National Defense Highway Act of 1956 unleashed bulldozers in cities across the nation. By 1973, newspapers were decrying even Moses's West Side Improvement as "an ugly traffic wall between city and river" while, across the nation, freeway revolts stalled new projects.[33]

In theory, accommodating the automobile promised to make cities more like the suburbs. In practice, it undermined the dense, walkable diversity that made cities attractive (and energy-efficient). Championed by Moses and others as liberating, the urban freeway accommodated affluent Americans' love of the automobile. But reliance on the automobile and the accompanying decline of public transportation also placed new burdens on the less affluent urbanites. Elevated or depressed roadways, sprawling cloverleaf off-ramps, parking lots, and gas stations and automobile repair shops created obstacles and dead zones, air and noise pollution, and toxic runoff. For those left in the city, freeways meant noise, dirt, ugliness, and respiratory ailments. "White men's highways," the complaint went, "through black men's bedrooms."[34]

The Meat Ax Eviscerates the Organic City

Caro's Pulitzer Prize–winning biography exaggerates Moses's singular responsibility for policies supported by everyone from the Chamber of

Commerce to the Communist Party. Recent scholars have argued that Moses's efforts to improve transportation, build middle-class housing, facilitate the expansion of universities and hospitals, and provide more parks and green space realized the dreams of New Deal liberals and laid the groundwork for the city's revitalization at the end of the century. But it is difficult to ignore that forcing freeways into the heart of the city eviscerated the urban organism and destroyed people's lives. Perhaps this is what Moses had in mind when he said that you need to "hack your way with a meat ax" through an "overbuilt metropolis."[35]

Caro examined the costs of the construction and operation of a single mile of the Cross Bronx Expressway (CBE), one of the 627 miles of roads Moses built in and around New York City. The CBE cut through a seven-mile stretch of New York City filled with sixty- to eighty-foot-high apartment houses and small businesses. Quite apart from the human lives involved, the CBE presented daunting engineering challenges. At the western end of the route, the freeway climbed out of a valley toward a ridge on top of which sat the Grand Concourse and its constant stream of automobiles. Rising above the Grand Concourse would produce a grade too steep for trucks, so the freeway had to dive beneath it, tunneling into the ridge, inside of which lay a storm sewer, a maze of utility lines, and a branch of the subway system.[36]

To get below the subway, the engineers drove deep into Fordham gneiss, an unusually hard bedrock known for its instability. They had to blast through rock while holding subway, concourse, and sewer and utility lines steady for months. The difficulty led one engineer to recall: "We took the stuff out with a teaspoon." To ensure the dive into this ridge would not itself be too steep, the freeway crossed the main valley in a deep cut, which meant another set of streets to be supported and held steady during the years of construction, including those with elevated rapid transit lines. In all, the CBE project negotiated 113 streets, hundreds of sewer and utility lines, a subway and three railroads, five elevated rapid transit lines, and seven other highways then being built by Moses.[37]

The project spoke to the heroic scale of Moses's ambition and the enormous capacity of the postwar United States. "It is impossible to be unmoved by it, or unconscious of the immense will and effort and talent," as one critic the city's transformation put it. But for all the physical challenges, Caro's story of the one mile focused on what the project meant for the neighborhood of East Tremont, for the people who lived there, and for the larger city. The demolition of fifty-four apartment buildings deprived New York City of significant tax revenues that would have been collected year after year. Those buildings meant even more to the largely Jewish garment industry employees who lived in East Tremont, people who had escaped the slums of Manhattan's Lower East Side but whose limited incomes still circumscribed their options.[38]

The population density of East Tremont, with approximately sixty thousand residents, marked the neighborhood as an "undesirable" location to federal housing officials. Few of the apartment houses had elevators, and their plumbing had begun to deteriorate. Although disparaged as tenements, the apartment buildings nevertheless provided large, airy, sunny rooms; thick, sound-deadening walls; broad windowsills; and courtyards in the back. City-instituted rent control made them affordable, even for families relying on one garment industry income. Modest rents enabled families to save for college tuition. The prospects for similar housing, at similar prices, were not good. Newer apartments rented for much more, and public housing, even if one's income was low enough to qualify, had long waiting lists.[39]

The neighborhood of East Tremont also offered crucial benefits to its residents, beginning with excellent public transportation that brought every job across the city within reach. Stay-at-home mothers valued the wide range of food and clothing shops within walking distance. The neighborhood lacked playgrounds, but Southern Boulevard's generous greensward provided play space for children and benches for their mothers. On the border of the neighborhood, Crotona Park did provide playgrounds, as well as tennis and basketball courts, baseball diamonds, and a swimming pool, all in a setting that residents recalled as safe even at night. Seven movie theaters and, a long walk or a short subway ride away, the Bronx Zoo and the New York Botanical Garden offered entertainment and educational opportunities.[40]

East Tremont sheltered extended families. The older generation could play chess or cards or volunteer at the East Tremont Young Men's Hebrew Association, which also provided day camps and other programs for children. The neighborhood's elementary and junior high schools maintained high standards and offered extracurricular programs, including music lessons. Family connections helped make the neighborhood a safe place. "Everyone seemed to help one another," one resident recalled. "If there was any trouble, everyone would do something for you if they could. They were always coming in and sharing what they had." While East Tremont suffered its share of religious and political divisions, it also enjoyed the informal networks and the continuity and connection that made for street-level public order, trust, and security.[41]

New York City needed neighborhoods such as East Tremont, which took in residents, assimilated them to the city's culture, and accommodated them to one another. A common consciousness developed among neighbors and extended outward to a sense of belonging to the city. The neighborhood served as a staging area where newcomers consolidated their gains, pushed for greater influence in the city, and launched their children into the world. East Tremont and neighborhoods like it also integrated urban populations. Successive waves of German, Irish, and Jewish immigrants moved into East Tremont in the nineteenth century, but some Germans persisted even as the Irish moved in, and some Irish persisted even as Jews moved in.[42]

Beginning in the early 1930s, the neighborhood attracted African American residents. The stability and amenities of the neighborhood forestalled white flight. "People here were good to us," recalled one of the first Black residents. After the war, Puerto Ricans began moving in. By 1950, 18 percent of the neighborhood was nonwhite. The leftist politics of many of East Tremont's Jews may have encouraged a welcoming attitude. But more than anything else, the neighborhood just had too many benefits to abandon. Longtime residents remained and new arrivals enjoyed opportunities for assimilation and integration.[43]

The fullest measure of East Tremont's value to the lives of its residents lies in the history of the East Tremont Neighborhood Association (ETNA). On December 4, 1952, Moses informed the residents they had ninety days to move. Tenants, convinced by sympathetic engineers of the feasibility of an alternative route that would save the threatened apartment buildings, formed an association to challenge Moses's plan. Lillian Edelstein, a thirty-nine-year-old housewife, emerged as the leader of ETNA. Building on the trust and solidarity the neighborhood nurtured, Edelstein mobilized hundreds of housewives to attend multiple meetings of various city agencies. She also raised money for a legal challenge, collecting dollar donations from hard-pressed families.[44]

The protests failed. Once the city took title to the apartment buildings on January 1, 1954, many of the buildings mysteriously lost heat and hot water. Superintendents moved out, and the city neglected the buildings. Most families stayed through the winter, but in the spring more and more began moving out. Older people, fearful but with fewer available options, made up a large percentage of those who stayed. As roofs and top floors began to come down, vacated apartments with boarded-up windows attracted vandals. Construction debris fueled bonfires; debris-filled pits endangered children; and rats multiplied. By November 1954, 90 percent of the residents had left, going where, no one knew.[45]

The rush had been unnecessary. Cost overruns and competing projects delayed completion of the East Tremont section of the Cross Bronx Expressway until 1960. Once underway, however, the construction damaged much of what was left of the neighborhood. Giant wrecking balls, called "skullcrackers," took down the buildings. Then came the explosions of dynamite to level the grade of the freeway. The explosions weakened adjacent buildings, necessitating hasty evacuations. Jackhammers, heavy drills, piledrivers, bulldozers, and other giant earth-moving equipment generated a constant roar. Pulverized debris filled the neighborhood; residents called it "fallout" and despaired of keeping it out of their apartments.[46]

Many of the ten thousand residents who lived closest to the construction site also began moving out. As desperate, impoverished, often African American residents moved in, landlords overcrowded the remaining buildings and skimped on maintenance. Break-ins and vandalism increased, but still residents clung to their neighborhood, adjusting—once the freeway opened—to the cloud of carbon monoxide and the deafening roar arising from the trench. As crime rose, so did insurance premiums. Merchants could no longer make a living. Vandalism and arson ravaged many of the remaining buildings. Newcomers made the best they could of the declining neighborhood.[47]

Urban Reconstruction as Image Making

Postwar urban renewal, however, had never been aimed at residents of central city neighborhoods. It had been aimed at the suburbanizing middle classes. In 1960, investigating the "image of the city," the urbanist Kevin Lynch interviewed suburbanized professionals and managers and learned that they understood little about what an attractive cityscape "can mean in terms of daily delight, or as a continuous anchor for their lives, or as an extension of the meaningfulness and richness of the world." The fifteen citizens he interviewed from suburban Los Angeles reported that the city seemed spread out, formless, without a center, an endless sprawl that produced disorientation and weariness. References to automobiles and highways and the daily battle with traffic dominated the interviews. One interviewee described commuting as taking a long time to get somewhere "and when you got there you discovered there was nothing there, after all."[48]

To Lynch's surprise, even historic Bunker Hill failed to impress itself on the interviewees. Rising from the northwestern corner of downtown Los Angeles, Bunker Hill offered that rare thing in Los Angeles: a walkable neighborhood. It began as an elite residential district in the 1880s and slid into slum status after World War I. As Bunker Hill's density rose and its buildings decayed after World War II, the Department of Building and Safety reported 60 percent of its structures as dangerous; its crime rate at twice the city average; and its cost to the city at seven times what it generated in taxes. Hollywood used Bunker Hill's decaying hotels and mansions (repurposed as cheap rooming houses) as the setting for stories about seedy, dangerous, and deteriorating cities.[49]

In 1956, city officials hung the crucial label "blighted" on Bunker Hill and slated it for urban renewal. Residents and a few activists opposed the plan and delayed its implementation. Like East Tremont, the neighborhood remained viable and provided easy access to downtown via the famous Angels Flight funicular. But the designers of the renewal plan thought little about the current residents. Success would be measured by attracting visitors and generating wealth.[50]

For the suburbanites the project sought to attract, Los Angeles combined a sense of danger and decay with the impression of formlessness noted by Lynch's interviewees. Nationally, critics described downtown LA as an "illusion" that created a "feeling of confusion." The renewal plan therefore made little effort to fit the redevelopment into the existing urban fabric. When the project finally got underway in the wake of the Watts riots of 1965, isolation from surrounding lower-income and minority neighborhoods became a top priority. The city even dismantled the Angels Flight funicular, only to later claim its trademark for marketing and merchandising efforts.[51]

The renewal plan thus sought to project a coherent image of a city for a suburbanizing middle class used to looking at it from the outside. The new Bunker Hill centered on gleaming high-rise towers in a stand-alone project. "The impact of building forms, particularly when the buildings are tall," the city's Design Department explained, "is felt far beyond their immediate surroundings" and "impress themselves upon even the most distant observer." Although "few of the high-rises will be architecturally distinguished," an admiring commentator wrote, "they will establish a convincingly urban downtown profile," generating the crucial image of rational order and predictability, cleanliness, and security.[52]

The Bunker Hill project reflected the eclipse of the remaining public and civic dimensions of urban renewal. Lynch recommended the creation of an open-ended visual order by engaging citizens in the planning process. In contrast, the renewal plan laid out a set of rules to guide developers in the creation of what one commentator called "a great dream city built entirely by private capital." Even as the analogy of community gave way to that of system in ecological science, the Bunker Hill project reimagined the city as a self-regulating system. Like those ecologists who also began to entertain technocratic ambitions, the designers of Bunker Hill embraced cybernetics (the study of how systems use messages to regulate themselves and communicate with other systems). Cybernetics promised to make the Bunker Hill redevelopment a machine that would run of its own.[53]

Early praise for the renewal plan highlighted the flow of traffic, funneling people into commercial opportunities. "Autos will move through the depressed streets into underground parking structures—where passengers will alight and move up stairways to the plaza areas," went one description. Moving sidewalks replaced the disorder and unpredictability of the streets with orderly, machine-like processes "making it an easy matter for shoppers and office tenants to get to the heart of the business center." The master plan would continually update itself, collecting information on the predictable behaviors of urban residents and translating them into new rules and guidelines for future redevelopment.[54]

When the bulldozers began to level the neighborhood in 1966, however, the aura of the machine had already begun to fade. Reversing his earlier optimism about technological innovation, Mumford complained that urban renewal brought not life and sun and air into the city but sterility and "the lowest possibility of active, autonomous, fully sentient life: just so much life as will conform to the requirements of the machine." Urban renewal projects struck the urbanist Jane Jacobs as a means of reducing the sidewalk to a single function, destroying the "moving chaos" that gave cities their vitality. A critic of urban renewal in New York City similarly lamented the loss of the old city's "planless variety" and "incongruity of accident," which was now "threatened by the new homogeneity arising about us everywhere." Such complaints suggested that the city as elaborate machine and predictable system might not be the keys to urban revitalization. If too carefully managed and controlled, the city lost its attractiveness.[55]

Everything Is Connected and the Bulldozer Is at the Center

The loss of urban vitality joined racial tensions, decaying neighborhoods, and disruptive highway and renewal projects in pushing the white middle class toward the suburbs. A desire to live closer to nature, however, also played an essential role in pulling people to the suburbs and had done so since the nineteenth century. Yet suburbanites soon found, to their dismay, that the same bulldozers remaking the city were also threatening the very things they came to enjoy. Expanding cities, President Lyndon Johnson observed in 1965, "reach out into the countryside, destroying streams and trees and meadows as they go." Everywhere Americans looked, the *Saturday Evening Post* reported in 1966, they saw bulldozers engaged in "the rape of the land." Machines disrupted life not just in cities, the *Post* continued, but also in "the suburbs, the countryside, at the seashore." For suburbanites, the landscape writer J. B. Jackson added, the "bulldozer is the very embodiment of ruthless destruction."[56]

Postwar suburbanization brought rapid change to what had once been called the "suburban countryside." At the turn of the twentieth century, the urban edge hosted a range of uses as residents grew their own food, farms persisted, and industry began to move in. By the 1920s, however, "suburban" increasingly implied residence and a search for pristine rather than working nature. Public health officials drained swampy areas, regulated outhouses and wells, and discouraged the keeping of farm animals and the sale of animal products. Land use zoning protected affluent enclaves from factories and shanties. Limits on hunting and fishing and the creation of forest reserves and parks made the urban edge less "countrylike" and more a distinct place: suburbia.[57]

In the postwar period, residential developers nevertheless banked on suburbia's association with unspoiled nature. At the high end of the market, developers advertised "tree-studded" or "wooded" settings. But even Levitt and Sons, the pioneers of cheaper, mass-produced suburban housing, engaged in a great deal of planting and landscaping to sell their product. The mass production of suburban housing, however, brought troubling changes. Residential subdivisions meant fewer farms and smaller forests. Heavy machinery often effaced what remained of the natural landscape, not only eliminating the features (brooks and woods) that gave subdivisions their names, but also destroying much wildlife habitat and fragmenting what remained.[58]

Building on hillsides, wetlands, and floodplains led to soil erosion and flooding. The widespread use of septic tanks contaminated groundwater, spread disease, and led to the eutrophication of lakes (i.e., nutrient-fueled plant growth and decay that killed animals from oxygen depletion). In the 1950s and 1960s, new specialists in federal agencies began to address these issues. Flooding in subdivisions led the U.S. Geological Survey and

Soil Conservation Service to examine urban and suburban hydrology in relation to floods, erosion, and groundwater contamination. The Fish and Wildlife Service coordinated efforts to protect wildlife habitat.[59]

Many troubling developments also arose from the activities of suburbanites themselves and the businesses that followed them to the urban edge. As the density of population and economic activity increased, unrestricted dumping and burning, by both residents and businesses, spread air, water, and land pollution. On suburban Long Island, substances from household detergents to toxic industrial wastes compromised the aquifers that served as both water source and dump. In suburban Los Angeles, waste from oil refining and exhaust from automobile traffic combined with abundant sunshine to produce smog. Public health officials, priding themselves on their handling of organic wastes and infectious disease, only slowly awoke to the dangers of synthetic wastes and chronic, degenerative diseases of the heart and lungs.[60]

Environmental degradation led suburban activists to address the transformation happening in their midst. In 1957, sixty-five retrofitted bombers dumped vast quantities of DDT over large stretches of suburban Long Island. Designed to preserve forests from the gypsy moth, the campaign indiscriminately sprayed woods and gardens, pastures and lawns. Outraged citizens sued federal and local officials who orchestrated the spraying and the related mosquito eradication program. One activist lambasted the officials for launching an "engineering proposition" without regard for "the general ecological situation."[61]

The fragility and vulnerability of nature closest to hand, including their own bodies, led suburban activists to move past the conservation of distant places to focus on their immediate environment. Children led the way in their fascination with the remaining wild spaces near home. As in the earlier movement for municipal housekeeping, women also played a crucial role. The growing anxiety about water and air pollution illuminated the dangers of treating land, water, and air as a free, unregulated commons. The heedless dumping of wastes meant that toxins inevitably found their way into human bodies, a dangerous reminder of the human embeddedness in nature.[62]

Citizen activists seized on the term *environment* to describe and defend these places near to hand. Neither scientists nor specialists, "environmentalists" became generalists who, as municipal housekeepers once envisioned, combined inquiries from chemistry to meteorology to build a discipline of daily life. Local efforts led to municipal recycling, Earth Day clean-ups, lessons on pollution in the public schools, and protests at nuclear plants. Citizen activism, with women often in the lead, also produced national results. The Water Quality Act of 1965 and the Water Pollution Control Act of 1972 regulated the use of septic systems, required local plans for controlling pollutants, and provided federal subsidies for the construction of suburban sewer systems. The National Environmental Policy Act of 1970 required an environmental impact statement for all federal projects and established a Council on Environmental Quality.[63]

The Council on Environmental Quality's first annual report delivered a stinging critique of the mass production of housing. The report underscored the lack of land use regulations as the central issue. "Building and construction practices, together with the quickened pace of development," the report explained, "often end in severe abuse of the land and are ultimately costly to the public." Legal scholars argued for restrictions on property rights as various states experimented with land use regulations in the early 1970s. "Property does not exist in isolation," wrote one legal scholar. "Particular plots are tied to one another in complex ways, and property is more accurately described as being inextricably part of a network of relationships." Such ecological thinking spread quickly, dismissing artificial divides. "We now realize," another scholar argued, that "one parcel of land is inextricably intertwined with other parcels, and that causes and effects flow across artificially imposed divisions in the land without regard for legal boundaries. The land simply cannot be neatly divided into mine and yours."[64]

As the debate over land use regulation suggests, the ecological maxim that "everything is connected" became the watchword of the new environmental movement. But environmentalists did not make every connection and often alienated potential supporters. They ignored criticisms of corporate and absentee ownership of rural land, including those launched by the National Coalition for Land Reform (NCLR) in 1973. The coalition documented the role of the land monopoly in economic inequality and environmental destruction. While the NCLR suffered from its own anti-urban bias, suburban environmentalists showed little interest in productive landscapes, concentrating on a politics of consumption centered on recycling, energy efficiency, and outdoor recreation.[65]

Affluent environmentalists also offended their less fortunate neighbors. Disdaining the "massive, monotonous ugliness" of lower-income subdivisions, they ignored the larger ecological footprint of their own sprawling developments. Such snobbishness pushed many modest homeowners into opposition to land use regulations that threatened to price them out of the suburban market. When a combination of construction and development interest groups defeated national land use regulation in 1974, they benefited from having small property owners in support. Only a few scattered experiments—most notably, in Governor Nelson Rockefeller's New York State—survived. Even there, large developers shaped the regulations.[66]

Anti-sprawl and Its Limits

A critique of urban sprawl stood at the center of the case for land use regulation and offered environmentalists their best opportunity to build an inclusive movement. Sprawl cost everyone—urban, suburban, or rural. Sprawl increased the cost of sewer and water systems and highway construction, much of it subsidized by urban taxpayers for the benefit of suburban commuters. Sprawl also contributed to the hollowing out of central cities, as well as their declining tax bases and soaring debt. Suburban and rural residents suffered, too. By increasing reliance on the automobile and fossil fuels, sprawl generated many forms of pollution, including, it eventually became clear, the greenhouse gasses responsible for climate change. Sprawl also gobbled up open space in and around suburban subdivisions and increased the tax burden on agricultural land, forcing farmers to sell out.[67]

The opposition to sprawl thus provided an opportunity to repair the relationship between city and country. The Congress for the New Urbanism (CNU), the most influential anti-sprawl organization, held that the "metropolis has a necessary and fragile relationship to its agrarian hinterland and natural landscapes." The CNU's founding charter held that "farmland and nature are as important to the metropolis as the garden is to the house." Anti-sprawl activists, including farmers themselves, bemoaned the loss of productive farmland close to city markets. The landscape architect Ian McHarg joined in highlighting the need to preserve agricultural soils in his influential primer *Design with Nature* (1969). Critics also warned about the loss of rural population and rural values and the lost opportunity for metropolitan people to have some "sense of rural life."[68]

Portland, Oregon, conducted the most important and inclusive experiment in addressing sprawl in the late 1970s. Environmentalists there built a regional coalition that included downtown interests and neighborhood activists, as well as suburbanites and farmers. They did so, first, by linking downtown preservation with neighborhood renovation. Then, to encourage infill and protect open space and agricultural land, environ-

mentalists advocated for an urban growth boundary. The Portland experiment enhanced an already livable and beautiful city, limiting sprawl
and encouraging denser, mixed-use development.[69]

Not having experienced extensive sprawl or racial division, however,
Portland provided a relatively easy test. Even so, the effort produced
unintended consequences. The urban growth boundary pushed development beyond the regulated area, even across the state border into Washington State, from which came sixty thousand commuters. The urban
growth boundary also increased land values and thus contributed to gentrification. Protection of agricultural land represented another partial
failure, as affluent residents purchased large tracts, called them farms,
and built McMansions.[70]

The mixed results of the Portland experiment revealed the limitations
of the anti-sprawl movement. Critics of the movement argued that *sprawl*
became a code word for whatever one did not like about suburbs. It is
more accurate to say that the movement did too little to transcend suburban concerns. Suburban critics of sprawl opposed some consequences,
such as traffic, pollution, and loss of open space, but remained indifferent
to others, such as urban disinvestment and concentrated poverty. They
also paid too little attention to rural concerns. Given the pressures sprawl
put on agricultural land values and the tendency of landfills and toxic
waste sites to proliferate in rural areas, rural residents might have proved
strong allies. From the perspective of rural communities suffering from
economic decline, however, urban sprawl might also mean jobs and easier access to metropolitan opportunities. Critics of sprawl showed too
little sensitivity to such matters.[71]

A lack of attention to matters of social justice further limited the reach
of the anti-sprawl movement. While environmentalists worried about the
polluted air and water that all shared, they did less to address the danger
of buried toxic wastes, often localized in factory districts in poorer communities. Beginning in the 1970s, Black activists built an environmental
justice movement to address this neglect. Viewing mainstream organizations with suspicion, the environmental justice movement documented
that the location of landfills, incineration plants, and toxic waste dumps
disproportionately burdened Black districts. But the anti-sprawl movement showed little interest in urban pollution, focusing instead on the
protection of open space, natural habitat, and quality of life in suburban
communities. As an anti-sprawl activist put it dismissively in 1965: "We
can affirm our strong support for pollution [control] and move on."[72]

Above all, the anti-sprawl movement left the debate too much about aesthetics and private consumer choice. Critics of sprawl did too little to highlight its civic costs and its tendency to sort citizens by income and race, provide the affluent with better public goods, and concentrate poverty in cities. The passage of clean air and clean water legislation showed that Americans could be moved by arguments about the public good. An appeal to the public good might have supported massive reinvestment in cities to address racial and economic inequality while also drawing some middle-class suburbanites back to the city and thus complementing efforts to reduce sprawl at the periphery. Ironically, the urbanist William Whyte, who first called public attention to the dangers of sprawl, did have civic issues in mind. Whyte worried about the civic consequences of raising "a whole generation that will never have known the city at all." He insisted that the city remained a "better place to raise children than suburbia," for it "exposes children to all kinds of people, colored and white, young and old, poor and rich."[73]

A robust vision of a just city and region might have overcome the tendency of segregation and jurisdictional fragmentation to discourage coalition building. In 1966, McHarg captured the challenge in arguing that "proponents of nature emphasize preservation, a negative position, one of defense, which excludes positive participation in the real and difficult tasks of creating noble and ennobling cities in fair landscapes." To speak of noble cities in fair landscapes is to recognize the interdependence of all settlements, urban, suburban, and rural. It is also to suggest that our goals need to be something more, and more positive, than simply preservation and sustainability. The building of noble cities amid fair landscapes awaited an alliance across geographic, class, and racial divides to challenge a set of policies that at once sacked neighborhoods and drenched the countryside in poison.[74]

8

The Origins of Urban Sustainability

From City Streets to Home and Garden

In the 1960s, as suburbanites launched an environmental movement, a potentially complementary interest in urban sustainability also emerged. The work of two prominent thinkers—the urbanist Jane Jacobs and the science writer Rachel Carson—suggested the potential for an alliance. From different starting points, Jacobs and Carson each criticized the technocratic project of designing a rational, efficient, and predictable world. In *The Death and Life of Great American Cities* (1961), Jacobs condemned urban renewal as nothing less than "the sacking of cities," while Carson's *Silent Spring* (1962) warned about the danger of using DDT and other chemicals to eradicate pests and disease at the cost of the "contamination of man's total environment."[1]

Jacobs's indictment of urban renewal and Carson's exposure of the heedless spewing of dangerous toxins pointed to the same source: the economic and political power of corporate capital allied with a technocratic elite. In a letter to Jacobs, the urbanist Lewis Mumford condemned "the age of wreckers and exterminators." Even if few others did, Mumford saw the links between urban officials using wrecking balls to renew cities, suburban developers turning fields and forests into prefab communities, and scientific experts deploying toxic sprays to eradicate insects and disease. Taken as two sides of a greater whole, Jacobs and Carson had much to offer those who would rethink the relationship between city and country.[2]

Jacobs and Carson provided a new and indispensable ecological language to critics of the wreckers and exterminators. The ecological sensibility that underlay Jacobs's defense of lively urban streets helped activists defend threatened places. Carson's warnings about the poisons accumulating in our bodies supported campaigns against pesticides and other toxins polluting the suburban countryside. But the great divides made it difficult to see their analyses as parts of a greater whole. The difficulty partly stemmed from their own work. Although Jacobs later rethought the relationship between cities and regions, *The Death and Life* said little about the countryside, even as cities filled with rural migrants. Carson linked her indictment of indiscriminate aerial spraying to the nuclear threat hanging over cities. But she framed her masterpiece in a pastoral mode ("There was once a town in the heart of America where all life seemed to live in harmony with its surroundings," *Silent Spring* begins) that was mismatched with the urban-industrial society she hoped to change.[3]

Jacobs and Carson are not to blame for the failure to build an environmental movement across the divides of city and country. Their work contributed to a larger effort to build such a coalition in the mid-1960s, when the Civil Rights Movement and President Lyndon Johnson's War on Poverty intersected with the growing interest in urban sustainability. As urban activists attempted to undo the damage of postwar metropolitan transformation, they addressed divisions of race and class and began to rethink the relationship between city and country. In the late 1960s and early 1970s, the counterculture interest in alternative technologies and healthy food strengthened the interest in reuniting city and country.[4]

By the mid-1970s, however, the stalling of the Civil Rights Movement and the end of the War on Poverty had transformed the movement for urban sustainability. In the new political atmosphere, the movement's critique of big government projects (urban renewal, freeways) came to the fore. Despite its potential for rethinking the ways we live, the counterculture also contributed to the skepticism about "big government." What one disgruntled planner called Jacobs's "laissez-faire theory of urban renewal" may have found its truest expression in the counterculture; the same might be said of Carson's pastoral dream of harmony with nature. As a counterculture movement rather than a political one, urban sustainability meshed all too easily with a neoliberal indictment of all public action. Increasingly a matter of private efforts focused on home and garden, urban sustainability laid itself open to the charge of being the dream of a white-collar, gentrifying middle class.[5]

Mean Streets: An Anti-urban Sociology

Jacobs's indictment of urban renewal centered on the multiple uses of city streets and sidewalks. In celebrating the "daily ballet" of urban sociability, Jacobs challenged an anti-urban bias with a long history. In the eighteenth century, city life already appeared to undercut the sympathy and fellow feeling celebrated by the economist and moral philosopher Adam Smith and other Scottish moralists. In nineteenth-century cities, explosive population and economic growth, the spread of impersonal market relations, and the influx of immigrants and migrants appeared to further undermine the sympathy that arose spontaneously in families. The landscape architect Frederick Law Olmsted thus designed public parks to "completely shut out the city" and "stimulate and keep alive the more tender sympathies" associated with family life.[6]

In the early twentieth century, settlement house leaders argued that small public and semipublic spaces could overcome suspicion and cultivate new sociable bonds of friendship across class and racial lines. Public interaction in the settlement house and its coffeehouses, gymnasiums, playgrounds, and museums would promote a richer understanding and appreciation of one's fellow urbanites. Sociological research aided this process by undercutting racial and ethnic identities imposed by others. As a young scholar active in the settlement movement, W. E. B. Du Bois extended the settlement strategy to a group who were often ignored: African Americans. He used personal stories in his study *The Philadelphia Negro* (1899) to promote sympathy and fellow feeling across lines of race.[7]

Activists who tried to create a democratic public through City Beautiful spaces, civic forums, and social centers extended the settlements' efforts. The political theorist and activist Mary Parker Follett recognized sociable encounters in city neighborhoods as the building blocks of democratic participation. Rather than a danger, she argued, heterogeneous neighborhoods provided the "stimulus and bracing effect of many different experiences and ideals." But neither the settlement movement nor the efforts to create a democratic public survived intact the American entry into World War I and the drive for "one-hundred-percent" Americanization. Between the wars, few urbanists championed the value of sociability on city streets and in public spaces.[8]

Instead, urban sociologists emerged as the foremost interpreters of urban life in the interwar period. Judging urban relationships to be "empty of content," the ubiquitous Chicago sociologists thought urbanites incapable of forming "bonds of kinship" or even "neighborliness." Adopting the distinction between primary and secondary relations central to the sociological tradition, they treated the spread of secondary relations as the source of social disorder. In contrast to the intimate, primary relations of the family, the city produced only "superficial, transitory, and segmental" secondary relationships. City dwellers fell prey to a "spirit of competition, aggrandizement, and mutual exploitation" and the social pathologies to which it gave rise.[9]

Inspired by their leader, Robert E. Park, the Chicago sociologists used the city as their laboratory, tramping its streets and immersing themselves in its various social worlds. But they looked elsewhere for their intellectual apparatus. Just as they seized on plant ecology as the foundation of their human ecology, they supplemented their theory of primary and secondary relations with the rural sociology of the village communities from which so many of Chicago's immigrants and migrants hailed. They theorized that the collapse of village order under urban conditions of size, density, and heterogeneity produced social disorder and disorganization. Little of value, it seemed, could come from secondary relations on city streets and in public spaces.[10]

Treating village communities as normative, the Chicago sociologists worked with city planners to re-create village conditions in big cities. After meeting with the Chicago sociologists, the sociological director of the Regional Plan of New York and Its Environs urged planners to "discover the physical basis for that kind of face-to-face association which characterized the old village community and which the large city finds it so difficult to re-create." The planner Clarence Perry's neighborhood unit idea, what he called "a scheme of arrangement for a family-life community," promised to make the city safe for primary relations. He scaled the neighborhood unit to support a single elementary school and bounded it by arterial streets to limit cross-neighborhood traffic.[11]

The Williamsburg Houses, opened in Brooklyn in 1937, reflected the new strategy. Set off at a forty-five degree angle from the urban grid, the project boasted of a village character and family atmosphere. As the federal publication advertising the project explained, Williamsburg had once been "a thriving farming community" and now "offered a quiet haven to persons desiring snugness and privacy." Focused inward on enhanced domestic spaces, the project emphasized intimate, familial, primary relations over the superficial, transitory, secondary relations of city streets and public spaces. The influential project set the tone for postwar public housing and urban renewal, sacrificing public gathering places, local streets, and small businesses in favor of sheltered, private, and intimate spaces.[12]

Betty Smith's novel *A Tree Grows in Brooklyn* (1943) questioned the strategy behind the Williamsburg Houses. Set in the period before the bulldozers arrived, the novel follows young Francie Nolan through public encounters in Williamsburg's streets, stores, libraries, and playgrounds. These encounters made Francie feel "a definite part of something, part of a community." When she tried to describe her experiences to a friend from outside the neighborhood, however, she could not get beyond "there's a *feeling*." To explore that feeling, the novel lingers on the public encounters Francie enjoys. Near the end of the story, the narrator laments that "there would be no old neighborhood to come back to" because "the city was going to tear down the tenements." In their place would be "a model housing project," a "place of living where sunlight and air were to be trapped, measured and weighed, and doled out so much per resident."[13]

Despite Smith's critique, an anti-urban sociology continued to shape public housing projects. In the wake of the 1949 National Housing Act's promise of "a decent home and suitable living environment for every U.S. family," no place felt the impact more than East Harlem. Federal funding enabled local agencies to construct sixteen housing projects in the neighborhood during the 1950s, displacing 100,000 low-income residents. Great enthusiasm greeted the projects initially as slums gave way to new buildings with sunlight, air, and modern kitchens. By the late 1950s, however, the "gigantic masses of brick, of concrete, of asphalt," as one reporter put it, with their "planned absence of art, beauty, and taste" seemed only to have "institutionalized our slums." Neighborhood leaders decried the "lack of imagination in planning" and the "failure to recreate the social institutions which have held the old community together."[14]

The social capital of the many relationships that city streets and neighborhoods supported found no place in the anti-urban sociology that shaped public housing. Instead, the focus on privacy at the expense of streets, small commercial enterprises, and public spaces destroyed those relationships. East Harlem had become "a civic and social wasteland," a neighborhood leader complained, because the projects "provided air and plumbing but destroyed the social structure that largely held the community together. Stores disappeared, neighbors scattered, and the traditional gathering places vanished." By 1965, much of the old neighborhood had been leveled, replacing mixed-use streetscapes with single-use superblocks. A quarter of the population, mostly poor parents with young children, lived isolated in the high-rise projects with little connection to the wider city.[15]

Humanizing Human Ecology

William Kirk of East Harlem's Union Settlement tried to convince policy makers of the importance of public interaction and sociability. In 1955, he approached the editors of *Architectural Forum* and found a willing partner in Jane Jacobs. Kirk took Jacobs on tours of East Harlem to see what she recognized as the "social poverty" produced by the projects. Jacobs wrote that Kirk taught her a "way of seeing," of "understanding the intricate social and economic order under the seeming disorder of cities." Cities might not promote intimacy, Jacobs concluded, but in their streets and public spaces they could develop sociable relations that built trust and made it easier to negotiate racial, ethnic, and other differences.[16]

In developing a human ecology that recognized the value of sociability, Jacobs drew on many sources. She learned from protests that decried the modernist remaking of the city as "alienating" and "inauthentic." Jacobs gave expression to the "urban discovery narratives" of antimodernist young professionals who, in gentrifying New York's decaying brownstone districts, sought a middle landscape between "phony" modernist city and "conformist" suburbs. Jacobs also joined and learned from a group of journalists who celebrated the value of diversity, density, and mixed-use districts. As they explored city streets, small public spaces, and sociable encounters, these journalists defended places slated for demolition. Their writings intersected with and complemented the work of "community" ecologists who argued that cooperation should rank with competition as key biological forces. Community ecologists filled scientific journals with examples of instinctive "proto-cooperation," plants and animals modifying the environment and associating with one another in ways that promoted vitality for all.[17]

In 1951, Rachel Carson's three-part profile of the sea in the *New Yorker* explicitly linked community ecology to city life. Carson compared gregariousness among species at the seashore with that of people in the city's public spaces, each expressing an instinct for valuing the presence of others. What happened to one member of the city's "odd community of creatures," Carson wrote, "may well determine what happens" to another member. The *New Yorker* also reviewed the curator Albert Parr's exhibits at the American Museum of Natural History that depicted proto-cooperation in the natural world. Like Carson, Parr urged visitors to link ecology to city life and embrace the "pleasures that do not end with the museum visit but repeat themselves a million times in everyday life beyond its walls."[18]

All these writers provided language to challenge those who thought of slum clearance or highway construction as simple problems. Jacobs urged city planners to recognize the complex order that lay beneath the apparent disorder of city streets. In the place of the planners' bird's-eye views, Jacobs recommended walking and looking at what people did in the city. Both Jacobs and her editor at *Fortune*, William Whyte, developed a human ecology based on observation. "It's very interesting to watch how people manipulate chairs," Whyte's documentary film *The Social Life of Small Urban Spaces* explained. Both Whyte's films and his commentary ("Here you can sort of tell there's going to be a rather aggressive movement") resembled wildlife documentaries on the social rituals of other species.[19]

As urban renewal disrupted the city's fragile order and millions of Black people migrated from the U.S. South to the cities of the North and West, the defense of diverse neighborhoods that contributed to sociability and trust took on special force. The Black novelists Richard Wright and Nella Larson dramatized how racial segregation frustrated the development of sociability and trust. "We live here and they live there," the fictional Bigger Thomas fumes in Wright's *Native Son* (1940). "We black and they white. They got things and we ain't. They do things and we can't. . . . Half the time I feel like I'm on the outside of the world peeping in through a knothole in the fence." Segregation could sour intraracial relationships, as well. In Larson's novel *Quicksand* (1928), the migrant Helga Crane initially gives herself up to the "miraculous joyousness of Harlem." But ultimately segregation leads her to "lose confidence in the fullness of her life." Feeling "shut in, trapped," she "drew away from those contacts which had so delighted her."[20]

Jacobs, like the gentrifying middle class, romanticized city neighborhoods. She said little about poverty, and nothing about blockbusting, firebombing, and other expressions of racial tension. In addressing the challenges of East Harlem, however, Jacobs did acknowledge the role of discrimination. Moreover, her recommendations on physical design, recommending low-rise, walk-up buildings to be mixed in with the high-rises, undercut segregation. Orienting housing projects outward, toward busy streets, instead of inward would support small commercial establishments, provide safety and interest, encourage public encounters, and dramatize interdependence. Poor neighborhoods, Jacobs concluded, needed the "highly communal and cooperative" interactions that city streets and public spaces made possible.[21]

Confronting the Concrete Monsters

The defense of urban sociability also informed the growing opposition to freeway construction. Protesters rebelled against "freeways that barge along in a straight line, knocking down everything in their path," slashing "great gashes through residential or business districts." Beginning in the mid-1950s, freeway revolts spread to dozens of cities until the pace of construction slowed in the early 1970s. Although not always successful, freeway revolts broke the postwar consensus about automobiles and freeways. Where freeway projects threatened cross-class and cross-racial constituencies, they could be stopped. The participation of civil rights and environmental activists and the veto power of local political officials added to the chances for success. Although the National Defense Highway Act of 1956 provided massive funding for freeways, other federal legislation provided crucial assistance in the revolts. The Federal Highway Act of 1962 required state road departments to cooperate with local governments and provide relocation assistance for families and businesses. The creation of the Department of Transportation in 1966 increased supervision over highway engineers and empowered voices in favor of multimodal transportation strategies.[22]

Where proponents acted fast and opposition remained scattered, however, freeways still gutted cities. In 1968, Miami's central Black neighborhood, Overtown, known as the Harlem of the South for its cultural and social capital, disappeared under multiple freeways, a four-level interchange, and urban renewal projects. Business and political leaders, tourism advocates, local newspapers, even the local Urban League all united behind the project. No Civil Rights Movement yet existed in the city to stop it, and no state law gave local officials veto power. Proceeding without public hearings, the project displaced more than ten thousand residents, swelling Miami's expanding second ghetto on the northwestern edge of the city.[23]

Freeway opponents, however, steadily gained new tools. The Federal Highway Act of 1968 required adequate relocation housing prior to property acquisition. In 1970, the National Environmental Policy Act (requiring environmental impact statements) and the Federal Clean Air Act provided new avenues for legal challenges. In 1971, anti-freeway activists launched the Highway Action Coalition (HAC) at the national level to stop freeways, discourage suburban sprawl, and promote mass transit. Targeting the highway lobby's strongest congressional supporters, the HAC also went after the federal Highway Trust Fund. The Federal Highway Act of 1973 opened the Trust Fund to mass-transit projects.[24]

Baltimore provides an example of how even the most powerful freeway advocates could be stymied. In 1944, Baltimore hired New York's much esteemed Robert Moses to develop a freeway plan. Moses recommended an east-west "mid-city" freeway that split the heart of Black Baltimore. He insisted that a "modern city artery must be built for every man, woman and child *on every conceivable errand*." Business leaders embraced Moses's plan as a "powerful force toward restraining decentralization and rehabilitating blighted areas." The freeway would displace nineteen thousand people and gut a neighborhood of theaters, churches, and schools that provided the foundation for Black civil rights and electoral efforts. Moses nevertheless dismissed "slum areas" as a "disgrace to the community," adding that "the more of them that are wiped out the healthier Baltimore will be in the long run."[25]

Over the next twenty years of shifting plans, the proposal to run a freeway through the heart of Black Baltimore remained the one constant. The project stalled for lack of funds until the mid-1950s. Here as elsewhere, the 1956 interstate act generated new and more ambitious plans. In 1961, a new plan included additional freeways that threatened white working-class areas and required a huge downtown interchange and a fourteen-lane bridge over the Inner Harbor. Four thousand dwellings and many small businesses would be cleared in districts judged to be blighted. Large crowds attended a series of public meetings, and sentiment grew for no freeways at all. Crucially, Baltimore's home rule charter stipulated that only the City Council could condemn property and determine whether projects meshed with the city's master plan.[26]

In 1966, with delays exasperating federal officials and nothing yet built, the Baltimore chapter of the American Institute of Architects called for more environmentally sensitive roads. This led to a new study from an "urban design concept team." Although intended to replace one set of experts with another, the urban design team did not turn out that way. Professional architects met with neighborhood residents in a process that resembled Mumford's regional survey. Residents gained technical understanding while the experts gained perspective. After six months, as the urban design team questioned whether it was possible "to lace tubes of traffic through vital parts without unduly disturbing the living organism of the city," state officials curtailed the meetings with residents. But now newspapers picked up the cause. "'Blending' a six or eight-lane highway into the fabric of Baltimore," one reporter put it, "is about as promising an assignment as 'blending' a buzz saw and a Persian rug."[27]

Even a scaled-down plan met with determined opposition bolstered by an energized Civil Rights Movement. Baltimore's new Relocation Action Movement (RAM) stepped up organizing efforts and united middle- and working-class Black people against freeways. Critics expressed outrage that the heart of Black Baltimore, long slated for demolition and left in limbo, had become an "environmental wasteland" of "boarded up houses, rats, and fire department sirens." Documenting that between 1951 and 1964 89 percent of displaced Baltimoreans came from low-income, Black areas, RAM made fair replacement value for Black homeowners a key lever in the fight. Relocation provided another lever, as activists charged that city officials were unprepared to deal with the displaced.[28]

By the end of the 1960s, white working-class homeowners in threatened neighborhoods had added their voices to the opposition. The Movement against Destruction (MAD), a biracial coalition of more than thirty Baltimore neighborhoods, reflected citizens' growing technical understanding of freeway planning and their long and painful experience with urban redevelopment. Mobilizing its own experts to confront and confound highway engineers, MAD charged that planners "do not have a corner on the 'imagination market'" and "citizens have a right to make their opinions known." The coalition first opposed the east-west freeway, then came out against all the proposed freeways. "There is a growing realization that expressways are being built in cities not for the sake of the people who live there," MAD argued, "but for the sake of cement, tire, oil, automobile, and other private interests."[29]

In the end, however, Baltimore's successful freeway revolt depended on the courts rather than public deliberation. Opposing the seizure of property for a "public use," MAD questioned whether freeways served an appropriate public purpose, not least because such projects destroyed crucial public spaces used by all. Using new federal legislation, MAD filed various lawsuits to protect parks, historic districts, and air quality. Ultimately, only one north-south freeway cut through the city. Baltimore never completed the east-west freeway. But long uncertainty about its future and the construction of a two-mile stretch of the "highway to nowhere" left the heart of Black Baltimore badly damaged. Cross-class and multiracial alliances made a difference in Baltimore. But the shift to the courts cut short a valuable interracial conversation about freeway planning, urban inequality, and the protection of neighborhoods and public spaces.[30]

Ecological Thinking and the Struggle for Public Space

A freeway revolt in New Orleans also deployed the new thinking about human ecology. In 1958, the New Orleans City Planning Commission unveiled plans for a six-lane elevated riverfront freeway (first suggested by the ubiquitous Moses in 1946) that skirted the city's famed French Quarter. Advocates argued that the freeway would revitalize the city commercially and relieve traffic congestion in the French Quarter. The promise of reduced traffic led the French Quarter's preservation community to support the highway if it could be built at grade level. Initially, only scattered voices warned that "the automobile is a monster" and that accommodating it would turn the French Quarter into a "slum."[31]

A preexisting lack of connection between the riverfront and the French Quarter dampened opposition. After the Civil War, the municipality had provided land at the riverfront to entice railroads into the city, establishing a barrier between neighborhood and river. During the Progressive era, the city added massive warehouses, further commercializing the riverfront and severing it from the French Quarter. In the 1950s, the Army Corps of Engineers built a twelve-and-a-half-foot-high floodwall, creating an even starker border between city and river.[32]

In 1962, however, geologists warned that the shifting river was undermining the riverfront structures. Demolition of those structures created an opportunity to reconnect city and river. While the federal Bureau of Roads still pushed the project, the new interest in human ecology and the growing national revolt against freeways galvanized local opposition. Planners and engineers, Jacobs argued, found it easier to deal with the "simple needs of automobiles" than the "complex needs of cities," conflating mobility and vitality. In 1965, a public meeting to discuss the freeway attracted seven hundred people who called for alternative routes and efforts to reconnect the river to the city.[33]

As the controversy unfolded, the Vieux Carré Commission (VCC), the state-sanctioned preservation agency, asserted its right to oversee any construction involving the French Quarter. Since its creation in 1936, the commission had focused only on the built environment and ignored the river. But reflecting the new human ecology, the VCC now claimed the riverfront as an integral part of the French Quarter. The preservationists sought federal allies and found one in Secretary of the Interior Stewart Udall, who considered designating the entire area a National Historic Landmark. Highway proponents countered that the freeway would protect the French Quarter from commercial development extending from the riverfront.[34]

In January 1966, the federal highway administrator approved the original project. Local opponents mobilized national allies, generated debate in Congress, and combed federal transportation and preservation law for ways to stop the road. As the fight took shape, the local Bureau of Government Research (BGR), a pro-development watchdog group, joined the fray. Initially interested only in minimizing the freeway's impact, the BGR began to worry that the noise and shadow of the freeway might harm the French Quarter and limit riverfront development. The freeway, the BGR argued, might upset the "tout-ensemble," the "sum total effect, buildings plus environment." While embracing the new ecological language, the BGR hoped to capitalize on the city's charm by creating a landscape of consumption that would boost tourism. Meanwhile, new plans to extend the roadway into the affluent Garden District broadened the opposition.[35]

In the end, New Orleans's freeway fighters won a partial victory. In January 1969, after defeating a compromise proposal for a grade-level freeway, opponents attended a public meeting to press for the cancellation of the whole project. The decision fell to President Richard Nixon's Secretary of Transportation John Volpe, a strong advocate of freeways. After gauging opinion in the city, however, Volpe cancelled the project, citing the BGR's case for economic development (although the decision may also have signaled declining federal aid to cities). While citizens gained access to the riverfront for the first time in generations, commercial development turned the waterfront into part theme park, part tourist trap. The mostly white, middle-class activists also failed to prevent another freeway from plowing through an African American neighborhood along Claiborne Avenue, destroying a stand of oak trees and a public space that hosted the city's largest African American Mardi Gras parade.[36]

The interest in economic revitalization that drove the BGR's intervention into New Orleans's freeway fight also shaped the struggle over Seattle's publicly owned Pike Place Market. In 1963, Seattle's Central Association (CA) of downtown business leaders put forward a revitalization plan focused on the area around the public market. Determined to attract suburban consumers, the CA proposed to remake the downtown with an eye to "improved accessibility," an effort anchored by "major parking garages." The public market would be demolished and replaced with an upscale hotel, apartment complex, office tower, and hockey arena. Escalators, all-weather protection, and canopies over sidewalks would entice suburban shoppers to an updated retail complex.[37]

The CA described its 1963 plan as crucial to sustaining the city's future in a suburbanized metropolis. In the same year, however, the Seattle Art Museum hosted an exhibition that offered a different vision of sustainability. Intersecting with a local freeway fight, the exhibition, "Mark Tobey and the Seattle Public Market," featured the local painter Mark Tobey, who described his paintings as a political act in favor of those "who live in awareness of man's relationship to nature, and who cherish the values of the past as a vital part of the present." The exhibition highlighted the public market's blend of nature and commerce. A public space shaped by citizens themselves, the public market supported a city that was a living but endangered organism. "Our homes are in the path of freeways," Tobey wrote. "Old landmarks, many of rare beauty, are sacrificed to the urge to get somewhere in a hurry."[38]

Opened in 1907, Pike Place Market brought urban consumers face to face with rural producers. The city constructed the stalls at public expense and rented them for a nominal price to local retailers. Only those who raised the food could sell at the market; farmers rose early to bring produce into the city. In the 1910s, the city added substantial market buildings. The city discouraged chain retailers, kept rents low, and eased standards for renovation and housekeeping to aid small retailers. Later improvements eased access for farmers' trucks.[39]

Pike Place Market also represented successful regionalism, an integration of urban and rural communities. Market produce came from the Kent Valley, an area of rich farmland stretching south of the city, tended by Italian and Japanese immigrants. World War II, however, brought the internment of the Japanese farmers. Then, after the war, supermarkets stopped buying locally, instead trucking in produce from consolidated farms in California. Meanwhile, small farm operations fell by half as zoning changes increased land values, pricing out those farmers who remained. Federal policies, from freeways and mortgage insurance to defense contracts, helped cover the rich soils of the Kent Valley with residential subdivisions and aerospace factories.[40]

By 1963, Pike Place Market had hit bottom. But Tobey and his "Friends of the Market" saw it as an "indicator species" of a broken relationship between city and country. Arguing that a revitalized market could again connect the city to the region, they launched a debate over alternative futures that again resembled Mumford's regional survey. Some defended the market for its gritty charm, its architecture, its sights and smells, and the pleasures of local produce, extolling the sense of place that came from the area's salvage and surplus stores, rooming houses, and small hotels. Others went further, arguing that the market nurtured a set of relationships built up over time. In the sociable exchanges between neighbors and retailers, the market promoted the trust, solidarity, and security that arose from knowing where goods came from and who produced them.[41]

But the Central Association only saw decay. Anxious to turn downtown into a pedestrian-friendly set of malls, the CA applied to the federal government for urban renewal funds. In 1964, a CA report described the "potential hazards to public health, welfare, and safety" at the public market. The area's "grunge"; its oddities and idiosyncrasies; and its gritty, run-down character seemed to point to everything wrong with the market. Neither safe nor, presumably, suburban enough for middle-class women, the market attracted the wrong kind of shoppers. The crucial designation of blight promised to unlock federal funds.[42]

Meanwhile, middle-class women, planning professionals, and, later, students and counterculture activists joined the opposition to the redevelopment plan. The CA's own survey revealed that women enjoyed the public market more than men, comparing it to the great markets of Europe and lauding its convenience over the supermarket. In 1968, a local activist nominated the public market for the National Register of Historic Places, citing its "unique living heritage" and its "sociological mixture of people." The nomination asserted that the "process of food preparation and the availability of local produce sold by the farmers who grew it" became part of the "dramatic experience of people acting out their daily existence through face-to-face involvement, in contrast to the sterile, dehumanizing environment that has grown to be typical of much of our urban world."[43]

In the late 1960s, as the market's defenders reached out to civil rights and environmental activists, the protests linked defense of the public market to broader criticism of postwar metropolitan development. Concerns about democracy, social justice, citizenship, and diversity all become more prominent. As anti-redevelopment protesters marched on City Hall in 1969, Seattle passed its first open-housing ordinance. In that context, the public market gained in stature as a place where races, ages, and classes mixed. During public hearings on the redevelopment plan in 1969, a University of Washington professor presented a diagram, modeled on ecological studies, showing how goods and money moved through the market. In contrast, the supermarket embodied the lack of diversity or sense of place, as well as the industrialized food system and the dysfunctional relationship between city and country.[44]

In 1971, a successful ballot initiative created a preservation district of seven acres covering the whole area. The victory, again, was partial. As in New Orleans, growing concerns about economic decline and the effort to attract tourist dollars shaped the resolution. Just months before the vote, the renowned architectural critic Ada Louise Huxtable wrote that efforts to preserve historic landmarks "are not the work of little old ladies playing house, but of unsentimental business interests." She marveled how long it took Seattle's business leaders to recognize the market as a valuable tourist attraction. "What greater pleasure," she concluded, "than fresh salmon and strawberries with a view of the Sound?"[45]

Environmental Reform as Participatory Democracy

The concern with attracting tourist dollars in New Orleans and Seattle reflected tightening economic conditions and declining federal support for cities. But for as long as it lasted, President Johnson's War on Poverty helped to link sustainability efforts to racial and social justice and to participatory democracy. The War on Poverty served as a partial counterweight to federal policies that promoted suburbanization and shored up urban real estate while leaving central city neighborhoods to fend for themselves. Unwilling to launch a major effort at structural change or economic redistribution, the architects of the War on Poverty banked on the idea that civic participation and political power would enable the poor to secure government aid to help them help themselves. The Economic Opportunity Act of 1964 thus mandated "maximum feasible participation" of citizens in the War on Poverty.[46]

Although never adequate to the need, the War on Poverty enabled minority citizens to direct local programs and demand that municipal officials address social needs. Federally funded community action projects provided the vehicle. Paralleling changes in the Civil Rights Movement, the community action projects shifted attention from integration to self-help and self-determination, improving communities from the inside. As grassroots mobilization arose in central city neighborhoods, community action projects launched comprehensive efforts to address the physical and social costs of urban renewal, deindustrialization, infrastructure decay, mounting pollution, and demographic change.[47]

The city of Cleveland, a pioneer in the antidelinquency programs that provided the first model for the War on Poverty, illustrates the War on Poverty's potential. As in other cities, federal funds employed Black activists and helped them develop the political skills of mobilization and negotiation. Carl Stokes, who grew up in a Cleveland housing project, rose through the ranks and, in 1967, won election as the first African American mayor of a major city. The following year, Stokes used federal poverty funds to create Neighborhood Opportunity Centers. The initiative enabled him to hire the young Black scholar and activist Bailus Walker to direct the centers. Pursuing a doctorate in public health, Walker linked poverty to environmental conditions. Pointing to smoke and carbon dioxide, abandoned automobiles, and rats, Walker concluded that "the environment of the urban ghetto child does more than depress him, injure him, or otherwise overwhelm him; it kills him as well."[48]

Cleveland's neighborhood centers organized citizens to demand attention to these hazards. By carrying a rat-infested couch to City Hall and laying dead rats on the steps, activists dramatized the larger issues of segregation, racism, unemployment, and concentrated poverty. In June 1969, Stokes visited one of Cleveland's central ghetto neighborhoods to enlist the residents' help in leveraging a federal grant to control rats. He explained that, beyond paying for rat poison, the money would train city workers and fund community education efforts. Federal funds also enabled activists to rehabilitate abandoned buildings, open clinics and preschools, plant community gardens, and publish community newspapers.[49]

Stokes repeatedly testified in Washington, DC, in support of War on Poverty programs. One of those programs, Model Cities, sought to coordinate the actions of multiple federal agencies and link physical rehabilitation to an attack on the social and political causes of poverty. "If we devour our countryside as though it were limitless, while our ruins—millions of tenement apartments and dilapidated houses—go unredeemed," President Johnson proclaimed in introducing Model Cities legislation in 1966, we will "become two people—the suburban affluent and the urban poor, each filled with mistrust and fear one for the other." Making our "great urban areas" into "masterpieces of our civilization," Johnson concluded, will require "an effort larger in scope, more comprehensive, more concentrated than any that has gone before."[50]

The nearly $1 billion Model Cities program reached more than sixty cities, large and small. One of the first projects focused on Seattle's Central District, a multiethnic area that included the heart of Black Seattle. Linking housing, recreation, and public health, the project conducted experiments in cooperative housing, small parks and open space, and mixed-use districts. One reporter aptly called it a "concentrated attack upon the ills of the total environment." Black activists insisted that the project should not just "decorate the neighborhood," but that "equally important will be the people's ability to earn sufficiently to maintain the improved property." By providing residents with work experience, training in public health, assistance in preparing for civil service exams, and "a career ladder," the project turned workers into "change agents." The project prided itself on moving people "from the status of ghetto-dwellers to full citizens of the city."[51]

The Central District project anticipated many of the elements of what we now call urban sustainability. They included building a local economy, developing innovative housing designs, and promoting public transit. But it did so with a strong focus on social and racial justice. Rejecting the designation of "blight" as prelude to slum clearance, the project worked to preserve and improve existing housing while securing low-income residents' access to it through alternative sources of mortgage financing. In yet another echo of Mumford's regional survey, innovative designs, from garden apartments and clustered housing to more open space and neighborhood parks, emerged from the grassroots. The project also sought to broaden transit options for a neighborhood with few automobile owners.[52]

The Central District project encouraged an ecological understanding of the city as more than the sum of its parts. "You can't build up health unless you can improve living conditions, and housing," the coordinator of the health effort insisted, and secure "improvement in the employment field." Treating rats as an indicator species, activists used them to focus attention on improper garbage disposal, overcrowding, burned-out structures, neglected properties, and absentee landlords. The project also trained participants for jobs in the city's Health Department and established a nonprofit company to oversee cleanup efforts.[53]

In the early 1970s, the development of a distinctively Black ecology and the associated movement for environmental justice added another set of potential allies to the movement for urban sustainability. Reflecting the experiences of African Americans, Black ecologists demanded redress for "the rats which attack their children, the lead in the peeling paints, which poison their babies, the decrepit housing conditions, the inadequate nutrition, and lack of open space." The first Earth Day, in 1970, included some activities focused on environmental justice. The federal Environmental Protection Agency, as well as some environmental organizations and unions, also took up the cause of environmental justice in cities. Protests centered on the location of landfills, incinerators, waste treatment facilities, and power plants in minority communities.[54]

Union activists added to the democratic agitation for environmental reform. Indeed, in the twenty-five years that followed World War II, labor unions stood in the vanguard of environmental politics. Often criticized for caring only about the wages, hours, and working conditions of its members, organized labor took up the issues of air and water pollution before the mainstream environmental movement did. Raising questions about public health and social justice, labor leaders reached constituencies that mainstream environmentalists did not. Environmental concerns even led workers to challenge management prerogatives. Steelworkers questioned the effects of their industry on air pollution; loggers objected to the unrestrained destruction of forests; and autoworkers criticized the environmental damage done by the internal combustion engine.[55]

Linking their status as workers to their roles as citizens, unionists prodded elected officials to address environmental issues. In 1948, in the wake of the "killer smog" in Donora, Pennsylvania, the United Steelworkers (USWA) urged local and federal officials to investigate and, when that failed, launched its own investigation. Once federal investigations of air and water pollution began, officials from the American Federation of Labor-Congress of Industrial Organizations (AFL-CIO) helped organize national conferences and testified before Congress. In 1961, even before the publication of *Silent Spring*, an AFL-CIO official warned Congress of the risks of "new and exotic industrial wastes." In 1963, as the first Clean Air Act worked its way through Congress, another AFL-CIO official told Congress that union members had "a vital interest in protecting the purity of the air around us, just as they have an interest in protecting the purity of America's water supply." In 1969, a USWA official testified in favor of stronger air pollution controls, insisting that his members *"want clean air."*[56]

In the late 1960s and early 1970s, environmentalists and labor unions worked together to pass key pieces of legislation. In 1970, they included the National Environment Policy Act and the Occupational Safety and Health Act. Working closely with environmentalists, the Oil, Chemical, and Atomic Workers Union (OCAW) linked hazardous substances in the workplace to pollution in the wider environment. When the OCAW struck against Shell Oil in 1973, environmentalists rallied in support. "Organized Labor must emphatically support environmental cleanup efforts," OCAW's president responded, "and must never get into the position of opposing such efforts on the grounds of economic hardship."[57]

While unions sometimes opposed preservation efforts that endangered jobs, two major lumber workers' unions in the Pacific Northwest supported wilderness preservation in defiance of their employers. Some forest lands, a union representative told a group of U.S. senators in 1958, should be protected as part of "a wilderness preservation system for the good of all people." In 1970, a USWA official testified to Congress in favor of stronger air pollution standards, stating: "If it is necessary to lose 300 or 400 jobs to save the lives of 3,000 or 4,000 people, then that is what is going to happen."[58]

Under the leadership of Walter Reuther, the United Automobile Workers (UAW) made the connection to urban sustainability explicit. Reuther first proposed the Model Cities program to President Johnson in 1965, describing it as "an urban TVA to stop erosion of cities and people." At a conference on clean water in 1965, Reuther expressed his hope for the "beginning of a massive mobilization of citizens . . . , not only for clean water, but also for cleaning up the atmosphere, the highways, the junkyards and the slums and for creating a total living environment worthy of free men." In 1967, another UAW official testified to Congress in favor of emission controls, arguing that autoworkers were "first and foremost American citizens" who had "to breathe the same air and drink and bathe in the same water" as everyone else.[59]

In 1970, Reuther demanded that environmental issues become part of labor-management negotiations. "I think the environmental crisis has reached such catastrophic proportions," he told the press, that "the labor movement is now obligated to raise this question at the bargaining table in any industry that is in a measurable way contributing to man's deteriorating living environment." In the same year, the UAW joined several environmental organizations in a letter to Congress calling for "air pollution control standards so tough they would banish the internal combustion engine from autos within the next five years." Eager to "guarantee every American a safer, cleaner atmosphere by 1975," UAW officials spoke of "auto free zones" in cities and retooling the industry for mass transit.[60]

The UAW led other unions in advocating for the larger community. All other issues are pointless, a UAW official told Congress in 1969, "if we continue to poison and destroy the life supports of the world." He continued: "Better we tear the factories to the ground, abandon the mines, plug the petroleum holes and fill the fuel tanks of our cars with sugar than continue this doomsday madness." A year later, a USWA official told the same subcommittee that his own rank and file blasted him for compromising on pollution controls that might cost jobs. "We felt we weren't around just for the purpose of negotiating wages, hours and working conditions," he explained, "but we must concern ourselves with the affairs of not only our members but the people in the community."[61]

Neoliberalism, Flexism, and the Decline of Political Activism

Toward the end of the 1960s, however, the rightward shift in American politics had begun to erode support for environmental reform. The fate of Model Cities signaled the shift. In 1971, as Seattle's successful Model Cities project spread to other neighborhoods, the administration of President Richard Nixon chose Seattle as one recipient of its "planned variations" program. Like the community block grants that soon followed, the planned variations program advanced Nixon's decentralizing new federalism. Reducing federal oversight and grassroots mobilization, the new initiative worked through established local governments rather than neighborhood activists. This pleased mayors, City Councils, planners, engineers, and business and civic leaders who had never embraced grassroots activism. The emphasis also shifted from social activism to brick-and-mortar projects such as convention centers, hotels, and commercial infrastructure that were more pleasing to business interests and middle-class voters.[62]

In 1974, the Housing and Community Development Act put an end to Model Cities. Despite its successes, critics linked Model Cities to the civil disturbances of the long, hot summers (the program's initial designation, Demonstration Cities, had been rejected as implying capitulation to urban unrest). As white suburbanites wrote off the city and tax revolts spread, the new law prohibited the use of community block grant funds for social services. As an appeal to anti-tax, anti-urban homeowner populism became crucial to electoral success, urban spending declined under both Democrats, beginning with President Jimmy Carter, and Republicans. Nixon's new federalism thus helped to sever the link between the movement for urban sustainability and the struggle for social and racial justice.[63]

Nixon's new federalism and the decline in urban spending also signaled the rise of a new neoliberal consensus, spreading skepticism about government action and an exaggerated faith in markets. The triumph of neoliberalism coincided with a new regime of capitalist accumulation, each reinforcing the other. Over the course of the 1970s, new marketing strategies combined with larger changes in corporate behavior to give rise to a new strategy known as flexible accumulation. Saturated mass markets, a series of oil shocks, and new competition, especially from the reviving economies of Western Europe and East Asia, led to declining profits and undermined the old regime of mass production. The new conditions demanded corporate flexibility in product lines, supply chains, and labor relations. Assembly line, one-size-fits-all mass production gave way to niche markets and batch production, outsourcing, subcontracting, temporary and nonunion labor, and, in places, a return to cottage industry and sweatshop conditions. Just-in-time inventory, containerization, air freight, computer design, and digitalization all served the needs of mobile, flexible capital.[64]

Neoliberalism and flexism made for a toxic mix, as corporate leaders and neoliberal politicians branded federal regulations, union contracts, and the social safety net costly luxuries. Corporate leaders also opposed new environmental legislation and challenged existing regulations in the courts. Meanwhile, mobile capital left aging, union-dominated cities for suburbs, the Sunbelt, and overseas, always shopping for tax breaks, subsidies, and cheaper labor. As capital became more mobile, metropolitan elites willing to link the fates of their enterprises to the broader prosperity of their regions became scarcer. Such elites once championed the infrastructure of water and sewers, transit and ports, and parks and parkways that made the metropolis a prosperous, healthful, and invigorating place. But in the 1970s, civic and business leaders limited their local concerns to the downtown core and associated corporate and cultural assets. New investment in aging factory and residential districts diminished to a trickle, accelerating the growth of inequality.[65]

In the 1990s, as metropolitan leaders struggled to compete in a global economy, regionalism made a partial comeback. The contrast between robust regional economies and faltering urban cores recommended regional cooperation, especially on education, housing, and transportation. In 1999, Chicago's Mayor Richard M. Daley argued: "We, the city and the suburbs, are all in this together. Only by working together will we be able to tackle the big issues." But the response of one suburban mayor suggested the obstacles: "The guy who wrote this [the regional plan Daley touted] must be from Moscow. These people are centralized planners, and they are not on our side." Alongside the jurisdictional war between city and suburbs, the withdrawal of key firms to the suburbs and the takeover of local firms by out-of-town corporations frustrated the drive for regional cooperation. Moreover, top-tier corporate leaders, focused on global matters, tended to sit out the effort.[66]

Meanwhile, the rise of flexism put organized labor on the defensive. In 1976, the UAW convened the Working for Environmental and Economic Justice and Jobs conference. A last gasp of insurgent sustainability efforts, the conference brought together hundreds of civil rights, labor, and environmental activists to address the interrelationships among racial, economic, and environmental justice. In the face of corporate opposition to environmental regulation that one conferee called "environmental blackmail," discussion centered on a federal jobs program to promote renewable energy. But already stagflation, reduced public spending, and the corporate assault on organized labor had changed the political situation. With growth and prosperity, or even steady employment, no longer assured, working people proved more receptive to the corporate indictment of environmentalism as a job killer.[67]

By the early 1990s, civil rights, labor, and environmental activists had gone their separate ways. Left to themselves, minority communities faced difficult choices as a once promising coalition splintered. When the First National People of Color Environmental Leadership Summit convened in 1991, labor unions—their ranks decimated over the previous decade—played little role. In the same year, during a struggle over the Greater Detroit Resource Recovery Facility (the "Detroit Incinerator"), the Black mayor (Coleman Young) and Black City Council of the financially strapped city found few allies among white, middle-class environmentalists. The city's sale of the incinerator to a financial services subsidiary of the tobacco giant Philip Morris helped Detroit pay down its massive budget deficit. But the now privatized incinerator saddled Black residents of Detroit with a host of health issues as it processed waste from white, wealthy suburbs.[68]

With the shifting national context, some activists interested in urban sustainability turned to local politics. Organizing at the neighborhood level, they kept environmental issues alive but focused less on metropolitan and regional perspectives. Others turned away from politics entirely in favor of a counterculture sustainability centered on home and garden. In rural communes as well as urban neighborhoods, counterculture environmentalism addressed issues of food, shelter, and energy, with an eye to the dangers of monocultures, deteriorating soils, and toxic chemicals.[69]

At its best, the counterculture suggested what a combination of the insights of Jacobs and Carson might bring. Challenging the separation of production and consumption, the focus on home and garden turned the household from a consumer retreat into a center of production. It also rejected the alienation, gender segregation, and environmental costs of the bedroom suburb. The attention to day-to-day practical issues even addressed the great divide between city and country. "The final barrier to alternative agriculture," a counterculture activist explained, is the "isolation . . . between urban and rural cultures." The "decaying urban condition," he concluded, "has its origins in the decaying rural condition."[70]

Counterculture activists raised chickens and rabbits, installed solar collectors, built rooftop and backyard gardens, dug aquaculture ponds, and tended bees. They religiously composted, even experimenting with composting toilets, to address the metabolic rift. Separating technology from technocracy, the counterculture challenged the pessimistic belief that human intervention inevitably destroyed nature. As environmental concerns faded from political debate, counterculture activists preserved ecological consciousness and combined it with a do-it-yourself bravado that emphasized human ingenuity and potential.[71]

The *Whole Earth Catalog*, first published in 1968, offered "access to tools" for this regeneration. The brainchild of the ecologically educated Stewart Brand, the *Whole Earth Catalog* originated in his LSD-inspired belief that an image of the whole Earth from outer space would change everything by giving people a sense of our collective dependence on a fragile planet. Brand's practical advice on how to repair the planet through individual effort appealed to young leftists tired of endless meetings and electoral defeat. The opening section of the catalog on "whole systems" encouraged personal responsibility and appropriate technology. The catalog was a hymn to "doing the most with the least," the credo of Brand's mentor, the designer Buckminster Fuller.[72]

The idea of the self-sufficient homestead resonated with much in the American tradition. But the homestead could also be isolating and divisive, skating the line between personal liberation and gentrification. In promising what the counterculture press called "privacy from the street," the new focus on home and garden also meant retreat from the larger public and political world. The logic of the movement held that, as one adherent put it, "choices about the right technology, both useful old gadgets and ingenious new tools, are crucial," but "choices about political matters are not."[73]

In the end, the counterculture reinforced the declining faith in government and the turn toward individual, market solutions. Faced with the decline of public spending, counterculture activists took less interest in repairing existing institutions than in building new, off-grid networks and relationships. The retreat from politics also resonated with the more entrepreneurial mood ushered in by neoliberalism, as solidarity fell by the wayside. The arcadian impulse to escape could be fueled either by a concern for an endangered planet or an optimistic belief in a new post-scarcity world. But either way, survival or self-sufficiency, it left politics behind.[74]

The retreat from politics left the search for alternative approaches to food, shelter, and energy a matter of consumer choices unavailable to many. Not everyone, however, gave up on politics. Challenging regulations and orchestrating free trade deals, neoliberals successfully removed more and more obstacles to the relentless exploitation of the biosphere. Capital accumulation rolled on, churning up the earth. A privatized vision of urban sustainability thus risked the fate that the literary historian Leo Marx assigned to the dream of the garden. Writing in 1964, Marx already feared that "an inspiring vision of a humane community has been reduced to a token of individual survival." His words capture much about the arc of the sustainability movement. Now that even individual survival is in doubt, we must return to politics.[75]

III

The Challenges before Us

Environmental and Political Repair

In mid-May 1975, as night fell, I found myself far out on the northwestern side of Phoenix, Arizona, at Bell Road and North 26th Avenue. Today that area is completely built over and packed with car dealers, donut and coffee shops, and sports bars. At the time, it was nothing but desert, dissected by a single line of asphalt. I had hitchhiked back to Phoenix from San Francisco to visit friends I had met two months earlier. My last ride dropped me off at the then desolate exit off Interstate 17.

I walked a mile east to the next major avenue, 19th, and tried to hitch a ride south into town. But no luck. I kept walking east, hoping to hit Central Avenue and walk south into town, estimating it would be six or seven miles. My destination, the Romney Motor Lodge, was actually more than sixteen miles away. Two months earlier, I had washed dishes at the Romney, one of the long-gone, enchanting, neon-lit motels that lined the four overlapping U.S. highways along Van Buren Street. In the years before the interstates, this stretch of motels beckoned weary desert travelers as a multicolor, air-conditioned oasis replete with swimming pools. It beckoned me because I knew my friend Phyllis would be working in the hotel's coffee shop, ready to sneak me a free meal.[1]

I kept walking east and after about two miles I hit an intersection with a lonely, one-light gas station. It was probably North 7th Street, which passes through North Mountain Park on its way south. I tried hitchhiking again and felt enormous gratitude when a young man in a pickup truck stopped. As he drove south, we crested the mountains and Phoenix appeared, spread out in all its glory. A "beautiful mass of lights (urban sprawl)," I wrote in the diary I kept that year. Looking back now, forty-eight years later, I am surprised I even knew the term *urban sprawl*. I could not have imagined that Phoenix would soon swallow up the desert that I had just walked through.

I trace the beginnings of my political consciousness to the six formative weeks I spent in Phoenix in February and March 1975. I arrived as a clueless college dropout, some variant of a counterculture green, having spent the previous six months hitchhiking across the country and backpacking in various national parks, forests, and wilderness areas. I took in a great deal of experience in those weeks as I waited out the winter and replenished my funds. I caddied at the Phoenix Country Club (for, among others, members of the Goldwater family) and picked oranges with migrant laborers from Latin America. In-between, I worked as a telephone solicitor, selling tickets to the fireman's ball at the Westward Ho Hotel, and washed dishes at the Romney.

I lived just off Van Buren Street in a flophouse on 1313 East Fillmore Street. Most of the motels had closed, and Van Buren had become a center of vice. It turned out that Chuck, the thirty-something manager, doubled as a pimp. A teenage couple, Andres and Maria, lived in the cramped upstairs. Andres belonged to a gang and tried to get me into nunchucks. The other downstairs tenants were two twenty-somethings, a guy who lived under the alias Sam Benson and his dodgy girlfriend, Phyllis. Chuck and Sam took me under their wings and tried to teach me something. Chuck's tutelage mainly involved how to successfully take LSD.

Sam offered a wider curriculum. A Vietnam vet from Detroit with a desire to punch out the guy who had signed him up as a seventeen-year-old to be an Army Ranger for a hitch that included the Tet Offensive (1968), Sam had returned from the war with a heroin addiction. He was now, or so he said, AWOL from an ill-advised second hitch. Sam later tried to convince me to join the Navy, submarine duty, with him. When not strung out, Sam talked nonstop. He told me about Vietnam, the armed forces, and Detroit and, less successfully, about how to make a living. Incredibly, he had us quit our phone solicitation jobs to find our fortune picking oranges. Through it all, Sam radicalized me.

Between the many jobs I held and the many talks with Sam, I had a lot to process. I felt everything passing me by, and I wanted to catch up. I see now that many of the developments examined in this book were just then gathering force, including the shift from the Fordist mass-production economy to the regime of flexible accumulation, the neoliberal rejection of governmental regulation, the assault on the social safety net, and the transformation of the movement for urban sustainability. The pace of global warming also began to accelerate, in significant part due to the growth of energy-intensive cities that mined and drilled their hinterlands. Phoenix lay at the heart of some of these developments and felt the impact of all of them.[2]

At the time, of course, I understood none of this. But I walked everywhere in the city. On arrival in Phoenix, I slept in a dive motel somewhere on the west side, off Van Buren Street. The next day I walked three miles to the downtown, through distressed neighborhoods, and then wandered northeast looking for an apartment. Once settled, I walked two-and-a-half miles to work on most days, first to the Phoenix Country Club and then to the Romney. Several times Sam stranded me in various parts of the city while he scored his drugs, once at a poolroom near the old Motorola plant on the northeastern side, now a superfund site soaked with chlorinated solvents. On this and other occasions I walked back to Fillmore Street, seeing a sizable cross-section of the city.

I also gained a vague sense of the city's embeddedness in a larger region, even before that May night in the desert. In the months preceding my arrival, I had backpacked in New Mexico's mountainous Gila Wilderness area, the source of the Gila River that watered Phoenix. I had also hitchhiked down from the Colorado Plateau in northern Arizona, where the coal that energized Phoenix was mined. For the orange-picking job, Sam and I arrived at the unemployment office downtown well before dawn and boarded an old, empty school bus. We drove for what seemed like forever and finally stopped in the middle of an orchard, well outside the city. While we sat there with the bus's headlights illuminating the edges of the orchards, dozens of migrant workers materialized out of the trees and got onto the bus.

No wonder that when I returned to college, the idea of human ecology intrigued me. I saw so many different parts of the city and region and wondered how they fit together. Even though I knew little about the shameful slums stretching south of downtown, so divorced from the life of the city that they might have been on another planet, I did see a great deal of poverty and inequality, and I wondered about that, too. But I also simply loved the city, especially its downtown. Phoenix was not built for walking, but it enjoyed a beautiful, compact, walkable downtown. I spent a good deal of time wandering through it.

Flourishing just before and after World War II, downtown Phoenix featured several iconic buildings. They included the Mission-style Union Station, busy with passengers, express, and mail (agricultural produce and other freight moved through the railyards in the nearby Warehouse District), the swanky Westward Ho Hotel (now subsidized housing for the elderly), the Beaux-Arts Luhrs Building, and the Art Deco Luhrs Tower. Awnings shaded the sidewalks, and neon glowed, giving the desert city a bewitching mix of shadow and light. Bars, restaurants, movie theaters, and a "Millionaires Row" of Victorian mansions, along with more modest residences, brought life to downtown.[3]

As Phoenix sprawled outward eventually to cover five hundred square miles of desert, the downtown had already begun to decline in 1975. The streetcar system (torn up in 1948) gave way to automobiles, dispersing offices, retail, and residences. Substandard bus service could not duplicate the centralizing work of the streetcars. Passenger rail dwindled down to nothing. Urban renewal and slum clearance sped the decline. Superblocks, parking lots, and garages disrupted the streetscape. In 1972, the Phoenix Civic Plaza and Symphony Hall, made of concrete in the Brutalist style, arose downtown. A dying gasp of urban modernism, they displaced low-income housing and expanded the homeless population. Multinational conglomerates purchased downtown's employment anchors and moved the jobs to new sites on the periphery. Festival marketplaces and sports complexes failed to revive the downtown.[4]

I have never stopped thinking about Phoenix. With the help of some extraordinary scholarship on the city, especially Andrew Needham's illuminating *Power Lines: Phoenix and the Making of the Modern Southwest*, I now recognize the enormous costs of Phoenix's growth, both within the city and in distant places. Chapter 9 thus examines Phoenix as an extreme case of the great divide between city and country. As one of the birthplaces of neoliberalism, Phoenix also illustrates the dangers of the shrinking of the public realm. Phoenix's potentially catastrophic predicament, moreover, offers an instructive complement to the uniformitarian decay of the Rust Belt with which this study began.[5]

In an indirect way, Phoenix also figures in the final, concluding chapter of this book. Those six weeks in Phoenix, and my ragtag set of friends, proved enormously stimulating. Although I could not have expressed it at the time, Phoenix—for all its faults—gave my young self a sense that, if we but share our social heritage more equitably, we might secure an engaging, satisfying life for all. Returning to college, I had that sense powerfully reinforced by the historian Christopher Lasch. As my teacher and mentor, Lasch communicated the promise of American life, although it came embedded in an incisive criticism of how far short of that promise we had fallen.

Lasch located much of that promise in the populist tradition. Although now used to describe various authoritarian movements across the world, populism—in Lasch's telling—stood for something closer to the opposite, the widest possible distribution of political and economic responsibility. In opposition to a progressive tradition that defined democracy in terms of ever increasing standards of material comfort, the populist tradition measured the success of democracy in terms of the mind and character of the citizens it produced. Lasch's populists championed a society of self-reliant (not necessarily self-sufficient), responsible, and competent citizens, a whole world of heroes. As so many of the movements and thinkers examined in this study suggest, lasting and effective environmental reform will require just such citizens. Our greatest challenge remains getting control of ourselves.[6]

With that vision in mind, Chapter 10 argues for a reconsideration of the populist tradition, its virtues as well as its faults. As a term of contempt, *populism* provides a measure of the metropolitan dismissal of the legitimate concerns of rural and small-town America. Properly understood, however, the populist vision of democracy may help us address our political and environmental challenges. While the label itself may be tarnished beyond recovery, those who wish to reverse our political dysfunction and environmental degradation will benefit from a reconsideration of its history. Rather than a political slogan or label, I intend the term *green populism* as a provocation to an open-ended reconsideration of that tradition.

Finally, I learned from Lasch, as part of that populist tradition, about the real dangers of resentment. In defeat, too many late nineteenth-century American populists descended into ugly, racist, and anti-Semitic scapegoating. Undeniably, something of the sort besets us now as we face increasingly difficult prospects. In a short Epilogue, I therefore explore what resources we might have for mutual understanding and resilience in the face of the challenges ahead. These resources may aid us in bearing our troubles while helping us avoid the worst outcomes.

9

Whither Phoenix?

A Desert Metropolis and the
Fate of Civilization

The city of Phoenix, Arizona, is built on the ruins of the Hohokam civilization. Living in a desert with only eight inches of rain a year, the Hohokam tapped the water of the Salt and Gila rivers that flow out of the Rocky Mountains to the east. By 650 C.E., the Hohokam had begun constructing an elaborate series of irrigation canals. A main canal twelve miles long, sixteen feet deep, and eighty feet wide fed 180 miles of trunk lines and hundreds, perhaps even thousands, of miles of secondary canals. Intensive cultivation of corn, beans, and squash, and the harvesting of two hundred species of edible plants, supported a larger self-sufficient population than the desert does today.[1]

Population peaked at forty thousand, a level that threatened disaster in an unpredictable climate. Drought set in around 1100 C.E., stressing resources, forcing people out of upland districts, and concentrating them along the rivers. Overexploitation left few trees or small game, while infant mortality rose and infectious disease spread. Deteriorating conditions to the north led to substantial in-migration, sparking ethnic-based social conflicts. A series of floods in the middle of the fourteenth century damaged the canal system. Salinization of soils from irrigation added to the Hohokam's troubles. By 1450, the civilization had collapsed. Later peoples living amid the abandoned canals dubbed the lost civilization "the Hohokam," which meant "all used up."[2]

More than four hundred years later, Jack Swilling, a Confederate veteran, prospector, and frontier entrepreneur, took note of the abandoned canals. In 1867, he organized an irrigation company that turned the Salt River Valley into productive farmland. One of Swilling's associates predicted that a triumphant new civilization would "spring Phoenix-like from the ruins and ashes of the old" and gave the new city its name. In the first decades of the twentieth century, with the aid of federal spending on water infrastructure and extensive use of immigrant labor, Phoenix bloomed out of the ruins of the doomed Hohokam.[3]

Modern Phoenix is an extreme case of the great divide between city and country. Its population, growing by more than 100,000 a year in the first decade of the twenty-first century, approached 1.5 million in the 2010 U.S. Census, making it the sixth-largest city in the United States. Today it is the fifth, with a metropolitan population nearing five million. Importing virtually everything necessary to sustain itself, this desert city developed an especially exploitative relationship with its hinterland. Phoenix itself is 517 square miles, but its ecological footprint (the area necessary to sustain it) is thirty thousand square miles.[4]

Water is the crucial resource for this desert city. Phoenix now gets most of its water from the $4 billion Central Arizona Project (CAP), a 335-mile canal that delivers Colorado River water to the metropolitan area. The Colorado River originates more than eight hundred miles to the northeast of Phoenix in the snowmelt of the central Rocky Mountains and travels 1,450 miles to its (mostly dry) delta at the Gulf of California in Mexico. The CAP, begun in 1973 and completed in 1993, uses coal-fired electric pumps to lift river water nearly three thousand feet over the course of the system. The CAP is, as the historian Marc Reisner put it, "a man-made river flowing uphill in a place of almost no rain."[5]

Water is not, however, Phoenix's only challenge. Despite abundant opportunities for solar and wind generation, most of Phoenix's electricity comes from fossil fuels and nuclear generation. The Four Corners Generating Station, located on the Colorado Plateau in northwestern New Mexico, more than 350 miles from Phoenix, consumes 4,200 tons of coal per day. In the 1960s, the Mercury astronauts reported the plume of smoke rising from the plant as one of two man-made features visible from space. With the closing in 2019 of the Navajo Generating Station, which was even larger than the Four Corners plant, Arizona's Palo Verde Nuclear Generating Plant, the largest in the nation, picked up the slack. Phoenix ranks among the world's top contributors to greenhouse gases. The city also suffers from poor air quality, aquifers poisoned with high-tech waste, an intense heat island effect (as built-up areas absorb heat and radiate it after the sun goes down), and at least twelve toxic waste Superfund sites.[6]

Phoenix's most dangerous condition, however—and one that helps explain its dire environmental prospects—is its neoliberal resistance to environmental regulation. After careful study and dozens of interviews, the sociologist Andrew Ross dubbed Phoenix "the world's least sustainable city." Rather than embrace environmental reform, Phoenix decision makers prefer to discuss risk management. At the state level, even risk management gives way to a blind faith in technology. "Phoenix Man," one of Ross's interviewees explained, is resistant to talk about regulating growth, making Phoenix "almost a perfect example of how to incentivize and encourage lifestyles and business practices that cannot be sustained."[7]

Historically, arid regions engage in extensive cooperation to manage a scarce resource. But in this "land of laissez-faire," as Phoenix came to be known in the 1980s, a "minimalist conception of government responsibilities" meant "it's every man for himself." The Salt River Valley, in which Phoenix sits, has its own buried traditions of cooperation dating back to the Hohokam, through Spanish settlements, to the early twentieth-century Salt River Project (SRP) that initiated Phoenix's twentieth-century rise. But today, the Salt River Valley contains dozens of competing jurisdictions and 120 water providers, frustrating cooperation. Anti-regulation attitudes make cooperation even more difficult. Moreover, the legal doctrine of "prior appropriation," which is prominent in the western states, grants first users the right to divert water. The resulting "use it or lose it" attitude encourages hoarding, waste, and overconsumption.[8]

As environmental stresses intensify, these multiple jurisdictions, water providers, and "private-enterprise governments" such as the SRP will need to cooperate to avoid economic collapse and social chaos. Private-enterprise governments, the most common form of local government in the United States, proliferate in the edge cities and gated communities that surround Phoenix and other cities. They also fill the vacuum created by the neoliberal assault on public authority. In his influential study *Edge City* (1991), the urbanist Joel Garreau used Phoenix to illustrate the rise of private-enterprise governments. Almost always unelected or representing property interests rather than citizens, these shadow governments enjoy a quasi-public stature, exercising governmental powers with fewer constraints.[9]

A provider of water and electricity, the SRP exercises enormous power. Over its history, it has operated as a for-profit corporation; an unregulated, investor-owned utility; a tax-levying political subdivision of the state; and a conduit for federal funds. Promoting water conservation and subsidizing the cost of water, building coal-fired generators, and investing in nuclear power plants, the SRP has more impact on the Arizona environment than perhaps any other entity. Public oversight comes only through an electorate composed of owners of irrigated land—one acre, one vote. Effective in pursuing private interests, private enterprise governments such as the SRP are less attentive to environmental and social equity.[10]

The SRP is only one arm of Phoenix's relentless growth machine that reaches far and wide for water, energy, and other resources. As the city stresses far-flung ecosystems, it is not difficult to imagine the region's ecological collapse. Water shortages are likely as lakes and reservoirs on the Colorado River, and the river itself, are badly depleted. Disaster scenarios, invoking the fate of the Hohokam, occasionally make their way into the local press. In such scenarios, water shortages lead to rationing, a doubling or more of prices, and armed water police patrolling neighborhoods, shutting off service. Then the real estate market collapses, and with it the city's finances, setting in motion escalating conflicts with Mexico over water rights. Finally, the population abandons the city and heads toward water.[11]

Such scenarios are not inevitable but chosen. "When we talk about sustainability," Phoenix's official archeologist explains, "we talk about decision making. Nothing just happens." Thousands of individual decisions, taken without cooperation or coordination and driven by ethnic conflicts, sped the Hohokam's collapse. Their story is not unique. Jared Diamond's best-selling study of the environmental collapse of past civilizations is subtitled "How Societies *Choose* to Fail or Succeed." The same thing could happen in Phoenix, where green lawns and golf courses shimmer in the middle of a desert while public officials delay making difficult choices.[12]

Phoenix provides a stress test for the creation of a socially and environmentally just and sustainable region. As Arizona State University's Global Institute of Sustainability puts it, Phoenix is "sustainability's test bed," not only for American cities, but also for huge, expanding, semiarid cities across the globe. This test will be conducted in one of the birthplaces of the neoliberal assault on the regulatory/social welfare state. After World War II, Phoenix boosters rolled back taxes, regulations, and labor protections to promote a "favorable business climate" to compete with other regions for new investment. Like other Sunbelt cities, Phoenix redirected local, state, and federal funds to benefit business interests, subsidizing the construction not only of roads, subdivisions, utilities, and universities, but also manufacturing facilities themselves.[13]

As they orchestrated Phoenix's growth in the three decades after 1945, the boosters' pro-business, anti-union, low-tax, deregulatory, hyper-growth policies became a national model, disseminated through their monthly newsletter, *Whither Phoenix?* In the process, the boosters re-shaped the Republican Party, the federal bureaucracy, and the federal courts. Although Arizona is still one of the fastest-growing states in the Union, the second and third generation of boosters are losing their grip on city, state, and national politics. Metropolitan Phoenix continues to dominate state politics, but it is divided by urban, suburban, exurban, and rural interests, making it a microcosm of the nation at large. Desperately in need of regional cooperation, Phoenix provides a window on the prospects for American civilization in an era of environmental degradation.[14]

Public Projects and Regional Conflicts

Although Phoenix became an incubator and bastion of neoliberal opposition to intrusive government, its rise depended on public works. In 1902, the National Reclamation Act established the U.S. Bureau of Reclamation. Two visions animated the bureau. The first was to irrigate the Southwest and people it with a democracy of small farmers to preempt speculation. That vision began with John Wesley Powell, later director of the U.S. Geological Survey, who explored the Colorado River basin in the 1870s. Powell's subsequent report *The Arid Lands of the United States* argued for cooperative irrigation in support of communities of small farmers.[15]

The second vision involved stupendous engineering projects to tame western rivers for irrigation, hydroelectric power, and urban development. The pro-growth policy won out and favored big agriculture and, eventually, big industry and urban real estate. Unfettered but subsidized private development supplanted cooperative irrigation. The bureau built hundreds of major dams and thousands of smaller ones on every river in the U.S. West, including fifteen on the main stem of the Colorado River. In 1911, the bureau completed its first important project, the [Theodore] Roosevelt Dam on the Salt River. An adjustment of the legislative stipulation that development focus on unclaimed public lands allowed private landowners to establish the Salt River Valley Water Users' Association in exchange for repaying the costs of construction of the dam.[16]

Even as it increased the federal presence in the Salt River Valley, the Bureau of Reclamation continued the nineteenth-century practice of placing natural resources in private hands. Renamed the Salt River Project, the water users' association turned Phoenix into a center of irrigated agriculture. During World War I, large landowners cashed in on the cotton boom. When cotton prices plummeted after the war, the SRP promoted crop diversification and electrification of farms for the pumping of irrigation water. By the late 1930s, the SRP was boasting that it watered "the largest block of electrified farmland in the world."[17]

Yet Phoenix remained a colonial outpost of the industrial heartland, a supplier of the "Four Cs": copper, cattle, cotton, and climate (i.e., an exotic vacation spot for tired or tubercular easterners). The profits flowed east, leaving the city short of capital. An insular local elite spent its time protecting the city's tourist reputation and fighting the labor legislation that might assist its polyglot working population. Working families clustered on the underserviced, wrong side of the railroad tracks south of downtown Phoenix.[18]

When economic conditions worsened during the Great Depression, President Franklin Roosevelt identified the Southwest as a desert adjunct to the impoverished South that he deemed "the nation's #1 economic problem." A local banker described Depression-era Phoenix as a "very hot, desolate place," probably "as close to Hell as you could be while being on Earth." But the National Resources Planning Board believed the Southwest possessed all "the essentials for greater growth and progress." New Deal agencies funded improvement of Phoenix's local airport along with other infrastructure projects. But in this heyday of regional thinking, the Roosevelt administration had bigger ambitions than the fortunes of a single city.[19]

As with every region, the constellation of natural resources and opportunities, and human imagination in exploiting them, shaped the Southwest's development. Beneath the ground, enormous veins of coal, a product of decayed vegetation from an ancient shallow sea, waited to be exploited. Seventy million years ago, tectonic forces pushed the Rocky Mountains above the sea. Over millions of years, rivers flowing out of the mountains carved deep canyons, leaving most of the land arid. But where the rivers exited the canyons and their currents slowed, as in the Salt River Valley and Southern California's Imperial Valley, they deposited vast quantities of rich soil, sometimes a foot or two deep. The Bureau of Reclamation recognized the deep, narrow canyons as perfect sites for dams that could make the valleys bloom.[20]

The Roosevelt administration embraced reclamation projects as a means of transforming the Southwest into a prosperous region and bastion of the New Deal. Championing the Bureau of Reclamation's most ambitious project, the unfinished Hoover Dam along the Arizona-Nevada border, Roosevelt proclaimed that the Southwest would no longer be an "unpeopled, forbidding desert." When Hoover Dam opened in 1936, it brought fragmented settlements into a regional web of interdependence. Combating both floods and drought, Hoover Dam promised to diversify the southwestern economy. Providing water and energy for a region stretching over seven states, the dam, theoretically, would support a high-wage, unionized workforce and modernized agriculture while addressing inequalities within and between rural and urban communities.[21]

Even before it opened, however, Hoover Dam revealed fractures within the emerging region by setting in motion uneven patterns of development. The project focused the attention of federal officials on the Navajo Reservation in northern Arizona and western New Mexico. In the nineteenth century, sheep herding had enabled the Navajo to secure an increase in population, an expanded reservation, and a measure of autonomy. The herds provided stable subsistence, supplemented with occasional wage work and the mining of visible coal seams on the reservation. The expansion of the herd, however, led to overgrazing and conflicts with competing Anglo and Hispanic stock raisers.[22]

Now federal officials worried that the overgrazing would lead to soil erosion and fill Hoover Dam with silt. Between 1934 and 1938, the Bureau of Indian Affairs (BIA) drastically reduced the sheep herds, buying some animals and slaughtering others. The BIA also established new restrictions on mining while promising new jobs that never materialized. With few alternatives, the Navajo faced disaster. When Phoenix's boosters began to eye the huge deposits of coal beneath the reservation as a source of electricity, the Navajo faced difficult choices between poverty and out-migration or potentially devastating environmental change.[23]

The new dam also generated conflicts between Phoenix and its powerful neighbor to the west. As planning for Hoover Dam began, the chief engineers of water and power in Los Angeles promised Congress that the city would "be a very large customer." Los Angeles's private utilities once feared that inexpensive public power would lead to the municipalization of utilities. But when the Bureau of Reclamation agreed to sell power to private utilities, Los Angeles's boosters became the greatest promoters, and the greatest beneficiaries, of the project. Defense contracts also flowed to Los Angeles, making it a favored recipient of New Deal assistance in the West.[24]

While Los Angelenos rejoiced, Phoenicians worried. Situated 270 miles northwest of Phoenix (and 290 miles east of Los Angeles), Hoover Dam turned flowing water into property. Phoenix boosters feared their city would not get its share. In the 1922 interstate agreement dividing the waters of the Colorado River, Arizona's bid for 44 percent of the river's flow, based on the proposition that the state contained 44 percent of the land drained by the river, had been rejected. Instead, the agreement divided the water between upper basin and lower basin states, placing Arizona in the lower basin with water-hungry California. Phoenix remained a decidedly junior partner, a backward appendage to the empire of Los Angeles.[25]

The Valley of the Sun and the Rise of Neoliberalism

A rising new generation of business leaders in Phoenix abhorred the New Deal and its favoring of Los Angeles. Rejecting the New Deal's expansion of the regulatory/social welfare state, these young, ambitious entrepreneurs rejuvenated the Phoenix Chamber of Commerce and recast it as their base of operation. Led by the native Arizonan retailer Barry Goldwater and the Chicago transplant banker Walter Bimson, the chamber men quickly dropped the Salt River Valley moniker for the more alluring Valley of the Sun. Traveling in wider national business networks than Phoenix's old mining and agricultural elite, the chamber men felt confident of their ability to shake off Phoenix's colonial status and bend government largess to their needs. The tight-knit group worked in the walkable downtown core of twelve square blocks; lunched at the Arizona Club; and socialized at the Kiva Club, the Hotel Westward Ho, and the Phoenix Country Club.[26]

Although the chamber men preached individual initiative and the free market, they had no compunction about using public funds to stimulate growth. The largess of the Federal Housing Administration (FHA) encouraged Bimson to place full-page newspaper ads announcing that his Valley National Bank was "prepared to loan money on homes." Meanwhile, he urged his employees to "Make loans!" to all comers from small businesses to individuals purchasing houses, cars, or appliances. Freed from the caution of his former Chicago colleagues, Bimson built his bank into one of the most powerful in the West and won praise in business circles and national magazines.[27]

Walter's brother Carl Bimson helped write the enabling legislation for the FHA. As he toured the country touting the FHA, Carl assured business groups that the program "is being operated by business men for the benefit of business men." Following his brother in seeking to privatize the New Deal, he told loan applicants that this "is private money, not government money." Yet by the end of the 1930s, the developer Del Webb (whose later Sun City retirement complex would also benefit from residents' Social Security pensions) acknowledged that "construction is no longer a private enterprise, it is a subsidiary of the national government."[28]

The chamber men knew the future of the Valley of the Sun depended on water and energy, provision of which outstripped the capacities of local capitalists. "The natural thing to which to turn," Goldwater recalled, "was the capitalization of our climate, our natural beauties, and the romance of the desert." To attract wealthy migrants who could help jump-start the local economy, they promoted "outdoor living" and "Golf! Year-Round." They also transformed the dull engineering journal *Arizona Highways* into a lush photographic advertisement for the sublime landscapes of the region. The boosters used nationwide junkets and magazine articles to tout Phoenix as a chance to reinvent oneself and become "a lot more of an *individual*."[29]

As they built alliances with national business leaders and the conservative movement, the chamber men set their eyes on attracting "clean," smoke-free industry that would fit their image of the Valley of the Sun. Prewar manufacturing consisted mainly of agricultural processing; stockyards, rendering plants, and other noxious enterprises clustered in the squalid neighborhoods south of downtown. Emblematic of the uneven successes of urban environmental reform, these neighborhoods reeked with "the odors of a fertilizer plant, an iron foundry, a thousand open privies and the city sewage disposal plant." Awash in polluted water and industrial wastes, the area shouldered the additional burdens of new freeways and, after 1945, an expanded airport, adding air pollution and toxic runoff.[30]

The growth of the electronics, aerospace, and computer industries distracted attention from the squalor south of downtown. Like other Sunbelt cities, Phoenix advertised itself as an industrial garden conducive to worker health and satisfaction. Leveled, irrigated farmland stood ready to provide space for single-story, green-fringed industrial parks interspersed amid residential neighborhoods. Wartime defense contracts provided the foundation as the federal government built four air training centers and several desert warfare training sites in and around Phoenix. The chamber men praised the region's low humidity for preventing corrosion in delicate electronic switches and 320 annual days of sunshine for aviation testing and training. A boom in the manufacturing of airplane parts and electrical components, as well as aluminum and steel production, followed.[31]

When postwar demobilization and canceled federal contracts stalled the boom, the chamber men seized on New Deal labor and regulatory policies as the key obstacle to growth. They now looked to reform government and provide a business-friendly atmosphere. With the Chamber of Commerce in the lead, voters passed a referendum in 1946 that amended the state constitution to ban the closed union shop, making Arizona a right-to-work state. In 1948, the chamber men also led the effort to rewrite the city's charter, providing for a professional city manager and nonpartisan, at-large elections. Two years later, dissatisfied with the persistence of anti-charter officials, the chamber successfully ran a slate of candidates it pledged would be more sympathetic to "the intent of the city charter revisions."[32]

Over the next two decades, chamber-supported officials dismantled New Deal support for unionization, business regulation, and the social safety net. As Cold War and Korean War defense spending grew, high-tech firms flocked to the city and took over government plants, fattening on defense contracts and branching out into consumer product manufacturing. Meanwhile, federal matching grants turned Sky Harbor Airport into one of the busiest and fastest-growing airports in the country. The policy of dispersing defense installations to reduce vulnerability to a nuclear strike also favored Phoenix. So did President Dwight Eisenhower's "New Look" defense strategy that emphasized the Air Force. Defense contracts covered costs for recruiting and resettling skilled workers, feeding a housing boom and turning Phoenix itself into a major consumer market.[33]

Energizing the Postwar Growth Machine

Arguing that growth benefited everyone, the chamber men orchestrated a growth machine that included municipal officials, developers, utilities, retailers, newspapers, and unions. Growth politics in Phoenix did not, however, lift all boats but, instead, contributed to social polarization. As the chamber men redirected government largess toward the needs of high-tech industry, they lavished funds on cultural institutions "to attract the type of people that Phoenix wants." The chamber men also combined the GI Bill and corporate funding for laboratories, equipment, and faculty to develop a technocratic Arizona State University. But by lowering taxes on manufacturers, city officials shifted the burden to homeowners in the subdivisions marching northward into the desert. They showed even less concern for the minority and low-income neighborhoods south of downtown, insisting that "spending money on housing isn't our business."[34]

Housing the more fortunate, however, became central to Phoenix's economy. "More house per dollar," the pitch went, "than in any other section of the country." The expansion of the housing sector began soon after the war, in part due to veterans who remembered the region from their training. Walter Bimson encouraged investors to purchase millions of dollars' worth of mortgages through the New Deal's Federal National Mortgage Association (Fannie Mae), freeing up his own bank's capital to make more loans. City officials pursued an aggressive annexation policy that traded water, sewers, and police for the collection of property taxes. Thus primed, the housing industry developed a momentum of its own as developers turned farmland into subdivisions while purchasing land farther out in the desert. Then trading that desert land for irrigated land closer in, developers left it to farmers to prepare graded and irrigated land for future subdivisions.[35]

By the late 1950s, developers were constructing more than ten thousand single-family residences a year. Each new subdivision, like each new high-tech factory, added to the energy demand. The chamber men's most important contribution to a business-friendly environment thus came in securing enough energy to fuel Phoenix's growth. Another New Deal initiative, the Public Utility Holding Company Act (PUHC) of 1935, facilitated their capture of Phoenix's major utility, the Central Arizona Light and Power Company. The PUHC took aim at national holding companies that owned multiple utilities, manipulated prices, and evaded regulations across state lines. Central Arizona Light and Power had been owned by just such a holding company, the largest in the nation, infamous for padding consumer bills with excessive management charges. Local control, reformers hoped, would end such abuses.[36]

When the PUHC secured the dissolution of the Central Arizona Light and Power Company in 1945, the chamber men put together fifteen or twenty local investors and offered them a fifty-cent stock discount in their new venture. Absorbing other local utilities, the new company began doing business as Arizona Public Service (APS) in 1952. The company reached far and wide to fuel Phoenix's growth, expanding its network of power lines from 803 to 3,255 miles by 1970. In a strategy of "build and grow," APS built new power plants fired by natural gas from western Texas to stay ahead of demand. The utility supplied the subdivisions of northern Phoenix but also sent power across the state, cementing Phoenix's position as Arizona's principal city. To finance all this expansion, APS linked back up with the same Wall Street speculators who gave the holding companies a bad name.[37]

Escalating demand for electricity secured APS's profitability. "The most important elements that determine our loads," a utility executive explained, "are not those that happen but those we project—that we invent—in the broad sense of the term 'invention.'" Marketing electrical use in the household for every conceivable purpose, APS created a cartoon mascot, Reddy Kilowatt, who promised to "do five loads of laundry, vacuum the house for a month, do the dishes for two days or provide five full evenings of radio entertainment," all for a nickel. Ignoring wartime experiments in solar power and energy conservation, the FHA facilitated utility growth by instituting new standards for residential wiring to accommodate large appliances and guaranteeing loans for home modernization.[38]

Domestic consumption of energy in Phoenix grew more than tenfold in the fifteen years after 1945. The electric home, replacing regional forms of architecture in Phoenix, as elsewhere, anchored a high-energy lifestyle. Profits for APS soared, while the SRP shifted its emphasis from agriculture to suburban consumers and functioned, an analyst reported, "essentially as private companies function." Advertisements for the SRP promoted the "electric valentine" husbands could send their wives in the form of the fully electric house with washers and dryers, vacuum cleaners, and ranges that "will help her get more fun out of life by making her homemaking easier."[39]

Air conditioning overcame the excessive heat that discouraged settlement in Phoenix. "Phoenicians do not move to new localities when they desire a climatic change," a booster explained. "They change the climate!" Although still limited to the affluent into the 1960s, climate control became central to the city's reputation. "I awaken in my air-conditioned home in the morning," a local banker enthused in 1961. "I take a dip in my swimming pool. I dress and get into my air-conditioned automobile and drive to the air-conditioned garage in the basement of this building. I work in an air-conditioned office, eat in an air-conditioned restaurant and perhaps go to an air-conditioned theater."[40]

Electrical shortages, however, had already begun by the late 1950s, blacking out the city and requiring purchases of energy from California utilities. Initially, manufacturing's constant use of electricity complemented and balanced the intermittent, peak usage in residential areas, enabling utilities to run near maximum capacity. Differential rates meant that residential customers subsidized manufacturers. But when natural gas production in Texas began to slow, both APS and the SRP lacked the fuel to run the new plants they needed.[41]

In 1955, APS turned to California's Stanford Research Institute for a study of energy potential in the region. The institute's report concluded that natural gas supplies would remain limited, and generator efficiency had reached its limit. But the report also pointed to major coal deposits on the Navajo Reservation, yet untapped due to rugged terrain and transportation difficulties. Recent improvements in transmission technology, however, meant that the energy could now be produced on-site and efficiently delivered through long-distance wires. "Coal by wire," the Bureau of Reclamation called it, a supply to "last one thousand years."[42]

"Almost Everybody Wins": Electrical Integration and the Not-so-Placeless Market

While Phoenix boosters reaped the benefits of abundant electricity, the costs of Phoenix's electrical grid would be paid, in large part, by the already impoverished Navajo. Ignoring a national debate about the best path forward for the Navajo (integration and assimilation versus self-determination and self-sufficiency), Phoenix's chamber men looked to the reservation's coal deposits as the solution to their city's expanding energy needs. Fed up with federal oversight of Indian affairs, they sought a freer hand in dealing with the Navajo and their resources. "One of your first and most important measures," Goldwater told Arizona's governor, "should be to unlock the natural resources known to exist on the reservations." That, Goldwater concluded, should "make our so-called Indian problems simple enough."[43]

With Republicans ascendant in the state and nation after the 1952 elections, the chamber men took aim at the barriers that were blocking development of the resources on the Navajo Reservation. Walter Bimson's Valley National Bank produced a report that recommended extending private leases of tribal land from five to twenty-five years and easing the renewal process. A mining corporation proposed strip mining operations on the reservation that would supply an on-site APS power plant. When payments for exploration rights began, Navajo leaders simply thanked "Divine Providence" for the "unexpected wealth." Soon, however, they sought to become partners in business operations and inserted into contracts the demand that companies "make special efforts to work Navajo tribal members into skilled, technical, and other higher level employment."[44]

The energy corporations and the chamber men, however, outmaneu-
vered tribal leaders. The contracts included no timetables or quotas, and
automatically renewable leases fixed the price of coal at its twentieth-
century nadir. After Walter Bimson offered advice on how to attract business with "the basics of our labor and taxation principles," the Tribal
Council passed a harsher "right-to-work" law than Arizona's and agreed
to ninety-nine-year leases. Subordinating tribal needs to its shareholders
and consumers, APS wrote protections against complaints about land, air,
and water pollution into its contract with the Navajo.[45]

By 1963, the new Four Corners Generating Station had become the
largest energy supplier in the region. Over the next decade, three more
giant coal-fired power plants ringed the Navajo Reservation, providing
most of the electricity for consumers across the Southwest. But whereas
the Four Corners plant had sent electricity directly to a substation in
Phoenix, the new plants became part of an integrated system of hydroelectric and coal-fired plants. Electricity, like grain in nineteenth-century
Chicago, became a fungible commodity, sent in any direction, depending
on demand.[46]

The efficiency of the new integrated system led boosters to declare that
"almost everybody wins." An integrated system meant that coal plants,
costly to turn off and on, could provide the base load while the more flexible hydropower plants could handle peak demands. The pooling arrangements reduced the need for new power plants and lowered prices for more
reliable service. Even environmentalists rejoiced as the shift to coal lessened the need for new dams.[47]

The environmental movement's growing opposition to dams relied on
the exploitation of the coal deposits on the Navajo Reservation. The integrated system might suggest the wonders of the placeless market, but
that remained a matter of perspective. By the mid-1960s, national publications had begun to question "the High Cost of Arizona" and to criticize
"the state's breathtaking political audacity in trying to seize hold of natural resources and put them to its own use." But environmentalists worried first and foremost about dams and the destruction of the "sacred"
spaces of western canyons. They had little to say about the day-to-day
damage of air, soil, and water pollution inflicted on the Navajo Reservation by coal-fired plants.[48]

Meanwhile, the exploitation of coal deposits set off debates within the
Navajo Nation. Many young people defended the Navajo's traditional
culture and complained about colonial exploitation that destroyed the
environment. "The Whiteman will do anything for money and greed,"

activists charged. "His cities have dirty, filthy air. We Indians used to have clean air and no traffic jams and noise of the city." Others complained that urban consumers "destroyed our land so they can use electric can openers and tooth brushes." City people "didn't want pollution," activists concluded. "So we got it. Is it worth it? Only a fool would say poisonous air was worth it."[49]

While Phoenix enjoyed a new abundance of energy, enormous machines ripped at Navajo land; constant explosions dislodged coal; toxic tailing piles buried grazing land; and waterholes became acidic ponds. With few alternatives, however, tribal leaders looked to the energy shortage and the rise of the Organization of Petroleum Exporting Countries as a model for building up the power of the Navajo Nation. "We have seen our land scarred by mine sites," tribal leaders admitted, "so that the giant cities of our country can be too cool in summer and too warm in winter." But they wanted to control mining, not end it. "It is obscene for energy to be produced on Indian lands and yet see our own people deprived of the very barest necessities of civilized life." The Navajo Nation had to settle for taxation, extracting a somewhat larger share of profits from energy development it had little hand in directing.[50]

Energy development in the Southwest again illustrates the great divide between city (Phoenix and its high-energy lifestyle) and country (the blasted landscape of the Navajo Reservation). But the great divide also ran down the middle of Phoenix. Homebuyers who sought "country-style living" located "on choice citrus lots" not only evaded the coal-fouled skies and toxic mining landscapes of Navajo Nation. They also distanced themselves from the impoverished Black and Mexican neighborhoods stretching south of downtown. As new subdivisions continued to spread north across irrigated agricultural fields, they promised not only clear skies, open space, and outdoor recreation, but also segregation from pollution and poverty.[51]

As elsewhere, federal housing policies and local prejudice enforced segregation. Of the 31,000 FHA-insured homes constructed by three major builders in northern Phoenix, "not one," a civil rights activist testified to a federal commission in 1962, "has been sold to a Negro." South of downtown, the *New Republic* reported in 1965, unpaved streets, unconnected sewers, inadequate public utilities, and low incomes produced "a squalid slum." Residents recalled never seeing a white person in southern Phoenix, while they themselves feared to venture north of Van Buren Street. "Apartheid is complete," the *New Republic* concluded. "The two cities look at each other across a golf course."[52]

Not everyone won from the new integrated power system that made Phoenix's high-energy lifestyle possible. Perhaps, as some young Navajos suspected, even the privileged residents of suburban Phoenix might entertain doubts about the high cost of Arizona. "Some of us have gone to college," a young Navajo explained in 1968, "but our education, if it was a good one, has pointed out to us that we do not want and will not live the life of an ulcerated white, middle-class Christian suburbanite." Growth politics in Phoenix, as elsewhere, produced fewer winners than expected.[53]

Phoenix Noir: Life in the Neoliberal City

Phoenix's explosive postwar growth built on its reputation as an escape from the dark and dangerous cities of the East. "People who come to Phoenix don't want to move into an inner city," an observer noted. "They've come to get away from that." In film noir, Hollywood captured this postwar pessimism about the nation's older and grittier cities collapsing under the weight of physical, economic, and moral decay. Phoenix's sunshine offered the antidote to noir's darkness. "Phoenix has the sun in the morning and the moon at night," the national press reported in the 1950s. The "sunniest city in the U.S.A.," without "slum apartments" or "much of a legacy of race feeling," Phoenix had "none of its past to bury."[54]

The chamber men's effort to maintain Phoenix's attractions clashed, however, with their efforts to attract industry by reducing corporate taxes. Only residential property taxes from unregulated sprawl enabled the city to make ends meet. In 1953, municipal officials documented how leapfrog development and scattered industry escalated the cost of utilities and services while encouraging a dangerous reliance on private sewage disposal. The construction of recreation facilities also lagged. Boosters organized a Phoenix Growth Committee and put before municipal voters a $70 million bond issue to invest in water, sewage, and traffic improvements, as well as parks and libraries. In 1958, Phoenix voters overwhelmingly approved the bond issue.[55]

A growing homeowner populism, however, soon challenged the chamber men's leadership. In Phoenix, as across the Sunbelt, homeowner populists rejected both corporate welfare and social welfare as antithetical to property rights, individual initiative, and free enterprise. Deploying the chamber men's own rhetoric of limited government, they complained that their property taxes and utility fees subsidized corporate tax breaks and utility rates. By the early 1960s, homeowner populism was frustrating chamber-led improvement plans. Facing what they called "a Frankenstein monster which no longer does their bidding," the chamber men's grip on local politics loosened.[56]

The final victory of the chamber men came in 1968 with federal approval of the Central Arizona Project. After a decades-long struggle, Arizona bested California in securing an enlarged share of Colorado River water. As the Bureau of Reclamation's last great project, the CAP should have supported irrigated agriculture. But with farmland rapidly turning into subdivisions, the water instead made a new wave of urban sprawl possible, which remained unregulated due to homeowners' opposition to public oversight.[57]

By the 1970s, as homeowner populism began to undermine the "friendly business environment," high-tech industry began to leave. With the economy increasingly reliant on residential construction, everything depended on the city's attractions. Municipal purchase removed some of the mountainous areas within the city from the residential market, adding to the city's public parks and preserving something of the city's attractiveness and healthfulness. Phoenix's mild winters also continued to attract. "Every winter that plunges below normal temperatures brings ten thousand new recruits to Phoenix," a reporter noted. Phoenix also retained its reputation as one of the best places to retire.[58]

But unregulated sprawl and a shrinking public realm began to bring to Phoenix many of the pathologies associated with the noir city. In the 1970s, Phoenix suffered from some of the nation's highest rates of mental illness, divorce, substance abuse, and suicide. Even affluent residents, a national study reported, suffered from "an intense loneliness accompanied by deteriorating health, marital discord, lethargy, depression, insomnia." "I was literally appalled," a visitor noted in 1976, "at the number and severity of the problems, particularly suicide, substance abuse and the chronically mentally ill who are roaming the streets here without food and basic living expenses." Even the climate seemed to turn against the city. The "heat creates a lot of stress," a local psychologist explained, "because it is so consistent."[59]

As Hohokam ruins disappeared and centuries-old saguaros fell to bulldozers clearing subdivisions, newcomers treated Phoenix as a disposable commodity. They also shied away from charitable, cultural, and public projects. "Newcomers are slow to feel the sense of belonging associated with an interest and involvement in community affairs," a local paper reported in 1982. The air-conditioned lifestyle and longer commute times left little opportunity or time for conversing with neighbors, who likely had a cement-block wall around their yard anyway. "People don't see their neighbors that much, they don't talk to them that much, everybody's kind of doing their own thing," an observer noted in 1987. By the end of the century, metropolitan Phoenix had the greatest number of gated communities in the nation.[60]

As everyone wanted to be the last migrant to the Valley of the Sun, an anti-growth opposition emerged. The environmental activist Edward Abbey, himself an early postwar migrant to Arizona, complained of the "cancer of growth," which he likened to "a mad amoeba . . . egged on by the Chamber of Commerce." Everyone wanted new freeways to ease congestion, just not in their own backyard. Urban sprawl resulted in a growing prevalence of smog, fouling the region's clear, bright skies. Phoenicians now complained of the same "shadowy, smudgy cobweb of smog" that marred older cities.[61]

Phoenix remained an especially bad place to be poor, as rates of public spending on social services and education ranked near the nation's lowest. Slum neighborhoods shouldered a disproportionate number of hazardous waste sites and the nation's highest incidences of asthma. In a chilling illustration of environmental injustice, 40 percent of hazardous emissions in the region came from one zip code south of downtown. Meanwhile, downtown redevelopment demolished cheap single-room occupancy rooming houses without providing new low-income housing. The city's homeless established makeshift camps where they could, including in the dry bed of the Salt River. Police action to break up the camps and subsequent protests focused unwelcome national attention on Phoenix.[62]

By the end of the twentieth century, Phoenix had spawned its own literary subgenre of desert noir. Unlike noir's Philip Marlowe, Phoenix's detectives did not walk the mean streets but drove through them in air-conditioned vehicles. But like earlier noir detectives, they exposed the underside of the sunshine myth. "Maryvale! Fortunate home of the American dream," begins Jon Talton's *Dry Heat* (2004):

A single-family detached house in the suburbs: three bedrooms, living room, den, all-electric kitchen and carport, laid out in a neat rectangle of a one-story ranch house. We've got thousands of 'em, ready to sell, on safe winding streets in brand-new Phoenix. . . . Leave behind the old dingy cities of the East and Midwest, with their crime and racial trouble. Time for a fresh start, thanks to a VA mortgage and the FHA. You've earned it: backyard lifestyle with a new swimming pool.

"Until you go out one fine day," the passage ends, "and find a body face down in the green water of what was once the swimming pool."[63]

Maryvale, an early subdivision west of downtown, began life as the signature project of the developer John Long, postwar Phoenix's largest home builder. With help from Walter Bimson's bank, Long adapted William Levitt's mass-production techniques to Phoenix's irrigated farmland. But as subdivisions marched northward, Maryvale went downhill. Cut off from central and eastern Phoenix in the 1960s by the deep trench of the north-south Interstate 17, Maryvale also suffered from its proximity to the industrial zone stretching along West Van Buren Street. The district combined industrial pollution with heavy doses of DDT from its agricultural past to produce a death rate from childhood leukemia that was twice the national average. It also suffered from one of the highest crime rates of any neighborhood in the nation.[64]

Where Phoenix Went Wrong: Sustainability as Reclamation

Whither Phoenix remains a crucial question. The chamber men's neoliberalism has curdled into an anti-immigrant and antigovernment populism wielded by angry homeowners and rural representatives in the Arizona State Legislature. The New Deal dream of a diversified economy with a regional balance of high-wage, unionized workforce and modernized agriculture is long gone. But the ideal of reclamation, of repair and reparation, still offers a path to a different future. It will take more than green buildings and xeriscaping in upscale parts of the city, however, to reduce the city's enormous ecological footprint or alleviate the eco-apartheid that leaves too many people out in the heat and toxicity.[65]

The 2008 recession hit Phoenix especially hard and deepened the city's challenges. Housing values fell by half; lenders foreclosed on seventy thousand homes; and unemployment passed 10 percent. Millions of dollars in home equity disappeared, and millions of square feet of commercial real estate went vacant. The growth psychology, however, survived. Ignoring climate change, as well as vacancy rates, the pro-growth State Legislature placed a freeze on all development-impact fees in 2009. In a reprise of the fate of the Hohokam, mounting frustration focused on immigrants. Maricopa County voters elected the notorious Sheriff Joe Arpaio to five consecutive terms between 1993 and 2016. Sweeping neighborhoods in search of the undocumented, Arpaio housed the arrested in huge tent cities and put them to work in chain gangs.[66]

For all the denial of climate change and other environmental threats, anti-immigrant animus suggested an implicit acknowledgment of the potential for disaster. Anti-immigrant activists, some with backgrounds in the environmental movement, assert that "immigration-related population growth" is the "principal cause" of urban sprawl and declining public resources. The argument is specious, as migrants to Phoenix live in central city neighborhoods and contribute more to government coffers than they take. In truth, immigrants are victims of high-carbon, climate-destabilizing policies. The North American Free Trade Agreement of 1994 contributed to the collapse of subsistence agriculture south of the border, increasing the numbers of desperate immigrants.[67]

Sustainability, however, has been much on the mind of Phoenix's recent municipal leaders. A succession of mayors have pledged to make Phoenix "the greenest city in America" by promoting bike lanes and curbside recycling, reducing local emissions and water use, capturing methane from city landfills, using biodiesel to run city buses, and encouraging zero waste retail. The recession also prompted some talk about solar energy. The city hoped to cash in on the $60 billion in stimulus funds earmarked for clean energy. Other initiatives addressed eco-apartheid, such as planting trees, creating gardens, installing water fountains, and other measures to reduce the heat island effect in low-income neighborhoods.[68]

A few initiatives addressed wider regional issues. One of the most innovative, the Tres Rios Wetland Project southwest of downtown, uses wastewater to recharge the wetlands at the intersection of the Gila, Salt, and Agua Fria rivers. But the biggest battles remain to be fought. New leapfrog development continues, even as vacant city lots await reclamation and green development. Solar power can tap the region's defining resource, but private utilities resist incentives for household production. Neighborhood activists win some struggles against pollution and toxic wastes and rescue gang members and ex-convicts through urban agriculture. But the distribution of hazards and opportunities is still deeply unequal. Above all, regional cooperation on water, energy, growth management, and immigration is largely absent.[69]

Sustainability must focus on reclamation and reparation, on rectifying damaged relationships between one another and the rest of nature. A way forward may be glimpsed in the 2004 water settlement between the Gila River Indian Community (GRIC) and the federal government. The Pima, the majority tribe in the GRIC, earned the title "Good Samaritans of the Desert" in the nineteenth century by saving both federal troops and California-bound migrants from starvation. Their riverine oasis just south of Phoenix built on techniques of the Hohokam and produced a bounty of fruit, vegetables, grains, and fish. But white settlers began siphoning off the water in the 1880s, perhaps even intentionally wasting it to starve out the Pima. The tribe declined rapidly while federal officials pressured the Pima to relocate to Oklahoma.[70]

The Pima persisted and fought a nearly one hundred-year legal battle to secure adequate water. A settlement in 2004 provided the tribes with 653,500 acre-feet of water annually and provided funds for the rehabilitation, operation, and maintenance of water infrastructure on the reservation. Yet in the intervening years, non-Indian outsiders had built an industrialized agriculture system on the land, undercutting the health of both the land and the Pima who subsisted on government rations. Although the water settlement would be fulfilled with CAP water, and the Gila River itself did not again flow through the community, the settlement nevertheless provided an opportunity to revive traditional agriculture. Pima activists did just that, using federal funds to build a new system of irrigation canals on top of the Hohokam ruins.[71]

In 2006, however, Arizona's Proposition 206 defined zoning and environmental regulations as a taking of property that required compensation. The neoliberal law undercut efforts to shield desert land from the growth machine, including the 372,000 acres of the GRIC, the largest undeveloped tract contiguous to a major metropolis in the United States. As urban sprawl advanced toward the GRIC, pressure mounted for the Tribal Council to lease part of the water it won in the 2004 settlement for new development. Intratribal debate on whether to sell water and invite development continues, while elsewhere in the region small farmers are still being displaced.[72]

Still, the Pimas' irrigation project demonstrates the potential to revive the abandoned Bureau of Reclamation dream of small farmers cooperating on arid land. More than offering the latest gizmo or gated community to the affluent, the future of sustainability rests on such efforts to address injustice, preserve resources, and find pathways out of poverty for the marginalized. If Phoenix can take the lead in the coming decades to repair human and environmental relationships across the city and region, it might yet provide a model for a new and better civilization rising from the ashes.

10

Reclaiming a Democratic Tradition

What Would Green Populism Look Like?

In the United States, as elsewhere across the globe, the defining challenge of our time is the deep division between urban and rural communities. Our current political situation is fluid and volatile, making prediction or prescription a fraught enterprise. But this study suggests that a political movement sensitive to both urban and rural concerns might transform the electoral map and unleash our public powers. Only then could we fully address the escalating challenges of environmental degradation and social inequality. In the wake of their successes in the 2018 elections, Democrats moved to create just such a movement, issuing an inclusive call for a Green New Deal. A bold set of initiatives, the Green New Deal targeted "deindustrialized communities," "depopulated rural communities," and "indigenous peoples."[1]

A shift to 100 percent renewable energy and an update of the power grid stood at the center of the Green New Deal. The plan also included the retrofitting of all buildings to reduce energy and water usage; the renovation of existing industrial plants; the promotion of clean manufacturing; and the overhaul of transportation infrastructure with zero emission vehicles, public transit, and high-speed rail. The vision extended beyond the metropolitan core to include support for family farming, the reduction of pollution in agriculture, and the restoration of soil health. Cleaning up hazardous wastes, promoting reforestation, and restoring natural ecosystems rounded out its ambitious environmental agenda.[2]

The Green New Deal also proposed publicly financed elections and government-sponsored health insurance, housing, and public utilities (solar heat, clean water, and universal broadband). Twenty years hence, in this vision, young Americans would find good, high-paying, unionized jobs building the infrastructure necessary to make their communities more resilient. Without student debt, they would work a thirty-six-hour week and enjoy high-speed rail, good public parks and beaches, concerts and other public arts, and locally sourced food. Young entrepreneurs would be able to start businesses without worrying about paying for their employees' health care.[3]

The creation of decent, well-paid jobs; first-rate, affordable education; and high-quality health care, combined with action on climate change and other environmental challenges, would seem to be a winning proposition in voting booths and legislative halls. Polling conducted in late 2018 revealed that large majorities, including many young Republicans, believe climate change is real and favor public support for clean energy. A solid and stable majority of Americans, including many moderate Republicans, favor green building codes and enhanced efforts to reduce air and water pollution. Polls taken at the end of 2018 revealed that the Green New Deal had overwhelming bipartisan support. Even after months of relentless partisan criticism, it still won the support of nearly 60 percent of likely voters in the summer of 2019.[4]

Yet the broad democratic majority needed to tackle the vested interests that stand in the way of the ambitious agenda of the Green New Deal never materialized. In the summer of 2022, Congress did pass the Inflation Reduction Act, which included a few important environmental initiatives, including $34 billion for conservation and clean energy initiatives in rural communities. But the law made major concessions to fossil fuel interests, including support for new pipelines and for experiments in carbon capture that will provide justification for prolonging the use of fossil fuels.[5]

An angry and nihilistic right-wing authoritarianism stands as a major obstacle to bolder action and can only deepen our troubles. But any effort to overcome the threat of authoritarianism will require the political imagination to see that, however ugly, the small town and rural anger that props up authoritarianism is, in significant part, the product of the dysfunctional relationship between city and country. The strategy of dismissing those who vote for right-wing authoritarians as "a basket of deplorables" is not a winning one.[6]

Too many small towns and rural communities suffer from declining standards of living and life expectancies, along with boarded-up main streets with little sign of economic activity. Economic growth over the past twenty years has been almost entirely located in metropolitan counties. As recently as the early 1990s, 71 percent of new business growth occurred in smaller, rural counties. That percentage fell to 51 percent in the wake of the 2002–2003 recession, and to 19 percent following the Great Recession of 2007–2008. Small towns and rural communities suffer from downward trends in everything from success in school and work to health, sobriety, and staying on the right side of the law. With opportunity disappearing, a plague of methamphetamines and opioids, so-called drugs of despair, deepen the damage.[7]

Yet in the wake of the 2016 elections that revealed the depth of rural discontent, disgruntled Democrats complained that areas lagging economically dictated policy to more dynamic areas. Democrats pointed out that their presidential candidate carried only 16 percent of counties, but those counties generated two-thirds of U.S. gross domestic product. The median income of Democratic-held districts in the House of Representatives, moreover, was $8,000 greater than in Republican-held districts. The trend toward greater divergence continued over the next four years. But few pundits or scholars asked whether metropolitan centers had anything to offer rural areas—or, indeed, whether they bore any responsibility for their plight.[8]

The electoral consequence of this neglect of rural concerns is that, even as Democrats build up majorities in every major metropolitan area, they often fail to win even 25 percent of the vote in rural districts. As recent elections have been extremely tight, Democrats have followed Republicans in shifting from persuading undecided voters to mobilizing their base. This has resulted in ever more strident partisanship, inflaming divisions. Here and there politicians, such as Ohio's Democratic Senator Sherrod Brown, have tried a different strategy by appealing to rural communities with a combination of economic development and environmental protection. The electoral appeal of the left-wing populist Bernie Sanders in rural areas, both in Vermont and nationally in the 2016 primaries, suggests the potential of such a strategy.[9]

None of this is to minimize the shameful conditions in the ghettoes of our central cities. Unemployment is 5–15 percentage points higher among young Black men than white men, and the gap reaches 25 percent for the nineteen-to-twenty-four age bracket. Mass incarceration, especially pronounced among young Black men, destroys individual lives, as well as families and communities. Young Black men are regularly harassed and worse by the police and are victimized by crime far more often than young white men. Nor can we ignore the plight of women of whatever color. Women still earn less than 80 percent of what men do for comparable work. Women also face constant threats of sexual harassment and worse. While some women have joined the authoritarian right, they are much more likely to be the objects of its resentments.[10]

Women, minorities, and environmentalists, however, may find a coalition that includes the working classes and independent proprietors from small town and rural communities more willing, and more able, to address social inequality and environmental degradation than one dominated solely by the affluent metropolitan classes. But the prospects for such a coalition are limited as long as rural despair fuels right-wing authoritarianism. Improving prospects for rural Americans is crucial not only for reasons of social justice and environmental repair, but also to isolate right-wing authoritarians, deny them more recruits, preserve democracy, and avoid further civil strife.[11]

Right-wing authoritarians have little to offer rural America. The promises to restore the family farm and return mining and manufacturing jobs are empty. Indeed, the great replacement theory (that elites are recruiting minorities to replace whites) misses its mark. Right-wing authoritarians enact tax policies that encourage robotics and automation, eliminating the jobs they pledged to save. One robot reduces the employment of approximately six workers, often white men without a college education. Jobs that rely on brawn, repetitive physical activity, and basic data management are disappearing. The next wave of innovation is targeting wholesale and retail trade, warehousing, and transport, further reducing employment options for blue-collar workers.[12]

Right-wing authoritarians ill serve their constituents in other ways, as well. Even as the number of American farmers dwindles, they have done nothing to slow the concentration of agricultural land in fewer and often absentee hands. Right-wing authoritarians who refused the federal monies appropriated for an expansion of Medicaid endanger not only the health of their constituents but their employment prospects, as well. One in seven jobs in rural areas are in hospitals, 130 of which have closed in the past decade. Six hundred others are in danger of closing. Spreading skepticism about the COVID-19 vaccines, moreover, has cost lives of many of their constituents.[13]

Many obstacles stand in the way of overcoming right-wing authoritarianism, including partisan redistricting, primary elections that amplify the power of extremes of left and right, and the echo chambers of media and social media. But nothing stands in the way of offering rural voters a more hopeful vision. It will help to recognize that rural politics are more complex than we think. Right-wing authoritarianism serves social reactionaries and red-state corporate powers, the latter monopolizing economic assets, from agricultural land to fast food restaurants and car dealerships. Authoritarianism succeeds by drawing back into politics the dispossessed rural classes and inflaming their economic and cultural grievances against politicians, urbanites, and minorities. But the many good and decent people in rural America have legitimate concerns about the future of the country. In appropriating the populist label, right-wing authoritarians, however cynically, address these concerns by promising to rescue the democratic process from corrupt interests; defend communities threatened by outside interests; and preserve opportunities for small, independent proprietors.[14]

In other words, we need a clearer and less dismissive understanding of the populist tradition, its strengths as well as its weaknesses. The label *populist* itself, long used as a term of derision, may be tainted beyond redemption. But the positive aspects of the populist tradition are still worth reclaiming from those who now use its negative aspects as a tool to perpetuate plutocracy. Recent populist insurgencies have taken two forms: political populism aimed at governmental elites and economic populism aimed at corporate elites. If the *anti-government* populism that now paralyzes public action can be submerged in *anti-corporate* populism, we might still reclaim the tradition. In the wake of the 2016 election, the pollster Guy Molyneaux found 64 percent approval, across party lines, for the following message:

> We need to take back our government so that it works for all Americans, not just billionaires and special interests. The size of government is less important than who it works for. Instead of giving tax breaks and subsidies to big corporations, we should create jobs, improve education, lift wages, and help people retire with dignity. And we should get big money out of politics, so that our government is accountable to the people.

As this message suggests, economic populism lies just beneath the surface of political populism. A democratic movement that advances an economic populist message may uncover unsuspected agreement.[15]

If we are to avoid the worst outcomes, environmentally and politically, we also need a clearer understanding of the limits of the New Deal model. The regional and green initiatives of the original New Deal, from the Tennessee Valley Authority to the Soil Conservation Service, recommend it as a model for some of what we need. So, too, do the social movements for sharing our wealth, securing labor's right to organize, and protecting the elderly that emboldened the original New Deal. But the New Deal's support for highways and suburbanization increased the economy's dependence on fossil fuels. On the Great Plains, New Deal policies failed to stop the spread of dangerous monocultures while its crop subsidies, now ensconced in the Farm Bill, sped the industrialization of agriculture across the nation. Most telling, the original New Deal only fitfully took on concentrated wealth. With the richest 1 percent of Americans controlling nearly one-third of all wealth and chief executive-to-employee compensation rising to more than 350 to 1, that task is more pressing than ever. A combination of the two traditions, populist and New Deal, will best serve our needs.[16]

The Green New Deal and Green Populism

In their effort to revive public initiative, advocates of the Green New Deal promised to engage in transparent and inclusive consultation with local communities and develop collaborative partnerships rather than issue directives. They also insisted that taxpayers get an ownership stake and appropriate return on public investments. These are useful suggestions. As a precedent for such efforts, advocates pointed to mobilization during World War II via a government-business partnership as evidence that great transformations are possible in a short time. They also lauded the mixed public-private partnerships of the Eisenhower era when federal initiatives sparked economic prosperity. The foundations of the digital economy, including computers and the internet, satellite technology and artificial intelligence, semiconductors and transistors, fiber options and data transmission, all came out of federal laboratories.[17]

But these precedents may not fully match the challenges we face. Federal intervention into the economy during World War II rationed many essential goods, disciplined corporations, and ultimately exercised control over almost 25 percent of manufacturing. But federal largess also subsidized significant modernization of physical plants and supported ample profits. The postwar private-public partnerships of the Eisenhower administration proceeded on the famous dictum that what was good for business was good for the United States. This time around, with so many industries dependent on fossil fuels and so many proven reserves of fossil fuels still available for exploitation, stronger federal measures, perhaps even criminal sanctions against the uncooperative, will be neces-sary to wean us from fossil fuels.[18]

The late nineteenth-century populist revolt provides a better model of challenging concentrated wealth than the New Deal. Populists assailed railroad corporations, national banks, and giant manufacturing firms as outsiders that destroyed local communities. Populist energies did animate parts of the New Deal, from new regulations on commercial banks and Wall Street brokers to President Franklin Roosevelt's indictment of "eco-nomic royalists" and congressional hearings on monopoly power. But by the end of the 1930s, most New Dealers had abandoned the effort to rein in monopoly and promote a more democratic economy. Postwar New Dealers embraced the less intrusive strategy of using fiscal policy (taxing and spending) to even out the business cycle and promote steady eco-nomic growth.[19]

Originating in rural communities, the populist revolt may also pro-vide lessons for those who would build an inclusive democracy across the great divides. Attempting to overcome divisions of race, party, and geog-raphy, populists tried to make common cause with a Colored Farmers' Alliance; sought to bury Civil War–era resentments; and sent out orga-nizers to every corner of the republic, both urban and rural. The failure of these efforts also provides a cautionary tale. "You are kept apart that you may be separately fleeced of your earnings," the populist insurgent Tom Watson told white and Black farmers in 1892. "You are made to hate each other because upon that hatred is rested the keystone of the arch of financial despotism which enslaves you both." That Watson him-self became a virulent racist after the defeat of the populist insurgency underscores the costs of failure. Populism without African Americans, then as now, is a doomed populism.[20]

Bringing together a Black movement for social justice with a largely white movement for environmental reform will not be easy. "I have been trying to bridge this divide for nearly a decade," the Black activist Van Jones wrote in 2008. But nothing else will do. The effort must start by reversing some of the discriminatory effects of the original New Deal and postwar policies. Federal mortgage insurance, support for redlining and restrictive covenants, urban renewal, and expressway construction all combined to destroy Black neighborhoods and deepen racial inequality. At the end of World War II, Miami's Overtown, West Oakland, South Central in Los Angeles, Detroit's Black Bottom, Cincinnati's West End, Chicago's Bronzeville, New York's Harlem, and many other Black com-munities provided the foundation for a concerted struggle for Black equality. Such communities are now either gone or gentrified. If the environmental reforms we need are to be greeted by African Americans as something other than a new round of gentrification and dispossession, care must be taken to preserve and invest in minority neighborhoods to rekindle that earlier promise.[21]

A parallel effort will be necessary to overcome the urban-rural divide. Here again, the legacy of the New Deal is mixed. For all the New Deal's experimentation with rural resettlement, farm security, and soil conservation, its agricultural subsidies, production limits, and support for scientific and technological research favored large-scale commercial operators and agricultural processers. When these large operators secured an exemption for agricultural produce from the regulations of the Motor Carrier Act of 1935, the rise of the independent, nonunion, unregulated trucking industry followed. Independent trucking enabled large operators to both decentralize and tap wider markets, setting off another wave of consolidation in farming and processing. Nonunion truckers, often rural men forced off the land, became expendable cogs at the mercy of large interests, abandoned by both unions and government regulators.[22]

No green economy is possible without an overhaul of industrialized agriculture. That effort will intersect with the racial divide as New Deal and postwar agricultural policies discriminated against Black farmers and Black communities, continuing a pattern with roots stretching back to slavery. The green economy will also require extensive mining of metals necessary for the technologies of renewable energy. We must therefore also overhaul our approach to mining (and other extractive industries). Such a bold set of initiatives cannot have much chance of passage without a robust political coalition that includes support from rural Americans.[23]

Reclaiming Populism

Over the past century, historians and other commentators have contested the definition of populism, identifying leftist populists and rightist populists, authentic populists and shadow populists, hard populists and soft populists, modernist populists and antimodernist populists. Discounting much of the criticism of populism as disguising a contempt for the self-described "plain people," the historian Christopher Lasch recast American history as a contest between populist and progressive traditions. Lasch's populists challenged a progressive tradition willing to forgo democratic participation in favor of a material abundance produced by hierarchical corporations and distributed by a centralized, bureaucratized state. He identified a diverse set of populists (urban and rural, artisans and farmers) united by a commitment to a republic of small producers. These populists believed that democracy required the broadest possible distribution of economic and political responsibility, a condition promoted by widespread property ownership and a limit to economic inequality.[24]

Late nineteenth-century populism consisted of a powerful amalgam of conservatism and radicalism. As conservatives, populists sought to preserve independent proprietorship and traditional crafts, including farming, and the civic virtues they nurtured. Yeoman farmers, artisans, small shopkeepers all defended the free labor ideal vindicated in the Civil War but disappearing in the Gilded Age. They opposed concentrated wealth as an alien, disruptive force. As radicals, however, populists did not shy away from the need for dramatic change, including federal support for cooperatives and the regulation of banks and railroads, as necessary to the preservation of a republic of small producers. Populists took on monopolistic corporations in the name of the commonwealth; championed greater citizen participation in government; and demanded the direct election of senators, a nonpartisan ballot, and a graduated income tax.[25]

For most metropolitan liberals, *populism* is a term of contempt for uneducated bumpkins. But urban populism has a longer and richer history than is acknowledged. Late nineteenth-century urban populists in the labor movement shared many of the concerns of rural populists. Embracing the cooperative movement as a means of preserving small producers, urban populists also saw large corporations as threats to the republic and virtuous citizens as the only defense. "Shall these great corporations control the government," a leader of the Knights of Labor asked, "or shall they be controlled by government?" Republics, added another labor leader, "must depend for their stability and success upon the virtue and intelligence of the masses."[26]

In the early twentieth century, followers of the self-described urban populist Henry George revitalized urban democracy. Taking power in several cities, they continued George's effort to raise tax revenues from rising land values and other socially produced forms of wealth to improve and extend public services and urban amenities. Along with the more celebrated "sewer socialists," the Georgists turned "the amazing power of a city to create wealth" toward "the essential needs of the city dweller." Eager to increase popular participation in municipal politics, the Georgists also worked to purge city politics of special interests. In the 1930s, the philosopher and activist John Dewey found inspiration in urban populism. Dewey lauded George for recognizing that, while the city made possible "a wider, fuller, and more varied life for all," monopoly "renders one-side and inequitable the people's share in these higher values." The socialization of ground rent, Dewey concluded, "means socialization of fundamental opportunity."[27]

In recent years, the resurgence of populist movements here and abroad renewed the debate about this mercurial phenomenon. Left-wing populism, the journalist John Judis argues, mobilizes the people against an economic elite while right-wing populism mobilizes the people against a political elite *that is favoring a third group, below them at the bottom of society.* A commitment to justice and equality thus competes with resentment and scapegoating for the soul of populist politics—hence, the aversion to a society of "tramps and millionaires," long a hallmark of populist politics. Speaking for the middle ranks, populists always face the temptation to blame those beneath them and embrace a reactionary politics of racial and ethnic resentment. But at its best, the aversion to tramps and millionaires treated both ignorant mass and leisured elite as threats to the republic. Populists favored a world where no one escaped the necessity of labor, and all enjoyed the opportunity to learn.[28]

The Civil Rights Movement offers the best example of populism that resisted resentment in favor of self-discipline and self-respect. True to populism, the Civil Rights Movement demanded for African Americans the right to participate and the chance to be responsible citizens. The backbone of the movement, the preachers and teachers, the radio stations and taxi companies, the churches and universities, rested on a lower middle class of small proprietors, artisans, and independent professionals patiently built up in the years since the end of the Civil War. Its leaders sought to enlist the broad middle class, and the impoverished masses below them, in a disciplined movement that would resist the temptation to turn toward hate and destructive violence.[29]

Refusing the privileged status as victims and acknowledging their own moral dilemmas, civil rights activists resolved to hate the sin, not the sinner. Drawing on the populist tradition, Martin Luther King Jr. also brought the Protestant theologian Reinhold Niebuhr's spiritual defense against resentment to the movement. "If social cohesion is impossible without coercion," Niebuhr asked in 1932, "and coercion is impossible without the creation of social injustice, and the destruction of injustice is impossible without the use of further coercion, are we not in an endless cycle of social conflict?" Speaking extemporaneously at the start of the Montgomery bus boycott in 1955, King provided the following answer.[30]

Asserting that his people had "no alternative but to protest," King cautioned that "our actions must be guided by the deepest principles of our Christian faith. Love must be our regulating ideal." King continued: "If we fail to do this our protest will end up as a meaningless drama on the stage of history, and its memory will be shrouded with the ugly garments of shame. In spite of the mistreatment that we have confronted we must not become bitter and end up by hating our white brothers." If, however, "you will protest courageously, and yet with dignity and Christian love," King concluded, "when the history books are written in future generations, the historians will have to pause and say, 'There lived a great people—a Black people—who injected new meaning and dignity into the veins of civilization.' This is our challenge and our overwhelming responsibility."[31]

Shamefully, the white resistance that greeted the Black demand for equality reflected the resentful strain of populism. So did much of the homeowner populism that fueled the late twentieth-century tax revolts. Following the mortgage crisis in 2008, this ugly strain of populism again came into prominence and is still with us. But the rise of populist politics has always signaled political volatility, a breakdown of ruling assumptions. In the 1890s, it signaled the demise of laissez-faire. In the 1960s, it anticipated the collapse of Jim Crow. In the 1970s and the 1980s it sped the unraveling of the New Deal order. In the aftermath of the 2008 recession, the neoliberal consensus came under fire. In the presidential campaign of 2016, populists of the left and the right blamed financial deregulation and global trade agreements for the recession and growing economic inequality. They shifted public debate as both parties stopped attacking entitlements and demanding balanced budgets and instead promised to regulate Wall Street and scrutinize future trade deals.[32]

Few of the promises of 2016 have been kept, but the erosion of the neoliberal consensus continues. The mobility of capital, the decline of domestic manufacturing, and the growing irresponsibility of the financial and high-tech sectors of the economy all exacerbate economic inequality. Yet misplaced populist anger has enabled a plutocratic gutting of government regulations and protections. Whether trust in public action can be successfully rekindled remains to be seen. But a proper understanding of populism challenges the nihilism of right-wing authoritarianism. "We believe that the powers of government—in other words, of the people—should be expanded," the Populist Party announced in 1892, "as rapidly and as far as the good sense of an intelligent people and the teachings of experience shall justify, to the end that oppression, justice, and poverty shall eventually cease in the land." This populist conviction may help us overcome our political paralysis and deploy public powers to address our mounting troubles.[33]

Existential threats, such as war, economic depression, and natural disaster, often call forth public mobilization and shared sacrifice. This has not happened yet with environmental degradation, but tapping into populist energy can still make it happen. There is widespread recognition that the ballooning profits enjoyed in financial and high-tech sectors over the past forty years have come at the cost of ignoring more productive activities. The simplistic fixation on economic growth as the measure of social well-being must be overcome. The buoyant stock market, and the ballooning wealth of billionaires, in the early years of the social disaster of COVID-19 should have made it clear that maximizing the gross national product only further enriches plutocrats. Social needs and planetary health must become our primary concerns.[34]

The Lost Soul of the Democratic Party

Democrats must recover the populist convictions that once connected them with working-class and farm families. Speaking in a populist mode, Franklin Roosevelt recognized concentrated economic wealth as a threat to political democracy in his 1932 campaign for the presidency. Defining private property as limited to the legitimate accumulation of a family, Roosevelt argued that concentrated, corporate wealth represented a potentially dangerous power that must be treated as a public trust. The continued "enjoyment of that power by any individual or group," Roosevelt thundered, "must depend upon the fulfillment of that trust."[35]

In the middle years of the 1930s, populist-minded Democrats struggled, with only partial success, to break up concentrations of corporate wealth. The regulation of the stock market and large banks, the dissolution of giant utility corporations, and the restraining of unfair competition marked their efforts. These initiatives earned the support of farmers and workers by delivering concrete benefits. But such efforts declined in the immediate postwar decades as Democrats embraced economic growth as the answer to all questions. By the early 1970s, in the context of an unpopular war in Vietnam and the Watergate scandal, a younger generation of Democrats began to see the federal government as just as culpable as big corporations in the ills of American society. Unmarked by the Depression-era labor struggles, these younger Democrats also judged the white working class as reactionary and racist in its support for the war in Vietnam and resistance to integration.[36]

The post–Watergate Democratic Party built a coalition based less on farmers and workers than on college-educated whites, women, and minorities. This Democratic coalition took on many forms of discrimination and intolerance and made the United States a better, more inclusive place. But at the same time, Democrats failed to prevent, and in some cases abetted, a dramatic concentration of economic power. They found merit in neoliberal arguments about how government regulation and antitrust policies discouraged investment. The idea of concentrated economic power as a public trust, or a threat to democracy, fell by the wayside.[37]

Entranced by neoliberalism, Democrats trusted the free market to correct excessive monopoly profits. Their embrace of global free trade agreements reflected this faith. They also contributed to the spread of deregulation and the relaxing of antitrust laws that began under Democratic President Jimmy Carter and accelerated under Republican President Ronald Reagan. Subsequent administrations, Democratic as well as Republican, continued the neoliberal tack. Economic concentration continued while rural and blue-collar prospects darkened.[38]

For a time during Bill Clinton's presidency, buoyed by the digital boom, the new Democratic coalition held on to enough white, working-class votes to win elections. But white working-class and farm families' long-term drift from the Democratic Party resumed soon enough, particularly in the South, as the promised benefits of neoliberal policies failed to materialize. Yet not even the mortgage crisis and recession of 2008 changed Democratic strategy. The Dodd-Frank Wall Street Reform Act of 2010 veered away from any populist condemnation of financial irresponsibility. As a new wave of economic concentration followed the recession, declining voter turnout reflected growing cynicism about politics. The debt finally came due in 2016 when the Democratic Party lost key elements of its onetime base, particularly blue-collar voters without college degrees.[39]

The sense Americans already had in the 1990s that the institutions that shaped their lives were beyond reach is now pervasive. Americans have little control over the economic giants—Amazon, Google, Walmart, Cargill, Tyson, Archer Daniels Midland—that transform their communities without local input. Political institutions appear equally unresponsive as frustration over the power of money in politics pushes the reputation of Congress to all-time lows. The question is not big government or small but the desperate need to establish some control over the institutions, public and private, that exert so much control over our lives.[40]

In addressing social inequality, Democrats will have to balance a commitment to minorities with a more universal appeal. In her recent study *The Sum of Us: What Racism Costs Everyone and How We Can Prosper Together*, the activist and scholar Heather McGhee marshals an imposing body of evidence to suggest that, although white people suffer from the absence of good public schools, safe and functioning infrastructure, public health and health care, a clean environment, ample parks and playgrounds, and good union jobs that pay decent wages, too many white people would rather go without than share these things with people of color. Racism makes it difficult for us to secure the public goods and the benefits of solidarity that none of us can provide on our own.[41]

Eager to address the plight of African Americans and other minorities, McGhee calls for a "targeted universalism," a commitment to universal goals that considers the specific circumstances of various populations. McGhee concedes that this may be a hard sell to white Americans. But if her strategy also considers the struggles of blue-collar and rural whites, it may provide a way forward. A green populism can stand for the larger public good while also paying close attention to necessary reparations, both social and environmental, urban and rural, Black and white.[42]

More powerfully than an expanded social welfare state, a green populism that links socially useful work to a generous public realm can turn anger into commitment and a shared sense of purpose. In the wake of the 2009 bailout of irresponsible banks judged "too big to fail," the neoliberal case against public initiative is bankrupt. The billions in public funds subsidizing industries from fossil fuels to food processing makes neoliberal talk of free markets a sham. The choice is not between a laissez-faire economy and a regulated one, or between liberty and regimentation, but between different sets of values and policies aimed at different outcomes. Green populists should invest in fields essential to social well-being, such as teaching and nursing, and provide a federal job guarantee that offers alternatives (wetlands restoration, retrofitting buildings, community gardens, care for the young and old, etc.) to low-paid work in carbon-intensive retail and fast food. Shifting labor out of extractive industries will require different incentives. But oil, gas, and coal workers can be won over to socially useful opportunities in the transition to cleaner energy.[43]

Crossing Great Divides

Above all, green populists must be prepared to listen and to learn. No one can pretend to have any full and complete understanding of the needs and concerns of rural and blue-collar citizens. But a few modest suggestions can be ventured. And here, the New Deal model may serve. The New Deal's Civilian Conservation Corps (CCC) provided socially useful work for millions of unemployed young men while repairing and restoring damaged landscapes. Supporters chose the name "corps" to provide a sense of common purpose much needed during the Great Depression. Despite some controversy and missteps, the CCC proved to be one of the more popular New Deal initiatives.[44]

An expanded version of the CCC can dramatize green populism's commitment to both socially useful work and the public good. The term *conservation* can also help green populists cross partisan and geographic divides. Conservation-minded hunters, for example, have many of the same concerns as environmentalists. Members of the 116th Congress (2019–2020) introduced multiple CCC-style proposals. Sanders made it an important part of his 2020 presidential campaign, calling for $171 billion to "provide good-paying jobs building green infrastructure, planting billions of trees," "rebuilding wetlands," and "cleaning up plastic pollution."[45]

A new CCC can provide an opportunity for engaging our divisions. Veterans of the original CCC recalled that it taught them how to get along with different types of people. Although largely segregated, the original CCC experimented with integration outside the South. Some white recruits even staged protests when federal officials enforced segregation. Rural communities initially feared the influx of reckless city boys but quickly embraced the camps when it became clear they brought an infusion of cash. Great benefits could come from a thoroughly integrated program, taking on urban as well as rural projects and enlisting young women as well as men.[46]

Atlanta's current remaking of the Chattahoochee Riverlands suggests some of the possibilities of a new CCC. A participatory design process is now underway to build an environmentally sensitive 125-mile trail along the Chattahoochee River. Reducing water pollution, providing new recreational opportunities, and encouraging understanding of an ecosystem, the trail will link a million people across urban, suburban, and rural Georgia. "We all know how divided the state is," the leader of the design process explains. "My question is, Can we do with landscape what we can't do with political ideology or the internet? Can we mend things, ecologically, and also repair the social world?" Linking urban, suburban, and rural communities, river systems offer unique opportunities for crossing divides. Such projects can even create a new generation of ecologically minded citizens who recognize themselves as agents of change, embrace an obligation to nonhuman nature, and enjoy a connection and commitment to place.[47]

Nor does a public works program need to focus exclusively on the young. The original CCC employed "experienced men" to guide and train the recruits. With the help of experienced women and men, young people can, for example, begin to retrofit all existing buildings for more efficiency in the use of energy and water. In the process, young Americans will learn important new skills. Combined with other initiatives to invest in human resources, education, and care for the elderly, the effort can also provide an opportunity to improve public schools, support minority and rural businesses, and close the gender gap in income.[48]

A new CCC will also acquaint a cross-section of young Americans with the challenges of impoverished urban and rural communities through direct engagement. Poverty and environmental injustice are found everywhere and in all colors, in small towns and rural areas, as well as cities and suburbs. More Americans need to understand this. Green populists must make clear that local communities, urban and rural, are under attack from outside interests who reap the benefits and leave the costs to workers and taxpayers.[49]

Too many young people of whatever color or gender feel lost in a world that does not value or foster diligence, integrity, or loyalty. A populist determination to defend local communities will best reach young people who, above all, want to be asked to do something important. The politics of resentment feeds on the sense that work is no longer valued; that greater market rewards stem from a spuriously defined "merit." We need to recognize, support, and reward the work that is essential to social well-being.[50]

Green Populism and Agriculture

Green populists will need to address agriculture, which stands at the center of the great divide between city and country. The future health of rural—and urban—communities will hinge on it. The dystopian case can be seen in California's "prison alley," thirteen prisons stretching across the length of the Central Valley. After World War II, huge, mechanized cotton growers, with ties reaching back to plantation slavery, monopolized Bureau of Reclamation water, squeezed out small family farmers, and slashed their labor force. In the 1980s, a series of droughts and declining reserves of irrigation water caused the growers to leave more and more land idle and pocket federal subsidies for *not* growing surplus crops. Faced with idle land and capital, growers hit on a prison fix. In what must be the most perverse expression of flexism, they helped to orchestrate the transfer of the surplus population of the urban unemployed, caught up in mass incarceration, to for-profit prisons on idled rural land, hiring unemployed farmers as prison guards.[51]

That nightmare scenario highlights the dangers of the monopolization of land. Although the original New Dealers too often ignored the plight of Black and tenant farmers, they recognized the need for land reform. They provided land, training, loans, and communal infrastructure to some of the poorest farmers in the country. The original populists also made land reform a priority, demanding the end of absentee ownership. In 1973, the populist National Conference on Land Reform tried to revive the issue. One conferee argued that economic inequality, environmental degradation, and "the deterioration of our cities" all "have their roots in the land, or more precisely, in the lack of access to productive land ownership by the poor, the young, and the non-white." Green populists must embrace that insight.[52]

The monopolization of farmland has skyrocketed in recent decades, further crowding out small, Black, and indigenous farmers. The wealthiest 1 percent of Americans now own 40 percent of land value. The concentration of land ownership has led to heedless extraction in agriculture, made all the easier as depopulation leaves rural democracies demoralized and vulnerable. Industrialized agriculture is careless about the health of soils and is drawing down both the nutrients and the water necessary to success. All farmers interested in conservation must get federal assistance, as preserving soil helps us all. More acres are enrolled in conservation plans than ever, involving half a million farmers protecting soil, water, and air. But we need more, as the care of our disappearing topsoil is crucial. Federal crop insurance must come with a requirement for a conservation plan.[53]

The African American role in agriculture, urban and rural, needs to be recognized and supported. After centuries of enslavement, Black farmers continued to suffer from violence and discrimination after emancipation, including at the hands of the U.S. Department of Agriculture. But they have also been responsible for much of the success of American agriculture, from pioneering new crops to creating community land trusts that preserve land for small farmers. Landownership and food production have always been central to the Black freedom struggle, from the demand for forty acres and a mule and training programs at Tuskegee and other schools through the Federation of Southern Cooperatives and various Black nationalist drives for self-sufficiency and self-determination. Black farmers' patient efforts since emancipation to secure property and build cooperatives deserve federal assistance, as do recent calls for young people, Black and white, to return to farming. Such efforts can complement the journalist Charles Blow's call for African Americans to return to the South, challenge white supremacy, and remake the electoral map.[54]

Central to social justice, the future of American farms is also linked to broader environmental issues, including climate change and public health. When all greenhouse gas emissions (GHGs) are tallied, our food system accounts for a third or more. Tilling the land always releases carbon, but industrialized agriculture also adds GHGs from chemical fertilizers, pesticides, farm machinery, food processing, packing, and transport. In 1940, every calorie of fossil fuel energy produced 2.3 calories of food. Today, ten calories of fossil fuel energy are needed for every—often unhealthful—calorie found in the supermarket. "The oil we eat," the historian Richard Manning explains, can be found in "the rings of fat around our necks and waists."[55]

That fat has more than a little to do with rising health care costs, from 5 percent of national income in 1960 to nearly 18 percent in 2017. Heart disease, stroke, type 2 diabetes, and cancer, four of the top ten killers, all are linked to our diets. Industrialized agriculture produces an abundance of cheap calories. But as spending on food has declined, spending on health care has risen in response. Policies designed to increase production at all costs have come at the expense of the health of soil, the planet, and ourselves. The vast subsidies still provided to corn-soybean-sugar-feedlot-meat monocultures have stymied food reformers.[56]

Those monocultures supplanted an older pattern of agriculture based, first and foremost, on sunshine and photosynthesis rather than fossil fuels. Crop diversity and rotation, pasturage of animals, and cover crops in the winter all helped to replenish soil and control pests. The fertilizers (made from natural gas) and the pesticides (made from petroleum) now used so extensively are quite recent additions to our farms, products of the repurposing of wartime explosives and nerve gases after 1945. Federal subsidies make it possible to sell grain for less than the cost of producing it, giving rise to another monoculture of feedlots. This turned the valuable fertilizer of animal manure, once the staple of small farms, into a concentrated form of pollution on factory feedlots.[57]

The resolarization of American agriculture should be a prime goal of green populists. The package of legislation known as "the Farm Bill" provides the federal government with vast leverage over agriculture. Passed roughly every five years, with roots in the New Deal, the Farm Bill expired in September 2023 and as of this writing, in October, has not yet been renewed. Green populists should work to amend the bill to encourage greater reliance on sunshine and less reliance on fossil fuels, artificial fertilizers, and pesticides. Diversification will help. Currently, if farmers take crop subsidies for corn and soybeans, they are prohibited from growing fruit and vegetables (a prohibition extracted by produce growers in California and Florida). This must change, and animals must be returned to farms. With intelligent rotation, land can be moved from pasture to crops over an eight-year cycle, without artificial fertilizers or pesticides. The use of cover crops is also crucial, reducing erosion and enriching soil. Composting will add to fertility, retain water, reduce drought, and likely improve the nutritional quality of food. It will also reduce the cost and environmental danger of municipal landfills.[58]

Over the next fifty years, the boldest efforts must shift our agriculture from annual grains to perennial grains. Every healthy ecosystem in the world supports perennial species in mixtures, building soil in the process. Annual monocultures do the opposite, drawing down soil fertility while necessitating vast quantities of artificial fertilizers and pesticides. The Land Institute's "A 50-Year Farm Bill" proposes gradual, systemic change over ten consecutive five-year farm bills, shifting subsidies and programs toward perennial polycultures. The institute's perennial grain, Kernza, is already commercially viable. It helps to sequester carbon, reduce dependence on fossil fuels, and protect soil from erosion. Its spread will limit toxins, reduce water waste, shrink dead zones in the Gulf of Mexico, and rebuild farm communities. Industrialized agriculture is also responsible for 70 percent of water contamination. The Green Lands Blue Waters coalition, an initiative of reformers from land grant colleges and environmental organizations founded in 2004, seeks to perennialize the entire Mississippi River basin. Such efforts deserve public support.[59]

Another example of regenerative agriculture is the effort to end concentrated animal feeding operations, which can survive only with the help of federal policies that subsidize the cost of grain, grant approval for the use of antibiotics (undermining their effectiveness for humans), and exempt such operations from the sewage treatment regulations that apply to cities with comparable waste loads. Here again government has enormous leverage. Remove those supports, and animals will return to farms. The price of meat will rise, but this is a good thing for human and environmental health, the welfare of animals, and dwindling sources of fresh water (producing a pound of meat requires five thousand gallons of water).[60]

These regenerative forms of agriculture must replace a system that is damaging the health and fertility of both our soils and our bodies. If the same research and development that made industrialized agriculture possible is applied to diversified, solar-based agriculture, the already impressive yields of organic farmers can be enhanced. Studies suggest that, per acre, organic farmers in the United States already produce 80 percent as much food as conventional farms. Nutrition must also be considered alongside yield. Food of higher quality can be a boon to health and well-being. Turning less grain into animal feed and biofuel can also increase our food supply.[61]

Well-designed polycultures can eventually produce food in greater quantities, of higher quality, and more securely. The trick is that it will require more human labor. Farming without fertilizers and pesticides is labor- and skill-intensive. Our two million farmers will not be enough. With the average age of the American farmer near sixty, we are going to need many more farmers and more gardeners, too, and this will require a reversal of policy. Instead of reducing labor through technology and fossil fuels, our land grant (and other) colleges need to inspire and train more students to embrace farming and gardening as respected and well-paid vocations. Such efforts, consistent with the original purpose of the land grant colleges, will expand the ranks of small proprietors central to the vision of the original populists.[62]

Nothing can bring the city and the country closer together than regional food systems. We had them not so long ago. "Instead of being competitive with agriculture," the study *The Suburban Trend* reported in 1925, "great cities actually create conditions under which increasing agricultural populations are brought in to people rural suburbs." But postwar urban sprawl and industrialized agriculture disrupted these systems. Prime agricultural land within a day's drive of big urban centers of population must be preserved, an imperative clear to activists fifty years ago but too often ignored by metropolitan planners today. Fair prices for nutritious foods benefit both rural producers and urban consumers, as Seattle's Pike Place Market and other public markets demonstrate. Regional food systems will help reduce transit distances, slow climate change, and repair the metabolic rift.[63]

The cause of healthy food can help us build new, stronger relationships among urban, suburban, and rural places. The need for healthy food also crosses ideological boundaries, as the family meal is as important to conservatives as to liberals, who also share a skepticism about giant agrobusinesses. Farm activists have sometimes made common cause with the Black Congressional Caucus (in favor of spending on nutrition), labor unions (focused on the common interests of farmers and workers), and the environmental movement (against pesticides and soil abuse). Passage of the Farm Bill always depends on urban representatives concerned about nutrition. Indeed, the Farm Bill is one of the few places urban and rural Americans cooperate. Healthy food can also bring broader cultural change. Fast food is part of our culture of manic, mindless consumption and is no way to live. Rethinking our most basic relationship to the natural world can move us toward the healthy transformation of daily life so essential to meeting our environmental challenges.[64]

Epilogue

The Need for Resilience

Religion, Science, and Philosophical Pragmatism

As a midwesterner, I have experienced extreme weather all my life, including blizzards, hailstorms, tornados, and, above all, thunderstorms that can make your heart skip a beat. Aside from the general inconvenience and occasional terror of driving in snow or negotiating a steep, icy rural driveway, I have loved it all, especially the thunderstorms. For many years in southeastern Indiana, I would sit on the ground on a steep hillside I cleared when we first moved there and watch the clouds roll in over the surrounding forest. I reveled as I felt the breeze pick up and cool, the leaves dance and fall, and the birds chirp and caw and smelled the air change to something moist and alive. I would sit there for the first minutes of the bracing, cooling rain, raising my arms skyward, peering straight up into the falling rain, and then duck under cover and watch the storm with ecstasy. I love thunderstorms.

Or, rather, I did. My joy is more complicated now. Several years ago, after moving to Cincinnati, I sat in my backyard and watched a thunderstorm roll in. At first, I enjoyed it as usual, feeling the air come alive as the birds and the squirrels darted nervously about. I welcomed the first drops and sat there contentedly as it built to a torrent. Then came a loud crack and dull thud. I passed through the gate into the front yard to find a huge limb, about the size of the barrel of an old cannon, lying on the ground. It came from the enormous silver maple, poised like a wrecking ball over the room where I sleep. No significant damage had been done—at least, not this time. But it left me with a keen sense of the precariousness of life and my own vulnerability.

Initially, I thought of this new feeling as loss. What a shame that, as climate change increases the frequency and severity of storms, we must fear nature. But then a friend pointed out Aldo Leopold's recollection of riding his horse on White Mountain in Arizona one summer. "Black gloom hung poised," Leopold recalled, while every living thing "cowered under the impending lash of lightning, rain, and hail." As the storm came on and lightning blasted rock and tree, Leopold saw "smoking slivers of stone" and splinters of pine, including one, fifteen feet long, "that stabbed deep into the earth at my feet and stood there humming like a tuning fork." Leopold continued: "When I hear anyone say he does not fear lightning, I still remark inwardly: he has never ridden the Mountain in July." For Leopold, fear was a central part of the experience. "It must be a poor life," he concluded, "that achieves freedom from fear."[1]

I now see my earlier, uncomplicated enjoyment of thunderstorms as a symptom of disorder, a complacency born of a false belief in our mastery of nature. My fear is a healthy acknowledgment of dependence and a path toward gratitude and resilience. We are all vulnerable. No one, regardless of location or financial security, no matter how carefully distanced from the common fate, is exempt from the capriciousness of nature. Should we somehow address the existential threats of deteriorating soils, declining supplies of fresh water, and climate change, we will not enter some Garden of Eden. The struggle to make our way in a world that cares little for our purposes will continue.[2]

We need to be resilient. Whether we rouse ourselves to address our environmental challenges or not, we face a rolling apocalypse, an uneven process of destabilizing change that will erase assumptions and strain, and quite likely break, social bonds. The billionaires may insulate themselves from the worst effects the best they can, for as long as they can, but the rest of us will be picking up the pieces from multiple disasters in the coming decades. Avoiding the worst will require cooperation.[3]

As extreme storms become more frequent, anxious audiences often ask the environmentalist Bill McKibben what they should to do prepare for life in an increasingly precarious world. McKibben advises them to live "anywhere with a strong community." They often ask, where do you find such communities? "You make them," is McKibben's reply. Here, too, we will not suddenly resolve, once and for all, the many issues that divide us. But it will surely help to overcome our alienation, loneliness, mutual suspicion, and animosity and rediscover our capacity to act collectively and support one another.[4]

We have important cultural resources that might promote cooperation and resilience. Many of us look first to religion as a source of resilience in the face of adversity. Others look first to science. We will need them both. That "nature" now plays the role in the lives of many Americans who consider themselves entirely secular that "God" plays for those who are religious suggests there may be greater space for dialogue along this divide than we think. The many evangelical Christians who embrace environmentalism—as well as Pope Francis, whose 2015 encyclical *Laudato Si'* joined spirituality and science—have begun to open that space.[5]

My own religious convictions leave me free of the dismissive attitude too many metropolitan Americans take to matters of faith. But I also look to science—specifically, to evolutionary and ecological theory—to consider what it suggests about our prospects and options. I also look to our historical experience, including that captured and refracted through our national literature, as a guide to our options as we face the future.

Religion as a Source of Resilience: From Reverence to Wonder

My ancestors would have found nothing unusual in the fear I felt that day the thunderstorm crashed into our silver maple. I grew up in a divided household, held to the Catholic faith by my mother but also deeply influenced by the attenuated Calvinism of my agonistic father. Terror in the face of the capriciousness of nature figures prominently on both sides of my religious heritage. Caught in a violent thunderstorm that crashed all around him outside his Saxon village on July 2, 1505, the twenty-one-year-old and still Catholic Martin Luther prayed to Saint Anne to preserve him, promising to become a monk if he survived.[6]

Closer to home is the conversion experience of Jonathan Edwards, the eighteenth-century Puritan divine who played a central role in the Great Awakening of the 1830s. My Fairfield ancestors arrived in colonial New England in 1636 with a Geneva Bible in hand; the Calvinist theology Edwards sought to revitalize is in my blood. In his personal narrative of conversion, Edwards recalled his impatience with what he saw as the "terrible doctrine" of "God's sovereignty," choosing some for eternal life while "rejecting whom he pleased; leaving them eternally to perish, and be everlastingly tormented in hell." Thunderstorms brought that doctrine to Edwards's mind in all its horrible immediacy. From an early age, he remembered being "uncommonly terrified with thunder, and to be struck with terror when I saw a thunderstorm rising."[7]

The young Edwards struggled to accept the Calvinist doctrine of an omnipotent, inscrutable God and the powerlessness of depraved humanity. But then he underwent a conversion experience during a thunderstorm. Immediately, he recalled, the "appearance of everything was altered; there seemed to be, as it were, a calm, sweet cast, or appearance of divine glory, in almost everything. . . . in the sun, moon, and stars; in the clouds, and blue sky; in the grass, flowers, trees; in the water, and all nature." Nothing, Edwards continued, "among all the works of nature, was so sweet to me as thunder and lightning." "I felt God at the first appearance of a thunderstorm" and would "fix myself in order to view the clouds, and see the lightnings play, and hear the majestic and awful voice of God's thunder."[8]

Mixing divinity and the natural world, Edwards built his theology around his youthful encounters with thunder and lightning. Those encounters led to his unconditional embrace of God's majesty and justice, what he called "consent and good will to Being in general." Two centuries earlier, the Protestant reformer Jean Calvin also saw nature as a route to God. "We know the most perfect way of seeking God," he wrote, is "for us to contemplate him in his works whereby he rendered himself near and familiar to us, and in some manner, communicates himself." Calvin's respect for nature led him to concede "that it can be said reverently, provided it proceeds from a reverent mind, that nature is God."[9]

The theology of consent to being in general that Edwards preached must be distinguished from quietism or passivity. The Calvinist faith that everything that came our way was the work of God, and therefore good, provided Calvinists with immense resolve in the face of adversity. That resolve played out in their commitment, in conscious dissent from the Catholic monastic tradition, to transform the world by living in it. Calvinists embraced the most difficult tasks in the sure belief that God called them to do so. This is what Calvinists meant by a calling, a vocation, and the more difficult the calling, the surer one could be that God willed it. Consent to being in general, Edwards argued, brought a sense of gratitude and expressed itself in exuberance, courage, resolution, and vitality in the face of adversity. Embracing the gift of life in the teeth of its pains, Edwards enjoyed what we call resilience.[10]

More than a century later, the pragmatic philosopher William James grappled with the same questions of gratitude, fortitude, and resilience in a universe indifferent to human projects. The evangelical Protestant spir-it Edwards tried to promulgate had, however, degenerated into a gospel of commercial success, enlisting self-discipline in avarice. In the wake of Charles Darwin's *On the Origin of Species by Means of Natural Selection* (1859), James bid goodbye to a dogmatic theology that he found literally incredible. But he still took religion seriously and believed that a careful examination of the effects of religious belief on one's mind and character offered the best understanding of religious experience. Acknowledging the religious insight that only something outside a person's conscious control (i.e., grace) can bring about a real change in character, James located it not in "the beyond" but in "the beneath," something welling up from the subconscious.[11]

Locating religious impulses in the subconscious, however, did not rule out something beyond. However much James admired the psychological realism of the Puritan divines, he did not believe psychology could replace religion. Instead, he recognized that psychological understanding had always been one of the appeals of religion. James is thus best understood as the philosopher of wonder, someone who believed that the rational, scientific mind alone cannot explain everything; nor does it provide a sufficient guide and motive to life.[12]

The question of the conduct of life confronted James in a lifelong struggle to find his vocation. In following Edwards's injunction to embrace life in the face of its terrors, James sought the energy to overcome laziness and timidity, the craving for comfort and social approval, the fear of ridicule and excessive respect for social conventions that paralyzed the capacity for action. He struggled to overcome his disillusionment with an imperfect world and resolved to act in such a way as to reduce the sum of evil. Regarding his religious doubts, he consulted his experience, as befit his pragmatic philosophy. The evidence of religious experience, his own and that in recorded history, suggested some "superhuman consciousness" existed that was nevertheless "not all-embracing." God existed, James concluded, but is finite in power or knowledge or both.[13]

It's on Us: The Evolutionary Miracle of Consciousness and Its Consequences

The finitude of God left much in human hands. But James's keen appre-ciation of the limits of rational certainty and his embrace of wonder recommended caution and humility in our approach to the world. Cau-tion and humility governed James's approach to Darwin's theory, as well.

Environmental conditions, Darwin argued, determined which organisms would die and which would live to pass on those characteristics that helped them adapt. This made evolution a matter of chance, caprice, and variation and appeared to rob the universe of any intelligent design or divine purpose. But James resisted the social Darwinist urge to treat the "survival of the fittest" (a phrase Darwin did not use) as a guide to the organization of society. Survivors were not necessarily better. They merely lucked out.[14]

James drew a different lesson from evolutionary theory. Humans lucked out in the biggest way of all, because evolution brought us the gift of consciousness. Consciousness enabled us to transcend natural selection, not only to protect the weak and care for one another, but to manipulate the environment in extraordinary ways. Darwin's theory of natural selection rankled many Christians, then as now. James's view may also rankle. "There is intelligence in the universe," the cultural critic Louis Menand said, paraphrasing James's view. "It is ours." While James might not have put it that starkly, he had enormous respect for the miracle of consciousness. Nor did his view proceed from a lack of reverence. He would have endorsed his friend Chauncey Wright's adage. "Atheism is speculatively as unfounded as theism," Wright held, "and practically can only spring from bad motives."[15]

A thoroughgoing atheist, John Dewey took James's ideas a step further. More confidently than James, Dewey found human intelligence and experience sufficient guides to action. In "The Influence of Darwin on Philosophy" (1910), Dewey wrote that "nature, till it produces a being who strives and who thinks in order that he may strive more effectively, does not know whether it cares more for justice or for cruelty." But, Dewey continued, "when the sentient organism, having experienced natural values, good and bad, begins to select, to prefer, and to make battle for its preference; and in order that it may make the most gallant fight possible picks out and gathers together in perception and thought what is favorable to its aims and what hostile, then and there Nature has at last achieved significant regard for good."[16]

I can hold Dewey's brief for the sufficiency of human experience in tension with a belief in God. Others have and will find it jarring, even offensive, too anthropocentric. But the pragmatic view should not be confused with a belief in humanity standing outside or above nature (or, by extension, the divine). "Experience is *of* as well as *in* nature," Dewey argued. "It is not experience which is experienced, but nature—stones, plants, animals, diseases, health, temperature, electricity, and so on." Nor should the sufficiency of experience be understood as precluding a moral approach to the world. Through experience we not only discover the relationships (the knowledge) that are the concern of science; we also find moral traits that are as real as anything else. Just as things have color, sound, taste, and smell, Dewey explained, so, too, they are "poignant, tragic, beautiful, humorous, settled, disturbed, comfortable, annoying, barren, harsh, consoling, splendid, fearful."[17]

The pragmatic view also must not be confused with a belief in human mastery of nature. Like James, Dewey recognized the limits of rational certainty and human understanding. Among other traits, the universe displayed a high degree of precariousness and contingency that made human mastery of nature impossible. The belief in luck and the fears of primitive humanity provided evidence enough of an uncertain, dangerous, and fearful world. But reflective thought, another product of an uncertain world—indeed, the best evidence of it—represented a more fruitful response to precariousness than luck or fear.[18]

Reflective thought would, nevertheless, fall far short of mastery. While we put our ideals and desires in the balance against precariousness, Dewey knew that our hopes would often be blasted. But if we would avoid the stance of "ruthless overlord" as fully as we renounce that of "oppressed subject," reflective thought offered the best chance to make things better and perhaps avoid the worst. "When we have used our thought to its utmost and have thrown into the moving unbalanced balance of things our puny strength," Dewey concluded, we will know that we have at least placed all our energy, imagination, skill, and bravery in service of whatever we find good in existence.[19]

Darwin's theories left James, Dewey, and other pragmatists where recent ecological theory leaves us. Over the past forty years, ecologists have dismantled the belief in a harmonious, self-rejuvenating balance of nature. Ecological succession no longer seems to lead anywhere in particular but goes on forever, with no stability, no cohesive plant and animal communities, no trend toward maximizing biomass, and no increasing diversity of species. Ecologists find only patches, shifting mosaics of individual species but no emergent balance. The "concept of a highly structured, ordered, and regulated, steady-state ecological system," an influential ecologist concluded in 1990, was "wrong at local and regional levels." As ecologists reconsidered their own knowledge about fire, wind, invading microbes, pests, predators, grinding ice, devastating drought, and volcanic eruption, disturbance displaced balance at the center of the science.[20]

The belief in a harmonious balance of nature has proved difficult for both scientists and nonscientists to give up. The belief has long been central to religious and utopian impulses and to the rational hopes of planners and managers. But our most advanced science now describes an ecology of chaos, a world "full of surprising events," the environmental historian Donald Worster explains, that "keep hitting us in the face." We are now left with the disorienting fear that "chaos was the law of nature," as Henry Adams first put it in 1907, and "order was only the dream of man." While scientists try to find a hidden order in chaos, it is not clear what the new ecology, more managerial, seeing continual change in nature, will produce in the way of social theory. Postmodern skepticism about any sort of grand social theory may make it difficult to find anything.[21]

It is well to remember, however, that this is not the first time that our advancing scientific knowledge has left us seemingly adrift. When the theory of evolution appeared to rob the universe of any intelligent design, the pragmatists showed us the way forward by teaching us to rely on our experience. It is on us, within the limits imposed by nature and our own fallibility, to consult what is good and bad in our experience and to work toward maximizing the good and minimizing the bad. The pragmatic approach informs the "adaptive management" strategy that has emerged in ecosystem ecology over the past few decades. Recognizing uncertainty in ever changing systems, adaptative management relies on an experimental approach and collective inquiry. It is always open to revision based on new knowledge gained through the management experience.[22]

The Instrumental and the Intrinsic

Scientific and other forms of knowledge (including adaptive management) examine relationships, dividing experience into subject and object. This enables us to better understand and manage relationships and extract instrumental value from nature. But confusing this useful division with the totality of experience strips nature of qualities and leaves it what Dewey called an "indifferent, dead mechanism." Those ignored qualities include what we call the intrinsic value of nature. This distinction between the instrumental and the intrinsic value of nature also shapes our environmental debates. An anthropocentric conservationism manages nature for its instrumental use, while a biocentric deep ecology reveres nature for its intrinsic value.[23]

Dewey's discussion of knowledge (about relations) and qualities (about immediacies) reveals that our recognition of nature's intrinsic worth comes out of our experience as fully as does our knowledge of nature's instrumental uses. Nature's qualities are neither in the experiencer nor in the experienced. They reside in the experience itself. Although felt, Dewey explained, qualities are not just feelings. They are objective features of natural events, "things lovable and contemptible, beautiful and ugly, adorable and awful." By putting immediate qualities back into our understanding of experience, we might better balance the instrumental and intrinsic value of nature.[24]

This same tension between the instrumental and the intrinsic is explored in our national literature. Much of American literature celebrates the (intrinsic) beauty and majesty of the American landscape while launching a criticism of the (instrumental) society that arose upon it. This literature measured the achievements of American life against an ecological ideal, what the literary scholar Leo Marx called "the maintenance of a healthy life-enhancing interaction between man and the environment."[25]

This dynamic between the instrumental and intrinsic can be seen in Mark Twain's masterpiece, *Huckleberry Finn* (1884). Twain began the work in the mood of affirmation. His effort to recapture the "glory & grandeur" he recalled from his youth on the Mississippi River generated a burst of creative energy. In the summer of 1876, he quickly wrote the first fourth of *Huckleberry Finn*, up to a steamboat's smash of the raft that sent Huck and his friend Jim, a fugitive slave, deeper into the slave South. But then Twain put the work aside, frustrated by his inability to capture the right voice, not finishing it until 1884.[26]

Twain identified but did not resolve the difficulty of voice in "Old Times on the Mississippi," a series of reminiscences published in the *Atlantic Monthly* in 1875. The difficulty arose from a conflict between the intrinsic and the instrumental, captured in two ways of looking at the great river: that of the passengers on a steamboat and that of a steamboat's pilot. The passengers do not know the river instrumentally, but they know a literary tradition that tells them, however formulaically, how to see the river's intrinsic beauty. The pilot knows the river as natural fact, dangerous to boats, and can use that knowledge, sometimes heedlessly, as an instrument of commerce. But in so doing, the pilot loses his capacity for wonder and appreciation of beauty. In the essay, Twain appears to side with the pilot, who must memorize the landscape for safety's sake, against the inadequacy and staleness of the passengers' view.[27]

But Twain found neither the passengers' nor the pilot's view adequate to what he hoped to convey in *Huckleberry Finn*. He wanted to capture what Marx calls the "joyous, even reverent feeling for the landscape of the Mississippi as he had known it in his youth." The passengers' and the pilot's voices represented conflicting sets of values. The passengers' view is perhaps aesthetically pleasing and emotionally satisfying but based on an illusion. It not only fails to see nature for what it is but imagines nature as something apart from us, refusing the responsibility that comes with recognizing nature as an instrumental part of our existence. The pilot's view is effective and precise but treats nature as simply a storehouse of resources without intrinsic value, a means devoid of higher ends.[28]

Again, this echoes our environmental debates—not just conservation versus deep ecology but between what Worster calls the imperial (instrumental) and arcadian (intrinsic) traditions in ecological thinking. For Twain, however, the issue came down to the craft of writing. He wanted to capture both the passengers' delight and the pilot's perception. This could be done only by capturing the full human experience of the river, the intrinsic and the instrumental as they are bound up in experience, as a pragmatist would put it.[29]

Twain found the appropriate voice only when he made Huck his narrator. When he resumed work on the book, Twain shifted the focus to the tension between the idyllic experience of Huck and Jim on the raft and the cruelty and hypocrisy of a slave society. In an extraordinary passage, Twain infused new energy into the extravagant hopes long attached to the American landscape. Huck is describing "the way we put in the time." We "run nights, and laid up and hid day-times," the boy explains. After securing and hiding the raft, "We set down on the [river's] sandy bottom . . . and watched the daylight come," first just "a pale place in the sky." Before long, the "river softened up. . . . [S]ometimes you could hear a sweep screaking; or jumbled up voices, it was so still, and sounds come so far."[30]

By and by, Huck continues, "you could see a streak on the water which you know by the look of the streak there's a snag there in a swift current which breaks on it and makes the streak look that way." Across the river "you make out a log cabin in the edge of the woods . . . being a wood-yard likely, and piled by them cheats so you can throw a dog through it anywheres." Then "the nice breeze springs up, and comes fanning you from over there, so cool and fresh, and sweet to smell . . . but sometimes not that way, because they've left dead fish laying around, gars, and such, and they do get pretty rank; and next you've got full day, and everything smiling in the sun, and the song-birds just going it."[31]

What makes the passage (which ought to be read in full) so remarkable is that Huck is experiencing the river directly; he is *in* the river. He brings no received notions as to how the scene should be seen or described. The facts come through, but so do the qualities. "Everything is alive, everything is changing," Marx explains, "the locus of reality is neither the boy nor the river, neither language nor nature, neither the subject nor the object, but the unending interplay between them." Here is Dewey's point that qualities are neither in the experiencing subject nor the experienced object, but in the experience itself. Huck takes nature as he finds it, knows the bad parts (the snags, the cheats, the stinking dead fish) but can also find beauty in it (the pale place in the sky, the song-birds just going it).[32]

It is, as Marx argues, an extraordinary piece of art and a powerful moment in our literature. It suggests an environmental ethic, a simultaneous appreciation of the intrinsic and instrumental qualities of nature, of qualities and relationships, and an implicit recognition of our humble place within the natural world. For a brief, exhilarating moment Twain's story is wedded to a civic ideal. When Huck resolves to not turn in the fugitive Jim ("All right, then, I'll go to hell"), his appreciation of the natural world is joined to a vision of egalitarian, interracial comity. What "you want, above all things, on a raft," Huck thinks in anticipation of this moment, "is for everybody to be satisfied, and feel right and kind toward the others." A recognition of our place in nature is joined to an ethic of caring about other people. That moment, moreover, is embedded within a larger narrative that is sensitive to the limitations of human aspirations. "After all this long journey," Huck remarks, "here was it all come to nothing, everything all busted up and ruined." The limits are real, but so are the beauty and the caring.[33]

The Sufficiency of Experience

Of course, our national literature also dramatizes our destructive pushing against those limits, our attempted mastery of nature. Herman Melville's *Moby-Dick* (1851) hinges on Captain Ahab, a man with a dream of mastery so stupendous that he would "strike the sun if it insulted me." Ahab is determined to strike revenge against the great white whale that dismembered him. "Vengeance on a dumb brute," Ahab's first mate Starbuck challenges him, "that simply smote thee from blindest instinct! Madness! To be enraged with a dumb thing, Captain Ahab, seems blasphemous." But Ahab insists there is some "inscrutable malice" beneath "the unreasoning mask" of the whale. Ahab is determined to "strike, strike through the mask!" In doing so, he will bring disaster to his ship, the Pequod, and all aboard.[34]

In his chapter "Try-Works," Melville links Ahab's desire for mastery to that of the industrializing American republic. A combination of oak, hemp, masonry, and iron, the try-works is a small factory for rendering blubber that stands near the center of the Pequod. Ishmael, who has set to sea in disgust with life on land, "of week days pent up in lath and plaster—tied to counters, nailed to benches, clinched to desks," ruminates on the try-works. He considers how, once the try-works has been started with wood shavings, the burned pieces of the whale's own blubber provide the fuel. He watches as the "pagan harpooners" from the four corners of the globe tend the fire in the dead of night. Then the "rushing Pequod," Ishmael thinks, "freighted with savages, and laden with fire, and plunging into that blackness of darkness, seemed the material counterpart of her monomaniacal commander's soul."[35]

Melville uses the violent encounter with the whale to reveal the physical dependence, the plunder and heroics, that underpin our lives. His disquisition on the Manila rope of the whale line reminds us of our animal fate, our dependence on other living things for all our needs, as well as our sad vulnerability. The whale line is attached to the harpoon on one end and carefully coiled in a large tub at the other end. In between, it is laced through sailors and oars as to make them "seem as Indian jugglers, with the deadliest snakes sportively festooning their limbs." The line ties the men to the whale, all caught in the deadly consequences of life. As the harpoon strikes and the whale takes the men off on a Nantucket sleighride, the "least tangle or kink in the coiling would, in running out, infallibly take somebody's arm, leg, or entire body off." What "more to say," Ishmael concludes. "All men are enveloped in whale lines. All are born with halters round their necks, but it is only when caught in the swift, sudden turn of death, that mortals realize the silent subtle, everpresent perils of life."[36]

Like Huck's final decision to "light out for the territory," Ishmael embodies an escapist impulse born of disgust with organized society. Like so many of the heroes in American literature, they dream of a green land of felicity that exists only in their imagination. Their exploration of the possibilities of a harmonious relationship to nature, and their search for ultimate meaning in nature, comes to naught. "It was the whiteness of the whale," Ishmael tells us, "that above all things appalled me." He can find no final meaning in the white whale, neither good nor evil, and concludes that all colors, all qualities we find in nature, are "laid on from without," by us. What frightens him the most is the lack of meaning, a "dumb blankness" that leaves us alone in an uncaring universe.[37]

Writing in 1964, Leo Marx rejected the impossible dream of a green land of felicity no less than the fear of a meaningless universe. Neither served our "intricately organized, urban, industrial, nuclear-armed society." But six years later, writing in *Science* to sound the alarm on a growing environmental crisis, Marx amended that judgment. Our best writers' "heightened sensitivity to the unspoiled environment, and man's relation to it," he wrote, provide "the basis for an alternative to the established social order." That literature did not provide "a program to be copied," but it did dramatize a "far more restrained and accommodating" approach to nature than the "aggressive thrust" of expanding capitalism. It made "an alternative mode of experience credible" to a "commercial, optimistic, self-satisfied culture."[38]

That heightened sensitivity to an unspoiled landscape also figures prominently in F. Scott Fitzgerald's *The Great Gatsby* (1925). Nick Carraway, Fitzgerald's narrator, found "something gorgeous," an "extraordinary gift for hope," in the otherwise appalling schemer, Jay Gatsby. Near the end of the novel, Carraway imagines Gatsby's gaudy Long Island estate melting away and revealing "the fresh, green breast of the New World" that Dutch sailors first encountered as they approached Long Island. For perhaps the last time in history, Carraway thinks, man stood face to face with "something commensurate to his capacity for wonder." Gatsby's extraordinary gift for hope arose from this extraordinarily beautiful continent.[39]

A less fortunate son of this continent, the slave Paul D in Toni Morrison's *Beloved* (1987), experienced a different sort of heightened sensitivity to the landscape. Escaping from unspeakably cruel masters, Paul D asks the group of fugitive Cherokee with whom he has taken shelter how to find his way north. "Follow the tree flowers," they tell him. Paul D then races "from dogwood to blossoming peach," then on to "cherry blossoms, then magnolia, chinaberry, pecan, walnut and prickly pear," north toward freedom. At the end of the novel, Paul D recalls all his escapes and reluctantly admits that "he could not help being astonished by the beauty of the land that was not his. He hid in its breast, fingered its earth for food, clung to its banks to lap water and tried not to love it." Ordinarily he could make "himself not love it." But anything "could stir him" and then he had to try "hard not to love it."[40]

Morrison asks whether such feelings made any difference in a brutal world, whether—as Fitzgerald put it—a gift of hope retained any meaning in the "valley of ashes." Fitzgerald's valley of ashes is the ugly dump for the refuse of coal-fired electrical plants that Gatsby passed on his way to the city. That the dump is now Flushing Meadows Park, made so by no less a controversial figure than New York planner Robert Moses, suggests that perhaps hope is never completely misplaced. "We have more to work with than we ordinarily acknowledge," Raymond Williams wrote at the end of *The Country and the City*. He pointed to the surviving beauty even in "exceptionally industrialized and urbanized" Britain and to the many good people who worked to cultivate that beauty, to rebuild and repair what had been damaged, and to "make the cities cleaner and finer, to bring out and to build their best qualities." How much more so for us? Perhaps a resilient gift for hope, combined with our experience, the good as well as the bad, the nourishing rain as well as the destructive storms, may prove sufficient to guide our way forward.[41]

Acknowledgments

I have incurred enormous debts in writing this book. They range from the many brilliant scholars whose work I synthesize here and the anonymous peer reviewers who pushed me to improve and clarify my argument to Aaron Javsicas, editor-in-chief at Temple University Press, and his skilled staff. Three other people merit special mention. Larry Bennett, my series editor, shepherded this work from an early stage with equal measures of patience and insight. My young and talented Xavier University colleague Randolph Browne taught this old professor many things about the craft of writing and the process of publication. Finally, my greatest debt is to my soulmate and best friend, Rachel Chrastil, who lived and talked and loved through every stage of this process. I could never thank her enough.

Notes

INTRODUCTION

1. Richard Manning, "The Oil We Eat," *Harper's Magazine*, February 2004; Richard Manning, *Against the Grain: How Agriculture Has Hijacked Civilization* (New York: North Point, 2004); Janine M. Beyus, *Biomimicry: Innovation Inspired by Nature* (New York: William Morrow, 1997).

2. A. Duncan Brown, *Feed or Feedback: Agricultural, Population, and the State of the Planet* (Utrecht: International Books, 2003), 190–194, 202–203, 257–258, passim; Manning, "The Oil We Eat"; Manning, *Against the Grain*; Elizabeth Kolbert, "Phosphorus Saved Our Way of Life—and Now Threatens It," *New Yorker*, March 6, 2023, 24–27.

3. Raymond Williams, *The Country and the City* (New York: Oxford University Press, 1973), 279–306, quoted passages on 297–300; Christopher Lasch, *The True and Only Heaven: Progress and Its Critics* (New York: W. W. Norton, 1991), 84–87.

4. Williams, *The Country and the City*, 272–298, "delights" on 297; Robert Hatch, "Country Mice or City Mice—The Cat Doesn't Care," *The Nation*, December 3, 1973, 597–598.

5. Williams, *The Country and the City*, 272–298, quoted passages on 289, 293–294, 297; Donald Worster, *Nature's Economy: A History of Ecological Ideas* (Cambridge: Cambridge University Press, 1994); Leo Marx, *The Machine in the Garden: Technology and the Pastoral Ideal in America* (New York: Oxford University Press, 1964).

6. William Cronon, *Nature's Metropolis: Chicago and the Great West* (New York: W. W. Norton, 1992), 5–19.

7. John D. Fairfield, "Cincinnati's Hole in the Ground: Rapid Transit, City Planning, and the New Urban Discipline," *Old Northwest*, Fall 1988, 213–236.

8. Martin V. Melosi, "Humans, Cities, and Nature: How Do Cities Fit in the Material World?" *Journal of Urban History* 36 (2010): 3–21; Andrew Needham and Allen Dieterich-Ward, "Beyond the Metropolis: Metropolitan Growth and Regional Transformation in Postwar America," *Journal of Urban History* 35 (2009): 943–969; Fritjof Capra and Pier Luigi Luisi, *The Systems View of Life: A Unifying Vision* (New York: Cambridge University Press, 2014), 66–67, passim.

9. Lewis Mumford, "Regions—To Live in," *Survey Graphic* 54 (May 1, 1925): 151–152.

INTRODUCTION TO PART I

1. Zane L. Miller, *Boss Cox's Cincinnati: Urban Politics in the Progressive Era* (New York: Oxford University Press, 1968).

2. John Huston, dir., *The Asphalt Jungle*, DVD, Criterion Collection, New York, (1950) 2016. The opening frames are available at https://www.tcm.com /video/244936/asphalt-jungle-the-opening-dix.

3. Lewis Mumford, *The Culture of Cities* (New York: Harcourt, Brace, 1938), 4.

CHAPTER 1

1. Hillary Angelo and David Wachsmuth, "Urbanizing Urban Political Ecology: A Critique of Methodological Cityism," *International Journal of Urban and Regional Research* 39 (2015): 16–27; Rose George, *Ninety Percent of Everything: Inside Shipping, the Invisible Industry That Puts Clothes on Your Back, Gas in Your Car, and Food on Your Plate* (New York: Henry Holt, 2013), 91–95.

2. Nik Heynen, Maria Kaika, and Eric Swyngedouw, *In the Nature of Cities: Urban Political Ecology and the Politics of Urban Metabolism* (New York: Routledge, 2006); Hillary Angelo, "From the City Lens toward Urbanization as a Way of Seeing: Country/City Binaries on an Urbanizing Planet," *Urban Studies* 54 (2017): 158–178; Hillary Angelo, "The Greening Imaginary: Urbanized Nature in Germany's Ruhr Region," *Theory and Society* 48 (2019): 645–669; David Wachsmuth, "Three Ecologies: Urban Metabolism and the Society-Nature Opposition," *Sociological Quarterly* 53 (2012): 506–523; Raymond Williams, *The Country and the City* (New York: Oxford University Press, 1973); William Cronon, "The Trouble with Wilderness; or, Getting Back to the Wrong Nature," in *Uncommon Ground: Rethinking the Human Place in Nature*, ed. William Cronon (New York: W. W. Norton, 1995), 69–90; Richard White, "Are You an Environmentalist or Do You Work for a Living? Work and Nature," in Cronon, *Uncommon Ground*, 171–185.

3. Pope Francis, *Encyclical Letter Laudato Si': On Care for Our Common Home* (Vatican City: Libreria Editrica Vaticana, 2015).

4. Richard Manning, *Against the Grain: How Agriculture Has Hijacked Civilization* (New York: North Point, 2004); Adam Rome, *The Bulldozer in the Countryside: Suburban Sprawl and the Rise of American Environmentalism* (New York: Cambridge University Press, 2001), 8, passim; Jeffrey Craig Sanders, *Seattle and the Roots of Urban Sustainability: Inventing Ecotopia* (Pittsburgh: University of Pittsburgh Press, 2010); Robert R. Gioielli, *Environmental Activism and*

the Urban Crisis: Baltimore, St. Louis, Chicago (Philadelphia: Temple University Press, 2014); David Stradling and Richard Stradling, *Where the River Burned: Carl Stokes and the Struggle to Save Cleveland* (Ithaca, NY: Cornell University Press, 2015); David N. Pellow, *Garbage Wars: The Struggle for Environmental Justice in Chicago* (Cambridge, MA: MIT Press, 2002); David Wallace-Wells, *The Uninhabitable Earth: Life after Warming* (New York: Random House, 2019).

5. Naomi Klein, *This Changes Everything: Capitalism versus the Climate* (New York: Simon and Schuster, 2014); Bill McKibben, *Falter: Has the Human Game Begun to Play Itself Out?* (New York: Henry Holt, 2019); Paul Hawken, Amory Lovins, and L. Hunter Lovins, *Natural Capitalism: Creating the Next Industrial Revolution* (Boston: Little, Brown, 1999); Jeremy Rifkin, *The Third Industrial Revolution: How Lateral Power Is Transforming Energy, the Economy, and the World* (New York: Palgrave Macmillan, 2011); Michael Pollan, "Letter to Farmer in Chief," *New York Times*, October 12, 2008; Tom Vilsack, "Reconnecting with Rural America," *Democracy: A Journal of Ideas* 47 (Winter 2018), https://democracyjournal.org/magazine/47/reconnecting-with-rural-america; Jason Hickel, *The Divide: A Brief Guide to Global Inequality and Its Solutions* (London: William Heinemann, 2017); Jason Hickel, *Less Is More: How Degrowth Will Save the World* (London: Penguin, 2020).

6. Aldo Leopold, *A Sand County Almanac* (New York: Ballantine, 1966), 237–264; Richard Register, *Ecocities: Building Cities in Balance with Nature* (Gabriola Island, BC: New Society, 2006).

7. Heather McGhee, *The Sum of Us: What Racism Costs Everyone and How We Can Prosper Together* (New York: One World, 2021); George Monbiot, *Out of the Wreckage: A New Politics for an Age of Crisis* (New York: Verso, 2017); Amy Chua, *Political Tribes: Group Instinct and the Fate of Nations* (New York: Penguin, 2018).

8. Herman E. Daly and Joshua Farley, *Ecological Economics: Principles and Application* (Washington, DC: Island, 2011), 3–35, "moves" on 33; Raymond Williams, "Ideas of Nature," in *Problems in Materialism and Culture: Selected Essays*, by Raymond Williams (London: Verso, 1980), 67–95; Register, *Ecocities*, 7–14.

9. "What Does 10 Million Pounds of Trash Look Like?" Ocean Conservancy, May 14, 2013, https://oceanconservancy.org/blog/2013/05/14/what-does-10-million-pounds-of-trash-look-like; Kenneth A. Gould and Tammy L. Lewis, *Green Gentrification: Urban Sustainability and the Struggle for Environmental Justice* (New York: Routledge, 2017); Rebecca H. Walker, "Engineering Gentrification: Urban Redevelopment, Sustainability Policy, and Green Stormwater Infrastructure in Minneapolis," *Journal of Environmental Policy and Planning* 23, no. 5 (2021): 646–664; Pellow, *Garbage Wars*; Julie Sze, *Noxious New York: The Racial Politics of Urban Health and Environmental Justice* (Cambridge, MA: MIT Press, 2007).

10. Kent E. Portney, "Local Sustainability Policies and Programs as Economic Development: Is the New Economic Development Sustainable Development?" *Cityscape* 15 (2013): 45–62; James Svara, Tanya C. Watt, and Hee Soun Jang, "How Are U.S. Cities Doing Sustainability? Who Is Getting on the Sustainability Train, and Why?" *Cityscape* 15 (2013): 9–34; Sharon Zukin, *Landscapes of Power: From Detroit to Disney World* (Berkeley: University of California Press,

1991); "The Giant Pool of Money," *This American Life*, https://www.thisameri canlife.org/355/the-giant-pool-of-money.

11. John D. Fairfield, *Oakley: From Hamlet to the Center of Cincinnati* (Cincinnati: Commonwealth, 2018).

12. Ibid.

13. Ibid.; "Oakley Neighborhood in Cincinnati, Ohio," City-Data.com, http://www.city-data.com/neighborhood/Oakley-Cincinnati-OH.html; R. J. Smith, "The Two Faces of Oakley," *Cincinnati Magazine*, November 9, 2015, https://www.cincinnatimagazine.com/citywiseblog/the-two-faces-of-oakley.

14. Mark Curnutte, "City's Childhood Poverty Third Worst in the Nation," *Cincinnati Enquirer*, November 3, 2011; Charles Casey-Leininger, "Making the Second Ghetto in Cincinnati: Avondale, 1925–1970," in *Race and the City: Work, Community, Housing, and Protest in Cincinnati, 1820–1970*, ed. Henry Louis Taylor Jr. (Urbana: University of Illinois Press, 1993); Greater Cincinnati Urban League, *The State of Black Cincinnati 2015* (Cincinnati: Urban League of Greater Southwestern Ohio, 2015); Linda Vaccariello, "This Is How We Lose Them," *Cincinnati Magazine*, April 2015, http://www.cincinnatimagazine.com/citywise blog/infant-mortality-this-is-how-we-lose-them.

15. Dan Horn, "Is Recovery as 'Great' as the Great Recession? The Numbers Say No," *Cincinnati Enquirer*, March 27, 2019, https://www.cincinnati.com/story /news/politics/2019/03/28/numbers-before-and-after-great-recession/3290368002; "Dreams Detoured," *Cincinnati Enquirer*, December 17, 2019, https://www.cin cinnati.com/in-depth/news/the-long-hard-road/2019/03/27/long-hard-road-begin ning-80-miles-struggle-after-recession-heart-greater-cincinnati/2850397002; "Hidden in Plain Sight," *Cincinnati Enquirer*, December 17, 2019, https://www .cincinnati.com/in-depth/news/2019/12/04/hidden-plain-sight-need-rural-ameri ca-looks-different/2566525001.

16. Samuel P. Hays, "From the History of the City to the History of the Urbanized Society," *Journal of Urban History* 19 (August 1993): 3–24; Jari Niemela, ed., *Urban Ecology: Patterns, Processes, and Applications* (Oxford: Oxford University Press, 2011); D. B. Botkin and C. E. Beveridge, "Cities as Environments," *Urban Ecosystems* 1 (1997): 3–19.

17. Wachsmuth, "Three Ecologies," 506–510, Marx quoted on 507 (italics are Marx's).

18. Williams, *The Country and the City*, 12–54; Karl Polanyi, *The Great Transformation* (Boston: Beacon, 2001), 187–194; Carolyn Merchant, *The Death of Nature: Women, Ecology, and the Scientific Revolution* (San Francisco: Harper and Row, 1989).

19. Williams, *The Country and the City*, 142–152.

20. Ibid., passim, quoted passages on 37, 293–297; Christopher Lasch, *The True and Only Heaven: Progress and Its Critics* (New York: W. W. Norton, 1991), 82–119; Angelo, "From the City Lens toward Urbanization as a Way of Seeing."

21. Williams, *The Country and the City*, 279–306, quoted passages on 299–300; Aisa Kirabo Kacyire, "Addressing the Sustainable Urbanization Challenge," *UN Chronicle* 49, nos. 1–2 (June 2012), accessed June 17, 2021, https://www .un.org/en/chronicle/article/addressing-sustainable-urbanization-challenge; Mike Davis, *Planet of Slums* (New York: Verso, 2006), 1–11, 121–150, passim.

22. A. Duncan Brown, *Feed or Feedback: Agricultural, Population, and the State of the Planet* (Utrecht: International, 2003), 264–268, passim; Robert Costanza, Ralph d'Arge, Rudolf de Groot, and Stephen Farber et al., "The Value of the World's Ecosystem Services and Natural Capital," *Nature* 387 (May 15, 1997): 253–260; Jared Diamond, "The Last Americans: Environmental Collapse and the End of Civilization," *Harper's Magazine*, June 2003, 43–51.

23. Wallace-Wells, *The Uninhabitable Earth*; John W. Reid and Thomas E. Lovejoy, *Ever Green: Saving Big Forests to Save the Planet* (New York: W. W. Norton, 2022); Ben Rawlence, *The Treeline: The Last Forest and the Future of Life on Earth* (New York: St. Martin's, 2022); Daly and Farley, *Ecological Economics*; Leo Marx, "American Institutions and Ecological Ideals," *Science*, vol. 170, November 27, 1970, 945–952; Monbiot, *Out of the Wreckage*, 113–131; Kate Raworth, *Doughnut Economics: Seven Ways to Think Like a 21st Century Economist* (White River Junction, VT: Chelsea Green, 2017); Klein, *This Changes Everything*; Daniel Immerwahr, "Polanyi in the United States: Peter Drucker, Karl Polanyi, and the Midcentury Critique of Economic Society," *Journal of the History of Ideas* (July 2009): 445–466; Amitav Ghosh, *The Great Derangement: Climate Change and the Unthinkable* (Chicago: University of Chicago Press, 2016).

24. Monbiot, *Out of the Wreckage*, 1–28; Brian Hare and Vanessa Woods, *Survival of the Friendliest: Understanding Our Origins and Rediscovering Our Common Humanity* (New York: Random House, 2020). Cf. Ralph Waldo Emerson, "Compensation" (1841), EmersonCentral.com, https://emersoncentral.com /texts/essays-first-series/compensation.

25. Chris Arsenault, "Only 60 Years of Farming Left if Soil Degradation Continues," *Scientific American*, December 5, 2014, https://www.scientificamerican.com /article/only-60-years-of-farming-left-if-soil-degradation-continues; George Monbiot, "Mass Starvation Is Humanity's Fate if We Keep Flogging the Land to Death," *The Guardian*, December 11, 2017; "New NASA Data Show How the World Is Running Out of Water," *Washington Post*, May 24, 2019; Richard Manning, "The Oil We Eat: Following the Food Chain Back to Iraq," *Harper's Magazine*, February 2004; Bill McKibben, *Eaarth: Making a Life on a Tough New Planet* (New York: St. Martin's Griffin, 2011); Wallace-Wells, *The Uninhabitable Earth*.

26. Gwynne Dyer, *Climate Wars: The Fight for Survival as the World Overheats* (Toronto: Vintage Canada, 2009); McKibben, *Eaarth*; Wallace-Wells, *The Uninhabitable Earth*; McKibben, *Falter*; Ghosh, *The Great Derangement*; National Aeronautics and Space Administration, "Evidence: How Do We Know Climate Change Is Real?" *Global Climate Change: Vital Signs of the Planet*, n.d., https://climate.nasa.gov/evidence.

27. "Is Methane Hydrate the Energy Source of the Future?" *Atlantic Monthly*, December 24, 2013.

28. Donella H. Meadows, Dennis L. Meadows, Jørgen Randers, and William W. Behrens III, *The Limits to Growth* (New York: Universe, 1972); Global Footprint Network, "Ecological Footprint," n.d., https://www.footprintnetwork.org /our-work/ecological-footprint; David Wallace-Wells, "Beyond Catastrophe: A New Climate Reality Is Coming into View," *New York Times Magazine*, October 26, 2022 https://www.nytimes.com/interactive/2022/10/26/magazine/climate -change-warming-world.html.

29. Meadows et al., *The Limits to Growth*; McKibben, *Eaarth*, 90–93, "uncertain" on 93; McKibben, *Falter*.

30. Klein, *This Changes Everything*, 186; Christian Parenti, "'The Limits to Growth': A Book That Launched a Movement," *The Nation*, December 5, 2012; Costanza et al., "The Value of the World's Ecosystem Services and Natural Capital"; Nancy Golubiewski, "Is There a Metabolism of an Urban Ecosystem? An Ecological Critique," *Ambio* 41 (2012): 751–764; Matthew Gandy, "Rethinking Urban Metabolism: Water, Space, and the Modern City," *City* 8 (December 2004): 363–379.

31. Alexander C. Kaufman, "Trump's Military Response to Migrant Caravan Foreshadows a Dark Long-term Climate Policy," *Politics*, October 27, 2018; Coral Davenport and Campbell Robertson, "Resettling the First American 'Climate Refugees,'" *New York Times*, May 2, 2016; Klein, *This Changes Everything*, 31–95; Shannon Hall, "Exxon Knew about Climate Change Almost 40 Years Ago," *Scientific American*, October 26, 2015; McKibben, *Falter*, 72–80; Monbiot, *Out of the Wreckage*, 54–92.

32. David F. Damore, Robert E. Land, and Karen A. Danielson, *Blue Metros, Red States: The Shifting Urban-Rural Divide in America's Swing States* (Washington, DC: Brookings Institution Press, 2021); Garrett Dash Nelson, "What Makes a Place Rural?" *Dissent* (Fall 2019), 38–47; Sarah Jones, "Scapegoat Country," *Dissent* (Fall 2019): 23–29.

33. Robert Kuttner, "Hidden Injuries," *American Prospect* (Fall 2016): 97–104; Christopher Ketcham, "A Play with No End," *Harper's Magazine*, vol. 339, August 2019, 41–49, "concrete" on 43; Mark Lilla, "Two Roads for the New French Right," *New York Review of Books*, December 20, 2018.

34. Kuttner, "Hidden Injuries"; Arlie Russell Hochschild, *Strangers in Their Own Land* (New York: New Press, 2016); Monica Potts, "In the Land of Self-Defeat," *New York Times*, October 4, 2019.

35. Michael Rawson, *Eden on the Charles: The Making of Boston* (Cambridge, MA: Harvard University Press, 2010); Cronon, "The Trouble with Wilderness"; Richard White, *The Organic Machine: The Remaking of the Columbia River* (New York: Hill and Wang, 1995); Samuel P. Hays and Barbara D. Hays, *Beauty, Health, and Permanence: Environmental Politics in the United States, 1955–1985* (New York: Cambridge University Press, 1989).

36. White, "Are You an Environmentalist or Do You Work for a Living?"; Maril Hazlett, "Rachel Carson Scholarship—Where Next?" *Rachel Carson Center Perspectives*, no. 7 (2012): 59–65; Andrew Hurley, *Environmental Inequalities: Class, Race, and Industrial Pollution in Gary, Indiana, 1945–1980* (Chapel Hill: University of North Carolina Press, 1995); Andrew Hurley, "Fiasco at Wagner Electric: Environmental Justice and Urban Geography in St. Louis," *Environmental History* 2 (October 1997), 460–811.

37. Stanley K. Schultz, *Constructing Urban Culture: American Cities and City Planning, 1800–1920* (Philadelphia: Temple University Press, 1989); Jon C. Teaford, *The Unheralded Triumph: City Government in America, 1870–1900* (Baltimore: Johns Hopkins University Press, 1984); Harold L. Platt, *Shock Cities: The Environmental Transformation and Reform of Manchester and Chicago* (Chicago: University of Chicago Press, 2005); Stradling and Stradling, *Where the River Burned*; Gioielli, *Environmental Activism and the Urban Crisis*.

38. Philip McMichael, "In the Short Run Are We All Dead? A Political Ecology of the Development Climate," in *The Longue Durée and World-Systems Analysis*, ed. Richard E. Lee (New York: State University of New York Press, 2013), 137–160; John Bellamy Foster, "Marx's Theory of Metabolic Rift: Classical Foundations for Environmental Sociology," *American Journal of Sociology* 105 (September 1999): 366–405; Wachsmuth, "Three Ecologies"; Donald Worster, *Nature's Economy: A History of Ecological Ideas* (Cambridge: Cambridge University Press, 1994); Hazlett, "Rachel Carson Scholarship"; Maril Hazlett, "'Woman versus Man versus Bugs': Gender and Popular Ecology in Early Reactions to *Silent Spring*," *Environmental History* 9 (October 2004): 701–729; White, "Are You an Environmentalist or Do You Work for a Living?"; Cronon, "The Trouble with Wilderness."

39. Williams, "Ideas of Nature"; Worster, *Nature's Economy*, ix–xiii.

40. Steward T. A. Pickett, William R. Burch, Shawn E. Dalton, and Timothy W. Foresman et al., "A Conceptual Framework for the Study of Human Ecosystems in Urban Areas," *Urban Ecosystems* 1 (1997), 185–199; James P. Collins, Ann Kinzig, Nancy B. Grimm, and William F. Hagan et al., "A New Urban Ecology." *American Scientist* 88 (September–October 2000): 416–425. Cf. Lasch, *The True and Only Heaven*, 133–135.

41. Worster, *Nature's Economy*; Joel B. Hagen, *An Entangled Bank: The Origins of Ecosystem Ecology* (New Brunswick, NJ: Rutgers University Press, 1992); Sharon E. Kingsland, "Essay Review: The History of Ecology," *Journal of the History of Biology* 27 (Summer 1994): 349–357; Daly and Farley, *Ecological Economics*; J. R. McNeil, *Something New under the Sun: An Environmental History of the Twentieth-Century World* (New York: W. W. Norton, 2000), 325–356.

42. Lewis Mumford, *The Culture of Cities* (New York: Harcourt, Brace, 1938); Anne Whiston Spirn, *The Granite Garden: Urban Nature and Human Design* (New York: Basic, 1984); Thomas Parke Hughes, *Human-built World: How to Think about Technology and Culture* (Chicago: University of Chicago Press, 2004); Marina Alberti, *Advances in Urban Ecology* (New York: Springer, 2008); J. Morgan Grove, Mary Cadenasso, Steward Pickettt, Gary Machlis, and William R. Burch Jr., *The Baltimore School of Urban Ecology: Space, Scale, and Time for the Study of Cities* (New Haven, CT: Yale University Press, 2015); Niemela, *Urban Ecology*; John D. Fairfield, "Green Cities and Sustainability," in *The Congressional Quarterly Press Guide to Urban Politics and Policy*, ed. Christine Paulus and Richardson Dilworth (Thousand Oaks, CA: 2016), chap. 39, 403–410.

43. Alberti, *Advances in Urban Ecology*; Niemela, *Urban Ecology*; Andrea Wulf, *The Invention of Nature: Alexander Humboldt's New World* (New York: Vintage, 2015), 65–66, passim; George Perkins Marsh, *Man and Nature* (Cambridge, MA: Harvard University Press, 1965); Marc Reisner, *Cadillac Desert: The American West and Its Disappearing Water* (New York: Penguin, 1987); John F. Ross, "How the West Was Lost," *The Atlantic*, September 10, 2018.

44. Daly and Farley, *Ecological Economics*, 51–57; Louis Menand, *The Metaphysical Club* (New York: Farrar, Straus, and Giroux, 2001), 117–148.

45. Eugene Cittadino, "The Failed Promise of Human Ecology," in *Science and Nature: Essays in the History of the Environmental Sciences*, ed. Michael Short-

land (London: British Society for the History of Science, 1993), 251–283; Eugene Cittadino, "Ecology and American Social Thought," in *Religion and the New Ecology*, ed. David M. Lodge and Christopher Hamlin (Notre Dame, IN: University of Notre Dame Press, 2006), 73–115; Niemela, *Urban Ecology*; Martin V. Melosi, "Humans, Cities, and Nature: How Do Cities Fit in the Material World?" *Journal of Urban History* 36 (2010): 3–21.

46. Menand, *The Metaphysical Club*, 117–148.

47. Robert E. Park, Ernest W. Burgess, and Roderick McKenzie, *The City* (Chicago: University of Chicago Press, 1925); Milla Aissa Alihan, *Social Ecology* (New York: Columbia University Press, 1938), quoted passages on 206, 247–248; Robert Westbrook, *John Dewey and American Democracy* (Ithaca, NY: Cornell University Press, 1991), 33–149; Menand, *The Metaphysical Club*, 285–333.

48. Pickett et al., "A Conceptual Framework for the Study of Human Ecosystems in Urban Areas"; Collins et al., "A New Urban Ecology." On the behavioral sciences, see Hannah Arendt, *The Human Condition* (Chicago: University of Chicago Press, 1958); Lasch, *The True and Only Heaven*, 133; James Scott, *Seeing like a State: How Certain Schemes to Improve the Human Condition Have Failed* (New Haven, CT: Yale University Press, 1998).

49. Arendt, *The Human Condition*; Lasch, *The True and Only Heaven*, 133; Menand, *The Metaphysical Club*, 151–200; Brown, *Feed or Feedback*, 57–60, 247–297; Dorothy Ross, *The Origins of American Social Science* (New York: Cambridge University Press, 1991).

50. Brown, *Feed or Feedback*, 247–297. The question about *sapiens* is Brown's, posed on 297.

CHAPTER 2

1. Stanley Hedeen, *The Mill Creek: An Unnatural History of an Urban Stream* (Cincinnati: Blue Heron, 1994); Sharon Coolidge, "S. Fairmount's Lick Run Creek May Flow Again," *Cincinnati Enquirer*, June, 12, 2011; Dan Monk, "$122M Waterway Planned for the City," *Cincinnati Business Courier*, February 25, 2011; Cedric Rose, "The Ripple Effect," *Cincinnati Magazine*, September 2012, 62–69; Project Groundwork, "Lick Run Greenway," accessed December 2, 2015, http://projectgroundwork.org/projects/lowermillcreek/sustainable/lickrun; *Combined Sewer Overflow 5 Operated by the Metropolitan Sewer District of Greater Cincinnati*, video posted July 23, 2013, accessed December 2, 2015, https://www.youtube.com/watch?v=uty6OTt9ysk.

2. Rose, "The Ripple Effect"; Metropolitan Sewer District of Greater Cincinnati, "Consent Decree Fact Sheet," accessed December 16, 2015, http://www.msdgc.org/downloads/consent_decree/consent_decree_fact_sheet.pdf.

3. Rose, "The Ripple Effect"; David A. Keiser and Joseph S. Shapiro, "Consequences of the Clean Water Act and the Demand for Water Quality," Center for Agricultural and Rural Development Working Papers, January 2017, https://lib.dr.iastate.edu/cgi/viewcontent.cgi?article=1591&context=card_workingpapers, "zero" quoted on 1; Joel A. Tarr, *The Search for the Ultimate Sink: Urban Pollution in Historical Context* (Akron: University of Akron Press, 1996), 345–346.

4. A. Duncan Brown, *Feed or Feedback: Agricultural, Population, and the State*

of the Planet (Utrecht: International Books, 2003); John Bellamy Foster, "Marx's Theory of Metabolic Rift: Classical Foundations for Environmental Sociology," *American Journal of Sociology* 105 (September 1999): 366–405; Philip McMichael, "In the Short Run Are We All Dead? A Political Ecology of the Development Climate," in *The Longue Durée and World-Systems Analysis*, ed. Richard E. Lee (New York: State University of New York Press, 2013); David Wachsmuth, "Three Ecologies: Urban Metabolism and the Society-Nature Opposition," *Sociological Quarterly* 53 (2012): 506–523.

5. Siemens, "What Is Urban Sustainability," n.d., accessed June 2, 2021, https://assets.new.siemens.com/siemens/assets/public.1560756617.90627521 -4620-4b1d-9dc6-d94563b93a46.what-is-urban-sustainability-v1.pdf; Benjamin R. Barber, *If Mayors Ruled the World* (New Haven, CT: Yale University Press, 2013), 29–49, quoted passages on 35, 43; Verlyn Klinkenborg, "The Prophet," *New York Review of Books*, vol. 60, October 24, 2013; Levi Van Sant, "Land Reform and the Green New Deal," *Dissent* (Fall 2019): 64–70.

6. Joel Garreau, *Edge City: Life on the New Frontier* (New York: Doubleday, 1991), 10–15.

7. Ibid., 10–15, 364–365; Leo Marx, "American Institutions and Ecological Ideals," *Science*, vol. 170, November 27, 1970, 945–952, quoted passage on 948.

8. David F. Damore, Robert E. Land, and Karen A. Danielson, *Blue Metros, Red States: The Shifting Urban-Rural Divide in America's Swing States* (Washington, DC: Brookings Institution Press, 2021); John D. Fairfield, "Review of *Blue Metros, Red States: The Shifting Urban-Rural Divide in America's Swing States*," *Journal of Urban Affairs* 43, no. 8 (April 2021): 1207–1209.

9. Wachsmuth, "Three Ecologies"; Brown, *Feed or Feedback*, 1–32, passim. Cf. Jared Diamond, "The Worst Mistake in History," *Discover Magazine*, May 1, 1987, 64–66.

10. Brown, *Feed or Feedback*; McMichael, "In the Short Run Are We All Dead?"; Foster, "Marx's Theory of Metabolic Rift"; Brett Clark and Richard York, "Carbon Metabolism: Global Capitalism, Climate Change, and the Biospheric Rift," *Theory and Society* 34 (2005): 391–428.

11. Carolyn Merchant, "Mining the Earth's Womb," in *Machina Ex Deo: Feminist Perspectives on Technology*, ed. Joan Rothschild (New York: Pergamon, 1983), 99–117, Bacon quoted on 115, "mining" on 99; Carolyn Merchant, *The Death of Nature: Women, Ecology, and the Scientific Revolution* (San Francisco: Harper and Row, 1979); Donald Worster, *Nature's Economy: A History of Ecological Ideas* (Cambridge: Cambridge University Press, 1994), 1–55, passim.

12. Joel Tarr, "From Farm to City: Urban Wastes and the American Farmer," *Agricultural History* 49 (October 1975): 598–612; Harold L. Platt, *Shock Cities: The Environmental Transformation and Reform of Manchester and Chicago* (Chicago: University of Chicago Press, 2005), 70–72; Theodore Steinberg, *Gotham Unbound: The Ecological History of Greater New York* (New York: Simon and Schuster, 2014), 109–125; Foster, "Marx's Theory of Metabolic Rift"; McMichael, "In the Short Run Are We All Dead?"; Brown, *Feed or Feedback*; Wachsmuth, "Three Ecologies."

13. Rose George, *The Big Necessity: The Unmentionable World of Human Waste and Why It Matters* (New York: Henry Holt, 2014), Marx, from volume 3 of *Capital*, quoted on 156; Brown, *Feed or Feedback*, 57–81.

14. Tarr, "From Farm to City," Barnes quoted on 598; Foster, "Marx's Theory of Metabolic Rift"; McMichael, "In the Short Run Are We All Dead?"; Wachsmuth, "Three Ecologies."

15. Henry George, *Social Problems* repr. ed. (New York: Robert Schalkenbach Foundation, [1883] 1966), "cutting down" on 27; Henry George, *Progress and Poverty* (New York: Henry George, 1887), "haunting" on 5; Ebenezer Howard, *Garden Cities of To-morrow* (London: Swan Sonnenschein, 1902), 32–37; Brett Clark, "Ebenezer Howard and the Marriage of Town and Country," *Organization and Environment* 16 (March 2003): 87–97.

16. Tarr, "From Farm to City"; Tarr, *The Search for the Ultimate Sink*, 293–308, "running" on 187; Martin V. Melosi, *The Sanitary City* (Pittsburgh: University of Pittsburgh Press, 2008), 108; George, *The Big Necessity*, 156; Steinberg, *Gotham Unbound*, 117–118.

17. Lewis Mumford, *The City in History* (New York: Harcourt, 1961), 14.

18. U.S. Environmental Protection Agency, "Combined Sewer Overflows," n.d., accessed November 21, 2021, https://www.epa.gov/npdes/combined-sewer-overflows-csos; Abel Wolman, "The Metabolism of Cities," *Scientific American*, vol. 213, September 1965, 179–190; George, *The Big Necessity*, 155; Wachsmuth, "Three Ecologies."

19. Tarr, "From Farm to City"; Barry Commoner, *The Closing Circle: Nature, Man and Technology* (New York: Bantam, 1971), 186–187; Tarr, *The Search for the Ultimate Sink*, 293–308, quoted passage on 304; Steinberg, *Gotham Unbound*, 238–258; David Stradling and Richard Stradling, *Where the River Burned: Carl Stokes and the Struggle to Save Cleveland* (Ithaca, NY: Cornell University Press, 2015), 192–194.

20. George, *The Big Necessity*, 149–171; Elizabeth Royte, *Garbage Land: On the Secret Trail of Trash* (New York: Little, Brown, 2005); Federal Bureau of Investigation, Detroit Division "Former Synagro Executive Sentenced in Bribery Scheme Related to Detroit Sludge Contract," press release, November 30, 2009, https://www.fbi.gov/detroit/press-releases/2009/de113009.htm.

21. George, *The Big Necessity*, 157–171.

22. Butler County Water and Sewer, "Biosolids," n.d., accessed November 9, 2015, http://des.butlercountyohio.org/html/wastewater/Biosolids.cfm; Metropolitan Sewer District of Greater Cincinnati, "Removal of Excess Sludge Cakes, RFP #2015-001," May 18, 2015, http://msdgc.org/cip/2005/RFP2015001.htm.

23. "Unknown Health Impacts of Biosolids," Sierra Club Grassroots Network, April 20, 2015, https://content.sierraclub.org/grassrootsnetwork/team-news/2015/04/unknown-health-impacts-biosolids-spreading-serious-flaw-qua sar-energy-project; Michael Pollan, "Letter to Farmer in Chief," *New York Times*, October 12, 2008.

24. Richard Manning, "The Oil We Eat," *Harper's Magazine*, February 2004, 37–45; Richard Manning, *Against the Grain: How Agriculture Has Hijacked Civilization* (New York: North Point, 2004); Pollan, "Letter to Farmer in Chief."

25. Wendell Berry, *The Unsettling of America* (San Francisco: Sierra Club, 1977), 23–72, quoted passages on 42, 56.

26. Ibid., quoted passages on 56, 23.

27. Ibid., quoted passages on 24, 67–69.

28. Ibid., quoted passages on 67–68; "The Revolution in American Agriculture," *National Geographic*, February 1970, 147–185.

29. Berry, *The Unsettling of America*, quoted passages on 67–68, 24.

30. Marx, "American Institutions and Ecological Ideals," quoted passages on 945, 950; Raymond Williams, *The Country and the City* (New York: Oxford University Press, 1973), see esp. 297–298

31. John Tallmadge, *The Cincinnati Arch: Learning from Nature in the City* (Athens: University of Georgia Press, 2004), 183–205.

32. Ibid.; Greater Cincinnati Waterworks website, accessed July 8 2021, https://www.cincinnati-oh.gov/water.

33. Tallmadge, *The Cincinnati Arch*, 186–192.

34. Ibid.

35. Ibid.; Paul Hawken, *The Ecology of Commerce: A Declaration of Sustainability* (New York: Harper Business, 2010), 45–64; Greater Cincinnati Waterworks, "GCWW Launches UV Treatment Facility," October 3, 2013, http://www.cincinnati-oh.gov/water/news/gcww-launches-uv-treatment-facility.

36. Tallmadge, *The Cincinnati Arch*, 189–191; Hawken, *The Ecology of Commerce*, 45–64; Nathaniel Rich, *Second Nature: Scenes from a World Remade* (New York: Farrar, Straus and Giroux, 2021), 36–37.

37. Tallmadge, *The Cincinnati Arch*, 192–194; Mill Creek Alliance website, accessed February 14, 2016, http://groundworkcincinnati.org; Hedeen, *The Mill Creek*.

38. Tallmadge, *The Cincinnati Arch*, 192–194; Hedeen, *The Mill Creek*, 160–161; Stanley Hedeen, "Waterproofing the Mill Creek Flood Plain," *Queen City Heritage*, Spring 1998, 15–24.

39. Tallmadge, *The Cincinnati Arch*, 193–198; Hawken, *The Ecology of Commerce*, 45–64.

40. Tallmadge, *The Cincinnati Arch*, 196–199.

41. Ibid.

42. Ibid., 199–205; Hedeen, *The Mill Creek*, 95–136.

43. Tallmadge, *The Cincinnati Arch*, 199–205.

44. Ibid.; Project Groundwork, "Lower Mill Creek Partial Remedy," December 2014, http://www.projectgroundwork.org/projects/lowermillcreek/Lower_Mill_Creek_Partial_Remedy_December_2014.pdf; Amy Souers Kober, "Urban River Revival: Celebrating Ohio's Mill Creek," America Rivers, September 13, 2017, https://www.americanrivers.org/2017/09/urban-river-revival-celebrating-ohios-mill-creek; Coolidge, "S. Fairmount's Lick Run Creek May Flow Again"; Monk, "$122M Waterway Planned for the City"; Rose, "The Ripple Effect."

45. Project Groundwork, "Lower Mill Creek Partial Remedy"; Rose, "The Ripple Effect"; Kober, "Urban River Revival"; Randy A. Simes, "Cincinnati Receives Federal Approval for Innovative Green Infrastructure CSO Fix," *UrbanCincy*, July 10, 2013, https://www.urbancincy.com/2013/06/cincinnati-receives-federal-approval-for-innovative-green-infrastructure-cso-fix.

46. Mill Creek Alliance, "Twin Creek Preserve," accessed February 14, 2016, http://millcreekwatershed.org/what-we-do/projects/twin-creek-preserve; Kathy Poole, "Civitas Oecologie: Infrastructure in the Ecological City," *Harvard Archi-*

tectural Review 10 (1998): 126–145, "unfathomable" on 128. Cf. Anne Spirn, "Reclaiming Common Ground: Water, Neighborhoods, and Public Places," in *The American Planning Tradition*, ed. Robert Fishman (Baltimore: Johns Hopkins University Press, 2000), 297–313.

47. Stanley Hedeen, *Natural History of the Cincinnati Region* (Cincinnati: Cincinnati Museum Center, 2006); Hedeen, *The Mill Creek*; Steven J. Ross, *Workers on the Edge: Work, Leisure, and Politics in Industrializing Cincinnati, 1788–1890* (New York: Columbia University Press, 1985), 3–63.

48. Jon C. Teaford, *Cities of the Heartland: The Rise and Fall of the Industrial Midwest* (Bloomington: Indiana University Press, 1993), booster quoted on 2; Kim Gruenwald, *River of Enterprise: The Commercial Origins of Regional Identity in the Ohio River Valley, 1790–1850* (Bloomington: Indiana University Press, 2002); Jon Scharf and Rick Stager, "It All Started with Steamboats: The Niles Works and the Origins of Cincinnati's Machine Tool Industry," *Queen City Heritage*, Spring 1996, 34–47; David E. Nye, *Consuming Power: A Social History of American Energies* (Cambridge, MA: MIT Press, 1998), 44; Ross, *Workers on the Edge*, 13–41.

49. Teaford, *Cities of the Heartland*, quotation on 5; Nye, *Consuming Power*, 61–100; Ross, *Workers on the Edge*, 28–140.

50. Quotations are from Theodore W. Eversole, "The Cincinnati Cholera Epidemic of 1849," *Queen City Heritage*, Fall 1983, 21–30; Alan I. Marcus, *A Plague of Strangers: Social Groups and the Origins of City Services in Cincinnati, 1819–1870* (Columbus: Ohio State University Press, 1991).

51. Eversole, "The Cincinnati Cholera Epidemic of 1849"; Charles Cist, *Cincinnati in 1841: Its Early Annals and Future Prospects* (Cincinnati: Charles Cist, 1841), 146–148; Zane L. Miller, "Scarcity, Abundance, and American Urban History," *Journal of Urban History* 4 (February 1978): 131–155.

52. Hedeen, *The Mill Creek*; Zane L. Miller, *Boss Cox's Cincinnati: Urban Politics in the Progressive Era* (New York: Oxford University Press, 1968), quotation on 17.

53. David Stradling, *Smokestacks and Progressives: Environmentalists, Engineers and Air Quality in America, 1881–1951* (Baltimore: Johns Hopkins University Press, 1999); Tarr, *The Search for the Ultimate Sink*.

54. Steinberg, *Gotham Unbound*; Carol Sheriff, *The Artificial River: The Erie Canal and the Paradox of Progress, 1817–1862* (New York: Hill and Wang, 1996); Richard Florida, *The Rise of the Creative Class* (New York: Basic, 2002); Richard Florida, "How the Crash Will Reshape America," *The Atlantic*, March 2009, http://www.theatlantic.com/magazine/archive/2009/03/how-the-crash-will-reshape-america/7293/#.

55. Theodore Steinberg, *Nature Incorporated: Industrialization and the Waters of New England* (New York: Cambridge University Press, 1991); Nye, *Consuming Power*, 43–68.

56. Steinberg, *Nature Incorporated*.

57. Ibid.

58. Richard White, *The Organic Machine: The Remaking of the Columbia River* (New York: Hill and Wang, 1995), quoted passage on 78–79.

59. Frederick Jackson Turner, "The Significance of the Frontier in American History," *Annual Report of the American Historical Association for the Year 1893*

(Washington, DC: Government Printing Office, 1894), 197–227; Richard Wade, *The Urban Frontier* (Chicago: University of Chicago Press, 1959); David Stradling, "Cincinnati a Queen City? Only on the Frontier," *Indiana Magazine of History*, vol. 105, September 2009, 219–231; Raymond A. Mohl, "City and Region: The Missing Dimension in U.S. Urban History," *Journal of Urban History* 25 (November 1998): 3–21, esp. 12.

60. Martin V. Melosi, "Humans, Cities, and Nature: How Do Cities Fit in the Material World," *Journal of Urban History* 36 (2010): 3–21. Melosi quotes Craig E. Colten, ed., *Transforming New Orleans and Its Environs: Centuries of Change* (Pittsburgh: University of Pittsburgh Press, 2000), 3.

INTRODUCTION TO PART II

1. Chicago Park District, n.d., "Portage Park," https://www.chicagoparkdistrict.com/parks-facilities/portage-park.

2. Albert Hunter taught the course. Albert Hunter, "The Ecology of Chicago: Persistence and Change, 1930–1960," *American Journal of Sociology* 77 (1971): 425–444; Albert Hunter, "Why Chicago? The Rise of the Chicago School of Urban Social Science," *American Behavioral Scientist* 24 (1980): 215–227.

3. Jennifer Light, *The Nature of Cities: Ecological Visions and the American Urban Professions, 1920–1960* (Baltimore: Johns Hopkins University Press, 2014).

4. Mike Davis, *City of Quartz: Excavating the Future in Los Angeles* (New York: Version, 1990), 3–97, "pastel" on 6, "wreckage" on 14; Mike Davis, *Ecology of Fear: Los Angeles and the Imagination of Disaster* (New York: Vintage, 1999), 57–91; Michael J. Dear, *The Postmodern Urban Condition* (Oxford: Blackwell, 2000); Michael J. Dear, ed., *From Chicago to L.A.: Making Sense of Urban Theory* (Thousand Oaks, CA: Sage, 2002).

CHAPTER 3

1. Harold L. Platt, *Shock Cities: The Environmental Transformation and Reform of Manchester and Chicago* (Chicago: University of Chicago Press, 2005), 3–8, Tocqueville quoted on 5; Asa Briggs, *Victorian Cities* (New York: Harper and Row, 1965), 88–138.

2. Platt, *Shock Cities*, quotation on 7; Briggs, *Victorian Cities*; Robert Fishman, *Bourgeois Utopias: The Rise and Fall of Suburbia* (New York: Basic, 1987), 77.

3. Platt, *Shock Cities*, Tocqueville quoted on 7; Fishman, *Bourgeois Utopias*, "no town" on 83; Briggs, *Victorian Cities*.

4. Briggs, *Victorian Cities*, 56; Weber quoted in University of Illinois, Chicago, "Visitors on City Streets," 2017, https://maxwellhalsted.uic.edu/home/immigrants-in-chicago/visitor-observations.

5. Platt, *Shock Cities*; Henry George, *Progress and Poverty* (New York: Henry George, 1887), 211, passim.

6. Karl Polanyi, *The Great Transformation* (Boston: Beacon, 2001).

7. Briggs, *Victorian Cities*, quoted passages on 87, 56; Lewis Mumford, *The Culture of Cities* (New York: Harcourt, Brace, 1938), 143–222; Platt, *Shock Cities*.

8. Platt, *Shock Cities*, 17–19, 50–52, Engels and Briggs quoted on 17–18; Briggs, *Victorian Cities*, 17.

9. Briggs, *Victorian Cities*, on "insensate," 23–24, "no local government" on 89; Platt, *Shock Cities*, medical examiner quoted on 52; Mumford, *The Culture of Cities*, 143–222, "sweet" on 190, "essential" on 179.

10. Platt, *Shock Cities*, 3–25, Tocqueville quoted on 5–6, "plunging" on 25; Briggs, *Victorian Cities*, 88–97, "strange" is George Saintsbury, quoted on 96.

11. Platt, *Shock Cities*, 3–52, "regret" is from an 1878 reminiscence quoted on 51; Fishman, *Bourgeois Utopias*, 73–102.

12. Platt, *Shock Cities*, 3–70.

13. Ibid.

14. Fishman, *Bourgeois Utopias*, 73–102; Platt, *Shock Cities*, 41–56.

15. Fishman, *Bourgeois Utopias*, 84–94; Platt, *Shock Cities*, 41–74, "total" on 67.

16. Fishman, *Bourgeois Utopias*, 84–94, "abomination" on 92; Platt, *Shock Cities*, 41–74, "contagious" on 65–66.

17. Fishman, *Bourgeois Utopias*, 91–96, "bubbling" on 92; Platt, *Shock Cities*, 74–77.

18. Fishman, *Bourgeois Utopias*, 91–96, "object" on 95.

19. Ibid., 39–102, "land" on 49; Raymond Williams, *The Country and the City* (New York: Oxford University Press, 1973), 120–126.

20. Fishman, *Bourgeois Utopias*, 39–102, "divided" on 102.

21. Platt, *Shock Cities*, passim.

22. William Cronon, *Nature's Metropolis: Chicago and the Great West* (New York: W. W. Norton, 1992), 5–19, passim, "token" on 17.

23. Ibid.

24. Ibid., 5–19, 55–63; Gerald W. Adelmann, "Reworking the Landscape, Chicago Style," *Hastings Center Report* 28 (November–December 1998): S6–S11; Dominic A. Pacyga, *Chicago: A Biography* (Chicago: University of Chicago Press, 2009), 8–35, 104.

25. Cronon, *Nature's Metropolis*, 5–93, Herrick quoted on 15. For the more complete quotation used here, see Robert Herrick, *The Gospel of Freedom* (New York: Macmillan, 1898), 101–102; Platt, *Shock Cities*, 78–195; the term *manic artifice* is from Garry Wills, "Chicago Underground," *New York Review of Books*, October 21, 1993, 15–22.

26. Cronon, *Nature's Metropolis*.

27. Peter A. Coclanis, "Business of Chicago," *Encyclopedia of Chicago*, http://www.encyclopedia.chicagohistory.org/pages/198.html; Cronon, *Nature's Metropolis*, 55–93; Platt, *Shock Cities*, 78–195.

28. Cronon, *Nature's Metropolis*, 55–93; Platt, *Shock Cities*, 78–195.

29. Cronon, *Nature's Metropolis*, 55–93; Platt, *Shock Cities*, 78–195.

30. Cronon, *Nature's Metropolis*, 55–93; Platt, *Shock Cities*, 78–195.

31. Cronon, *Nature's Metropolis*, 55–93; Platt, *Shock Cities*, 78–134; Alfred Chandler, *The Visible Hand: The Managerial Revolution in American Business* (Cambridge, MA: Harvard University Press, 1977).

32. Cronon, *Nature's Metropolis*, 148–206.

33. Ibid., 207–259.

34. Ibid., 207–259, "nasty" on 235; Eric Schlosser, *Fast Food Nation: The Dark Side of the All-American Meal* (New York: Perennial, 2002).

35. Cronon, *Nature's Metropolis*, 207–259.

36. Ibid., 97–147.

37. Ibid., "body" on 119.

38. Ibid., 97–147.

39. Ibid., Morton Rothstein quoted on 125.

40. Ibid.

41. Ibid., quoted passages on 130–131.

42. Ibid.

43. Ibid., quoted passage on 142.

44. Ibid.; Naomi Klein, *This Changes Everything: Capitalism versus the Climate* (New York: Simon and Schuster, 2014), 168–174, on climate futures, 8.

45. Cronon, *Nature's Metropolis*, 5–54, 333–340, booster quoted on 35; Carl S. Smith, *Urban Disorder and the Shape of Belief* (Chicago: University of Chicago Press, 1995), anarchist quoted on 167; Elizabeth Grennen Browning, *Nature's Laboratory: Environmental Thought and Labor Radicalism in Chicago, 1886–1937* (Baltimore: Johns Hopkins University Press, 2022).

46. Polanyi, *The Great Transformation*; Jean-Christophe Agnew, *Worlds Apart: The Market and Theater in Anglo-American Thought, 1550–1750* (Cambridge: Cambridge University Press, 1986), 17–56; Herman E. Daly and Joshua Farley, *Ecological Economics: Principles and Application* (Washington, DC: Island, 2011), 3–35.

47. Karl Polanyi, "Our Obsolete Market Mentality," *Commentary* 3 (February 1947): 109–117; Polanyi, *The Great Transformation*, 42–44, 81–89, 171–200; Klein, *This Changes Everything*, 168–174; Daniel Immerwahr, "Polanyi in the United States: Peter Drucker, Karl Polanyi, and the Midcentury Critique of Economic Society," *Journal of the History of Ideas* 70 (July 2009): 445–466.

48. Polanyi, *The Great Transformation*.

49. Polanyi, "Our Obsolete Market Mentality," "bent" on 116.

50. Polanyi, *The Great Transformation*, "stark" on 3, 147; Immerwahr, "Polanyi in the United States"; Peter Drucker, *The End of Economic Man: A Study of the New Totalitarianism* (London: British Publishing Guild, 1943).

51. Cronon, *Nature's Metropolis*, 333–340.

52. Ibid.

53. Pacyga, *Chicago*, 65–109; Smith, *Urban Disorder and the Shape of Belief*, 19–98.

54. Fishman, *Bourgeois Utopias*, 95–102, quoted passages on 101; Platt, *Shock Cities*, 301–304.

55. Robert A. Woods and Albert J. Kennedy, eds., *Handbook of Settlements* (New York: Arno, 1970), Hull-House charter quoted on 53; Jane Addams, *Twenty Years at Hull-House* (New York: Macmillan, [1910] 1930), "dirty" on 81; Harold L. Platt, "Jane Addams and the Ward Boss Revisited: Class, Politics, and Public Health in Chicago, 1890–1930," *Environmental History* 5 (April 2000): 194–222; Robert Gottlieb, *Forcing the Spring: The Transformation of the American Environmental Movement* (Washington, DC: Island, 2005), 97–106.

56. Jane Addams, *Democracy and Social Ethics* (New York: Macmillan, 1907); Platt, "Jane Addams and the Ward Boss Revisited"; Platt, *Shock Cities*, 333–361.

57. Platt, "Jane Addams and the Ward Boss Revisited."

58. Ibid.; Residents of Hull-House, *Hull-House Maps and Papers*, repr. ed. (New York: Arno, [1895] 1970); Robert Hunter, *Tenement Conditions in Chicago: Report by the Investigating Committee of the City Homes Association* (Chicago: City Homes Association, 1901); Mary Jo Deegan, *Jane Addams and the Men of the Chicago School, 1892–1918* (New Brunswick, NJ: Transaction, 1988), 55–70; Gottlieb, *Forcing the Spring*, 97–105.

59. Platt, "Jane Addams and the Ward Boss Revisited"; Platt, *Shock Cities*, 333–361.

60. Addams, *Twenty Years at Hull-House*, "easy" on 201; Platt, *Shock Cities*, 342–350; Platt, "Jane Addams and the Ward Boss Revisited."

61. Platt, *Shock Cities*, 342–350; Platt, "Jane Addams and the Ward Boss Revisited."

62. Platt, *Shock Cities*, 348–361, pamphlet quoted on 350; Platt, "Jane Addams and the Ward Boss Revisited."

63. Platt, "Jane Addams and the Ward Boss Revisited"; Suellen M. Hoy, "'Municipal Housekeeping': The Role of Women in Improving Urban Sanitation Practices, 1880–1917," in *Pollution and Reform in American Cities, 1870–1930*, ed. Martin V. Melosi (Austin: University of Texas Press, 1980), 173–198; Maureen A. Flanagan, "The City Profitable, the City Livable: Environmental Policy, Gender, and Power in Chicago in the 1910s," *Journal of Urban History* 22 (January 1996): 163–190.

64. Platt, *Shock Cities*, 78–134, sanitarian quoted on 111; Martin V. Melosi, "'Out of Sight, Out of Mind': The Environment and Disposal of Municipal Refuse, 1860–1920," *The Historian* 35 (1973): 621–640, "intellectual awakening" on 632.

CHAPTER 4

1. A. Duncan Brown, *Feed or Feedback: Agricultural, Population, and the State of the Planet* (Utrecht: International, 2003), 83–95; Jared Diamond, *Guns, Germs, and Steel: The Fates of Human Societies* (New York: W. W. Norton, 2017), 195–214; Martin V. Melosi, *The Sanitary City: Urban Infrastructure from Colonial Times to the Present* (Baltimore: Johns Hopkins University Press, 2008), 4–5, passim.

2. John D. Fairfield, "A Populism for the Cities: Henry George, John Dewey, and the City Planning Movement," *Urban Design Studies* 8 (2002): 19–27, quotations on 19.

3. Stanley K. Schultz, *Constructing Urban Culture: American Cities and City Planning, 1800–1920* (Philadelphia: Temple University Press, 1989), 129–149, sanitarian quoted on 130; Stanley K. Schultz and Clay McShane, "To Engineer the Metropolis: Sewers, Sanitation, and City Planning in Late-Nineteenth-Century America," *Journal of American History* 65 (September 1978): 389–411, "need" on 395.

4. Schultz, *Constructing Urban Culture*; Schultz and McShane, "To Engineer the Metropolis"; Melosi, *The Sanitary City*, 11–68; Jon C. Teaford, *The Unheralded Triumph: City Government in America, 1870–1900* (Baltimore: Johns Hopkins

University Press, 1984), 217–250; Jon A. Peterson, *The Birth of City Planning in the United States, 1840–1917* (Baltimore: Johns Hopkins University Press, 2003), 188–222. "Worthy" is Clinton Rogers Woodruff, "Awakening America," American Park and Outdoor Art Association, *Proceedings* (1903): 75–81; "measure" is Frederic C. Howe, "The City as a Socializing Agency," *American Journal of Sociology* 17 (March 1912): 590–601; Kevin Mattson, *Creating a Democratic Public: The Struggle for Urban Participatory Democracy in the Progressive Era* (University Park: Pennsylvania State University Press, 1998).

5. Harold Platt, *Shock Cities: The Environmental Transformation and Reform of Manchester and Chicago* (Chicago: University of Chicago Press, 2005), 248–250; Sarah Jones and Emily Atkin, "Rural America's Drinking-Water Crisis," *New Republic*, February 12, 2018, https://newrepublic.com/article/147011/rural-amer icas-drinking-water-crisis; Catherine Coleman Flowers, *Waste: One Woman's Fight against America's Dirty Secret* (New York: New Press, 2020); Grey Brechin, *Imperial San Francisco: Urban Power, Earthly Ruin* (Berkeley: University of California Press, 1999); Donald Worster, *Rivers of Empire: Water, Aridity, and the Growth of the American West* (New York: Pantheon, 1985); Andrew Needham, *Power Lines: Phoenix and the Making of the Modern Southwest* (Princeton, NJ: Princeton University Press, 2014); Nelson Manfred Blake, *Water for the Cities: A History of the Urban Water Supply Problem in the United States* (Syracuse, NY: Syracuse University Press, 1956).

6. Blake, *Water for the Cities*; Steven P. Erie and Harold Brackman, *Beyond Chinatown: The Metropolitan Water District, Growth, and the Environment in Southern California* (Stanford, CA: Stanford University Press, 2006); Lucy Sante, *Nineteen Reservoirs: On Their Creation and the Promise of Water for New York City* (New York: The Experiment, 2022).

7. Lewis Mumford, *The Culture of Cities* (New York: Harcourt, Brace, 1938), 143–222; Platt, *Shock Cities*; Schultz, *Constructing Urban Culture*, 111–128; Martin V. Melosi, *Effluent America: Cities, Industry, Energy, and the Environment* (Pittsburgh: University of Pittsburgh Press, 2001), 23–48; Joel Tarr, *The Search for the Ultimate Sink: Urban Pollution in Historical Perspective* (Akron, OH: University of Akron Press, 1996), 7–35, passim.

8. Platt, *Shock Cities*, 70–74; Schultz, *Constructing Urban Culture*, 129–149.

9. David R. Goldfield, "The Business of Health Planning: Disease Prevention in the Old South," *Journal of Southern History* 42 (November 1978): 557–570; Platt, *Shock Cities*, 7–23; Schultz, *Constructing Urban Culture*, 111–149; Melosi, *The Sanitary City*, 40–67; Paul S. Boyer, *Urban Masses and Moral Order* (Cambridge, MA: Harvard University Press, 1978), 3–122; Platt, *Shock Cities*, 333–361; Tarr, *The Search for the Ultimate Sink*.

10. Platt, *Shock Cities*, 7–23; Schultz, *Constructing Urban Culture*, 111–149; Melosi, *The Sanitary City*, 40–67; Boyer, *Urban Masses and Moral Order*, 3–122; Platt, *Shock Cities*, 333–361; Tarr, *The Search for the Ultimate Sink*.

11. Schultz, *Constructing Urban Culture*, 35–91; Teaford, *The Unheralded Triumph*, 132–173, passim.

12. Schultz, *Constructing Urban Culture*, 35–91; Teaford, *The Unheralded Triumph*, 132–173, passim; Barton Bledstein, *The Culture of Professionalism* (New York: W. W. Norton, 1978).

13. Melosi, *The Sanitary City*, 71–112; Suellen Hoy, *Chasing Dirt: The American Pursuit of Cleanliness* (New York: Oxford University Press, 1996), 59–86; Teaford, *The Unheralded Triumph*, 123–141; Schultz, *Constructing Urban Culture*, 153–181; David Stradling, *The Nature of New York* (Ithaca, NY: Cornell University Press, 2010), 70–72, 116–118.

14. Platt, *Shock Cities*, 118–195; Schultz, *Constructing Urban Culture*, 170–173; Dominic A. Pacyga, *Chicago: A Biography* (Chicago: University of Chicago Press, 2009), 44–46; Teaford, *The Unheralded Triumph*, 217–226; Harold L. Platt, "Chicago, the Great Lakes, and the Origins of Federal Urban Environmental Policy," *Journal of the Gilded Age and Progressive Era* 1 (April 2002): 122–153.

15. Platt, *Shock Cities*, 118–126.

16. Ibid., 135–195, "fountain" on 188, "purity" on 137, "river" on 144; Platt, "Chicago, the Great Lakes, and the Origins of Federal Urban Environmental Policy."

17. Platt, *Shock Cities*, 118–195; Platt, "Chicago, the Great Lakes, and the Origins of Federal Urban Environmental Policy"; Pacyga, *Chicago*, 104–106.

18. Schultz, *Constructing Urban Culture*, 153–181; Teaford, *The Unheralded Triumph*, 219–227.

19. Melosi, *The Sanitary City*, 71–112; Hoy, *Chasing Dirt*, 59–86; Tarr, *The Search for the Ultimate Sink*.

20. Clay McShane, *Down the Asphalt Path* (New York: Columbia University Press, 1994); Boyer, *Urban Masses and Moral Order*, 220–251; Schultz, *Constructing Urban Culture*, 154–161.

21. John W. Reps, *The Making of Urban America: A History of City Planning in the United States* (Princeton, NJ; Princeton University Press, 1965); Schultz, *Constructing Urban Culture*, 154–161; Boyer, *Urban Masses and Moral Order*, 236–239; Anne Whiston Spirn, *The Granite Garden: Urban Nature and Human Design* (New York: Basic, 1984), 9–37, passim; Kenneth T. Jackson, *Crabgrass Frontier: The Suburbanization of the United States* (New York: Oxford University Press, 1985), 73–86.

22. Schultz, *Constructing Urban Culture*, 154–161; Teaford, *The Unheralded Triumph*, 142–147; Anne Whiston Spirn, "Reclaiming Common Ground: Water, Neighborhoods, and Public Spaces," in *The American Planning Tradition: Culture and Policy*, ed. Robert Fishman (Baltimore: Johns Hopkins University Press, 2000), 297–313.

23. Tarr, *The Search for the Ultimate Sink*.

24. Hoy, *Chasing Dirt*, 59–86; Melosi, *Effluent America*; Tarr, *The Search for the Ultimate Sink*, 77–98; Laura E. Baker, "Public Sites versus Public Sights: The Progressive Response to Outdoor Advertising and the Commercialization of Public Space," *American Quarterly* 59 (December 2007): 1187–1213.

25. Boyer, *Urban Masses and Moral Order*, 123–131, quotation on 126; Alfred Kazin, "Fear of the City, 1783–1983," *American Heritage* 34 (February–March 1983): 14–23; Jackson, *Crabgrass Frontier*, 70.

26. Jacob Riis, *How the Other Half Lives* (New York: Scribner's, 1890), quoted passages on 55, 273, 296; Boyer, *Urban Masses and Moral Order*, 123–131.

27. Boyer, *Urban Masses and Moral Order in America*, 123–131; Stanley K.

Schulz, *Constructing Urban Culture: American Cities and City Planning, 1800–1920* (Philadelphia: Temple University Press, 1989), 3–32.

28. Schulz, *Constructing Urban Culture*, 3–32, Bellamy quoted on 3.

29. Teaford, *The Unheralded Triumph*; Boyer, *Urban Masses and Moral Order*, 261–265; Mattson, *Creating a Democratic Public*, 14–20.

30. Schultz, *Constructing Urban Culture*, 3–32, novelist quoted on 25.

31. Peterson, *The Birth of City Planning in the United States*, 98–108; Schultz, *Constructing Urban Culture*, 3–32, utopian novelist quoted on 21; Leo Marx, *The Machine in the Garden: Technology and the Pastoral Ideal in America* (New York: Oxford University Press, 1964).

32. Frederick Law Olmsted, *Public Parks and the Enlargement of Towns*, repr. ed. (New York: Arno, [1870] 1970); John D. Fairfield, *The Mysteries of the Great City: The Politics of Urban Design, 1877–1937* (Columbus: Ohio State University Press, 1993), 41–49; Peterson, *The Birth of City Planning in the United States*, 39–54; William H. Wilson, *The City Beautiful Movement* (Baltimore: Johns Hopkins University Press, 1989), 14–22, "progress" on 19, "hard" on 20; Boyer, *Urban Masses and Moral Order*, 236–240, "pleasure" on 239, "harmonizing" on 238.

33. Wilson, *The City Beautiful Movement*, 22–33; Peterson, *The Birth of City Planning in the United States*, 29–73.

34. Wilson, *The City Beautiful Movement*, 22–33; Peterson, *The Birth of City Planning in the United States*, 29–73.

35. Alan Trachtenberg, *The Incorporation of America: Culture and Society in the Gilded Age* (New York: Hill and Wang, 1982), 208–234; Wilson, *The City Beautiful Movement*, 56–60; Schultz, *Constructing Urban Culture*, 209–217.

36. Thomas S. Hines, *Burnham of Chicago, Architect and Planner* (New York: Oxford University Press, 1974), 4–6, passim; Carl Smith, *The Plan of Chicago: Daniel Burnham and the Remaking of the American City* (Chicago: University of Chicago Press, 2006), 19–22, 32–33; Boyer, *Urban Masses and Moral Order*, 182–184, 269–271, quotations on 183.

37. Fairfield, *The Mysteries of the Great City*, Olmsted quoted on 42; Geoffrey Blodgett, "Frederick Law Olmsted: Landscape Architecture as Conservative Reform," *Journal of American History* 62 (March 1976): 869–889; Roy Rosenzweig and Elizabeth Blackmar, *The Park and the People: A History of Central Park* (Ithaca, NY: Cornell University Press, 1992), passim; Trachtenberg, *The Incorporation of America*, 208–234.

38. Peterson, *The Birth of City Planning in the United States*, 69–102; Wilson, *The City Beautiful Movement*, 56–64, Robinson quoted on 60; Trachtenberg, *The Incorporation of America*.

39. Peterson, *The Birth of City Planning in the United States*, 98–108, motto quoted on 103; Michele H. Bogart, *Public Sculpture and the Civic Ideal in New York City, 1890–1930* (Chicago: University of Chicago Press, 1989); Wilson, *The City Beautiful Movement*, 35–47; John D. Fairfield, "The City Beautiful Movement," in *Oxford Research Encyclopedia in American History*, ed. Jon Butler (New York: Oxford University Press, 2018), https://doi.org/10.1093/acre fore/9780199329175.013.558.

40. Peterson, *The Birth of City Planning in the United States*, 151–172; Wilson, *The City Beautiful Movement*, 1–112; Daniel Baldwin Hess, "Transportation Beautiful: Did the City Beautiful Improve Urban Transportation?" *Journal of Urban History* 32 (May 2006): 511–545.

41. Hess, "Transportation Beautiful," 511–545, Robinson quoted on 523–524; Peterson, *The Birth of City Planning in the United States*, 162–172; Wilson, *The City Beautiful Movement*, 1112; Matthew Gandy, *Concrete and Clay: Reworking Nature in New York City* (Cambridge, MA: MIT Press, 2003), 115–126.

42. Peterson, *The Birth of City Planning in the United States*, 181–222; Wilson, *The City Beautiful Movement*, 99–278; Daniel H. Burnham and Edward H. Bennett, *Plan of Chicago*, ed. Charles Moore (New York: Princeton Architectural Press, 1993); Smith, *The Plan of Chicago*.

43. Brechin, *Imperial San Francisco*, 13–70, passim.

44. Mario Manieri-Elia, "Toward an 'Imperial City,'" in *The American City: From the Civil War to the New Deal*, ed. Giorgio Ciucci, Francesco Del Co, Mario Manieri-Elia, and Manfredo Tafuri (New York: Granada, 1980), 1–142; Burnham and Bennett, *Plan of Chicago*, quoted passages on 80, 95; Smith, *The Plan of Chicago*; Peterson, *The Birth of City Planning in the United States*, 213–222.

45. Burnham and Bennett, *Plan of Chicago*, quoted passages on 66, 74, and 99; Peterson, *The Birth of City Planning in the United States*, 213–222; Fairfield, *The Mysteries of the Great City*, 119–124.

46. Burnham and Bennett, *Plan of Chicago*, "citizenship" on 123, "efficient" on 1; "Make no little plans" is often attributed to Burnham but there is no definitive source: see Smith, *The Plan of Chicago*, 98.

47. Burnham and Bennett, *Plan of Chicago*, "frequent" and "narrow" on 32, "influx" on 1, "Lake front" on 50; Smith, *The Plan of Chicago*, 11–37, 99–103, "singing" on 33; Maureen A. Flanagan, "The City Profitable, the City Livable: Environmental Policy, Gender, and Power in Chicago in the 1910s," *Journal of Urban History* 22 (January 1996): 163–190; Fairfield, *The Mysteries of the Great City*, 119–124.

48. Smith, *The Plan of Chicago*, 80–117, "serenely" is Smith's elegant phrase on 91; Burnham and Bennett, *Plan of Chicago*, "unified" on 100, "dominion" on 30.

49. Burnham and Bennett, *Plan of Chicago*, "menace" on 108; Smith, *The Plan of Chicago*, 34–53, Burnham quoted on 52; Laura E. Baker, "Civic Ideals, Mass Culture, and the Public," *Journal of Urban History* 36 (2010): 747–770.

50. Smith, *The Plan of Chicago*, 34–53; Baker, "Civic Ideals, Mass Culture, and the Public."

51. Smith, *The Plan of Chicago*, 116–125, 132–133; Thomas J. Schlereth, "Burnham's *Plan* and Moody's *Manual*: City Planning as Progressive Reform," *Journal of the American Planning Association* 47 (January 1981): 70–82; Baker, "Civic Ideals, Mass Culture, and the Public."

52. Baker, "Civic Ideals, Mass Culture, and the Public"; Wilson, *The City Beautiful Movement*, 99–278; David B. Brownlee, *Building the City Beautiful: The Benjamin Franklin Parkway and the Philadelphia Museum of Art* (Philadelphia: Philadelphia Museum of Art, 1989).

53. Baker, "Civic Ideals, Mass Culture, and the Public"; Baker, "Public Sites

versus Public Sights," 1187–1205, "sordid" is Frederick Law Olmsted Jr., son of the landscape architect, quoted on 1194; "din," shriek[ing], "riot," and "mob" on 1201; Mattson, *Creating a Democratic Public.*

54. Baker, "Public Sites versus Public Sights," 1199–1209, *Architectural Record* quoted on 1199; Baker, "Civic Ideals, Mass Culture, and the Public"; Smith, *The Plan of Chicago*, 118–121; David E. Nye, *Consuming Power: A Social History of American Energies* (Cambridge, MA: MIT Press, 1998), 257–258.

55. Mattson, *Creating a Democratic Public*, 14–30, "soothe" on 17, "spirit" on 18, "proprietary" on 19; Charles Mulford Robinson, *Modern Civic Art* (New York: Putman, 1909), "visibly" on 91; John D. Fairfield, *The Public and Its Possibilities: Triumphs and Tragedies in the American City* (Philadelphia: Temple University Press, 2010), 149–151; Smith, *The Plan of Chicago*, 126–129.

56. Mattson, *Creating a Democratic Public*, 14–30, "open-air" on 21; Peterson, *The Birth of City Planning in the United States*, "striving" on 113.

57. Peterson, *The Birth of City Planning in the United States*, 229–232; Robinson, *Modern Civic Art*, "sunless" on 257–258; Burnham and Bennett, *Plan of Chicago*, "degraded" on 109.

58. Flanagan, "The City Profitable, the City Livable," "broad" on 171–172; Susan Marie Wirka, "The City Social Movement: Progressive Women Reformers and Early Social Planning," in *Planning the Twentieth Century City*, ed. Mary Corbin Sies and Christopher Silver (Baltimore: Johns Hopkins University Press, 1996), 55–75.

59. Jane Addams, *Democracy and Social Ethics* (New York: Macmillan, 1902), 236; Suellen M. Hoy, "'Municipal Housekeeping': The Role of Women in Improving Urban Sanitation Practices, 1880–1917," in *Pollution and Reform in American Cities, 1870–1930*, ed. Martin V. Melosi (Austin: University of Texas Press, 1980), 173–198; Flanagan, "The City Profitable, the City Livable"; Eileen Maura McGurty, "Trashy Women: Gender and the Politics of Garbage in Chicago, 1890–1917," *Historical Geography* 26 (June 1998): 27–43; David Stradling, "Dirty Work and Clean Air: Locomotive Firemen, Environmental Activists, and Stories of Conflict," *Journal of Urban History* 28 (November 2001): 35–54; Peterson, *The Birth of City Planning in the United States*, 192–194; Gregory Alexander Donofrio, "Feeding the City," *Gastronomica* 7 (Fall 2007): 30–41; Harold L. Platt, "Jane Addams and the Ward Boss Revisited: Class, Politics, and Public Health in Chicago, 1890–1930," *Environmental History* 5 (April 2000): 194–222.

60. Wirka, "The City Social Movement," 55–70, "pictured" on 69; Peterson, *The Birth of City Planning in the United States*, 227–245; Fairfield, *The Mysteries of the Great City*, 119–157.

61. Wirka, "The City Social Movement," 68–75, Simkhovitch quoted on 72–73.

62. Peterson, *The Birth of City Planning in the United States*, 240–259, "sunlight" on 242, "social" on 253; F. L. Ackerman, "The Battle with Chaos," *Journal of the American Institute of Architects* 3 (1913): 444–447; Fairfield, *The Mysteries of the Great City*, 119–157; Fairfield, "A Populism for the Cities."

63. George Ford, "The City Scientific," *Proceedings of the Fifth National Conference on City Planning* (Boston: National Conference on City Planning, 1913), 31–41; George Ford, "What Planning Has Done for Cities," *Proceedings of the Sixteenth National Conference on City Planning* (Los Angeles: National Conference on City Planning, 1924), 27; John D. Fairfield, "The Scientific Manage-

ment of Urban Space: Professional City Planning and the Legacy of Progressive Reform," *Journal of Urban History* 20 (February 1994): 179–204.

64. Peterson, *The Birth of City Planning in the United States*, 255–259; Fairfield, *The Mysteries of the Great City*, 119–157; David M. P. Freund, *Colored Property: State Policy and White Racial Politics in Suburban America* (Chicago: University of Chicago Press, 2007), 45–97; Adam Rome, "'Political Hermaphrodites': Gender and Environmental Reform in Progressive America," *Environmental Reform* 11 (July 2006): 440–463, "effeminate" on 431.

CHAPTER 5

1. Stanley K. Schultz and Clay McShane, "To Engineer the Metropolis: Sewers, Sanitation, and City Planning Late-Nineteenth-Century America," *Journal of American History* 65 (September 1978): 389–410, sanitarian quoted on 402; Robert Claike, *Ellen Swallow: The Woman Who Founded Human Ecology* (Chicago: Follett, 1973); Jon A. Peterson, *The Birth of City Planning in the United States, 1840–1917* (Baltimore: Johns Hopkins University Press, 2003), 255–259; Sharon E. Kingsland, *The Evolution of American Ecology* (Baltimore: Johns Hopkins University Press, 2005); Jon C. Teaford, *The Unheralded Triumph: City Government in America, 1870–1900* (Baltimore: Johns Hopkins University Press, 1984); Nancy Golubiewski, "Is There a Metabolism of an Urban Ecosystem? An Ecological Critique," *Ambio* 41 (2012): 751–764.

2. Frederick Law Olmsted Jr., "Introduction," in *City Planning: A Series of Papers Presenting the Essential Elements of a City Plan*, ed. John Nolen (New York: D. Appleton, 1916), 1–18, quoted passages on 1, 2, 16; Peterson, *The Birth of City Planning in the United States*; Mike Davis, *Ecology of Fear: Los Angeles and the Imagination of Disaster* (New York: Vintage, 1999), 61–67.

3. Jennifer Light, *The Nature of Cities: Ecological Visions and the American Urban Professions, 1920–1960* (Baltimore: Johns Hopkins University Press, 2014); Greg Mitman, *The State of Nature: Ecology, Community, and American Social Thought, 1900–1950* (Chicago: University of Chicago Press, 1992), 3, 38–44, passim; Eugene Cittadino, "The Failed Promise of Human Ecology," in *Science and Nature: Essays in the History of the Environmental Sciences*, ed. Michael Shortland (London: British Society for the History of Science, 1993), 251–283; Eugene Cittadino, "Ecology and American Social Thought," in *Religion and the New Ecology*, ed. David M. Lodge and Christopher Hamlin (Notre Dame, IN: University of Notre Dame Press, 2006), 73–115.

4. Barrington Moore, "The Scope of Ecology," *Ecology* 1 (1920): 3–5; Stephen A. Forbes, "The Humanizing of Ecology." *Ecology* 3 (1922): 89–92, quoted passage on 89–90; Cittadino, "The Failed Promise of Human Ecology"; Cittadino, "Ecology and American Social Thought"; Matthias Gross, "Human Geography and Ecological Sociology: The Unfolding of a Human Ecology, 1890 to 1930— and Beyond," *Social Science History* 28 (2004): 575–605.

5. Kingsland, *The Evolution of American Ecology*, 1–16, 129–132; Samuel P. Hays, *Conservation and the Gospel of Efficiency: The Progressive Conservation Movement, 1890–1920* (Cambridge, MA: Harvard University Press, 1959); Gifford Pinchot, *Breaking New Ground* (New York: Harcourt, Brace, 1947);

Cittadino, "The Failed Promise of Human Ecology"; Cittadino, "Ecology and American Social Thought."

6. Jane Addams, *Women and Public Housekeeping* (New York: National Women Suffrage, 1910); Suellen M. Hoy, "'Municipal Housekeeping': The Role of Women in Improving Urban Sanitation Practices, 1880–1917," in *Pollution and Reform in American Cities, 1870–1930,* ed. Martin V. Melosi (Austin: University of Texas Press, 1980), 173–198; Maureen A. Flanagan, "The City Profitable, the City Livable: Environmental Policy, Gender, and Power in Chicago in the 1910s," *Journal of Urban History* 22 (January 1996): 163–190; Clarke, *Ellen Swallow*; Harold L. Platt, "Jane Addams and the Ward Boss Revisited: Class, Politics, and Public Health in Chicago, 1890–1930," *Environmental History* 5 (April 2000): 194–222.

7. Gerald L. Young, ed., *Origins of Human Ecology* (Stroudsburg, PA: Hutchinson Ross, 1983); Louis Wirth, "Urbanism as a Way of Life," *American Journal of Sociology* 44 (1938): 1–24, quoted passage on 1–2; Robert E. Park, Ernest W. Burgess, and Roderick McKenzie, *The City* (Chicago: University of Chicago Press, 1925); Cittadino, "The Failed Promise of Human Ecology"; Cittadino, "Ecology and American Social Thought."

8. Park et al., *The City*, "chronic" on 22; Robert E. Park, "The Concept of Position in Sociology," *Papers and Proceedings of the American Sociological Society* 20 (1926): 1–14; David Wachsmuth, "Three Ecologies: Urban Metabolism and the Society-Nature Opposition," *Sociological Quarterly* 53 (2012): 506–523; Milla Aissa Alihan, *Social Ecology* (New York: Columbia University Press, 1938); John D. Fairfield, *The Mysteries of the Great City: The Politics of Urban Design, 1877–1937* (Columbus: Ohio State University Press, 1993), 158–224; Cittadino, "The Failed Promise of Human Ecology," 262–271; John D. Fairfield, "The Alienation of Social Control: The Chicago Sociologists and The Origins of Urban Planning," *Planning Perspectives* 7 (October 1992): 418–434.

9. Park et al., *The City*; Light, *The Nature of Cities*. The quotation "change the changes" is from John Dewey, "The Need for a Recovery of Philosophy" (1917), in *The Middle Works of John Dewey, 1899–1924*, vol. 10 (Carbondale: Southern Illinois University Press, 1976–1983), 7–10; Lewis Mumford, *The Culture of Cities* (New York: Harcourt, Brace, 1938), 302; Ben A. Minteer, *The Landscape of Reform: Civic Pragmatism and Environmental Thought in America* (Cambridge, MA: MIT Press, 2006), 1–9, 51–80; Kingsland, *The Evolution of American Ecology*, 1–16; Neil W. Browne, *The World in Which We Occur: John Dewey, Pragmatist Ecology, and American Ecological Writing in the Twentieth Century* (Tuscaloosa: University of Alabama Press, 2007); Deron Boyles, "Dewey, Ecology, and Education: Historical and Contemporary Debates over Dewey's Naturalism and (Transactional) Realism," *Educational Theory* 62 (2012): 143–161; Kai Alhanen, *John Dewey's Ecology of Experience* (Helsinki: Books on Demand, 2018).

10. Mary Beard, *Woman's Work in Municipalities* (New York: Appleton, 1915); Addams, *Women and Public Housekeeping*; Alison Isenberg, *Downtown America: A History of the Place and the People Who Made It* (Chicago: University of Chicago Press, 2004), 13–41, "lamppost" on 17; Hoy, "'Municipal Housekeeping'"; Flanagan, "The City Profitable, the City Livable"; Clarke, *Ellen Swallow*; Platt, "Jane Addams and the Ward Boss Revisited"; Christopher Lasch

and Elisabeth Lasch-Quinn, *Women and the Common Life: Love, Marriage, and Feminism* (New York: W. W. Norton, 1997), 93–136.

11. Addams, *Women and Public Housekeeping*, 1; Flanagan, "The City Profitable, the City Livable"; Hoy, "Municipal Housekeeping"; Clarke, *Ellen Swallow*; Hannah Arendt, *The Human Condition* (Chicago: University of Chicago Press, 1958).

12. Isenberg, *Downtown America*, 26–30; Ellen H. Richards, *Conservation by Sanitation* (New York: Wiley, 1911), "duty" on v; Hoy, "Municipal Housekeeping"; Clarke, *Ellen Swallow*.

13. Ellen Swallow Richards, *Sanitation in Daily Life* (Boston: Whitcomb and Burrow, [1907] 1910), v–viii; Clarke, *Ellen Swallow*; Hoy, "Municipal Housekeeping."

14. Hoy, "Municipal Housekeeping."

15. Flanagan, "The City Profitable, the City Livable," quotations on 176, 182; Hoy, "Municipal Housekeeping"; Isenberg, *Downtown America*, 26–30.

16. Hoy, "Municipal Housekeeping," quotations on 187; Tiffany Lewis, "Municipal Housekeeping in the American West: Bertha Knight Landes's Entrance into Politics," *Rhetoric and Public Affairs* 14 (2011): 465–491.

17. Mitman, *The State of Nature*; Kristen R. Egan, "Conservation and Cleanliness: Racial and Environmental Purity in Ellen Richards and Charlotte Perkins Gilman," *Women's Studies Quarterly* 39 (Fall–Winter 2011): 77–92; Nancy Tomes, *The Gospel of Germs: Men, Women, and the Microbe in American Life* (Cambridge, MA: Harvard University Press, 1998); Alan Kraut, *Silent Travelers: Germs, Genes, and the "Immigrant Menace"* (Baltimore: Johns Hopkins University Press, 1994).

18. Egan, "Conservation and Cleanliness"; Ellen Richards, *Euthenics: The Science of Controllable Environments*, repr. ed. (New York: Arno, [1910] 1977); Adam Cohen, *Imbeciles: The Supreme Court, American Eugenics, and the Sterilization of Carrie Buck* (New York: Penguin, 2016); Roger Daniels, *Guarding the Golden Door: American Immigration Policy and Immigrants since 1882* (New York: Hill and Wang, 2004).

19. Charlotte Perkins Gilman, *Herland and Selected Stories* (New York: Signet, 1992); Egan, "Conservation and Cleanliness."

20. Egan, "Conservation and Cleanliness"; Gilman, *Herland and Selected Stories*.

21. Mary Corbin Sies, "The City Transformed: Nature, Technology, and the Suburban Ideal, 1877–1917," *Journal of Urban History* 14 (November 1987): 81–111.

22. Ibid., quoted passage on 89.

23. Ibid.; Egan, "Conservation and Cleanliness"; Gilman, *Herland and Selected Stories*.

24. Egan, "Conservation and Cleanliness"; Richards, *Euthenics*.

25. Egan, "Conservation and Cleanliness"; Richards, *Euthenics*.

26. Kingsland, *The Evolution of American Ecology*, 1–16, 129–154, quoted passage on 141; Ellsworth Huntington, *Civilization and Climate* (New Haven, CT: Yale University Press, 1915); Ellsworth Huntington, "The Control of Pneumonia and Influenza by the Weather," *Ecology* 1 (January 1920): 6–23; Cittadino, "The Failed Promise of Human Ecology," 250–259; Kraut, *Silent Travelers*;

Ellsworth Huntington, *Tomorrow's Children: The Goal of Eugenics* (New York: John Wiley, 1935).

27. The U.S. Supreme Court case against racial zoning is *Buchanan v. Warley* (1917). Isenberg, *Downtown America*, 32–41, "undesirable" on 34; David M. P. Freund, *Colored Property: State Policy and White Racial Politics in Suburban America* (Chicago: University of Chicago Press, 2007), 45–98; Christopher Silver, "The Racial Origins of Zoning: Southern Cities from 1910–1940," *Planning Perspectives* 6 (1991): 189–205.

28. Herman E. Daly and Joshua Farley, *Ecological Economics: Principles and Application* (Washington, DC: Island, 2011), 37–58; Mitman, *The State of Nature*, passim; Sharon E. Kingsland, "Essay Review: History of Ecology," *Journal of the History of Biology* 27 (Summer 1994): 349–357.

29. Robert Westbrook, *John Dewey and American Democracy* (Ithaca, NY: Cornell University Press, 1991), 33–149; Louis Menand, *The Metaphysical Club* (New York: Farrar, Straus, and Giroux, 2001), 59–148, 285–333.

30. Menand, *The Metaphysical Club*, 285–333, "organism" quoted on 297; Nick Salvatore, *Eugene V. Debs: Citizen and Socialist* (Urbana: University of Illinois Press, 1984).

31. Menand, *The Metaphysical Club*, 295–304, federal judge (William Howard Taft) quoted on 300.

32. Lester Ward, "Mind as a Social Factor," *Mind* 9 (October 1884): 563–573; Menand, *The Metaphysical Club*, 299–306; Jane Addams, "Hull-House, Chicago: An Effort toward Social Democracy," *Forum* 14 (October 1892): 227–228; Jane Addams, "A New Impulse to a New Gospel," *Forum* 14 (November 1892): 346; Mary Jo Deegan, *Jane Addams and the Men of the Chicago School, 1892–1918* (New Brunswick, NJ: Transaction, 1988).

33. Written in 1894, Addams's controversial essay would not appear in print until 1912. Menand, *The Metaphysical Club*, 307–316; Jane Addams, "A Modern Lear," *Survey* 29 (1912): 131–137; Deegan, *Jane Addams and the Men of the Chicago School*, 247–253.

34. John Dewey, "The Reflex Arc Concept in Psychology," *Psychological Review* 4 (July 1896): 357–370; Westbrook, *John Dewey and American Democracy*, 65–71; Menand, *The Metaphysical Club*, 316–330; William James, *The Principles of Psychology* (New York: Henry Holt, 1890), 66.

35. Dewey, "The Reflex Arc Concept in Psychology"; Westbrook, *John Dewey and American Democracy*, 65–71; Menand, *The Metaphysical Club*, 316–330; Browne, *The World in Which We Occur*, 1–19; Minteer, *The Landscape of Reform*; John D. Fairfield and William Widdowson, "Of Patterns and Publics: City Planning as Democratic Process," *Urban Design Studies* 6 (2000): 149–157; Timothy V. Kaufman-Osborne, "Pragmatism, Policy Science, and the State," *American Journal of Political Science* 29 (1985); Timothy V. Kaufman-Osborne, "John Dewey and the Liberal Science of Community," *Journal of Politics* 46 (1984): 1153–1159; Daly and Farley, *Ecological Economics*, 47–51.

36. William Rainey Harper, *The University and Democracy* (Chicago: University of Chicago Press, 1970); Kevin Mattson, *Creating a Democratic Public: The Struggle for Urban Participatory Democracy in the Progressive Era* (University Park: Pennsylvania State University Press, 1998), 26; Mitman, *The State of Nature*,

65–71; Westbrook, *John Dewey and American Democracy*, 361–366; Jamin Creed Rowan, *The Sociable City: An American Intellectual Tradition* (Philadelphia: University of Pennsylvania Press, 2017), 102–105; Ronald Engel, "Social Democracy, the Roots of Ecology, and the Preservation of the Indiana Dunes," *Journal of Forest History* 28 (January 1984): 4–13.

37. W. C. Allee, *Animal Life and Social Growth* (Baltimore: Williams and Wilkins, 1932), quoted passage on 149; Donald Worster, *Nature's Economy: A History of Ecological Ideas* (Cambridge: Cambridge University Press, 1994), 206–208; Ronald C. Tobey, *Saving the Prairies: The Life Cycle of the Founding School of American Plant Ecology, 1895–1955* (Berkeley: University of California Press, 1981), 102–104, passim; William Cronon, "Paradigm Shift," *Reviews in American History* 11 (March 1983): 93–98.

38. Henry Chandler Cowles, "The Ecological Relations of the Vegetation on the Sand Dunes of Lake Michigan," *Botanical Gazette* 27 (February 1899): 95–117, quoted passage on 96; Tobey, *Saving the Prairies*, 76–109; Engel, "Social Democracy, the Roots of Ecology, and the Preservation of the Indiana Dunes"; Mitman, *The State of Nature*, 15–20; Worster, *Nature's Economy*, 198–220; Eugene Cittadino, "A 'Marvelous Cosmopolitan Preserve': The Dunes, Chicago, and the Dynamic Ecology of Henry Cowles," *Perspectives on Science* 3 (Fall 1993): 520–559; Mitman, *The State of Nature*, 74–78; Engel, "Social Democracy, the Roots of Ecology, and the Preservation of the Indiana Dunes"; Cittadino, "Ecology and American Social Thought," 77.

39. W. C. Allee, *Animal Aggregations: A Study in General Sociology* (Chicago: University of Chicago Press, 1931), "group" on 375, "fundamental" on 355; W. C. Allee, *The Social Life of Animals* (Boston: Beacon, 1938), "problems" on 7; Allee, *Animal Life and Social Growth*, "beneficial" on 149.

40. Engel, "Social Democracy, the Roots of Ecology, and the Preservation of the Indiana Dunes," Cowles quoted on 10, Taylor quoted on 9. For complete testimony, see Stephen Mather, *Report on Sand Dunes National Park, Indiana* (Washington, DC: Government Printing Office, 1917); Cittadino, "A 'Marvelous Cosmopolitan Preserve'"; J. Ronald Engel, "Indiana Dunes," in *Encyclopedia of Chicago*, http://www.encyclopedia.chicagohistory.org/pages/634.html.

41. Engel, "Social Democracy, the Roots of Ecology, and the Preservation of the Indiana Dunes"; Cittadino, "A 'Marvelous Cosmopolitan Preserve.'"

42. Engel, "Social Democracy, the Roots of Ecology, and the Preservation of the Indiana Dunes," quotations on 8–9; Engel, "Indiana Dunes."

43. Kingsland, *The Evolution of American Ecology*, 1–16; Cittadino, "The Failed Promise of Human Ecology"; Cittadino, "Ecology and American Social Thought"; Thomas Bender, *New York Intellect* (Baltimore: Johns Hopkins University Press, 1987), 263–318; Tobey, *Saving the Prairies*, 122–127; Robert Gottlieb, *Forcing the Spring: The Transformation of the American Environmental Movement* (Washington, DC: Island, 2005), 82–115; National Park Service, "Indiana Dunes: Plants," https://www.nps.gov/indu/learn/nature/plants.htm.

44. Frederic E. Clements and Roscoe Pound, *The Phytogeography of Nebraska* (Lincoln: Botanical Survey of Nebraska, 1898); Frederic E. Clements, *Research Methods in Ecology* (Lincoln, NE: University Publishing, 1905); Frederic E. Cle-

ments, *Plant Succession: An Analysis of the Development of Vegetation* (Washington, DC: Carnegie Institution of Washington, 1916); Tobey, *Saving the Prairies*, 48–75, 122–127, passim; Cittadino, "The Failed Promise of Human Ecology"; Cittadino, "Ecology and American Social Thought."

45. Tobey, *Saving the Prairies*, 76–154; Worster, *Nature's Economy*, 205–220, Clements quoted on 214.

46. Worster, *Nature's Economy*, 215–217, 248–253.

47. Ibid., 205–253; Engel, "Indiana Dunes"; Kingsland, *The Evolution of American Ecology*, 129–154; Cittadino, "The Failed Promise of Human Ecology."

48. Worster, *Nature's Economy*, 205–253; Donald Worster, *Dust Bowl: The Southern Plains in the 1930s* (New York: Oxford University Press, 1979), 204–208; Robert E. Park and Ernest W. Burgess, *Introduction to the Science of Sociology* (Chicago: University of Chicago Press, 1921); Fairfield, *The Mysteries of the Great City*, 158–224; Park et al., *The City*.

49. Clements, *Plant Succession*, 4; Park et al., *The City*, 1–2, 45–79, "tendency" on 50, "inevitable" on 4, "forces" and "isolate" on 1–2.

50. Park and Burgess, *Introduction to the Science of Sociology*, 275; Park et al., *The City*, Burgess on 53, McKenzie on 63–65; Cittadino, "Ecology and American Social Thought."

51. Park et al., *The City*, "inevitable" on 4; Alihan, *Social Ecology*, quoted passages on 206, 247–248. See also Park's generous review of Alihan's sometimes harsh critique: Robert E. Park, "Social Ecology Milla Aissa Alihan," *Annals of the American Academy of Political and Social Science* 202 (1939): 264. Elizabeth Grennen Browning, *Nature's Laboratory: Environmental Thought and Labor Radicalism in Chicago, 1886–1937* (Baltimore: Johns Hopkins University Press, 2022).

52. William Cronon, *Nature's Metropolis: Chicago and the Great West* (New York: W. W. Norton, 1991); Harold Platt, *Shock Cities: The Environmental Transformation and Reform of Manchester and Chicago* (Chicago: University of Chicago Press, 2005). On urbanists who crafted more environmentally aware plans, see Davis, *Ecology of Fear*, 59–91; Bruce Stephenson, "Utopian Plans for the Modern World: John Nolen, Lewis Mumford, and the Origins of Sustainability," *Journal of Planning History* 17, no. 4 (2018): 281–299.

53. Scales are crucial to ecological science, but the Chicago sociologists tended to be careless about them: Park et al., *The City*, 53; Wachsmuth, "Three Ecologies."

54. Kingsland, *The Evolution of American Ecology*, 161–164, Clements quoted on 162; Worster, *Nature's Economy*, 205–253; Worster, *Dust Bowl*, 204–208. On the Chicagoans' limited collaboration, see Martin Bulmer, *The Chicago School of Sociology: Institutionalization, Diversity, and the Rise of Sociological Research* (Chicago: University of Chicago Press, 1986), 114–116. On the Chicago sociologists' skepticism about sentimental reform and desire for scientific standing, see Deegan, *Jane Addams and the Men of the Chicago School*. Park et al., *The City*, 1–2, passim; Alihan, *Social Ecology*; Cittadino, "The Failed Promise of Human Ecology," 262–271.

55. Park, "The Concept of Position in Sociology," "man's relation" on 2; Alihan, *Social Ecology*, 6; Park et al., *The City*, "junk" on 109; Light, *The Nature of Cities*;

Wachsmuth, "Three Ecologies"; Dorothy Ross, *The Origins of American Social Science* (New York: Cambridge University Press, 1991), 303–306, 435–437, passim; Fairfield, *The Mysteries of the Great City*, 158–224.

56. Mumford, *The Culture of Cities*, "web" on 302; Minteer, *The Landscape of Reform*, "terms" quoted on 64.

CHAPTER 6

1. Pare Lorenz, dir., *The River*, documentary film, Farm Security Administration, (Washington, DC, 1938), https://archive.org/details/TheRiverByPareLorentz. The text of the narrative is transcribed at https://archive.org/stream/riverparelorentz00lorerich/riverparelorentz00lorerich_djvu.txt.

2. Lewis Mumford, *Technics and Civilization* (Chicago: University of Chicago Press, 1934); Lewis Mumford, *The Culture of Cities* (New York: Harcourt, Brace, 1938); Carl Susman, ed., *Planning the Fourth Migration: The Neglected Vision of the Regional Planning Association of America* (Cambridge, MA: MIT Press, 1976); Mark Luccarelli, *Lewis Mumford and the Ecological Region: The Politics of Planning* (New York: Guilford, 1995); Ben A. Minteer, *The Landscape of Reform: Civic Pragmatism and Environmental Thought in America* (Cambridge, MA: MIT Press, 2006); Bruce Stephenson, "Utopian Plans for the Modern World: John Nolen, Lewis Mumford, and the Origins of Sustainability," *Journal of Planning History* 17, no. 4 (2018): 281–299. On conscious and conscientious, see Richard Register, *Ecocities: Rebuilding Cities in Balance with Nature* (Gabriola, BC: New Society, 2006), 80–83.

3. Howard Gillette Jr., "Film as Artifact: The City (1939)," *American Studies* 18 (1977): 71–83; Richard Griffith, "Films at the Fair," *Films* (November 1939): 61–75; William Alexander, *Film on the Left: American Documentary Film from 1931 to 1942* (Princeton, NJ: Princeton University Press, 1981), 247–257.

4. Gillette, "Film as Artifact"; Griffith, "Films at the Fair"; Joseph Arnold, *The New Deal in the Suburbs* (Columbus: Ohio State University Press, 1971).

5. William E. Leuchtenburg, "Roosevelt, Norris, and the 'Seven Little TVAs,'" *Journal of Politics* 14 (August 1952): 418–444, "to cover" is Norris, quoted on 418; David Lilienthal, *TVA: Democracy on the March* (New York: Harper, 1943); Howard Segal, "Down in the Valley: David Lilienthal's TVA: Democracy on the March," *American Scholar* 64 (Summer 1995): 423–427.

6. William E. Leuchtenburg, *Franklin Roosevelt and the New Deal* (New York: Harper and Row, 1963), 164–165; Steve Conn, *Americans against the City: Anti-urbanism in the Twentieth Century* (New York: Oxford University Press, 2014), 94–113; Arnold, *The New Deal in the Suburbs*; Rexford Tugwell, "The Meaning of the Greenbelt Towns," *New Republic*, February 17, 1937, 42–43.

7. Gillette, "Film as Artifact"; Griffith, "Films at the Fair"; Conn, *Americans against the City*, 64–70.

8. Jennifer Light, *The Nature of Cities: Ecological Visions and the American Urban Professions, 1920–1960* (Baltimore: Johns Hopkins University Press, 2014); Wendell E. Pritchett, "The 'Public Menace' of Blight: Urban Renewal and the Private Use of Eminent Domain," *Yale Law and Policy Review* 12 (Winter 2003):

1–52; Robert R. Gioielli, *Environmental Activism and the Urban Crisis: Baltimore, St. Louis, Chicago* (Philadelphia: Temple University Press, 2014).

9. Light, *The Nature of Cities*; Gioielli, *Environmental Activism and the Urban Crisis*; Kenneth T. Jackson, *Crabgrass Frontier: The Suburbanization of the United States* (New York: Oxford University Press, 1985), 190–218; Luccarelli, *Lewis Mumford and the Ecological Region*; Stephenson, "Utopian Plans for the Modern World"; John L. Thomas, "Lewis Mumford, Regionalist Historian," *Reviews in American History* 16 (March 1988): 158–172. Cf. Robert Fishman, "The Death and Life of American Regional Planning," in *Reflections on Regionalism*, ed. Bruce Katz (Washington, DC: Brookings Institution Press, 2000), 107–123.

10. Pare Lorenz, dir., *The Plow That Broke the Plains*, documentary film, Resettlement Administration, Washington, DC, 1936, https://archive.org/details/gov.archives.arc.13595; Michael C. Steiner, "Regionalism and the Great Depression," *Geographic Review* 73 (October 1983): 430–446.

11. Steiner, "Regionalism and the Great Depression"; John E. Miller, "Midwestern Regionalism during the 1930s: A Democratic Art with Continuing Appeal," *Mid-America* 83 (Summer 2001): 71–93; Conn, *Americans against the City*, 114–147; Robert L. Dorman, *Revolt of the Provinces: The Regionalist Movement in America, 1920–1945* (Chapel Hill: University of North Carolina Press, 1993); Thomas, "Lewis Mumford, Regionalist Historian"; John L. Thomas, "The Uses of Catastrophism: Lewis Mumford, Vernon L. Parrington, Van Wyck Brooks, and the End of Regionalism," *American Quarterly* 42 (June 1990): 223–252; Donald Worster, *Dust Bowl: The Southern Plains in the 1930s* (New York: Oxford University Press, 1979).

12. Sheila D. Collins, "The Rightful Heritage of All: The Environmental Lessons of the Great Depression and the New Deal Response," in *When Government Helped: Learning from the Successes and Failures of the New Deal*, ed. Sheila D. Collins and Gertrude Schaffner Goldberg (New York: Oxford University Press, 2014), 233–265, Roosevelt quoted on 247; John F. Sears, "Grassroots Democracy: FDR and the Land," in *FDR and the Environment*, ed. Harry L. Henderson and David B. Woolner (New York: Palgrave Macmillan, 2005), 7–17; Walter L. Creese, *TVA's Public Planning: The Vision, the Reality* (Knoxville: University of Tennessee Press, 1990); Douglas Brinkley, *Rightful Heritage: Franklin D. Roosevelt and the Land of America* (New York: Harper, 2016).

13. Collins, "The Rightful Heritage of All," Roosevelt quoted on 240; Sears, "Grassroots Democracy"; Brinkley, *Rightful Heritage*, 3–136.

14. Collins, "The Rightful Heritage of All"; Henderson and Woolner, *FDR and the Environment*, Roosevelt quoted on 136.

15. Robert Leighninger, *Long-Range Public Investment: The Forgotten Legacy of the New Deal* (Columbia: University of South Carolina Press, 2007), 11–34, "she, she, she" on 17; Neil M. Maher, *Nature's New Deal: The Civilian Conservation Corps and the Roots of the American Environmental Movement* (New York: Oxford University Press, 2008); Collins, "The Rightful Heritage of All"; Henderson and Woolner, *FDR and the Environment*.

16. Collins, "The Rightful Heritage of All"; Kevin Baker, "Where Our New World Begins: Politics, Power and the Green New Deal," *Harper's*, vol. 338, May

1, 2019, 25–36; Worster, *Dust Bowl*, 210–230; Brinkley, *Rightful Heritage*, 159–212.

17. Leighninger, *Long-Range Public Investment*; Collins, "The Rightful Heritage of All"; Adam Rome, *The Bulldozer in the Countryside: Suburban Sprawl and the Rise of American Environmentalism* (New York: Cambridge University Press, 2001), 189–252.

18. Leuchtenburg, *Franklin Roosevelt and the New Deal*, 54–55; Collins, "The Rightful Heritage of All"; Henderson and Woolner, *FDR and the Environment*, 181–194.

19. The historian James Scott used the term *metis* to describe the sort of local ecological knowledge the TVA ignored. Segal, "Down in the Valley"; James Scott, *Seeing like a State: How Certain Schemes to Improve the Human Condition Have Failed* (New Haven, CT: Yale University Press, 1998); Donald Davidson, *The Tennessee: The New River: Civil War to TVA* (New York: Rinehart, 1948); Brian Black, "Referendum on Planning: Imagining River Conservation in the 1938 TVA Hearings," in Henderson and Woolner, *FDR and the Environment*, 181–194; Creese, *TVA's Public Planning*. On dams more broadly, see Donald Worster, *Rivers of Empire: Water, Aridity, and the Growth of the American West* (New York: Pantheon, 1985), 308–326; Ben Knight and Travis Rummel, dirs., *DamNation*, DVD, Bullfrog Films, Oley, PA, 2014.

20. Black, "Referendum on Planning"; Collins, "The Rightful Heritage of All"; Baker, "Where Our New World Begins."

21. Leuchtenburg, "Roosevelt, Norris, and the 'Seven Little TVAs,'" 418–441, Roosevelt quoted on 418; Leuchtenburg, *Franklin Roosevelt and the New Deal*, 140–142, 164–166; Thomas, "Lewis Mumford, Regionalist Historian"; Black, "Referendum on Planning"; Steiner, "Regionalism and the Great Depression."

22. Minteer, *The Landscape of Reform*, 81–113, MacKaye quoted on 99; Mumford, *The Culture of Cities*, 306–322, "geographic" on 308, "spheres" on 315.

23. Lewis Mumford, "Regions—To Live In," *Survey Graphic* 54 (May 1, 1925): 151–152; Clarence Stein, "Dinosaur Cities," in *Planning the Fourth Migration: The Neglected Vision of the Regional Planning Association of America*, ed. Carl Sussman (Cambridge, MA: MIT Press, 1976), 65–74, "the few" on 66; Robert W. Bruere, "Giant Power—Region Builder," in Sussman, *Planning the Fourth Migration*, 111–120; Mumford, *The Culture of Cities*, 342–347; Edward K. Spann, *Designing Modern America: The Regional Planning Association of America and Its Members* (Columbus: Ohio State University Press, 1996); Minteer, *The Landscape of Reform*, 51–66.

24. Mumford, *The Culture of Cities*, "vegetative" on 304. Mumford first began to sketch out his regional vision in *The Story of Utopias* (New York: Viking, 1922); Casey Nelson Blake, *Beloved Community: The Cultural Criticism of Randolph Bourne, Van Wyck Brooks, Waldo Frank, and Lewis Mumford* (Chapel Hill: University of North Carolina Press, 1990), 208–218.

25. Mumford, *The Culture of Cities*, "theater" on 337, "distribute" on 300, "shadow" on 255–256.

26. Ibid., 322–342, 495–496; Blake, *Beloved Community*, 208–218; Sussman, *Planning the Fourth Migration*.

27. Mumford, *The Culture of Cities*, 300–304, "no longer" on 305, "barest"

on 304, "co-operative" on 302; Luccarelli, *Lewis Mumford and the Ecological Region*, 9–21.

28. Mumford, *The Culture of Cities*, 312–315, "primordial" and "emergent" on 311.

29. Ibid., 306–315, 366–371, "finished" and "solely" on 367, "conceiving" on 314; Robert Casillo, "Lewis Mumford and the Organicist Concept in Social Thought," *Journal of the History of Ideas* 53 (January–March 1992): 91–116; Mumford, *Technics and Civilization*, 316–320; Blake, *Beloved Community*, 187–201; Luccarelli, *Lewis Mumford and the Ecological Region*, 25–27. With Geddes, Mumford anticipated the efforts of Ian McHarg, Richard Register, and others to insert city building into evolutionary theory. See Patrick Geddes, *Cities in Evolution: An Introduction to the Town Planning Movement* (London: Williams and Norgate, 1915); Ian McHarg, *Design with Nature* (Garden City, NY: Doubleday, 1969); Anne Whiston Spirn, "Ian McHarg, Landscape Architecture, and Environmentalism: Ideas and Methods in Context," in *Environmentalism in Landscape Architecture*, ed. Michael Conan (Washington, DC: Dumbarton Oaks Research Library and Collection, 2000), esp. 109–110; Register, *Ecocities*; Murray Bookchin, *From Cities to Urbanization* (New York: Cassel, 1995).

30. Benton MacKaye, "The New Exploration: Charting the Industrial Wilderness," in Sussman, *Planning the Fourth Migration*, 94–110, "roots" on 101, "*mining*" on 106; Minteer, *The Landscape of Reform*, 81–113, MacKaye quoted on 98; Eugene Cittadino, "Ecology and American Social Thought," in *Religion and the New Ecology*, ed. David M. Lodge and Christopher Hamlin (Notre Dame, IN: University of Notre Dame Press, 2006), 73–115, esp. 90.

31. Minteer, *The Landscape of Reform*, 81–113, 130–135, MacKaye quoted on 96.

32. Ibid., 81–113, MacKaye quoted on 100, Royce quoted on 87. On Royce's view of "loyalty to loyalty," see Christopher Lasch, *The True and Only Heaven: Progress and Its Critics* (New York: W. W. Norton, 1991), 356–359; Howard W. Odum and Harry Estill Moore, *American Regionalism: A Cultural-Historical Approach to National Integration* (New York: Henry Holt, 1938), quotation on v; Cittadino, "Ecology and American Social Thought," 92.

33. Mumford, *The Culture of Cities*, 454–458.

34. Ibid.

35. Stein, "Dinosaur Cities"; Bruere, "Giant Power—Region Builder"; Mumford, *The Culture of Cities*, 322–347; John D. Fairfield, "A Populism for the Cities: Henry George, John Dewey, and the City Planning Movement," *Urban Design* 8 (2002): 19–27; Michael Sandel, *Democracy's Discontent: America in Search of a Public Philosophy* (Cambridge, MA: Harvard University Press, 1998), 250–273; Alan Brinkley, *The End of Reform: New Deal Liberalism in Recession and War* (New York: Alfred A. Knopf, 1995).

36. Mumford, *The Culture of Cities*, 336–358, 495–496, quoted passage on 348; Luccarelli, *Lewis Mumford and the Ecological Region*, 12–13; Steiner, "Regionalism and the Great Depression."

37. Mumford, *The Culture of Cities*, 348–349, 366–387, quoted passages on 384; Victor Branford and Patrick Geddes, *The Coming Polity: A Study in Reconstruction* (London: Williams and Norgate, 1917); Blake, *Beloved Community*,

190–201; Aaron Sachs, "Lewis Mumford's Urbanism and the Problem of Environmental Modernity," *Environmental History* 21 (October 2016): 638–659.

38. Mumford, *The Culture of Cities*, 348–349, 376–387, "opportunities" on 378, "immediate" on 384, "know" on 386.

39. Sandel, *Democracy's Discontent*, 266–273, Lilienthal quoted on 273; Mumford, *The Culture of Cities*, 380–383.

40. Minteer, *The Landscape of Reform*, 1–9, 51–80; John Dewey, *Logic: A Theory of Inquiry* (New York: Henry Holt, 1938); Mumford, *The Culture of Cities*, 376–379.

41. John Dewey, *The Public and Its Problems* (1927), in *John Dewey: The Later Works, 1925–1953*, ed. Jo Ann Boydston (Carbondale: Southern Illinois University Press, 1984), 344, 363–366; Mumford, *The Culture of Cities*, 376–379, "old" on 377; Timothy V. Kaufman-Osborne, "Pragmatism, Policy Science, and the State," *American Journal of Political Science* 29 (1985): 827–849; Timothy V. Kaufman-Osborne, "John Dewey and the Liberal Science of Community," *Journal of Politics* 46 (1984): 1153–1159; John D. Fairfield and William Widdowson, "Of Patterns and Publics: City Planning as Democratic Process," *Urban Design Studies* 6 (2000): 149–157; Robert Westbrook, *John Dewey and American Democracy* (Ithaca, NY: Cornell University Press, 1991), 313–314.

42. Walter Lippmann, *The Phantom Public* (New York: Harcourt, Brace, 1925); Dewey, *The Public and Its Problems*, 367; Spann, *Designing Modern America*, 50–55, 90–92, 120–124, MacKaye quoted on 91; Minteer, *The Landscape of Reform*, 74–78, 94–108.

43. Minteer, *The Landscape of Reform*, 105–152; Mumford, *The Culture of Cities*, 479–485, "treatises" on 479.

44. Light, *The Nature of Cities*, 1–35, 287–298.

45. Ibid., 6–11; Eugene Cittadino, "The Failed Promise of Human Ecology," in *Science and Nature: Essays in the History of the Environmental Sciences*, ed. Michael Shortland (London: British Society for the History of Science, 1993), 251–283, esp. 262–271; Dorothy Ross, *The Origins of American Social Science* (New York: Cambridge University Press, 1991), 357–367, 435–437. On the sociological tradition and community, see Lasch, *The True and Only Heaven*, 120–167.

46. Ernest Burgess, "Can Neighborhood Work Have a Scientific Basis?" in *The City*, by Robert E. Park, Ernest W. Burgess, and Roderick McKenzie (Chicago: University of Chicago Press, 1925), 148; Light, *The Nature of Cities*, 15–35, "grows" on 27, "Residential" is Harlan Paul Douglass quoted on 15.

47. Light, *The Nature of Cities*, 1–35, Burgess quoted on 26, see also 190, n. 86. On challenges to the model, see James A. Quinn, "The Burgess Zonal Hypothesis and Its Critics," *American Sociological Review* 5, no. 2 (1940): 210–218. In 1939, Adams and the ecologist Paul Sears invited Burgess and McKenzie to a scientific symposium, "On the Relations of Ecology to Human Welfare—The Human Situation." Neither Burgess nor McKenzie could attend. Light, *The Nature of Cities*, 8–35; Charles C. Adams, "The Relation of General Ecology to Human Ecology," *Ecology* 16 (July 1935): 316–335; Robert E. Park, "The City as a Social Laboratory," in *Chicago: An Experiment in Social Science Research*, ed. Thomas V. Smith

and Leonard D. White (Chicago: University of Chicago Press, 1929), 1; Cittadino, "The Failed Promise of Human Ecology," 274–276.

48. Pritchett, "The 'Public Menace' of Blight," 13–18; Light, *The Nature of Cities*, 22–68; Gioielli, *Environmental Activism and the Urban Crisis*, 14–17; Cittadino, "The Failed Promise of Human Ecology," 274–276; Adams, "The Relation of General Ecology to Human Ecology"; David M. P. Freund, *Colored Property: State Policy and White Racial Politics in Suburban America* (Chicago: University of Chicago Press, 2007), 45–98; Davarian L. Baldwin, "Chicago's 'Concentric Zones': Thinking through the Material History of an Iconic Map," in *Many Voices, One Nation: Material Culture Reflections on Race and Migration in the United States*, ed. Margaret Salazar-Porzio and Joan Fragasky Troyano (Washington, DC: Smithsonian Institution Scholarly Press, 2017), 179–191.

49. Light, *The Nature of Cities*, 36–68; Jackson, *Crabgrass Frontier*, 190–218; Pritchett, "The 'Public Menace' of Blight"; Richard Wade, *The Urban Frontier* (Chicago: University of Chicago Press, 1959); Light, *The Nature of Cities*, Ely quoted on 59; Donald Worster, *Nature's Economy: A History of Ecological Ideas* (New York: Cambridge University Press, 1994), 217–219; William Cronon, *Nature's Metropolis: Chicago and the Great West* (New York: W. W. Norton, 1991), 55–147, 302–308.

50. Cronon, *Nature's Metropolis*, 23–54; Light, *The Nature of Cities*, 22–28, "efficient" on 22; Worster, *Nature's Economy*, 216–220.

51. Clements excluded even the activities of Native Americans, whose hunting and burning did so much to shape the grasslands, from his theory of succession and climax. Worster, *Nature's Economy*, 221–253; Cronon, *Nature's Metropolis*, 55–147, 302–308; Worster, *Dust Bowl*, 78–97; History Museum, "The Oliver Chilled Plow Works," https://historymuseumsb.org/the-oliver-chilled-plow -works; Ted Genoways, *This Blessed Earth: A Year in the Life of an American Farm Family* (New York: W. W. Norton, 2018), on soybeans, 19–29, *Fortune* quoted on 23; William Shurtleff and Akiko Aoyagi, "Henry Ford and His Employees: Work with Soy," SoyInfo Center, 2004, https://www.soyinfocenter.com/HSS /henry_ford_and_employees.php.

52. Worster, *Dust Bowl*, 26–63; Genoways, *This Blessed Earth*, 19–29.

53. Maher, *Nature's New Deal*, 160–180, Leopold quoted on 167.

54. Worster, *Nature's Economy*, 221–253; Worster, *Dust Bowl*, 10–25; Collins, "The Rightful Heritage of All."

55. Worster, *Nature's Economy*, 221–253; Worster, *Dust Bowl*, 42–63; Collins, "The Rightful Heritage of All."

56. Worster, *Nature's Economy*, 221–253; Worster, *Dust Bowl*, 42–63; Collins, "The Rightful Heritage of All"; Henry Nash Smith, *Virgin Land: The American West as Symbol and Myth* (Cambridge, MA: Harvard University Press, 1950), 182–206.

57. Worster, *Nature's Economy*, 221–253; Worster, *Dust Bowl*, 56–59; Collins, "The Rightful Heritage of All."

58. One of the soil conservation districts in southwestern Wisconsin shaped the thinking of forester and conservationist Aldo Leopold. Worster, *Nature's Economy*, 221–253; Collins, "The Rightful Heritage of All"; Janine M. Benyus,

Biomimicry: Innovation Inspired by Nature (New York: Morrow, 1997), 11–58. On Leopold, see Minteer, *The Landscape of Reform*, 120–121.

59. Worster, *Nature's Economy*, 221–253, Great Plains Committee quoted on 231; Collins, "The Rightful Heritage of All"; John L. Shover, *Cornbelt Rebellion: The Farmers' Holiday Association* (Urbana: University of Illinois Press, 1965).

60. Worster, *Dust Bowl*, 198–230.

61. Ibid., 210–230.

62. Worster, *Nature's Economy*, 237–241, Clements quoted on 237; James Malin, *The Grasslands of North America: Prolegomena to Its History with Addenda*, rev. ed. (Lawrence, KS: James C. Malin, 1956); Worster, *Nature's Economy*, 242–249; Cittadino, "Ecology and American Social Thought," 93–94.

63. Arthur Tansley, "The Use and Abuse of Vegetational Concepts and Terms," *Ecology* 16 (1935): 284–307, quoted passages on 303; Worster, *Nature's Economy*, 237–241. Tansley might be seen as anticipating permaculture. On permaculture as part of a third-way environmentalism that navigates between deep ecology and an anthropocentric conservation, see Minteer, *The Landscape of Reform*, 153–170.

64. Tansley, "The Use and Abuse of Vegetational Concepts and Terms"; Henry Gleason, "The Individualistic Concept of the Plant Association," *Bulletin of the Torrey Botanical Club* 53 (1926): 7–26; Cittadino, "Ecology and American Social Thought," 80–82; Sharon Kingsland, *The Evolution of American Ecology* (Baltimore: Johns Hopkins University Press, 2005), 184–185; Worster, *Nature's Economy*, 362–372; Light, *The Nature of Cities*, 32–35.

65. Malin, *The Grasslands of North America*, 154–155; Worster, *Nature's Economy*, 237–249.

CHAPTER 7

1. Kenneth T. Jackson, *Crabgrass Frontier: The Suburbanization of the United States* (New York: Oxford University Press, 1985), 190–218; Jon C. Teaford, *The Rough Road to Renaissance: Urban Revitalization in America, 1945–1985* (Baltimore: Johns Hopkins University Press, 1990); Jennifer Light, *The Nature of Cities: Ecological Visions and the American Urban Professions, 1920–1960* (Baltimore: Johns Hopkins University Press, 2014); Robert R. Gioielli, *Environmental Activism and the Urban Crisis: Baltimore, St. Louis, Chicago* (Philadelphia: Temple University Press, 2014), 11–37.

2. Matthew Gandy, *Concrete and Clay: Reworking Nature in New York City* (Cambridge, MA: MIT Press, 2003); Light, *The Nature of Cities*; Leo Marx, *The Machine in the Garden: Technology and the Pastoral Ideal in America* (New York: Oxford University Press, 1964).

3. Robert Caro, *The Power Broker: Robert Moses and the Fall of New York* (New York: Random House, 1974); Jane Jacobs, *The Death and Life of Great American Cities* (New York: Random House, 1961).

4. Light, *The Nature of Cities*, 43–48, Ickes quoted on 47; Andrew M. Shanken, *194X: Architecture, Planning, and Consumer Culture on the American Home Front* (Minneapolis: University of Minnesota Press, 2009), 59–95, modernist architect Jose Luis Sert quoted on 65.

5. Donald Worster, *Nature's Economy: A History of Ecological Ideas* (New York: Cambridge University Press, 1994), 326–332, "isolationism" is the ecologist Ralph Gerard, quoted on 329; Gregg Mitman, *The State of Nature: Ecology, Community, and American Social Thought, 1900–1950* (Chicago: University of Chicago Press, 1992), 146–156.

6. Light, *The Nature of Cities*, 43–48, NRPB member George Renner quoted on 46; Mitman, *The State of Nature*, 6–8, 146–156, "totalitarian" is the paleontologist George Gaylord Simpson, quoted on 6; Sharon E. Kingsland, *The Evolution of American Ecology* (Baltimore: Johns Hopkins University Press, 2005), 161–164; Worster, *Nature's Economy*, 242–249; Shanken, *194X*, 96–195, "road to serfdom" is the economist Friedrich Hayek, quoted on 165, "inexhaustible" is the commercial publisher Thomas S. Holden, quoted on 166, Senator Frederick C. Smith quoted on 162; Les K. Adler and Thomas G. Paterson, "Red Fascism: The Merger of Nazi Germany and Soviet Russia in the American Image of Totalitarianism, 1930s–1950s," *American Historical Review* 75 (1970): 1046–1064. Nazi Germany's appalling grasp for living space and natural resources, and its ugly eugenic slaughter, also put ecological and organic thinking further on the defensive. Timothy Snyder, *Black Earth: The Holocaust as History and Warning* (New York: Tim Duggan, 2015).

7. Alan Brinkley, *The End of Reform: New Deal Liberalism in Recession and War* (New York: Alfred A. Knopf, 1995), 137–170, Henderson quoted on 164; Michael J. Sandel, *Democracy's Discontent: America in Search of a Public Philosophy* (Cambridge, MA: Harvard University Press, 1996), Kemler quoted on 269.

8. Lewis Mumford, *The Culture of Cities* (New York: Harcourt, Brace, 1938), 331–342, "moribund" on 341. Cf. Douglas W. Rae, *City: Urbanism and Its End* (New Haven, CT: Yale University Press, 2003), 1–31; Christopher C. Sellers, *Crabgrass Crucible: Suburban Nature and the Rise of Environmentalism in Twentieth-Century America* (Chapel Hill: University of North Carolina Press, 2012), 11–35.

9. Daniel Yergin, *The Prize: The Epic Quest for Oil, Money, and Power* (New York: Simon and Schuster, 1991); Richard Manning, "The Oil We Eat: Following the Food Chain Back to Iraq," *Harper's*, February 2004, Kennan quoted on 38.

10. Gandy, *Concrete and Clay*, 115–118; Mumford, *The Culture of Cities*, 486–493, quoted passage on 489; Yergin, *The Prize*, 389–560; Vandana Shiva, *Soil not Oil: Climate Change, Peak Oil and Food Insecurity* (London: Zed, 2008).

11. Jackson, *Crabgrass Frontier*, 190–218; Amy Hillier, "Redlining and the Home Owners Loan Corporation," *Journal of Urban History* 29 (May 2003): 394–420.

12. Jackson, *Crabgrass Frontier*, 190–218; Hillier, "Redlining and the Home Owners Loan Corporation," "inharmonious" is from the 1935 FHA *Underwriting Manual*, quoted on 403; Light, *The Nature of Cities*, 36–68.

13. Jackson, *Crabgrass Frontier*, 195–218; Hillier, "Redlining and the Home Owners Loan Corporation"; Jon C. Teaford, *The Metropolitan Revolution* (New York: Columbia University Press, 2006), 49–89; Robert O. Self, *American Babylon: Race and the Struggle for Postwar Oakland* (Princeton, NJ: Princeton University Press, 2003).

14. David M. P. Freund, *Colored Property: State Policy and White Racial Politics in Suburban America* (Chicago: University of Chicago Press, 2007), quotations

on 3, 375; Karl E. and Alma F. Taeuber, *The Negro in Cities: Residential Segregation and Neighborhood Change* (Chicago: Aldine, 1965), 199–201; William H. Frey, "Central City White Flight: Racial and Nonracial Causes," *American Sociological Review* 44 (June 1979): 425–448; Arnold Hirsch, *Making of the Second Ghetto: Race and Housing in Chicago, 1949–1960* (New York: Cambridge University Press, 1983), 1–39, passim; Thomas J. Sugrue, *The Origins of the Urban Crisis: Race and Inequality in Postwar Detroit* (Princeton, NJ: Princeton University Press, 1996); Heather McGhee, *The Sum of Us: What Racism Costs Everyone and How We Can Prosper Together* (New York: One World, 2021), 21–23.

15. Freund, *Colored Property*, 34–35, 99–240; David Stradling and Richard Stradling, *Where the River Burned: Carl Stokes and the Struggle to Save Cleveland* (Ithaca, NY: Cornell University Press, 2015); Hirsch, *Making of the Second Ghetto*, 1–39, passim; Self, *American Babylon*; Andrew J. Diamond, "The Long March toward Neoliberalism: Race and Housing in the Postwar Metropolis," *Journal of Urban History* 36 (November 2010): 922–928.

16. Stradling and Stradling, *Where the River Burned*; Gioielli, *Environmental Activism and the Urban Crisis*; Andrew Hurley, *Environmental Inequalities: Class, Race, and Industrial Pollution in Gary, Indiana, 1945–1980* (Chapel Hill: University of North Carolina Press, 1995); Andrew Hurley, "Fiasco at Wagner Electric: Environmental Justice and Urban Geography in St. Louis," *Environmental History* 2 (October 1997): 460–481.

17. Harold Cruse, *The Crisis of the Negro Intellectual* (New York: William Morrow, 1967); Davarian Baldwin, *Chicago's New Negroes: Modernity, the Great Migration, and Black Urban Life* (Chapel Hill: University of North Carolina Press, 2007); Isabel Wilkerson, *The Warmth of Other Suns: The Epic Story of America's Great Migration* (New York: Random House, 2010); Kenneth Clark, *Dark Ghetto: Dilemmas of Social Power* (New York: Harper and Row, 1965); Stradling and Stradling, *Where the River Burned*, "suspended" is from the *New York Times*, quoted on 53, "invisible" is the psychologist Kenneth Clark, quoted on 48; Self, *American Babylon*; Gioielli, *Environmental Activism and the Urban Crisis*.

18. Homer Hoyt, "Rebuilding American Cities after the War," *Journal of Land and Public Utility Economics* (October 1943): 364–368, quoted passage on 366; Homer Hoyt, "The Structure of American Cities in the Post-war Period," *American Journal of Sociology* 48 (1943): 475–481; Light, *The Nature of Cities*, 36–68, passim; Teaford, *The Rough Road to Renaissance*; Gioielli, *Environmental Activism and the Urban Crisis*, 11–37; Wendell E. Pritchett, "The 'Public Menace' of Blight: Urban Renewal and the Private Use of Eminent Domain," *Yale Law and Policy Review* 12 (Winter 2003): 1–52; Robert Fishman, "The Death and Life of American Regional Planning," in *Reflections on Regionalism*, ed. Bruce Katz (Washington, DC: Brookings Institution Press, 2000), 107–123; Jon C. Teaford, *Cities of the Heartland: The Rise and Fall of the Industrial Midwest* (Bloomington: Indiana University Press, 1993), 211–252; Teaford, *The Metropolitan Revolution*, 49–89; Chad Freidrichs, dir., *The Pruitt-Igoe Myth*, DVD, First Run Features, New York, 2011.

19. Light, *The Nature of Cities*, 36–68, 155–160, "represents" is from a 1953 *Indiana Law Journal* article, quoted on 151; Self, *American Babylon*; Gioielli, *Environmental Activism and the Urban Crisis*; Stradling and Stradling, *Where the*

River Burned; Pritchett, "The 'Public Menace' of Blight"; Hirsch, *Making of the Second Ghetto*; Teaford, *The Rough Road to Renaissance*; Rae, *City*.

20. Light, *The Nature of Cities*, 36–68, 155–160; Hirsch, *Making of the Second Ghetto*, 100–170; Gioielli, *Environmental Activism and the Urban Crisis*; Teaford, *The Metropolitan Revolution*, 112–124; Freidrichs, *The Pruitt-Igoe Myth*.

21. Light, *The Nature of Cities*, 60–68, 98–127, 155–160; Gioielli, *Environmental Activism and the Urban Crisis*, 13–25; Hirsch, *Making of the Second Ghetto*.

22. Light, *The Nature of Cities*, 36–68, 155–160; Self, *American Babylon*; Hirsch, *Making of the Second Ghetto*, 100–170; Gioielli, *Environmental Activism and the Urban Crisis*; Teaford, *The Metropolitan Revolution*, 112–124; Raymond A. Mohl, "Stop the Road: Freeway Revolts in American Cities," *Journal of Urban History* (July 2004): 674–706.

23. Light, *The Nature of Cities*, 36–68, 155–160; Hirsch, *Making of the Second Ghetto*, 100–170; Gioielli, *Environmental Activism and the Urban Crisis*, 18–29; Sellers, *Crabgrass Crucible*, 11–103; Thomas J. Nechyba and Randall P. Walsh, "Urban Sprawl," *Journal of Economic Perspectives* 18 (Fall 2004): 177–200; Peter Mieszkowski and Edwin S. Mills, "The Causes of Metropolitan Suburbanization," *Journal of Economic Perspectives* 7 (Summer 1993): 135–147; Edward L. Glaeser, "Are Cities Dying?" *Journal of Economic Perspectives* 12 (Spring 1998): 139–160.

24. Chris W. Wells, *Car Country: An Environmental History* (Seattle: University of Washington Press, 2013); Marshall Berman, *All That Is Solid Melts into Air: The Experience of Modernity* (New York: Simon and Schuster, 1982); Jane Holtz Kay, *Asphalt Nation: How the Automobile Took Over America, and How We Can Take It Back* (New York: Crown, 1997); Mark H. Rose, *Interstate: Express Highway Politics* (Knoxville: University of Tennessee Press, 1990); Owen D. Gutfreund, *Twentieth Century Sprawl: Highways and the Reshaping of the American Landscape* (New York: Oxford University Press, 2005).

25. Descriptions of the parkway are from Jay Downer, "Reclaiming a Polluted River," *American City* 22 (1920): 15, quoted in Gandy, *Concrete and Clay*, 118–123. The architect is Gilmore D. Clarke, who later worked for Moses. Cf. Kathy Poole, "Civitas Oecologie: Infrastructure in the Ecological City," *Harvard Architectural Review* 10 (1998): 126–145.

26. Gandy, *Concrete and Clay*, 126–137; Caro, *The Power Broker*, passim. See also Robert Leighninger, *Long-range Public Investment: The Forgotten Legacy of the New Deal* (Columbia: University of South Carolina Press, 2007); Berman, *All That Is Solid Melts into Air*.

27. Caro, *The Power Broker*, 342–343, 552–557, quoted passage on 554.

28. Ibid., "beautiful" on 555; Gandy, *Concrete and Clay*, 126–137.

29. Gandy, *Concrete and Clay*, 115–152, "ugly" on 117, "Unfortunately" on 132; Caro, *The Power Broker*, passim; Robert Fitch, *The Assassination of New York* (New York: Verso, 1993); Joel Schwartz, *The New York Approach: Robert Moses, Urban Liberals, and the Redevelopment of the Inner City* (Columbus: Ohio State University Press, 1993); Adam Rome, *The Bulldozer in the Countryside: Suburban Sprawl and the Rise of American Environmentalism* (New York: Cambridge University Press, 2001); Sellers, *Crabgrass Crucible*.

30. Alison Isenberg, *Downtown America: A History of the Place and the People Who Made It* (Chicago: University of Chicago Press, 2004); Hilary Ballon and Kenneth T. Jackson, *Robert Moses and the Modern City: The Transformation of New York* (New York: W. W. Norton, 2007); Samuel Zipp, *Manhattan Projects: The Rise and Fall of Urban Renewal in Cold War New York* (New York: Oxford University Press, 2010), "balm" on 352, 370; Robert Fogelson, *Downtown: Its Rise and Fall, 1880–1950* (New Haven, CT: Yale University Press, 2001); Suleiman Osman, *The Invention of Brownstone Brooklyn: Gentrification and the Search for Authenticity in Postwar New York* (New York: Oxford University Press, 2011), esp. 52–54; John F. Bauman, "The American Downtown: Sagas of Race, Place, and Space," *Journal of Urban History* 34 (March 2008): 520–531; Freidrichs, *The Pruitt-Igoe Myth*.

31. Teaford, *The Rough Road to Renaissance*, 10–43, "lessening" on 34; Isenberg, *Downtown America*; Fogelson, *Downtown*; Bauman, "The American Downtown"; Zipp, *Manhattan Projects*, 17–20, 195–205, passim; Osman, *The Invention of Brownstone Brooklyn*, 52–81.

32. Teaford, *The Rough Road to Renaissance*; Zipp, *Manhattan Projects*.

33. U.S. Congress, *Interregional Highways*, House doc. 379, 78th Cong., 2d sess. (Washington, DC: U.S. Government Printing Office, 1944), quoted in Gilmore D. Clarke, "The Design of Motorways," in *Highways in Our National Life: A Symposium*, ed. Jean Labatut and Wheaton J. Lane (Princeton, NJ: Princeton University Press, 1950), 308; Gandy, *Concrete and Clay*, 115–152, "ugly" on 117; Mohl, "Stop the Road"; Fitch, *The Assassination of New York*; Schwartz, *The New York Approach*.

34. Gandy, *Concrete and Clay*, 130–138; Caro, *The Power Broker*, 520–525, 850–894, passim; B. Drummond Ayres Jr., "Washington; 'White Roads through Black Bedrooms,'" *New York Times*, December 31, 1967, B7.

35. Caro, *The Power Broker*, 849–894, "hack" on 849; Gandy, *Concrete and Clay*, 138–152; Schwartz, *The New York Approach*; Ballon and Jackson, *Robert Moses and the Modern City*; Osman, *The Invention of Brownstone Brooklyn*, 52–81; Zipp, *Manhattan Projects*, 357–359.

36. Caro, *The Power Broker*, 839–843.

37. Ibid., "teaspoon" on 841.

38. Ibid., 843–894; Zipp, *Manhattan Projects*, "impossible" on 352.

39. Caro, *The Power Broker*, 843–856.

40. Ibid., 843–894.

41. Ibid., 843–856, quoted passage on 854; Jacobs, *The Death and Life of Great American Cities*; Jamin Creed Rowan, *The Sociable City: An American Intellectual Tradition* (Philadelphia: University of Pennsylvania Press, 2017), 98–153, passim.

42. Caro, *The Power Broker*, 856–859.

43. Ibid., "People" on 857.

44. Ibid., 859–884.

45. Ibid., 880–884.

46. Ibid., 885–894.

47. Ibid.

48. Kevin Lynch, *The Image of the City* (Cambridge, MA: MIT Press, 1960), 1–45, quoted passages on 2, 41.

49. Mike Davis, *City of Quartz: Excavating the Future in Los Angeles* (New York: Version, 1990), 229–232; Edward Dimendberg, *Film Noir and the Spaces of Modernity* (Cambridge, MA: Harvard University Press, 2004), 151–165; Eric Gordon, *The Urban Spectator: American Concept Cities from Kodak to Google* (Hanover, NH: Dartmouth College Press, 2009), 125–152; Eric Avila, "Popular Culture in the Age of White Flight: Film Noir, Disneyland, and the Cold War (Sub)urban Imaginary," *Journal of Urban History* 31 (November 2004): 3–22; David Reid and Jayne L. Walker, "Strange Pursuit: Cornell Woolrich and the Abandoned City of the Forties," in *Shades of Noir: A Reader*, ed. Joan Copjec (New York: Verso, 1993), 57–95.

50. Gordon, *The Urban Spectator*, 125–152; Davis, *City of Quartz*, 229–232; Dimendberg, *Film Noir and the Spaces of Modernity*, 151–165; Dean MacCannell, "Democracy's Turn: On Homeless Noir," in Copjec, *Shades of Noir*, 279–297.

51. Gordon, *The Urban Spectator*, 125–152; Davis, *City of Quartz*, 229–232; Eric Avila, *Popular Culture in the Age of White Flight: Fear and Fantasy in Suburban Los Angeles* (Berkeley: University of California Press, 2006), "illusion" and "confusion" on 55–56.

52. Gordon, *The Urban Spectator*, 125–152, "impact" on 139; Davis, *City of Quartz*, 229–232; Adam Shatz, "Mike Davis and the Politics of Disaster," *Lingua Franca* 7 (September 1997): 26–37.

53. Beginning with Arthur Tansley's idea of the ecosystem, the science turned toward the study of energy flows and the processing and transmission of information. Deploying sophisticated mathematical models (predator-prey oscillations, logistical curves), ecologists entertained technocratic ambitions. Gordon, *The Urban Spectator*, 125–152, "dream" on 146; Eugene Cittadino, "Ecology and American Social Thought," in *Religion and the New Ecology*, ed. David M. Lodge and Christopher Hamlin (Notre Dame, IN: University of Notre Dame Press, 2006), 73–115; Worster, *Nature's Economy*, 388–433. Cf. David F. Noble, *Forces of Production: A Social History of Industrial Automation* (New York: Alfred A. Knopf, 1984).

54. Fritjof Capra and Pier Luigi Luisi, *The Systems View of Life: A Unifying Vision* (Cambridge: Cambridge University Press, 2014); Gordon, *The Urban Spectator*, 125–152, "Autos" on 146, "making" on 147. Cf. Michel de Certeau, *The Practice of Everyday Life* (Berkeley: University of California Press, 1988), 91–110.

55. Gordon, *The Urban Spectator*, 125–152, Mumford quoted on 149, Jacobs on 150; Zipp, *Manhattan Projects*, 351–371, "planless" on 353; Fishman, "The Death and Life of American Regional Planning."

56. Rome, *The Bulldozer in the Countryside*, 15–43; Teaford, *The Metropolitan Revolution*, 90–124; Gioielli, *Environmental Activism and the Urban Crisis*, 11–37; Self, *American Babylon*; Thomas J. Sugrue, "Crabgrass-Roots Politics: Race, Rights, and the Reaction against Liberalism in the Urban North, 1940–1964," *Journal of American History* (September 1995): 551–578; Louis Mozingo, *Pastoral Capitalism: A History of Suburban Corporate Landscapes* (Cambridge, MA: MIT Press, 2011); Ben H. Bagdikian, "The Rape of the Land,"

Saturday Evening Post, June 18, 1966, 25–29, 86–94, quoted passage on 26; Sellers, *Crabgrass Crucible*, passim; Rome, *The Bulldozer in the Countryside*, 139–152, Johnson quoted on 140, Jackson quoted on 150; Mike Davis, *Ecology of Fear: Los Angeles and the Imagination of Disaster* (New York: Vintage, 1999), 59–91.

57. Sellers, *Crabgrass Crucible*, 11–35; Harlan Douglass, *The Suburban Trend* (New York: Century, 1925); Jackson, *Crabgrass Frontier*; Samuel P. Hays and Barbara D. Hays, *Beauty, Health, and Permanence: Environmental Politics in the United States, 1955–1985* (New York: Cambridge University Press, 1987).

58. The Depression years briefly revived subsistence and market farming, but the same residential security maps that redlined urban neighborhoods also marked these mixed-use areas as undesirable. African Americans and Hispanics joined the exodus to suburbia, although they enjoyed fewer choices and fewer protections from public officials; residential security maps also downgraded rural areas with minority populations. Sellers, *Crabgrass Crucible*, 39–240, "tree-studded" and "wooded" on 49; Rome, *The Bulldozer in the Countryside*, 87–219; Dianne Harris, ed., *Second Suburb: Levittown, Pennsylvania* (Pittsburgh: University of Pittsburgh Press, 2010).

59. Eutrophication is the result of nutrient-rich runoff that encourages dense blooms of plant life that deprive animal life of oxygen. Rome, *The Bulldozer in the Countryside*, 180–219; Sellers, *Crabgrass Crucible*, 39–240.

60. Sellers, *Crabgrass Crucible*, 39–240; Rome, *The Bulldozer in the Countryside*, 87–219; Rachel Carson, *Silent Spring* (Boston: Houghton Mifflin, 1962).

61. Sellers, *Crabgrass Crucible*, 102–136, quoted passage on 125, on a similar protest in Pasadena regarding air pollution, see 223–225; David Kinkela, "The Ecological Landscapes of Jane Jacobs and Rachel Carson," *American Quarterly* 61 (December 2009): 905–928.

62. Sellers, *Crabgrass Crucible*, 39–296; Hays and Hays, *Beauty, Health, and Permanence*.

63. Sellers, *Crabgrass Crucible*, 243–296; Christopher Sellers, "Suburban Nature, Class, and Environmentalism in Levittown," in Harris, *Second Suburb*, 281–313; Rome, *The Bulldozer in the Countryside*, 180–236.

64. Rome, *The Bulldozer in the Countryside*, 221–253, "Building" on 222–223, "isolation" and "realize" on 233.

65. Levi Van Sant, "Land Reform and the Green New Deal," *Dissent* (Fall 2019): 64–70.

66. Sellers, *Crabgrass Crucible*, 243–296, "ugliness" on 248; Rome, *The Bulldozer in the Countryside*, 242–270; Robert Bruegmann, *Sprawl: A Compact History* (Chicago: University of Chicago Press, 2006); Peter Siskind, "'Enlightened System' or 'Regulatory Nightmare'?: New York's Adirondack Mountains and the Conflicted Politics of Environmental Land-Use Reform during the 1970s," *Journal of Policy History* 31 (2019): 406–430; Peter Siskind, "Shades of Black and Green: The Making of Racial and Environmental Liberalism in Nelson Rockefeller's New York," *Journal of Urban History* 34 (January 2008): 243–265.

67. Robert W. Burchell, Anthony Downs, Barbara McCann, and Sahan Mukherji, *Sprawl Costs: Economic Impacts of Unchecked Development* (Washington, DC: Island, 2005); Gutfreund, *Twentieth-Century Sprawl*; Richard Register, *Ecocities:*

Building Cities in Balance with Nature (Gabriola Island, BC: New Society, 2006); Peter Calthrope, *The Next American Metropolis: Ecology, Community, and the American Dream* (Princeton, NJ: Princeton Architectural Press, 1993); Andres Duany, Elizabeth Plater-Zyberg, and Jeff Speck, *Suburban Nation: The Rise of Sprawl and the Decline of the American Dream* (New York: North Point, 2000); Jon C. Teaford, "Review Essay—Stopping Sprawl," *International Journal of Urban and Regional Research* 32 (September 2008): 745–757. See also Gregory Greene, dir., *The End of Suburbia: Oil Depletion and the Collapse of the American Dream*, documentary film, Electric Wallpaper, Toronto, 2004.

68. Adam Rome, "William Whyte, Open Space, and Environmental Activism," *Geographic Review* 88 (April 1998): 259–274, "sense" on 261; Rome, *The Bull-dozer in the Countryside*, 119–128, 181–188; Ian McHarg, *Design with Nature* (Garden City, NY: Natural History, 1969); Congress for the New Urbanism, "The Charter of the New Urbanism," 1999, https://www.cnu.org/who-we-are/charter-new-urbanism; Paul M. Weyrich, William S. Lind, and Andres Duany, "Conservatives and the New Urbanism: Do We Have Some Things in Common?" n.d., http://archive.cnu.org/sites/www.cnu.org/files/Conservatives&NewUrbanism.pdf; Matt K. Lewis, "The New Urbanism Isn't Just for Liberals—Conservatives Should Embrace It Too," *The Week*, January 10, 2015, http://theweek.com/articles/445510/new-urbanism-isnt-just-liberals--conservatives-should-embrace.

69. Fishman, "The Death and Life of American Regional Planning"; Bruegmann, *Sprawl*, 202–219.

70. Bruegmann, *Sprawl*; Gregory A. Galluzzo, "Organizing against Urban Sprawl: A New Model," *Race, Poverty and the Environment* 15, no. 2 (2008): 13–15.

71. Bruegmann, *Sprawl*; Galluzzo, "Organizing against Urban Sprawl"; Thomas Benton Bare, "Recharacterizing the Debate: A Critique of Environmental Democracy and an Alternative Approach to the Urban Sprawl Dilemma," *Virginia Environmental Law Journal* 21 (2003): 455–501; Andrew Needham and Allen Dieterich-Ward, "Beyond the Metropolis: Metropolitan Growth and Regional Transformation in Postwar America," *Journal of Urban History* 35 (2009): 943–969; Allen Dietrich-Ward, *Beyond Rust: Metropolitan Pittsburgh and the Fate of Industrial America* (Philadelphia: University of Pennsylvania Press, 2017); Michelle Nickerson, "Beyond Smog, Sprawl, and Asphalt: Developments in the New Suburban History," *Journal of Urban History* 41 (2015): 171–180.

72. Sellers, *Crabgrass Crucible*, 202–206, 243–296, "affirm" is Laurence Rockefeller, quoted on 254; Josiah Rector, *Toxic Debt: An Environmental Justice History of Detroit* (Chapel Hill: University of North Carolina Press, 2022); Robert D. Bullard, "The Threat of Environmental Racism," *Natural Resources and Environment* 7 (1993): 23–56; Martin V. Melosi, "Equity, Eco-racism and Environmental History," *Environmental History Review* 19, (1995): 1–16; Hurley, *Environmental Inequalities*; David N. Pellow, *Garbage Wars: The Struggle for Environmental Justice in Chicago* (Cambridge, MA: MIT Press, 2002); Kinkela, "The Ecological Landscapes of Jane Jacobs and Rachel Carson."

73. Thad Williamson, *Sprawl, Justice, and Citizenship: The Civic Costs of the American Way of Life* (New York: Oxford University Press, 2010); Bare, "Recharacterizing the Debate"; Mark Sagoff, "Economic Theory and Environmental

Law," *Michigan Law Review* 79 (June 1981): 1393–1419; William H. Whyte, *The Exploding Metropolis* (Berkeley: University of California Press, 1993), 7–19; Rome, *The Bulldozer in the Countryside*, 255–270; Fishman, "The Death and Life of American Regional Planning."

74. Williamson, *Sprawl, Justice, and Citizenship*; Ian L. McHarg, "Blight or a Noble City," *Audubon Magazine*, vol. 68, 1966, 47–52; Bare, "Recharacterizing the Debate"; Rome, *The Bulldozer in the Countryside*, 181–189; Kinkela, "The Ecological Landscapes of Jane Jacobs and Rachel Carson."

CHAPTER 8

1. David Kinkela, "The Ecological Landscapes of Jane Jacobs and Rachel Carson," *American Quarterly* 61 (December 2009): 905–928; Jane Jacobs, *The Death and Life of Great American Cities* (New York: Random House, 1961), "sacking" on 4; Rachel Carson, *Silent Spring* (Boston: Houghton Mifflin, 1962), "contamination" on 8.

2. Kinkela, "The Ecological Landscapes of Jane Jacobs and Rachel Carson," Mumford quoted on 912.

3. Jacobs did think regionally in much of her subsequent work—most notably, in *Cities and the Wealth of Nations* (New York: Random House, 1984). Carson, *Silent Spring*, quoted passage on 1; Kinkela, "The Ecological Landscapes of Jane Jacobs and Rachel Carson"; Jacobs, *The Death and Life of Great American Cities*; Maril Hazlett, "Rachel Carson Scholarship—Where Next?" *Rachel Carson Center Perspectives* (2012): 59–65; Maril Hazlett, "'Woman versus Man versus Bugs': Gender and Popular Ecology in Early Reactions to *Silent Spring*," *Environmental History* 9 (October 2004): 701–729; Robert Fishman, "The Death and Life of American Regional Planning," in *Reflections on Regionalism*, ed. Bruce Katz (Washington, DC: Brookings Institution Press, 2000), 107–123.

4. Suleiman Osman, *The Invention of Brownstone Brooklyn: Gentrification and the Search for Authenticity in Postwar New York* (New York: Oxford University Press, 2011); Samuel Zipp, *Manhattan Projects: The Rise and Fall of Urban Renewal in Cold War New York* (New York: Oxford University Press, 2010); Jeffrey Craig Sanders, *Seattle and the Roots of Urban Sustainability: Inventing Ecotopia* (Pittsburgh: University of Pittsburgh Press, 2010); Robert R. Gioielli, *Environmental Activism and the Urban Crisis: Baltimore, St. Louis, Chicago* (Philadelphia: Temple University Press, 2014); David Stradling and Richard Stradling, *Where the River Burned: Carl Stokes and the Struggle to Save Cleveland* (Ithaca, NY: Cornell University Press, 2015); Andrew G. Kirk, *Counterculture Green: The Whole Earth Catalog and American Environmentalism* (Lawrence: University of Kansas Press, 2007); Kinkela, "The Ecological Landscapes of Jane Jacobs and Rachel Carson."

5. Sanders, *Seattle and the Roots of Urban Sustainability*; Zipp, *Manhattan Projects*, 360–370, "laissez-faire" is on 367; Martin Anderson, *The Federal Bulldozer: A Critical Appraisal* (Cambridge, MA: MIT Press, 1964); Kirk, *Counterculture Green*.

6. Jacobs, *The Death and Life of Great American Cities*, 50–54; Jean-Christophe Agnew, *Worlds Apart: The Market and Theater in Anglo-American*

Thought, 1550–1750 (Cambridge: Cambridge University Press, 1986); Dana Brand, *The Spectator and the City in Nineteenth-Century American Literature* (New York: Cambridge University Press, 1991); John Kasson, *Rudeness and Civility: Manners in Nineteenth-Century Urban America* (New York: Hill and Wang, 1990); Jamin Creed Rowan, *The Sociable City: An American Intellectual Tradition* (Philadelphia: University of Pennsylvania Press, 2017), 2–3, 15–41, Olmsted quoted on 4–5.

7. Rowan, *The Sociable City*, 24–49; W. E. B. Du Bois, *The Philadelphia Negro* (Philadelphia: University of Pennsylvania, 1899).

8. Rowan, *The Sociable City*, 33–47; Kevin Mattson, *Creating a Democratic Public: The Struggle for Urban Participatory Democracy in the Progressive Era* (University Park: Pennsylvania State University Press, 1998), Follett quoted on 96; Mary Parker Follett, *The New State: Group Organization the Solution of Popular Government* (New York: Longman, 1918).

9. Rowan, *The Sociable City*, 42–74, "empty" is the political scientist Nicholas Spykman, an associate of the Chicago sociologists, quoted on 50. Other quotations are from Louis Wirth, "Urbanism as a Way of Life," *American Journal of Sociology* (July 1938): 1–24, quoted in Rowan, *The Sociable City*, 50–51; Robert E. Park, Ernest W. Burgess, and Roderick McKenzie, *The City* (Chicago: University of Chicago Press, 1925). See also Richard Sennett, *Classic Essays on the Culture of Cities* (Englewood Cliffs, NJ: Prentice Hall, 1969), esp. Georg Simmel, "The Metropolis and Mental Life," 47–60. On the primary-secondary distinction as fundamental to the sociological tradition, see Christopher Lasch, *The True and Only Heaven: Progress and Its Critics* (New York: W. W. Norton, 1991), 120–167.

10. Rowan, *The Sociable City*, 47–53. At least some of those immigrants came not from villages but from rural cities. See Rudolph J. Vecoli, "Contadini in Chicago: A Critique of *The Uprooted*," *Journal of American History* 51 (December 1964): 404–417.

11. Shelby Harrison, "Introduction," in Clarence Arthur Perry, "The Neighborhood Unit," one of the three monographs in the *Regional Survey of New York and Its Environs, Volume 7: Neighborhood and Community Planning* (New York: Regional Plan Association, 1929), Harrison quotation on 22–24, Perry quotation on 34; Rowan, *The Sociable City*, 53–61, Harrison and Perry are also quoted on 54–55. On Harrison's relationship with the Chicago sociologists, see John D. Fairfield, *The Mysteries of the Great City* (Columbus: Ohio State University Press, 1993), 203–210; Ernest Burgess, ed., *The Urban Community* (Chicago: University of Chicago Press, 1926).

12. Rowan, *The Sociable City*, 42–74.

13. Ibid., 75–97, Rowan quotes from Smith's novel, "definite" and "*feeling*," on 93, "old neighborhood" on 75.

14. Zipp, *Manhattan Projects*, 251–350, reporter quoted on 295; Rowan, *The Sociable City*, 124–153; Joel Schwartz, *The New York Approach: Robert Moses, Urban Liberals, and Redevelopment of the Inner City* (Columbus: Ohio State University Press, 1993), neighborhood leaders quoted on 274; "National Housing Act of 1949," *United States Statutes at Large*, vol. 63 (1949), 81st Cong., sess. 1, https://www.loc.gov/law/help/statutes-at-large/81st-congress/session-1/c81s1ch338.pdf.

15. Rowan, *The Sociable City*, 124–153; Schwartz, *The New York Approach*, 271–276, 293–294; Zipp, *Manhattan Projects*, 218–350, "wasteland" on 302.

16. Rowan, *The Sociable City*, 124–153; "social poverty" is from Jane Jacobs, "The Missing Link in City Redevelopment," *Architectural Forum* 104 (June 1956): 133; "way of seeing" and "understanding" are from Jacobs, *The Death and Life of Great American Cities*, 15–16, both quoted in Rowan, 125–126.

17. Building on the work of Henry Cowles and Warder Allee discussed in Chapter 7, the community ecologists showed how sociability could be based on physiological dependencies and gregarious instincts as much as physical familiarity and intersubjective emotions. They used urban metaphors to explain these natural communities. Rowan, *The Sociable City*, 75–123; Greg Mitman, *The State of Nature: Ecology, Community, and American Social Thought, 1900–1950* (Chicago: University of Chicago Press, 1992), 48–201; Zipp, *Manhattan Projects*, 360–368; Osman, *The Invention of Brownstone Brooklyn*, 52–117, "impersonal," "alienating," and "inauthentic" on 56–57, "phony" and "conformist" on 89.

18. Rowan, *The Sociable City*, 98–123, Carson quoted on 113, Parr quoted on 13; Mitman, *The State of Nature*, 48–201; Albert E. Parr, *Mostly about Museums* (New York: American Museum of Natural History, 1959).

19. Rowan, *The Sociable City*, 124–153; William H. Whyte, *The Social Life of Small Urban Spaces* (Washington, DC: Conservation Foundation, 1980); William H. Whyte, *The Exploding Metropolis* (Garden City, NY: Doubleday, 1958); Jacobs, *The Death and Life of Great American Cities*; Kinkela, "The Ecological Landscapes of Jane Jacobs and Rachel Carson."

20. Rowan, *The Sociable City*, 94–123, Wright and Larson's novels quoted on 94–97.

21. There is more recognition of race in *The Death and Life of Great American Cities*, especially in the section on "salvaging projects," than critics allow. Rowan, *The Sociable City*, 135–144; Jacobs, *The Death and Life of Great American Cities*; Osman, *The Invention of Brownstone Brooklyn*, 173–178; Zipp, *Manhattan Projects*, 360–368.

22. Anthony Flint, *Wrestling with Moses* (New York: Random House, 2011), 61–92; Raymond A. Mohl, "Stop the Road: Freeway Revolts in American Cities," *Journal of Urban History* 30 (July 2004): 674–706, quotation is from the *San Francisco Examiner*, quoted on 679; Gioielli, *Environmental Activism and the Urban Crisis*, 73–103; Jane Holtz Kay, *Asphalt Nation: How the Automobile Took Over America and How We Can Take It Back* (Berkeley: University of California Press, 1997), 221–294.

23. Flint, *Wrestling with Moses*, 61–92; Mohl, "Stop the Road"; Gioielli, *Environmental Activism and the Urban Crisis*, 73–103.

24. Mohl, "Stop the Road"; Gioielli, *Environmental Activism and the Urban Crisis*.

25. Gioielli, *Environmental Activism and the Urban Crisis*, 73–103, "artery" on 75–76 (italics added), "slum areas" and "disgrace" on 76; Mohl, "Stop the Road," "powerful" on 690.

26. Mohl, "Stop the Road"; Gioielli, *Environmental Activism and the Urban Crisis*.

27. Mohl, "Stop the Road," quotations on 693; Gioielli, *Environmental Activism and the Urban Crisis.*

28. Gioielli, *Environmental Activism and the Urban Crisis*, "wasteland" on 82; Mohl, "Stop the Road," "realization" on 696.

29. Gioielli, *Environmental Activism and the Urban Crisis*, "imagination" on 89; Mohl, "Stop the Road."

30. Gioielli, *Environmental Activism and the Urban Crisis*; Mohl, "Stop the Road."

31. Ari Kelman, *A River and Its City: The Landscape of New Orleans* (Berkeley: University of California Press, 2003), 197–221, opposition quoted on 198.

32. Ibid., 197–204.

33. Ibid., 200–209, Jacobs quoted on 205.

34. Ibid.

35. Ibid., 209–213, BGR quoted on 209.

36. Ibid., 213–221; Sanders, *Seattle and the Roots of Urban Sustainability*, 14; Timothy J. Conlan, *New Federalism: Intergovernmental Reform from Nixon to Reagan* (Washington, DC: Brookings Institution, 1988).

37. Sanders, *Seattle and the Roots of Urban Sustainability*, 16–22, quoted passages on 18.

38. Ibid., quoted passages on 16–17.

39. Nicholas Dagen Bloom, *Merchant of Illusion: James Rouse, America's Salesman of the Businessman's Utopia* (Columbus: Ohio State University Press, 2004), 174–179; Sanders, *Seattle and the Roots of Urban Sustainability*, 16–64.

40. Sanders, *Seattle and the Roots of Urban Sustainability*, 16–64.

41. Ibid. "Indicator species" is Sanders's term, on 31; Peter Calthorpe, *The Next American Metropolis: Ecology, Communities, and the American Dream* (New York: Princeton Architectural Press, 1993), 23–26.

42. Sanders, *Seattle and the Roots of Urban Sustainability*, 34–64, quotation on 35–36.

43. Ibid., quotations from the nomination on 51.

44. Ibid.

45. Ibid., Huxtable is quoted on 61–62.

46. Ibid., 1–15; Stradling and Stradling, *Where the River Burned*, 44–77; Allen J. Matusow, *The Unraveling of America: A History of Liberalism in the 1960s* (New York: Harper and Row, 1981), 243–272; Anneliese Orleck and Lisa Gayle Hazirjian, eds., *The War on Poverty: A New Grassroots History, 1964–1980* (Athens: University of Georgia Press, 2011); Robert O. Self, *American Babylon: Race and the Struggle for Postwar Oakland* (Princeton, NJ: Princeton University Press, 2003); Wendell Pritchett, *Brownsville, Brooklyn: Blacks, Jews, and the Changing Face of the Ghetto* (Chicago: University of Chicago Press, 2002); Bret A. Weber and Amanda Wallace, "Revealing the Empowerment Revolution: A Literature Review of the Model Cities Program," *Journal of Urban History* 38 (2012): 173–192. "Economic Opportunity Act of 1964," Public Law 88-452 (August 20, 1964), https://www.govinfo.gov/content/pkg/STATUTE-78/pdf/STATUTE-78-Pg508.pdf.

47. Sanders, *Seattle and the Roots of Urban Sustainability*, 1–130; Gioielli, *Environmental Activism and the Urban Crisis*, 29–37; Self, *American Babylon*;

John D. Fairfield, *The Public and Its Possibilities: Triumphs and Tragedies in the American City* (Philadelphia: Temple University Press, 2010), 256–261.

48. Matusow, *The Unraveling of America*, 107–116, 246; Stradling and Stradling, *Where the River Burned*, 44–77, Walker quoted on 59.

49. Stradling and Stradling, *Where the River Burned*, 44–63; Gioielli, *Environmental Activism and the Urban Crisis*, 33; Sanders, *Seattle and the Roots of Urban Sustainability*, 65–98.

50. Stradling and Stradling, *Where the River Burned*, 31–35; Sanders, *Seattle and the Roots of Urban Sustainability*, 65–98, Johnson quoted on 72–74; Self, *American Babylon*, 242–246, passim; Christopher Klemek, "Model Cities," in *Encyclopedia of American Urban History*, vol. 2, ed. David Goldfield (Thousand Oaks, CA: Sage, 2007), 485–486; Weber and Wallace, "Revealing the Empowerment Revolution." On Model Cities legislation, see "Demonstration Cities and Metropolitan Development Act of 1966," Public Law 89-754 (November 3, 1966), https://www.govinfo.gov/content/pkg/STATUTE-80/pdf/STATUTE-80-Pg1255 .pdf.

51. The Central District enjoyed its own chronicler in the painter and University of Washington professor Jacob Lawrence. Sanders, *Seattle and the Roots of Urban Sustainability*, 65–98, "concentrated" on 80, "decorate" on 75, "change" and "career" on 94, "status" on 77.

52. Ibid.

53. Ibid.

54. Nathan Hare, "Black Ecology," *Black Scholar* 1 (1970): 2–8; Gioielli, *Environmental Activism and the Urban Crisis*, 137–146, "rats" on 137; Scott Dewey, "Working for the Environment: Organized Labor and the Origins of Environmentalism in the United States, 1948–1970," *Environmental History* 3 (January 1998): 45–63; Julie Sze, *Noxious New York: The Racial Politics of Urban Health and Environmental Justice* (Cambridge, MA: MIT Press, 2007); David N. Pellow, *Garbage Wars: The Struggle for Environmental Justice in Chicago* (Cambridge, MA: MIT Press, 2002); Christopher C. Sellers, *Crabgrass Crucible: Suburban Nature and the Rise of Environmentalism in Twentieth-Century America* (Chapel Hill: University of North Carolina Press, 2012), 278–284.

55. Dewey, "Working for the Environment"; Robert Gottlieb, *Forcing the Spring: The Transformation of the American Environmental Movement* (Washington DC: Island, 2005), 270–306; Robert Gordon, "'Shell No!': OCAW and the Labor-Environmental Alliance," *Environmental History* 3 (1998): 460–487; Victor Silverman, "Sustainable Alliances: The Origins of International Labor Environmentalism," *International Labor and Working-Class History* 66 (2004): 118–135.

56. Dewey, "Working for the Environment," "exotic" on 49, "vital" on 48; Gordon, "Shell No!," *want* on 464.

57. Gordon, "Shell No!," quotation on 460; Dewey, "Working for the Environment."

58. Dewey, "Working for the Environment," 50–52, lumber official quoted on 51, USWA official quoted on 54.

59. Kevin Boyle, *The UAW and the Heyday of American Liberalism, 1945–1968*

(Ithaca, NY: Cornell University Press, 1995), 185–205, "TVA" on 202; Dewey, "Working for the Environment," 50–55, other quotations on 52.

60. Dewey, "Working for the Environment," 55–57, quoted passages on 56–57.

61. Ibid., USWA official quoted on 54, UAW official quoted on 56.

62. Sanders, *Seattle and the Roots of Urban Sustainability*, 95–98, 180–237; Weber and Wallace, "Revealing the Empowerment Revolution"; Conlan, *New Federalism*.

63. Sanders, *Seattle and the Roots of Urban Sustainability*, 95–98, 180–237; Conlan, *New Federalism*; Gioielli, *Environmental Activism and the Urban Crisis*, 137–146; Demetrios Caraley, "Washington Abandons the Cities," *Political Science Quarterly* 107 (Spring 1992): 1–30; Jon C. Teaford, *The Metropolitan Revolution* (New York: Columbia University Press, 2006), 125–164; "Housing and Community Development Act of 1974," Public Law 98-383 (August 22, 1974), https://www.hud.gov/sites/documents/CDBG_HCD_CAT_1974.PDF; Megan Randall, "Census of Governments Illustrates Declining Aid to Localities, Other Trends in State and Local Finance," Tax Policy Center, April 21, 2020, https://www.taxpolicycenter.org/taxvox/census-governments-illustrates-declining-aid-localities-other-trends-state-and-local-finance; Self, *American Babylon*; Kevin Phillips, *The Emerging Republican Majority* (New York: Doubleday, 1969).

64. Bennett Harrison and Barry Bluestone, *The Great U-turn: Corporate Restructuring and the Polarizing of America* (New York: Basic, 1993); David Harvey, *The Condition of Postmodernity: An Enquiry into the Origins of Cultural Change* (Cambridge, MA: Blackwell, 1990), esp. 164–188; David Harvey, "Flexible Accumulation through Urbanization; Reflections on 'Post-Modernism' in the American City," *Antipode* 19 (December 1987): 260–286; Philip Mirowski, ed., *The Road from Mont Pelerin: The Making of the Neoliberal Thought Collective* (Cambridge, MA: Harvard University Press, 2009); John P. Koval, Larry Bennett, Michael I. J. Bennett, and Fassil Demissie et al., eds., *The New Chicago: A Social and Cultural Analysis* (Philadelphia: Temple University Press, 2008); David Harvey, *A Brief History of Neoliberalism* (New York: Oxford University Press, 2011); Jason Hackworth, *The Neoliberal City: Governance, Ideology, and Development in American Urbanism* (Ithaca, NY: Cornell University Press, 2007); Sandel, *Democracy's Discontent*, 262–273; John Kenneth Galbraith, "The Affluent Society Ten Years After," *The Atlantic*, May 1969, 37–44; Dan La Botz, "Who Rules Cincinnati? A Study of Cincinnati's Economic Power Structure and Its Impact on Communities and People," Cincinnati Studies, 2008, https://www.uc.edu/cdc/urban_database/citywide_regional/who_rules_cincinnati.pdf.

65. Harrison and Bluestone, *The Great U-turn*; Harvey, *A Brief History of Neoliberalism*; Fishman, "The Death and Life of American Regional Planning"; Douglas W. Rae, *City: Urbanism and Its End* (New Haven, CT: Yale University Press, 2003); Harvey, *The Condition of Postmodernity*.

66. David Rusk, *Cities without Suburbs* (Washington. DC: Woodrow Wilson Center, 1993); Larry Bennett, "Regionalism in a Historically Divided Metropolis," in Koval et al., *The New Chicago*, 277–285, Daley and suburban mayor quoted on 277; Quinn Slobodian, *Globalists: The End of Empire and the Birth of Neoliberalism* (Cambridge, MA: Harvard University Press, 2018); Fishman, "The Death and Life

of American Regional Planning"; Gerald W. Adelmann, "Reworking the Landscape, Chicago Style" *Hastings Center Report* 28 (November–December 1998): S6–S11.

67. Josiah Rector, *Toxic Debt: An Environmental Justice History of Detroit* (Chapel Hill: University of North Carolina Press, 2022), 124–135, passim, "blackmail" on 132; Dewey, "Working for the Environment."

68. Rector, *Toxic Debt*, 144–171.

69. Robert Fisher, *Let the People Decide: Neighborhood Organizing in America* (Boston: Twayne, 1984); Zane L. Miller, *Suburb: Neighborhood and Community in Forest Park, Ohio, 1935–1976* (Knoxville: University of Tennessee Press, 1981); Sanders, *Seattle and the Roots of Urban Sustainability*, 131–237; Kirk, *Counterculture Green.*

70. Sanders, *Seattle and the Roots of Urban Sustainability*, 131–237, "barrier" on 144; Kirk, *Counterculture Green*; Portola Institute, *The Whole Earth Catalog: Access to Tools* (Menlo Park, CA: Portola Institute, 1968); Wendell Berry, *The Unsettling of America* (San Francisco: Sierra Club, 1977).

71. Kirk, *Counterculture Green*; Portola Institute, *The Whole Earth Catalog.*

72. Kirk, *Counterculture Green*, 1–73, "doing" on 57.

73. Sanders, *Seattle and the Roots of Urban Sustainability*, 180–214, "privacy" on 213; Kirk, *Counterculture Green*, 1–73, "choices" on 55.

74. Sanders, *Seattle and the Roots of Urban Sustainability*, 131–237; Sellers, *Crabgrass Crucible*, 278–284; Kirk, *Counterculture Green.*

75. Lisa McGirr, *Suburban Warriors: The Origins of the New American Right* (Princeton, NJ: Princeton University Press, 2001); Harvey, *A Brief History of Neoliberalism*; Leo Marx, *The Machine in the Garden: Technology and the Pastoral Ideal in America* (New York: Oxford University Press, 1964), 364.

INTRODUCTION TO PART III

1. Sadly, those neon-lit motels did not beckon everyone. See the depressing story of the African American Dr. Robert Foster, a member of the Great Migration, and his unsuccessful effort to find lodging. Isabel Wilkerson, *The Warmth of Other Suns: The Epic Story of America's Great Migration* (New York: Vintage, 2011), 205–211. John Talton, "Phoenix 101: Blue Highways," *Rogue Columnist* (blog), September 21, 2012, https://roguecolumnist.typepad.com/rogue_colum nist/2012/09/phoenix-101-blue-highways.html; Douglas Towne, "Phoenix's Street of Dreams: The Visual Extravaganza That Was Van Buren," *Modern Phoenix*, 2011, http://www.modernphoenix.net/vanburen/vanburensigns.htm.

2. Andrew Needham, *Power Lines: Phoenix and the Making of the Modern Southwest* (Princeton, NJ: Princeton University Press, 2014); Elizabeth Tandy Shermer, *Sunbelt Capitalism: Phoenix and the Transformation of American Politics* (Philadelphia: University of Pennsylvania Press, 2013); Jason Hackworth, *The Neoliberal City: Governance, Ideology, and Development in American Urbanism* (Ithaca, NY: Cornell University Press, 2007).

3. John Talton, "Phoenix 101: What Killed Downtown" (three parts), *Rogue Columnist* (blog), March 11–25, 2013, http://www.roguecolumnist.com/rogue _columnist/2013/03/phoenix-101-what-killed-downtown-part-i.html; John Talton, "Phoenix 101: Phoenix Union Station," *Rouge Columnist* (blog), January 11, 2010,

http://roguecolumnist.typepad.com/rogue_columnist/2010/01/phoenix-101-union
-station.html; John Talton, "The Warehouse District," *Rogue Columnist* (blog), January 26, 2016 https://www.roguecolumnist.com/rogue_columnist/2016/01/the
-warehouse-district.html.

4. Talton, "Phoenix 101: What Killed Downtown."

5. Daniel B. Higgins, "Review of *Bird on Fire*," *Review of Policy Research* 29
(2012): 439–440. On catastrophism and uniformitarianism, see Stephen Jay Gould,
*Time's Arrow, Time's Cycle: Myth and Metaphor in the Discovery of Geological
Time* (Cambridge, MA: Harvard University Press, 1987), 126–127, passim; Mike
Davis, *Ecology of Fear: Los Angeles and the Imagination of Disaster* (New York:
Vintage, 1998), 14–35.

6. Christopher Lasch, *The True and Only Heaven: Progress and Its Critics* (New
York: W. W. Norton, 1991), 29, passim; Christopher Lasch, *The Revolt of the Elites
and the Betrayal of Democracy* (New York: W. W. Norton, 1995).

CHAPTER 9

1. Michael F. Logan, *Desert Cities: The Environmental History of Phoenix
and Tucson* (Pittsburgh: University of Pittsburgh Press, 2006), 21–24; Andrew
Ross, *Bird on Fire: Lessons from the World's Least Sustainable City* (New York:
Oxford University Press, 2011), 25–28; Jared Diamond, *Collapse: How Societies
Choose to Fail or Succeed* (New York: Viking, 2005), 136–156; James Lawrence
Powell, *Dead Pool: Lake Powell, Global Warming, and the Future of Water in
the West* (Los Angeles: University of California Press, 2008), 32.

2. Logan, *Desert Cities*; Ross, *Bird on Fire*.

3. Diamond, *Collapse*, 136–156; Albert R. Bates, *Jack Swilling: Arizona's
Most Lied about Pioneer* (Tucson: Wheatmark, 2008); Ross, *Bird on Fire*, 28–50.

4. Ross, *Bird on Fire*, 212–250, passim; Office of Sustainability, City of Phoenix,
2015–2026 Sustainability Update, brochure, April 12, 2016, https://www.phoe
nix.gov/sustainabilitysite/Documents/Final%20COP%202015-16%20Sustainabil
ity%20Brochure%2003.27.17.pdf.

5. Ross, *Bird on Fire*, 21–50, Reisner quoted on 42; Andrew Needham, *Power
Lines: Phoenix and the Making of the Modern Southwest* (Princeton, NJ: Princeton University Press, 2014); Logan, *Desert Cities*, 137–157; "Plight of Phoenix:
How Long Can the World's 'Least Sustainable' City Survive?" *The Guardian*, U.S.
ed., March 20, 2018, https://www.theguardian.com/cities/2018/mar/20/phoenix
-least-sustainable-city-survive-water.

6. Ross, *Bird on Fire*, 21–50; Needham, *Power Lines*, 157–182, on Mercury
astronauts, 180; Jon Talton, *A Brief History of Phoenix* (Charleston, SC: History Press, 2015), 123–125; Central Arizona Project, "Your Water, Your Future,"
https://www.cap-az.com; U.S. Energy Information Administration, "Arizona State
Profile and Energy Estimates," accessed February 20, 2020, https://www.eia.gov
/state/analysis.php?sid=AZ; American Lung Association, "State of the Air," April
14, 2019, https://www.lung.org/media/press-releases/20th-sota-ca; AZCentral,
"Phoenix Is Tying Records for Highest Low Temperatures," July 21, 2020, https://
www.azcentral.com/story/news/local/arizona-environment/2020/07/21/phoenix
-night-temps-get-hotter-because-heat-island-climate-change/5472797002; Umair

Irfan, "100 Degrees for Days: The Looming Phoenix Heat Wave That Could Harm Thousands," *Vox*, September 9, 2019, https://www.vox.com/energy-and-environ ment/2019/9/9/20804544/climate-change-phoenix-heat-wave-deaths-extreme -weather; Arizona Department of Environmental Quality, "What Is a Superfund Site," May 16, 2018, https://azdeq.gov/NPL_Sites.

7. Bradford Luckingham, "Trouble in a Sunbelt City," *Journal of the Southwest* 33 (Spring 1991): 52–67, national journalist quoted on 65; Ross, *Bird on Fire*, 3–50, 116–147, interviewee quoted on 13; Daniel B. Higgins, "Review of *Bird on Fire*," *Review of Policy Research* 29 (2012): 439–440.

8. Luckingham, "Trouble in a Sunbelt City," quotations on 65; Patricia A. Simko, "Arizona: The Land of Laissez-Faire," in *Promised Lands*, ed. Dean M. Halloran (New York: Praeger, 1978); Ross, *Bird on Fire*, 42–50, 116–147, "use it" on 48; Powell, *Dead Pool*, 239–240; Joel Garreau, *Edge City: Life on the New Frontier* (New York: Doubleday, 1992), 183–208; Bradford Luckingham, *Minorities in Phoenix. A Profile of Mexican American, Chinese American, and African-American Communities, 1860–1992* (Tucson: University of Arizona Press, 1994).

9. Garreau estimated that 150,000 private-enterprise governments existed in the United States, far more than conventional local governments: Garreau, *Edge City*, 183–208, "private-enterprise government" on 185. See also Robert E. Lang and Jennifer B. LeFurgy, *Boomburbs: The Rise of America's Accidental Cities* (Washington, DC: Brookings Institution Press, 2007).

10. Garreau, *Edge City*, 183–208; Elizabeth Tandy Shermer, *Sunbelt Capitalism: Phoenix and the Transformation of American Politics* (Philadelphia: University of Pennsylvania Press, 2013), 185–188, passim; Needham, *Power Lines*, 37–42; Ross, *Bird on Fire*, 3–50.

11. Ross, *Bird on Fire*, 3–50, *Arizona Republic* on 22; Garreau, *Edge City*, 183–208; Needham, *Power Lines*, 37–42; Shermer, *Sunbelt Capitalism*, 185–188, 336–340, passim; Powell, *Dead Pool*, 239–240; Sarah Kaplan, "How America's Hottest City Will Survive Climate Change," *Washington Post*, July 8, 2020, https://www .washingtonpost.com/graphics/2020/climate-solutions/phoenix-climate-change-heat.

12. Ross, *Bird on Fire*, 21–50, archeologist on 27–29; Shermer, *Sunbelt Capitalism*; Diamond, *Collapse*, my italics; Karl W. Butzer, "Collapse, Environment, and Society," *Proceedings of the National Academy of Sciences* 109 (March 6, 2012): 3632–3639.

13. U.S. Senator (and presidential candidate) Barry Goldwater and U.S. Supreme Court justices William Rehnquist and Sandra Day O'Connor are Phoenix's most obvious contributors to national affairs. The city also nurtured the early political career of Ronald Reagan and helped make him president. Ross, *Bird on Fire*, 212–250, "test bed" on 249; Shermer, *Sunbelt Capitalism*, 49–55, 270–301, passim; Needham, *Power Lines*, 72–88.

14. Ross, *Bird on Fire*, 212–250; Shermer, *Sunbelt Capitalism*, 49–55, 270–301, passim, *Whither Phoenix?* on 78; Needham, *Power Lines*, 72–88; David F. Damore, Robert E. Land, and Karen A. Danielson, *Blue Metros, Red States: The Shifting Urban-Rural Divide in America's Swing States* (Washington, DC: Brookings Institution Press, 2021), 337–351, passim.

15. John Wesley Powell, *Report on the Arid Lands of the United States* (Cambridge, MA: Harvard University Press, [1878] 1962); Needham, *Power Lines*,

30–34; Donald Worster, *Rivers of Empire: Water, Aridity, and the Growth of the American West* (New York: Pantheon, 1985); Charles Wilkinson, *Crossing the Next Meridian: Land, Water, and the Future of the West* (Washington, DC: Island, 1992), 16–20, passim; David E. Nye, *Consuming Power: A Social History of American Energies* (Cambridge, MA: MIT Press, 1998), 157–215.

16. Wilkinson, *Crossing the Next Meridian*, 18, 255–286; Needham, *Power Lines*, 38–42; Shermer, *Sunbelt Capitalism*, 22–24; Nye, *Consuming Power*, 157–215.

17. Needham, *Power Lines*, 38–42, "largest" on 39; Shermer, *Sunbelt Capitalism*, 17–38; Worster, *Rivers of Empire*, 129–140.

18. Needham, *Power Lines*, 38–42; Shermer, *Sunbelt Capitalism*, 17–38.

19. Needham, *Power Lines*, 38–42; Shermer, *Sunbelt Capitalism*, 17–49, banker quoted on 17, "essentials" on 40.

20. Needham, *Power Lines*, 26–30.

21. Ibid., 23–26, Roosevelt quoted on 24; Shermer, *Sunbelt Capitalism*, 40–43.

22. Needham, *Power Lines*, 42–52.

23. Ibid., 42–52.

24. Ibid., 30–37, "very large" on 32; Shermer, *Sunbelt Capitalism*, 37–38.

25. Needham, *Power Lines*, 30–37.

26. Shermer, *Sunbelt Capitalism*, 49–90, 270–301; Needham, *Power Lines*, 57–88; Bradford Luckingham, *Phoenix: The History of a Southwestern Metropolis* (Tucson: University of Arizona Press, 1995), 136–176.

27. Shermer, *Sunbelt Capitalism*, 55–66, 278–282, "Make loans" on 56, "private" on 58; Needham, *Power Lines*, 57–72, "prepared" on 57.

28. Shermer, *Sunbelt Capitalism*, 55–66, 270–284, "operated" and "private" on 58; Needham, *Power Lines*, 57–72; Ann Markusen, *The Rise of the Gunbelt* (New York: Oxford University Press, 1991); Luckingham, *Phoenix*, Webb quoted on 107.

29. Shermer, *Sunbelt Capitalism*, 66–70, 184–221, 272–278, Goldwater quoted on 69; Needham, *Power Lines*, 60–63, "outdoor living" and "Golf" on 62, "*individual*" on 62.

30. Needham, *Power Lines*, 91–94, "odors" on 93; Shermer, *Sunbelt Capitalism*, 282–301; Bob Bolin, Sara Grineski, and Timothy Collins, "The Geography of Despair: Environmental Racism and the Making of South Phoenix, Arizona, USA," *Human Ecology Review* 12 (Winter 2005): 156–168.

31. Needham, *Power Lines*, 93–96, 115–120; Shermer, *Sunbelt Capitalism*, 97–115, passim; Ross, *Bird on Fire*, 62–68; Luckingham, *Phoenix*, 136–143; Michael Konig, "Phoenix in the 1950s: Urban Growth in the 'Sunbelt,'" *Arizona and the West* 24 (Spring 1982): 19–38; Logan, *Desert Cities*, 137–144. Cf. Robert O. Self, *American Babylon: Race and the Struggle for Postwar Oakland* (Princeton, NJ: Princeton University Press, 2003), 23–60.

32. Shermer, *Sunbelt Capitalism*, 97–141; Needham, *Power Lines*, 93–102, "intent" on 101; Luckingham, *Phoenix*, 136–157; Ross, *Bird on Fire*, 62–68.

33. Needham, *Power Lines*, 102–111, mayor quoted on 109, 111; Konig, "Phoenix in the 1950s."

34. Needham, *Power Lines*, 102–111, "attract" on 109, "spending" on 111; Shermer, *Sunbelt Capitalism*, 184–221; Ross, *Bird on Fire*, 176–177; Konig, "Phoenix in the 1950s."

35. Harvey Molotch, "The City as a Growth Machine: Toward a Political Economy of Place," *American Journal of Sociology* 82 (September 1976): 309–332; Needham, *Power Lines*, 66–72, "More" on 67; Konig, "Phoenix in the 1950s"; Jon C. Teaford, *The Metropolitan Revolution* (New York: Columbia University Press, 2006), 108–112.

36. Needham, *Power Lines*, 72–80; Shermer, *Sunbelt Capitalism*, 185–188.

37. Needham, *Power Lines*, 72–81.

38. Ibid., quotations on 78; Adam Rome, *The Bulldozer in the Countryside* (New York: Cambridge University Press, 2001), 45–86; Lizabeth Cohen, *A Consumers' Republic* (New York: Alfred A. Knopf, 2003).

39. Needham, *Power Lines*, 3–6, 79–83, "essentially" on 81, "valentine" on 80; Rome, *The Bulldozer in the Countryside*, 45–86.

40. Needham, *Power Lines*, 3–6, 79–83, banker quoted on 4 and 82; Shermer, *Sunbelt Capitalism*, 274–275; Konig, "Phoenix in the 1950s"; Logan, *Desert Cities*, 144–146, booster quoted on 145; Raymond Arsenault, "The End of the Long Hot Summer: The Air Conditioner and Southern Culture," *Journal of Southern History* 50, no. 4 (1984): 597–628.

41. Needham, *Power Lines*, 111–120.

42. Ibid., quotations on 118–119; Shermer, *Sunbelt Capitalism*, 188–192.

43. Needham, *Power Lines*, 129–145, Goldwater quoted on 138.

44. Ibid., 129–156, tribal chairman Paul Jones quoted on 146, contractual demand on 149.

45. Ibid., 145–156, Bimson quoted on 151.

46. Ibid., 130–159.

47. Ibid., 130–159, 179–210, 248, "almost" on 180.

48. Ibid., 185–212, "High Cost" on 185 and 199, "breathtaking" on 185.

49. Ibid., 213–229, quotations on 226.

50. Ibid., 148–150, 229–236, quotations on 231.

51. Ibid., 55–72, quotations on 69.

52. Ibid., 83–90, activist quoted on 84; Andrew Kopkind, "Modern Times in Phoenix," *New Republic*, vol. 153, November 6, 1965, 14–16; Konig, "Phoenix in the 1950s"; Bolin et al., "The Geography of Despair"; Petra Spiess, "Scientists and the City," *High Country News*, vol. 39, 2007, 6–7.

53. Needham, *Power Lines*, 217–229, quoted passage on 221.

54. Logan, *Desert Cities*, "inner city" on 161; Shermer, *Sunbelt Capitalism*, 272–278, national press quoted on 274; Eric Avila, "Popular Culture in the Age of White Flight: Film Noir, Disneyland, and the Cold War (Sub)urban Imaginary," *Journal of Urban History* 31 (November 2004): 3–22; Nicholas Christopher, *Somewhere in the Night: Film Noir and the American City* (New York: Free Press, 1997); Edward Dimendberg, *Film Noir and the Spaces of Modernity* (Cambridge, MA: Harvard University Press, 2004); Mike Davis, *City of Quartz* (New York: Vintage, 1992), 40–41.

55. Konig, "Phoenix in the 1950s," 35–38; Shermer, *Sunbelt Capitalism*, 184–221, 302–310.

56. Shermer, *Sunbelt Capitalism*, 302–310, "Frankenstein" on 302; Konig, "Phoenix in the 1950s," 36–38; Davis, *City of Quartz*, 151–219; Self, *American*

Babylon; Lisa McGirr, *Suburban Warriors: The Origins of the New Right* (Princeton, NJ: Princeton University Press, 2015).

57. Shermer, *Sunbelt Capitalism*, 188–192; Needham, *Power Lines*, 187–191.

58. Shermer, *Sunbelt Capitalism*, 302–335; Luckingham, "Trouble in a Sunbelt City," 52–67, "winter" on 53.

59. Shermer, *Sunbelt Capitalism*, 336–340; Ross, *Bird on Fire*, 50–74; Luckingham, "Trouble in a Sunbelt City," 52–67, "intense" on 64, "appalled" on 60, "heat" on 53; Logan, *Desert Cities*, 160–170, 170–172; Spiess, "Scientists and the City"; Needham, *Power Lines*, 221–229; Carl Abbot, "Southwestern Cityscapes: Approaches to an American Urban Environment," in *Essays on Sunbelt Cities and Recent Urban America*, ed. Robert Fairbanks and Kathleen Underwood (College Station: Texas A&M Press, 1990), 59–86.

60. Luckingham, "Trouble in a Sunbelt City," "People" on 53, "Newcomers" on 55; Shermer, *Sunbelt Capitalism*, 130–146; Talton, *A Brief History of Phoenix*, 123–130.

61. Needham, *Power Lines*, 246–251, "shadowy" on 246.

62. Luckingham, "Trouble in a Sunbelt City"; Shermer, *Sunbelt Capitalism*, 306–335; Ross, *Bird on Fire*, 116–147, 239–250; Bolin et al., "The Geography of Despair."

63. Ross, *Bird on Fire*, 47–50; Powell, *Dead Pool*, 239–240; Kaplan, "How America's Hottest City Will Survive Climate Change"; Shermer, *Sunbelt Capitalism*, 336–340; Jon Talton, *Dry Heat* (Scottsdale, AZ: Poisoned Pen, 2004), 1; David William Foster, "The Desert Noir Detective Novels of Jon Talton," *Rocky Mountain Review of Language and Literature* 61 (Spring 2007): 73–83; Catherine Armstrong, "This Neighborhood in Arizona Was One of the Most Dangerous Places in the Nation," *Only in Your State*, August 21, 2017, https://www.onlyinyourstate.com/arizona/maryvale-az-dangerous-neighborhood; Patrick Millikin, ed., *Phoenix Noir* (New York: Akashic, 2009).

64. Maryvale is named after Long's wife. Needham, *Power Lines*, 66–72; Ross, *Bird on Fire*, 128–131; Armstrong, "This Neighborhood in Arizona Was One of the Most Dangerous Places in the Nation."

65. Shermer, *Sunbelt Capitalism*, 336–340; Ross, *Bird on Fire*, 55–62, 148–184, 239–250.

66. John Judis, *The Populist Explosion: How the Great Recession Transformed American and European Politics* (New York: Columbia Global Reports, 2016); Ross, *Bird on Fire*, 55–62, 148–250, "attrition" on 196, "reasonable" on 190.

67. Ross, *Bird on Fire*, 185–211, "growth" and "cause" are from a 2010 report from the Federation for American Immigration Reform, founded by a former Sierra Club activist, quoted on 189; Shermer, *Sunbelt Capitalism*, 336–340; "Immigrants in Arizona," American Immigration Council, August 6, 2020, accessed October 31, 2021, https://www.americanimmigrationcouncil.org/research/immigrants-in-arizona.

68. Ross, *Bird on Fire*, 239–250, "greenest" is Mayor Phil Gordon in 2009, quoted on 245; Office of Sustainability, City of Phoenix, *2015–2026 Sustainability Update*; John J. Berger, "Phoenix, AZ: A Blue City in a Red State Is Going

Green," *HuffPost*, November, 29, 2017, https://www.huffpost.com/entry/phoe
nix-aza-blue-city-in-a-red-state-is-going-green_b_5a1cd0fbe4b09413e786ae84;
City of Phoenix, "Phoenix Continues to Reduce Greenhouse Gas Emissions," June
10, 2020, https://www.phoenix.gov/newsroom/environmental-programs/1330;
Kaplan, "How America's Hottest City Will Survive Climate Change"; Katie Couric,
"Transforming the World's Least Sustainable City," *Yahoo News*, August 9, 2017,
https://news.yahoo.com/transforming-worlds-least-sustainable-city-221217694
.html.

69. "Welcome to Tres Rios," City of Phoenix, n.d., https://www.phoenix.gov/wa
terservices/tresrios; Ross, *Bird on Fire*, 212–250; Shermer, *Sunbelt Capitalism*, 336–
340; Needham, *Power Lines*, 246–257.

70. Ross, *Bird on Fire*, 212–240, "Samaritans" on 231.

71. Ibid., 212–250; U.S. Department of Justice, "Gila River Community Water
Rights Settlement," updated May 14, 2015, accessed August 12, 2022, https://
www.justice.gov/cnrd/gila-river-indian-community.

72. Ross, *Bird on Fire*, 212–250; Emily Davis, "'A Raging Crisis': Metro Phoenix
Is Losing Its Family Farms and Local Food Sources," *AZCentral*, August 17, 2020,
https://www.azcentral.com/story/news/local/phoenix/2020/08/16/metro-phoenix
-losing-its-family-farms-development/3315284001.

CHAPTER 10

1. U.S. Congress, House, *Recognizing the Duty of the Federal Government to
Create a Green New Deal*, HR 109, 116th Cong., introduced February 7, 2019,
https://www.congress.gov/bill/116th-congress/house-resolution/109 (hereafter,
HR 109); U.S. Congress, Senate, *A Resolution Recognizing the Duty of the Federal
Government to Create a Green New Deal*, SR 59, 116th Cong., introduced February 7, 2019, https://www.congress.gov/bill/116th-congress/senate-resolution/59
(hereafter, SR 59).

2. HR 109; SR 59; Kate Arnoff, "With the Green New Deal Here's What the
World Could Look like for the Next Generation," *The Intercept*, December 8, 2018,
https://theintercept.com/2018/12/05/green-new-deal-proposal-impacts.

3. Arnoff, "With the Green New Deal Here's What the World Could Look like
for the Next Generation"; Katrina Vanden Heuvel, "Why the Time Has Come for
the Green New Deal," *Washington Post*, December 18, 2018; Chelsea Whyte, "A
Green Deal That Could Save the Planet," *New Scientist*, vol. 240, December 12,
2018, 25; Naomi Klein, "A Message from the Future with Alexandria Ocasio-
Cortez," *The Intercept*, video posted April 17, 2019, https://www.youtube.com
/watch?v=d9uTH0iprVQ; Naomi Klein, *On Fire: The (Burning) Case for the Green
New Deal* (Toronto: Alfred A. Knopf, 2019).

4. Alec Tyson, Brian Kennedy, and Gary Funk, "Gen Z, Millennials Stand Out
for Climate Change Activism, Social Media Engagement with Issue," Pew Research
Center, May 26, 2021, https://www.pewresearch.org/science/2021/05/26/gen
-z-millennials-stand-out-for-climate-change-activism-social-media-engagement
-with-issue; David Roberts, "U.S. Public Opinion Supports Action on Climate
Change—and Has For Years," *Vox*, June 23, 2020, https://www.vox.com/ener
gy-and-environment/2020/6/23/21298065/climate-clean-energy-public-opinion

-poll-trends-pew; Alexander C. Kaufman, "Green New Deal Has Overwhelming Bipartisan Support, Polls Find—At Least, for Now," *HuffPost*, December 18, 2018, https://www.huffpost.com/entry/green-new-deal-poll_n_5c169f2ae4b 05d7e5d8332a5; "Fox News Has United the Right against the Green New Deal, the Left Remains Divided," *Vox*, April 22, 2019, https://www.vox.com/energy -and-environment/2019/4/22/18510518/green-new-deal-fox-news-poll; Robinson Meyer, "It's Younger and Cooler than a Carbon Tax: The Green New Deal Is Surprisingly Popular," *The Atlantic*, June 21, 2019, https://www.theatlantic.com/sci ence/archive/2019/06/green-new-deal-may-be-more-popular-carbon-tax/592201; Miranda Green, "GOP Pollster Luntz: Majority of Younger Republicans Worried by Party Stance on Climate Change," *The Hill*, June 12, 2019 https://thehill .com/policy/energy-environment/448162-gop-pollster-luntz-majority-of-younger -republicans-worried-by-party-stance-on-climate-change; Zoya Teirstein, "Poll: The Green New Deal Is as Popular as Legalizing Weed," *Grist*, July 22, 2019, https://grist.org/article/poll-the-green-new-deal-is-as-popular-as-legalizing-weed; Robinson Meyer, "The Democratic Party Wants to Make Climate Policy Exciting," *The Atlantic*, December 5, 2018.

5. U.S. Congress, "Inflation Reduction Act of 2022," HR 5376, 117th Cong., introduced September 27, 2021, https://www.congress.gov/bill/117th-congress /house-bill/5376; Ben Thomas, "Four Big Ways the Inflation Reduction Act Invests in Rural America," Environmental Defense Fund, November 22, 2022, https:// www.edf.org/blog/2022/11/22/4-big-ways-inflation-reduction-act-invests -rural-america; Bill McKibben, "For the Third Time in Three Decades, Congress Punts on Serious Climate Legislation," *New Yorker*, July 16, 2022, https://www .newyorker.com/news/daily-comment/for-the-third-time-in-three-decades-con gress-punts-on-serious-climate-legislation.

6. Michael Lerner, "Stop Shaming Trump Supporters," *New York Times*, November 9, 2016, https://www.nytimes.com/interactive/projects/cp/opinion /election-night-2016/stop-shaming-trump-supporters; Michael Sandel, "What Liberals Got Wrong about Work," *The Atlantic*, September 2, 2020, https://www .theatlantic.com/ideas/archive/2020/09/contributive-justice-and-dignity-work/61 5919.

7. David F. Damore, Robert E. Land, and Karen A. Danielson, *Blue Metros, Red States: The Shifting Urban-Rural Divide in America's Swing States* (Washington, DC: Brookings Institution, 2021); Michael Tomasky, "The Midterms: So Close, So Far Apart," *New York Review of Books*, December 20, 2018; "An Extremely Detailed Map of the 2020 Election," *New York Times*, n.d., https:// www.nytimes.com/interactive/2021/upshot/2020-election-map.html; William A. Galston, *Anti-pluralism: The Populist Threat to Liberal Democracy* (New Haven, CT: Yale University Press, 2018); Economic Innovation Group, *The New Map of Economic Growth and Recovery*, report, May 2016, https://eig.org/wp-content /uploads/2016/05/recoverygrowthreport.pdf; Arlie Russell Hochschild, "Male Trouble," *New York Review of Books*, October 11, 2018; Nick Reding, *Methland: The Death and Life of an American Small Town* (New York: Bloomsbury, 2009).

8. Damore et al., *Blue Metros, Red States*; Ronald Brownstein, "The Prosperity Paradox Is Dividing the Country in Two," CNN, January 23, 2018, https://www .cnn.com/2018/01/23/politics/economy-prosperity-paradox-divide-country-voters

/index.html; Michael Tomasky, "Democrats Win?" *New York Review of Books*, December 17, 2020, https://www.nybooks.com/articles/2020/12/17/election -2020-what-did-democrats-win; Mark Muro, Eli Byerly-Duke, Yang You, and Robert Maxim, "Biden-Voting Counties Equal 70% of American Economy," Brookings Institution, updated February 26, 2021, https://www.brookings.edu/blog/the-ave nue/2020/11/09/biden-voting-counties-equal-70-of-americas-economy-what-does -this-mean-for-the-nations-political-economic-divide; Madeline Hein, "Democrats Made Early Moves on High-Speed Internet, but at Local Level It's Not Partisan," *Politifact*, December 28, 2021, https://www.politifact.com/factchecks/2021/dec/28 /jon-erpenbach/democrats-made-early-moves-high-speed-internet-acc.

9. Tomasky, "The Midterms"; "An Extremely Detailed Map of the 2020 Election." For a recent examples of Brown's efforts, see "Brown Announces Nearly $2.4 Million for Rural Development in Eastern Ohio," press release, June 8, 2022, https://www.brown.senate.gov/newsroom/press/release/brown-24-million-for -rural-development-eastern-ohio. For a broader understanding of his approach and strategy, see Michael Kazin, "Working Too Hard for Too Little: An Interview with Senator Sherrod Brown," *Dissent* 64, no. 3 (2017): 25–31; John Halpin and Ruy Teixeira, "The Base Mobilization Fallacy," *Liberal Patriot*, August 10, 2021, https://theliberalpatriot.substack.com/p/the-base-mobilization-fallacy; Sandel, "What Liberals Got Wrong about Work"; "Does Bernie Sanders Have 'Strong Support' in Rural and Red Vermont?" *Politifact*, February 20, 2020, https://www .politifact.com/factchecks/2020/feb/21/jane-omeara-sanders/does-bernie-sanders -have-strong-support-rural-and-; "Detailed Maps of Where Trump, Cruz, Clinton, and Sanders Have Won," *New York Times*, October 4, 2016, https://www.nytimes .com/elections/2016/national-results-map.

10. U.S. Bureau of Labor Statistics, *Labor Force Statistics from the Current Population Survey*, https://www.bls.gov/web/empsit/cpsee_e16.htm; Danielle Sered, *Until We Reckon: Violence, Mass Incarceration, and a Road to Repair* (New York: New Press, 2019); Michelle Alexander, *The New Jim Crow* (New York: New Press, 2012); Ta-Nehisi Coates, "The Black Family in the Age of Mass Incarceration," *The Atlantic*, October 1, 2015, 60–84; Nikki Graf, Anna Brown, and Eileen Patten, "The Narrowing, but Persistent, Gender Gap in Pay," Pew Research Center, March 22, 2019, https://www.pewresearch.org/fact-tank/2019/03/22/gender-pay -gap-facts.

11. James L. Wunsch, "The Suburban Cliché," *Journal of Social History* 28 (Spring 1995): 643–658; Tomasky, "The Midterms."

12. Patrick Wyman, "American Gentry," *The Atlantic*, September 23, 2021, https://www.theatlantic.com/ideas/archive/2021/09/trump-american-gentry -wyman-elites/620151; Nick Bowlin, "Joke's on Them: How Democrats Gave Up on Rural America," *The Guardian*, February 22, 2022, https://www.theguard ian.com/us-news/2022/feb/22/us-politics-rural-america; Thomas B. Edsall, "The Robots Have Descended on Trump Country," *New York Times*, December 13, 2018; Hochschild, "Male Trouble."

13. Eric O'Keefe, "Bill Gates: America's Top Farmland Owner," *Land Report*, January 11, 2021, https://landreport.com/2021/01/farmer-bill; Wyman, "American Gentry"; Heather McGhee, *The Sum of Us: What Racism Costs Everyone and How*

We Can Prosper Together (New York: One World, 2021), 53–61; "The Crisis in Rural Health Care," Saving Rural Hospitals, accessed September 11, 2022, https://ruralhospitals.chqpr.org.

14. Damore et al., *Blue Metros, Red States*; Scott Tong and Serena McMahon, "White, Employed and Mainstream: What We Know about the Jan[uary] 6 Rioters One Year Later," WBUR, January 3, 2022, https://www.wbur.org/hereand now/2022/01/03/jan-6-rioters-white-older; Wyman, "American Gentry"; Bowlin, "Joke's on Them"; Farah Stockman, *American Made: What Happens to People When Work Disappears* (New York: Random House, 2021).

15. Guy Molyneaux, "A Tale of Two Populisms," *American Prospect*, June 1, 2017, https://prospect.org/labor/tale-two-populisms; Robert Kuttner, *The Stakes: 2020 and the Survival of American Democracy* (New York: W. W. Norton, 2019).

16. Lizabeth Cohen, *Making a New Deal: Industrial Workers in Chicago, 1919–1939* (Cambridge: Cambridge University Press, 1990); Steven Fraser, *Labor Will Rule: Sidney Hillman and the Rise of American Labor* (Ithaca, NY: Cornell University Press, 1993); Alan Brinkley, *Voices of Protest: Huey Long, Father Coughlin, and the Great Depression* (New York: Alfred A. Knopf, 1982); William E. Leuchtenburg, *Franklin Roosevelt and the New Deal* (New York: Harper and Row, 1963); Ellis Hawley, *The New Deal and the Problem of Monopoly: A Study in Economic Ambivalence* (Princeton, NJ: Princeton University Press, 1966); Alan Brinkley, *The End of Reform: New Deal Liberalism in Recession and War* (New York: Alfred A. Knopf, 1995), 175–200; Lawrence Mishel and Jori Kandra, "CEO Pay Has Skyrocketed 1,322% since 1978," Economic Policy Institute, August 10, 2021, https://www.epi.org/publication/ceo-pay-in-2020; Alexandre Tanzi and Mike Dorning, "Top 1% of U.S. Earners Now Hold More Wealth than All of the Middle Class," Bloomberg, October 8, 2021, https://www.bloomberg.com/news /articles/2021-10-08/top-1-earners-hold-more-wealth-than-the-u-s-middle-class.

17. HR 109; Mariana Mazzucato, *The Entrepreneurial State: Debunking Public versus Private Sector Myths* (London: Anthem, 2011); Stephen S. Cohen and James Bradford DeLong, *Concrete Economics: The Hamilton Approach to Economic Growth and Policy* (Boston: Harvard Business Review Press, 2016); Win McCormack, "The Green New Deal: A Capitalist Plot (Part 1)," *New Republic*, July 1, 2019, 68; Samuel Miller McDonald, "The Green New Deal Can't Be Anything like the New Deal," *New Republic*, May 31, 2019; Greg Jackson, "Prayer for Just War; Finding Meaning in the Climate Fight," *Harper's*, June 2021, 35–38, 59–69.

18. Cohen and DeLong, *Concrete Economics*, 83–120; McDonald, "The Green New Deal Can't Be Anything like the New Deal"; Kenneth T. Jackson, *Crabgrass Frontier: The Suburbanization of the United States* (New York: Oxford University Press, 1985), 157–282; Allan M. Winkler, *Home Front U.S.A.: America during World War II* (Hoboken, NJ: Wiley-Blackwell, 2012); Lizabeth Cohen, *A Consumers' Republic* (New York: Alfred A. Knopf, 2003); Brinkley, *The End of Reform*, 175–200.

19. Lawrence Goodwyn, *Democratic Promise: The Populist Moment in America* (New York: Oxford University Press, 1976); Robert C. McMath Jr., *American Populism: A Social History, 1877–1898* (New York: Hill and Wang, 1993); Christopher Lasch, *The True and Only Heaven: Progress and Its Critics*

(New York: W. W. Norton, 1991), 168–224, passim; Omar H. Ali, *In the Lion's Mouth: Black Populism in the New South, 1886–1990* (Jackson: University Press of Mississippi, 2012); John D. Fairfield, "A Populism for the Cities: Henry George, John Dewey, and the City Planning Movement," *Urban Design Studies* 8 (2002): 19–27; John D. Fairfield, *The Public and Its Possibilities* (Philadelphia: Temple University Press, 2010), 151–154; Leuchtenburg, *Franklin Roosevelt and the New Deal*; Hawley, *The New Deal and the Problem of Monopoly*; Brinkley *The End of Reform*; Cohen, *A Consumers' Republic*.

20. Thomas E. Watson, "The Negro Question in the South," *The Arena* 6 (October 1892): 540–550, quoted passage on 548; Ali, *In the Lion's Mouth*; Kenneth Janken, "Organizing the Black Political Insurgency," *Journal of the Gilded Age and Progressive Era* 11 (April 2012): 297–299; C. Vann Woodward, *Tom Watson, Agrarian Rebel* (New York: Macmillan, 1938).

21. Van Jones and Ariane Conrad, *The Green-Collar Economy: How One Solution Can Fix Our Two Biggest Problems* (New York: HarperOne, 2008), 106; Jackson, *Crabgrass Frontier*, 190–230; Thomas J. Sugrue, *The Origins of the Urban Crisis: Race and Inequality in Postwar Detroit* (Princeton, NJ: Princeton University Press, 1996); Robert O. Self, *American Babylon: Race and the Struggle for Postwar Oakland* (Princeton, NJ: Princeton University Press, 2003); N. D. B. Connolly, "Colored, Caribbean, and Condemned: Miami's Overtown District and the Cultural Expense of Progress, 1940–1970," *Caribbean Studies* 34 (January–June 2006): 3–60; Davarian Baldwin, *Chicago's New Negroes: Modernity, the Great Migration, and Black Urban Life* (Chapel Hill: University of North Carolina Press, 2007).

22. Shane Hamilton, *Supermarket USA: Food and Power in the Cold War Farms Race* (New Haven, CT: Yale University Press, 2018); Shane Hamilton, *Trucking Country: The Road to America's Wal-Mart Economy* (Princeton, NJ: Princeton University Press, 2008).

23. Pete Daniel, *Dispossession: Discrimination against African American Farmers in the Age of Civil Rights* (Chapel Hill: University of North Carolina Press, 2013); Audrea Lim, "We Shall Not Be Moved," *Harper's*, July 2020, 47–51; Tadlock Cowan and Jody Feder, "The *Pigford* Cases: USDA Settlement of Discrimination Suits by Black Farmers," *Congressional Research Service*, May 29, 2013, http://nationalaglawcenter.org/wp-content/uploads/assets/crs/RS20430.pdf; Andrew Needham, *Power Lines: Phoenix and the Making of the Modern Southwest* (Princeton, NJ: Princeton University Press, 2014); Shirley Burns, *Bringing Down the Mountain* (Morgantown: University of West Virginia Press, 2007); Ernest L. Schusky, *Culture and Agriculture: An Ecological Introduction to Traditional and Modern Farming Systems* (New York: Bergin and Garvey, 1989); Kate Logan and Shay Totten, "The Seeds of Progressive Populism," *Dissent* (Fall 2019), 71–77; Garrett Dash Nelson, "What Makes a Place Rural?" *Dissent* (Fall 2019): 38–47; Levi Van Sant, "Land Reform and the Green New Deal," *Dissent* (Fall 2019): 64–70; Ned Mamula, "Balancing America's Environment, Mining and the Green New Deal," *The Hill*, March 1, 2019, https://thehill.com/blogs/congress-blog/energy-environment/432066-balancing-americas-environment-mining-and-the-green; Brent Patterson, "Why Mining Justice Must Be Central to

the Green New Deal," *Rabble.Ca*, May 10, 2019, http://rabble.ca/blogs/bloggers /brent-patterson/2019/05/why-mining-justice-must-be-central-green-new-deal.

24. If we recognize the populists' determination to preserve an economy of small producers *on a new foundation*, Goodwyn's and Lasch's anti-progressive populists are not so different from Postel's modernizing populists. Lasch, *The True and Only Heaven*, 168–225, 445–465; Goodwyn, *Democratic Promise*; McMath, *American Populism*; Michael Sandel, *Democracy's Discontent: America's Search for a Public Philosophy* (Cambridge, MA: Harvard University Press, 1996); Charles Postel, *The Populist Vision* (New York: Oxford University Press, 2009); Robert C. McMath Jr., "Another Look at the 'Hard Side' of Populism," *Reviews in American History* 36 (June 2008): 209–217; Mary Summers, "Putting Populism Back In: Rethinking Agricultural Politics and Policy," *Agricultural History* 70 (Spring 1996): 395–414.

25. Lasch, *The True and Only Heaven*; Michael Kazin, *The Populist Persuasion: An American History* (Ithaca, NY: Cornell University Press, 2017), quoted passages on 2–40; Daniel Walker Howe, *The Political Culture of the American Whigs* (Chicago: University of Chicago Press, 1979), 801; Sandel, *Democracy's Discontent*, 168–200.

26. Lasch, *The True and Only Heaven*, 217–225; Sandel, *Democracy's Discontent*, quotations on 185–187.

27. Fairfield, "A Populism for the Cities," Dewey quoted on 21; Fairfield, *The Public and Its Possibilities*, 151–154, "amazing" and "essential" from the Georgists' journal *The Public*, quoted on 153.

28. "From the same prolific womb of governmental injustice," the Populist Party platform of 1892 charged, "We breed the two great classes—tramps and millionaires": "National People's Party Platform, 1892," *History Matters: The U.S. Survey Course on the Web*, American Social History Project, Center for Media and Learning, Graduate Center, City University of New York, and the Roy Rosenzweig Center for History and New Media, George Mason University, Fairfax, VA, n.d., http://historymatters.gmu.edu/d/5361; John B. Judis, *The Populist Explosion: How the Great Recession Transformed American and European Politics* (New York: Columbia Global Reports, 2017); John Judis, "Us versus Them: The Birth of Populism," *The Guardian*, October 13, 2016; Donald I. Warren, *The Radical Center: Middle Americans and the Politics of Alienation* (Notre Dame, IN: University of Notre Dame Press, 1976); Charles Postel, "If Trump and Sanders Are Both Populists, What Does Populist Mean?" *American Historian*, February 2, 2016, https://www.oah.org/tah/february-2/if-trump-and-sanders-are-both -populists-what-does-populist-mean; Lasch, *The True and Only Heaven*, 369–411; Christopher Lasch, *The Revolt of the Elites and the Betrayal of Democracy* (New York: W. W. Norton, 1995), 50–79, passim.

29. Lasch, *The True and Only Heaven*, 369–411. For a contrasting account of King and the movement that defines its radicalism in more social democratic terms, see the review essay (and the books reviewed) in Annette Gordon-Reed, "MLK: What We Lost," *New York Review of Books*, November 8, 2018.

30. Lasch, *The True and Only Heaven*, 369–411; Harry C. Boyte, "Populism or Socialism? The Divided Heart of the Green New Deal," *MinnPost*, March 1,

2019, https://www.minnpost.com/community-voices/2019/03/populism-or-socia
lism-the-divided-heart-of-the-green-new-deal; Reinhold Niebuhr, *Moral Man and
Immoral Society: A Study in Ethics and Politics* (New York: Scribner's, 1932), 231.

31. Peter B. Levy, ed., *Documentary History of the Modern Civil Rights Movement* (New York: Greenwood, 1992), 59.

32. Numan V. Bartley, *The Rise of Massive Resistance: Race and Politics in
the South during the 1950s* (Baton Rouge: Louisiana State University Press, 1969);
Judis, *The Populist Explosion*, 39–87; Judis, "Us versus Them."

33. Judis, *The Populist Explosion*, 154–163; "National People's Party Platform, 1892."

34. Jackson, "Prayer for Just War"; Arnoff, "With the Green New Deal Here's
What the World Could Look like for the Next Generation"; Michael Lewis, *The
Big Short: Inside the Doomsday Machine* (New York: W. W. Norton, 2011); Kev-
in Phillips, *Bad Money: Reckless Finance, Failed Politics, and the Global Crisis
of American Capitalism* (New York: Viking, 2008); Naomi Klein, *This Changes
Everything: Capitalism versus the Climate* (New York: Simon and Schuster, 2014),
230–255; Jason Hickel, *The Divide: A Brief Guide to Global Inequality and Its
Solutions* (London: William Heinemann, 2017); Jason Hickel, *Less Is More: How
Degrowth Will Save the World* (London: Penguin, 2020).

35. Roosevelt, quoted in Matt Stoller, "How Democrats Killed Their Populist Soul," *The Atlantic*, October 24, 2016, https://www.theatlantic.com/politics
/archive/2016/10/how-democrats-killed-their-populist-soul/504710; Mark Lilla,
The Once and Future Liberal: After Identity Politics (New York: HarperCollins,
2017); Sandel, *Democracy's Discontent*.

36. Hawley, *The New Deal and the Problem of Monopoly*; Stoller, "How
Democrats Killed Their Populist Soul."

37. Stoller, "How Democrats Killed Their Populist Soul." Brinkley, *The End of
Reform*, traces the origins of these developments back at least a generation further
than Stoller.

38. Stoller, "How Democrats Killed Their Populist Soul"; Bennett Harrison
and Barry Bluestone, *The Great U-turn: Corporate Restructuring and the Polarizing of America* (New York: Basic, 1993), 76–108.

39. A fifteen-point decline in the percentage of non-college-educated white
voters in 2016 compared with 2012 doomed the Democrats electorally. Stoller,
"How Democrats Killed Their Populist Soul"; Gary Gerstle, *The Rise and Fall of
the Neoliberal Order* (New York: Oxford University Press, 2022); George Packer,
The Unwinding (London: Faber and Faber, 2013), 284–295, 259–273, passim;
Lilla, *The Once and Future Liberal*; Jonathan Rauch, "Speaking as a . . . ," *New
York Review of Books*, November 9, 2017.

40. Stoller, "How Democrats Killed Their Populist Soul"; Barry C. Lynn,
"The Big Tech Extortion Racket," *Harper's*, September 2020, https://harpers.org
/archive/2020/09/the-big-tech-extortion-racket; Rauch, "Speaking as a . . ."; Sandel, *Democracy's Discontent*; Lasch, *The Revolt of the Elites*.

41. McGhee, *The Sum of Us*, esp. 271–279; John D. Fairfield, "Race and the Cost
of Public Goods," *Black Perspectives*, September 24, 2021, https://www.aaihs.org
/race-and-the-cost-of-public-goods/?utm_source=rss&utm_medium=rss&utm
_campaign=race-and-the-cost-of-public-goods.

42. McGhee, *The Sum of Us.*

43. McDonald, "The Green New Deal Can't Be Anything like the New Deal"; Dan Merica, "Jay Inslee Proposes Ending Fossil Fuel Subsidies in Latest Proposal to Combat Climate Crisis," *CNN Politics*, June 24, 2019, https://www.cnn.com/2019/06/24/politics/jay-inslee-fossil-fuels/index.html; "Federal Farm Subsidies: What the Facts Say," USA Facts, June 4, 2019, https://usafacts.org/reports/farm-subsidies-usda-ccc-crop-insurance; Mike Collins, "The Big Bank Bailout," *Forbes*, July 14, 2015, https://www.forbes.com/sites/mikecollins/2015/07/14/the-big-bank-bailout/#6040fa9e2d83; Packer, *The Unwinding*; John Dewey, "Liberty and Social Control," *Education Review* 1 (December 1935): 13–15.

44. Robert Leighninger, *Long-Range Public Investment: The Forgotten Legacy of the New Deal* (Columbia: University of South Carolina Press, 2007), 11–34.

45. Randall Williams, "Green Voters, Gun Voters: Hunting and Politics in Modern America," Ph.D. diss., University of Montana, Missoula, 2015. Sanders's plan, quoted in Paul J. Baicich, "A Green New Deal Needs a 21st-Century Civilian Conservation Corps," *Jacobin*, August 11, 2020, https://jacobinmag.com/2020/08/fdr-green-new-deal-ccc.

46. Leighninger, *Long-Range Public Investment*; Baicich, "A Green New Deal Needs a 21st-Century Civilian Conservation Corps."

47. "Explore the Chattahoochee Riverlands," *Chattahoochee Riverlands*, n.d., accessed August 13, 2021, https://chattahoocheeriverlands.com; Eric Klinenberg, "Manufacturing Nature," *New Yorker*, August 9, 2021, 18–24, Kate Orff quoted on 24.

48. Leighninger, *Long-Range Public Investment*, 11–34; Graf et al., "The Narrowing, but Persistent, Gender Gap in Pay."

49. Wunsch, "The Suburban Cliché"; "Poverty in the United States: Percentage of People in Poverty by State: 2015," U.S. Bureau of the Census, n.d., https://www.census.gov/library/visualizations/2016/comm/cb16-158_poverty_map.html; Jillean McCommons, "Appalachian Hillsides as Black Ecologies: Housing, Memory, and the Sanctified Hill Disaster," *Black Perspectives*, June 16, 2020, https://www.aaihs.org/appalachian-hillsides-as-black-ecologies-housing-memory-and-the-sanctified-hill-disaster-of-1972; Robert Neubauer, "For an Ecological Populism," *Policy Alternatives*, July 2, 2019, https://www.policyalternatives.ca/publications/monitor/ecological-populism.

50. Danielle Allen's eloquent account of her imprisoned cousin's embrace of firefighting in California's forests makes a powerful case for the redemptive value of socially useful work. Hochschild, "Male Trouble"; Sandel, "What Liberals Got Wrong about Work"; Danielle Allen, *Cuz: The Life and Times of Michael A.* (New York: Livermore, 2017).

51. In truth, few locals got the prison jobs. Ruth Wilson Gilmore, *Golden Gulag: Prisons, Surplus, Crisis, and Opposition in Globalizing California* (Berkeley: University of California Press, 2007). For a radically different approach to the future of agriculture, and one that has shaped the argument here, see Kathleen Smythe, *Whole Earth Living: Reconnecting Earth, History, Body, and Mind* (London: Dixi, 2020).

52. Van Sant, "Land Reform and the Green New Deal," "deterioration" on 68; Eliza Griswold, "People in Coal Country Worry about the Climate, Too," *New*

York Times, July 13, 2019; Mamula, "Balancing America's Environment, Mining and the Green New Deal"; Patterson, "Why Mining Justice Must Be Central to the Green New Deal"; Tom Vilsack, "Reconnecting with Rural America," *Democracy* 47 (Winter 2018), https://democracyjournal.org/magazine/47/reconnecting-with -rural-america.

53. Sant, "Land Reform and the Green New Deal"; Vilsack, "Reconnecting with Rural America"; Richard Manning, "The Oil We Eat," *Harper's*, February 2004; Richard Manning, *Against the Grain: How Agriculture Has Hijacked Civilization* (New York: North Point, 2004).

54. Daniel, *Dispossession*; Lim, "We Shall Not Be Moved"; Cowan and Feder, "The *Pigford* Cases"; Monica M. White, *Agricultural Resistance and the Black Freedom Movement* (Chapel Hill: University of North Carolina Press, 2018); Leah Penniman, *Farming while Black: Soul Fire Farm's Practical Guide to Liberation on the Land* (White River Junction, VT: Chelsea Green, 2018); Brian Donahue, *Go Farm, Young People, and Help Heal the Country* (Middlebury, VT: New Perennials, 2022); Charles Blow, *The Devil You Know: A Black Power Manifesto* (New York: Harper, 2021); Lisa Capretto, "Meet Will Allen, the Urban Farmer Starting His Own Revolution," *HuffPost*, December 6, 2017, https://www.huff post.com/entry/will-allen-urban-farmer-growing-power_n_7183926; Andrew Ross, *Bird on Fire: Lessons from the World's Least Sustainable City* (New York: Oxford University Press, 2011), 222–229.

55. Vilsack, "Reconnecting with Rural America"; Manning, "The Oil We Eat," "eat" on 39; Manning, *Against the Grain*; A. Duncan Brown, *Feed or Feedback: Agricultural, Population, and the State of the Planet* (Utrecht: International, 2003); Michael Pollan, "Letter to the Farmer in Chief," *New York Times Magazine*, October 12, 2008; Schusky, *Culture and Agriculture*.

56. Pollan, "Letter to the Farmer in Chief"; Manning, *Against the Grain*; Centers for Medicare and Medicaid Services, "N[ational] H[ealth] E[xpenditures] Fact Sheet," CMS.gov, n.d., https://www.cms.gov/research-statistics-data-and-sys tems/statistics-trends-and-reports/nationalhealthexpenddata/nhe-fact-sheet.html; Michael Pollan, "The Food Movement, Rising," *New York Review of Books*, May 20, 2010; Nicole Rasul, "How School Food Purchases Are Moving the Needle for the Local Food Movement," *Forbes*, August 24, 2018, https://www.forbes .com/sites/nicolerasul/2018/08/24/how-school-food-purchases-are-moving-the -needle-for-the-local-food-movement/#4ea93e86400f; Gracy Olmsted, "Has the Sustainable Food Movement Failed?" *American Conservative*, June 23, 2015, https://www.theamericanconservative.com/olmstead/has-the-sustainable-food -movement-failed.

57. Pollan, "Letter to the Farmer in Chief"; Wendell Berry, *The Unsettling of America: Culture and Agriculture* (San Francisco: Sierra Club, 1977); Hamilton, *Supermarket USA*.

58. Pollan, "Letter to the Farmer in Chief"; Matthew Weaver, "Work on New Farm Bill Continues during House Upheaval," *Capital Press*, October 20, 2023, https://www.capitalpress.com/nation_world/nation/work-on-new-farm-bill-contin ues-during-house-upheaval/article_a80ea788-6ed8-11ee-b5d2-df596393edc7.html.

59. Land Institute, "A 50-Year Farm Bill," June 2009, https://landinstitute.org /wp-content/uploads/2016/09/FB-edited-7-6-10.pdf; Dee Kim, "Can the Climate-

Friendly Grain Kernza Finally Hit the Big Time?" *Civil Eats*, October 15, 2020, https://civileats.com/2020/10/15/can-the-climate-friendly-grain-kernza-finally -hit-the-big-time.

60. Pollan, "Letter to the Farmer in Chief"; Gidon Eshel, Alon Shepon, Taga Shaket, and Brett D. Cotler et al., "A Model for 'Sustainable' U.S. Beef Production," *Nature Ecology and Environment* 2 (January 2018): 81–85; Gidon Eshel, Paul Stainier, Alon Shepon, and Akshay Swaminathan, "Environmentally Optimal, Nutritionally Sound, Protein and Energy Conserving Plant Based Alternative to U.S. Meat," *Scientific Reports*, August 8, 2019, https://doi.org/10.1038 /s41598-019-46590-1.

61. Farmer's Footprint website, accessed August 4, 2022, https://farmersfoot print.us; Pollan, "Letter to the Farmer in Chief"; Steven Savage, "The Lower Productivity of Organic Farming: A New Analysis and Its Big Implications," *Forbes*, October 9, 2015, https://www.forbes.com/sites/stevensavage/2015/10/09/the-organ ic-farming-yield-gap/#7e06b5875e0e; George Anifandis, Katerina Katsanaki, Georgia Lagodonti, and Christina Messini et al., "The Effect of Glyphosate on Human Sperm Motility and Sperm DNA Fragmentation," *International Journal of Environmental Research and Public Health* 30 (May 2018): 1117.

62. Pollan, "Letter to the Farmer in Chief"; Ross, *Bird on Fire*, 212–238.

63. Harlan Paul Douglass, *The Suburban Trend* (New York: Century, 1925), 61; Wunsch, "The Suburban Cliché," Wunsch also quotes Douglass on 651. Among the commentators who spoke to the need to preserve farmland, see Leo Marx, "American Institutions and Ecological Ideals," *Science*, vol. 170, November 27, 1970, 948; William H. Whyte, *The Exploding Metropolis* (Garden City, NY: Doubleday, 1958), 133–139. Cf. the discussion of development of the Gulfton neighborhood in Houston, a place that, the authors note in passing, had been "mostly farmland" in the 1940s, in Bruce Katz and Jennifer Bradley, *The Metropolitan Revolution: How Cities and Metros Are Fixing Our Broken Politics and Fragile Economy* (Washington, DC: Brookings, 2013), 88–91.

64. Pollan, "Letter to the Farmer in Chief"; Pollan, "The Food Movement, Rising"; Summers, "Putting Populism Back In"; Alexandra Norris, "The Agricultural Iron Triangle," *DLJ Online*, May 26, 2018, https://dartmouthlawjournal.org /dljonline/?p=104.

EPILOGUE

1. I am indebted to Sean Comer for the reference to Leopold. Aldo Leopold, *Sand County Almanac* (New York: Ballantine, 1970), 130–134; National Climate Assessment, "Extreme Weather," U.S. Global Change Research Program, n.d., https://nca2014.globalchange.gov/highlights/report-findings/extreme-weather.

2. Naomi Klein, *This Changes Everything: Capitalism versus the Climate* (New York: Simon and Schuster, 2014), 175.

3. Ibid., 28; Greg Jackson, "Prayer for Just War: Finding Meaning in the Climate Fight," *Harper's*, June 2021, 35–38, 59–69; Stephen Leahy, "Hidden Costs of Climate Change Running Hundreds of Billions a Year," *National Geographic*, September 27, 2017; Jim Dobson, "Billionaire Bunkers: Exclusive Look inside the World's Largest Planned Doomsday Escape," *Forbes*, June 12, 2015; Olivia Carville, "The Super Rich

of Silicon Valley Have a Doomsday Escape Plan," *Bloomberg News*, September 5, 2018; Noah Gallagher Shannon, "Climate Chaos Is Coming—and the Pinkertons Are Ready," *New York Times*, April 10, 2019; Evan Osnos, "Doomsday Prep for the Super Rich," *New Yorker*, January 30, 2017; George Monbiot, *Out of the Wreckage: A New Politics for an Age of Crisis* (New York: Verso, 2017), 182–186, passim.

4. McKibben, quoted in Verlyn Klinkenborg, "The Prophet," *New York Review of Books*, vol. 60, October 24, 2013.

5. "An Interview with William Cronon," *Scapes*, no. 5 (Fall 2006): 34–45. See the many articles at the website of the Evangelical Environmental Network, New Freedom, PA, https://creationcare.org; Pope Francis, *Encyclical Letter Laudato Si': On Care for Our Common Home* (Vatican City: Libreria Editrica Vaticana, 2015). For evidence of the unfortunate divide between secular and religious environmentalists, see Andrew Spencer, "Three Reasons Why Evangelicals Stopped Advocating for the Environment," *Christianity Today*, June 14, 2017, https://www.christian itytoday.com/ct/2017/june-web-only/three-reasons-evangelicals-dont-advocate-for -environment.html.

6. Carlos M. N. Eire, *Reformations: The Early Modern World, 1450–1650* (New Haven, CT: Yale University Press, 2016), 133.

7. Henry Rodgers, Sereno Edwards Dwight, and Edward Hickman, eds., *The Works of Jonathan Edwards* (London: W. Ball, 1839), liv; Perry Miller, *Errand into the Wilderness* (New York: Harper and Row, 1956); Christopher Lasch, *The True and Only Heaven: Progress and Its Critics* (New York: W. W. Norton, 1991), 246–256; Connie Fairfield Ganz, *The Fairfields of Wenham* (Newberg, OR: Allegra Print and Imaging, 2013).

8. Rodgers et al., *The Works of Jonathan Edwards*, li–lvi; Miller, *Errand into the Wilderness*, 185.

9. Mark Stoll, *Protestantism, Capitalism, and Nature in America* (Albuquerque: University of New Mexico Press, 1997), 55–76, passim; Mark Stoll, *Inherit the Holy Mountain: Religion and the Rise of American Environmentalism* (New York: Oxford University Press, 2015), 10–53, passim, Calvin quoted on 21; John Murdock, "Christian, Conservative, Treehugger," On Being Project, January 27, 2019, https://onbeing.org/blog/christian-conservative-treehugger; Leo Marx, "The Idea of Nature in America," *Daedalus* 137, no. 2 (Spring 2008): 8–21.

10. Eire, *Reformations*, 294–317; Lasch, *The True and Only Heaven*, 246–256.

11. Miller, *Errand into the Wilderness*, 48–98, 185–203; Mark A. Noll, *God and Mammon: Protestants, Money, and the Market, 1790–1860* (New York: Oxford University Press, 2002); Charles Grier Sellers, *The Market Revolution: Jacksonian America, 1815–1846* (New York: Oxford University Press, 1991), 202–236; Costi W. Hinn, *God, Greed, and the (Prosperity) Gospel: How Truth Overwhelms a Life Built on Lies* (Grand Rapids, MI: Zondervan, 2019); Miller, *Errand into the Wilderness*, 200; Stoll, *Protestantism, Capitalism, and Nature in America*, 55–96; Marx, "The Idea of Nature in America," 9–11; Charles Darwin, *On the Origin of Species by Means of Natural Selection* (London: Oxford University Press, [1859] 2018); Louis Menand, *The Metaphysical Club* (New York: Farrar, Straus, and Giroux, 2001), 117–148; William James, *Varieties of Religious Experience: A Study in Human Nature* (New York: Modern Library, 2002); Lasch, *The True and Only Heaven*, 282–295.

12. Lasch, *The True and Only Heaven*, 282–295.

13. Abandoning the "smirking reason" that he judged a childish desire for certainty, James embraced a "philosophy of wonder." Ibid., 282–295, James quoted on 294, "smirking" is Benjamin Paul Blood's take on James, quoted on 286; Menand, *The Metaphysical Club*, 73–95.

14. Darwin did not have the benefit of our understanding of genetic inheritance. Darwin, *On the Origin of Species by Means of Natural Selection*; Menand, *The Metaphysical Club*, 117–148.

15. Menand, *The Metaphysical Club*, "intelligence" on 146, Wright quoted on 212.

16. John Dewey, *The Influence of Darwin on Philosophy and Other Essays* (New York: Henry Holt, 1910), 21–45, quoted passage on 43; Robert Westbrook, *John Dewey and American Democracy* (Ithaca, NY: Cornell University Press, 1991), 319–373.

17. Ben A. Minteer, *The Landscape of Reform: Civic Pragmatism and Environmental Thought in America* (Cambridge, MA: MIT Press, 2006), 1–9; John Dewey, *Experience and Nature* (1929), in *John Dewey: The Later Works, 1925–1953*, vol. 1, ed. Jo Ann Boydston (Carbondale: Southern Illinois University Press, 1984), 12–13, 82, passim; Westbrook, *John Dewey and American Democracy*, 319–366. For a critical assessment of Dewey's thought that nevertheless shares much of the view expressed here, see John P. Diggins, *The Promise of Pragmatism: Modernism and the Crisis of Knowledge and Authority* (Chicago: University of Chicago Press, 1994).

18. John Dewey, *Experience and Nature*, repr. ed. (New York: Dover, [1929] 1958); Westbrook, *John Dewey and American Democracy*, 341.

19. Dewey, *Experience and Nature* (1958), 420–421; Westbrook, *John Dewey and American Democracy*, 340–341.

20. Eugene Cittadino, "Ecology and American Social Thought," in *Religion and the New Ecology*, ed. David M. Lodge and Christopher Hamlin (Notre Dame, IN: University of Notre Dame Press, 2006), 98–106; Donald Worster, *Nature's Economy: A History of Ecological Ideas* (Cambridge: Cambridge University Press, 1994), 388–433, "concept" is Daniel Botkin, quoted on 397; Daniel Botkin, *Discordant Harmonies: A New Ecology for the Twenty-first Century* (New York: Oxford University Press, 1990).

21. Cittadino, "Ecology and American Social Thought"; Worster, *Nature's Economy*, 388–433, "full" on 405, Adams paraphrased on 407; Botkin, *Discordant Harmonies*.

22. For a fictional dramatization of some of these ideas, see Daniel Quinn, *Ishmael: A Novel* (New York: Bantam, 2017). On pragmatism and "adaptive management, see Bryan Norton, "Integration or Reduction: Two Approaches to Environmental Values," in *Environmental Pragmatism*, ed. Andrew Light and Eric Katz (London: Routledge, 1996), 105–138; Bryan Norton, "Pragmatism, Adaptive Management, and Sustainability," *Environmental Values* 8 (1999): 451–466.

23. Dewey, *Experience and Nature* (1958), "indifferent" on 21; Westbrook, *John Dewey and American Democracy*, 321–327; Minteer, *The Landscape of Reform*, 1–9; Worster, *Nature's Economy*, 1–55, passim.

24. Dewey, *Experience and Nature* (1958); Westbrook, *John Dewey and American Democracy*, 321–327, "lovable" is from the second edition of *Experience and Nature*, quoted by Westbrook on 326.

25. Leo Marx, "American Institutions and Ecological Ideals," *Science*, vol. 170, November 27, 1970, 945–952, quoted passage on 945.

26. Leo Marx, *The Machine in the Garden: Technology and the Pastoral Ideal in America* (New York: Oxford University Press, 1964), 319–341.

27. Ibid.

28. Ibid., quoted passage on 323.

29. Mark Twain, *Huckleberry Finn* (New York: Harper and Brothers, 1912), 163–164; Marx, *The Machine in the Garden*, 331–332; Minteer, *The Landscape of Reform*, 1–9.

30. Twain, *Huckleberry Finn*, 163–164.

31. Ibid.

32. Marx, *The Machine in the Garden*, quoted passage on 333.

33. Twain, *Huckleberry Finn*, "hell" on 297, "everybody" on 174, "long journey," 294; Marx, *The Machine in the Garden*, 333–339.

34. Herman Melville, *Moby-Dick* (New York: W. W. Norton, [1851] 2002), 136–142; Marx, *The Machine in the Garden*, 277–319.

35. Melville, *Moby-Dick*, 325–328; Marx, *The Machine in the Garden*, 277–319.

36. Melville, *Moby-Dick*, 227–229; Marx, *The Machine in the Garden*, 277–319.

37. Twain, *Huckleberry Finn*, 405; Melville, *Moby-Dick*, 159–165; Marx, *The Machine in the Garden*, 277–319.

38. Marx, *The Machine in the Garden*, 364; Marx, "American Institutions and Ecological Ideals," 950.

39. Marx, *The Machine in the Garden*, 359–360; F. Scott Fitzgerald, *The Great Gatsby* (New York: Scribner, [1925] 2020), "gift" on 2, "breast" on 180.

40. Toni Morrison, *Beloved* (New York: New American Library, 1987), "flowers" on 112, "astonished," 268.

41. Roger Starr, "The Valley of Ashes: F. Scott Fitzgerald and Robert Moses," *City Journal*, Autumn 1992, https://www.city-journal.org/html/valley-ashes-f-scott-fitzgerald-and-robert-moses-12680.html; Raymond Williams, *The Country and the City* (New York: Oxford University Press, 1973), 301–302.

Index

John D. Fairfield is Professor of History at Xavier University. He is the author of *The Public and Its Possibilities: Triumphs and Tragedies in the American City* (Temple), *The Mysteries of the Great City: The Politics of Urban Design, 1877–1937,* and *Oakley: From Hamlet to the Center of Cincinnati,* as well as the coeditor of *Bringing the Civic Back In: Zane L. Miller and American Urban History* (Temple).

Also in the series *Urban Life, Landscape, and Policy*: